George Long

The discourses of Epictetus;

With the Encheiridion and fragments

George Long

The discourses of Epictetus;
With the Encheiridion and fragments

ISBN/EAN: 9783337818395

Printed in Europe, USA, Canada, Australia, Japan

Cover: Foto ©ninafisch / pixelio.de

More available books at **www.hansebooks.com**

THE DISCOURSES OF EPICTETUS;

WITH THE

ENCHEIRIDION AND FRAGMENTS.

TRANSLATED,

WITH NOTES, A LIFE OF EPICTETUS, AND A VIEW OF HIS PHILOSOPHY,

BY GEORGE LONG.

"The important question, What is the rule of Life? is lost out of the world."—BP. BUTLER.

"Consider thyself to be dead, and to have completed thy life up to the present time; and live according to Nature the remainder which is allowed thee."—M. ANTONINUS, vii. 56.

LONDON: GEORGE BELL AND SONS, YORK STREET, COVENT GARDEN.

1877.

LONDON:

PRINTED BY WILLIAM CLOWES AND SONS,
STAMFORD STREET AND CHARING CROSS.

TO

ESTHER LAWRENCE,

A DILIGENT READER OF EPICTETUS,

TO WHOM THE TRANSLATOR OWES MANY

USEFUL REMARKS.

CONTENTS.

BOOK I.

CHAP. PAGE

I. Of the Things which are in our Power, and not in our Power 3

II. How a Man on every occasion can maintain his Proper Character 8

III. How a Man should proceed from the principle of God being the Father of all Men to the rest 12

IV. Of Progress or Improvement 13

V. Against the Academics 17

VI. Of Providence 19

VII. Of the use of Sophistical Arguments and Hypothetical, and the like 23

VIII. That the Faculties are not safe to the Uninstructed 28

IX. How from the Fact that we are akin to God a Man may proceed to the Consequences . . . 30

X. Against those who eagerly seek Preferment at Rome 35

XI. Of Natural Affection 37

XII. Of Contentment 41

XIII. How Everything may be done acceptably to the Gods 45

XIV. That the Deity oversees All Things 46

XV. What Philosophy promises 49

XVI. Of Providence 50

XVII. That the Logical Art is necessary 52

XVIII. That we ought not to be Angry with the Errors (Faults) of others 55

XIX. How we should behave to Tyrants 60

XX. About Reason and how it contemplates itself . 63

XXI. Against those who wish to be Admired . . . 66

XXII. Of Praecognitions 66

XXIII. Against Epicurus 69

CHAP. PAGE

XXIV. How we should struggle with Circumstances . 70
XXV. On the same 73
XXVI. What is the Law of Life 77
XXVII. In how many ways Appearances exist, and what Aids we should provide against them . . . 80
XXVIII. That we ought not to be Angry with Men; and what are the Small and the Great Things among Men 83
XXIX. On Constancy (or Firmness) 87
XXX. What we ought to have ready in Difficult Circumstances 96

BOOK II.

I. That Confidence (Courage) is not inconsistent with Caution 97
II. Of Tranquillity (Freedom from Perturbation) . 103
III. To those who recommend Persons to Philosophers 106
IV. Against a Person who had once been detected in Adultery 107
V. How Magnanimity is consistent with Care . . 108
VI. Of Indifference 112
VII. How we ought to use Divination 116
VIII. What is the Nature (ἡ οὐσία) of the Good . 118
IX. That when we cannot fulfil that which the Character of a Man promises, we assume the Character of a Philosopher 123
X. How we may discover the Duties of Life from Names 127
XI. What the Beginning of Philosophy is 130
XII. Of Disputation or Discussion 133
XIII. Of Anxiety (Solicitude) 136
XIV. To Naso 140
XV. To or against those who obstinately Persist in what they have determined 144
XVI. That we do not strive to use our Opinions about Good and Evil 147
XVII. How we must adapt Preconceptions to particular Cases 153
XVIII. How we should struggle against Appearances . 158
XIX. Against those who embrace Philosophical Opinions only in Words 162
XX. Against the Epicureans and Academics . . 167

CHAP. PAGE
XXI. Of Inconsistency 173
XXII. Of Friendship 176
XXIII. On the Power of Speaking 182
XXIV. To (or against) a Person who was one of those who were not valued (esteemed) by him . . 188
XXV. That Logic is necessary 192
XXVI. What is the Property of Error 192

BOOK III.

I. Of Finery in Dress 195
II. In what a Man ought to be exercised who has made Proficiency; and that we neglect the Chief Things 201
III. What is the Matter on which a Good Man should be employed, and in what we ought chiefly to employ ourselves 204
IV. Against a Person who showed his Partizanship in an unseemly way in a Theatre 207
V. Against those who on account of Sickness go away Home 209
VI. Miscellaneous 211
VII. To the Administrator of the Free Cities who was an Epicurean 213
VIII. How we must exercise ourselves against Appearances (φαντασίαι). 218
IX. To a certain Rhetorician who was going up to Rome on a Suit 219
X. In what Manner we ought to bear Sickness . 222
XI. Certain Miscellaneous Matters 225
XII. About Exercise 225
XIII. What Solitude is, and what Kind of Person a Solitary Man is 228
XIV. Certain Miscellaneous Matters 233
XV. That we ought to proceed with Circumspection to Everything 234
XVI. That we ought with Caution to enter into Familiar Intercourse with Men 236
XVII. Of Providence 238
XVIII. That we ought not to be disturbed by any News 239
XIX. What is the Condition of a Common Kind of Man and of a Philosopher 240

CHAP. PAGE

XX. That we can derive Advantage from all External Things 241

XXI. Against those who readily come to the Profession of Sophists 244

XXII. About Cynism 248

XXIII. To those who read and discuss for the sake of Ostentation 264

XXIV. That we ought not to be moved by a Desire of those Things which are not in our Power . 270

XXV. To those who fall off (desist) from their Purpose 287

XXVI. To those who fear Want 289

BOOK IV.

I. About Freedom 295

II. Of Familiar Intimacy 322

III. What Things we should Exchange for other Things 324

IV. To those who are desirous of passing Life in Tranquillity 325

V. Against the Quarrelsome and Ferocious . . 333

VI. Against those who lament over being Pitied . 339

VII. On Freedom from Fear 345

VIII. Against those who hastily rush into the Philosophic Dress 351

IX. To a Person who had been changed to a Character of Shamelessness 357

X. What Things we ought to Despise and what Things we ought to Value 360

XI. About Purity (Cleanliness) 366

XII. On Attention 372

XIII. Against or to those who readily Tell their own Affairs 375

The Encheiridion or Manual 379

Fragments 405

Index . . . 441

EPICTETUS.

Very little is known of the life of Epictetus. It is said that he was a native of Hierapolis in Phrygia, a town between the Maeander and a branch of the Maeander named the Lycus. Hierapolis is mentioned in the epistle of Paul to the people of Colossae (Coloss. iv. 13); from which it has been concluded that there was a Christian church in Hierapolis in the time of the apostle. The date of the birth of Epictetus is unknown. The only recorded fact of his early life is that he was a slave in Rome, and his master was Epaphroditus, a profligate freedman of the emperor Nero. There is a story that the master broke his slave's leg by torturing him; but it is better to trust to the evidence of Simplicius, the commentator on the Encheiridion or Manual, who says that Epictetus was weak in body and lame from an early age. It is not said how he became a slave; but it has been asserted in modern times that the parents sold the child. I have not, however, found any authority for this statement.

It may be supposed that the young slave showed intelligence, for his master sent or permitted him to attend the lectures of C. Musonius Rufus, an eminent Stoic philosopher. It may seem strange that such a master should have wished to have his slave made into a philosopher; but Garnier, the author of a Mémoire sur les ouvrages d'Epictète, explains this matter very well in a communication to Schweighaeuser. Garnier says: "Epictetus, born at Hierapolis of Phrygia of poor parents, was indebted apparently for the advantages of a good education to the whim, which was common at the end of the Republic and under the first emperors, among the great of Rome to reckon among their numerous slaves Grammarians, Poets, Rhetoricians, and Philosophers, in the same way as rich financiers in these later ages have been led to form at a great cost rich and numerous libraries. This supposition is the only one which can explain to us, how a wretched child, born as poor as Irus, had received a good education, and how a rigid Stoic was the slave of Epaphroditus, one of the officers of the Imperial guard. For we cannot suspect that it was through predilection for the Stoic doctrine and for his own use, that the confidant and the minister of the debaucheries of Nero would have desired to possess such a slave."

Some writers assume that Epictetus was manumitted by his master; but I can find no evidence for this statement. Epaphroditus accompanied Nero when he fled from Rome before his enemies, and he aided the miserable tyrant in killing himself. Domitian (Sueton. Domit. 14) afterwards put Epaphroditus to death for this service to Nero. We may conclude that Epictetus in some way obtained his freedom, and that he began to teach at Rome; but after the expulsion of the philosophers from Rome by Domitian A.D. 89, he retired to Nicopolis in Epirus, a city built by Augustus to commemorate the victory at Actium. Epictetus opened a school or lecture room at Nicopolis, where he taught till he was an old man. The time of his death is unknown. Epictetus was never married, as we learn from Lucian (Demonax, c. 55, Tom. ii. ed. Hemsterh. p. 393).[1] When Epictetus was finding fault with Demonax and advising him to take a wife and beget children, for this also, as Epictetus said, was a philosopher's duty, to

[1] Lucian's 'Life of the Philosopher Demonax.'

leave in place of himself another in the Universe, Demonax refuted the doctrine by answering, Give me then, Epictetus, one of your own daughters. Simplicius says (Comment. c. 46, p. 432, ed. Schweigh.) that Epictetus lived alone a long time. At last he took a woman into his house as a nurse for a child, which one of Epictetus' friends was going to expose on account of his poverty, but Epictetus took the child and brought it up.

Epictetus wrote nothing; and all that we have under his name was written by an affectionate pupil, Arrian, afterwards the historian of Alexander the Great, who, as he tells us, took down in writing the philosopher's discourses (the Epistle of Arrian to Lucius Gellius, p. 1). These discourses formed eight books, but only four are extant under the title of Ἐπικτήτου διατριβαί. Simplicius in his commentary on the Ἐγχειρίδιον or Manual, states that this work also was put together by Arrian, who selected from the discourses of Epictetus what he considered to be most useful, and most necessary, and most adapted to move men's minds. Simplicius also says that the contents of the Encheiridion are found nearly altogether and in the same words in various parts of the Discourses. Arrian also wrote a work on the life and death of Epictetus. The events of the philosopher's studious life were probably not many nor remarkable; but we should have been glad if this work had been preserved, which told, as Simplicius says, what kind of man Epictetus was.

Photius (Biblioth. 58) mentions among Arrian's works Conversations with Epictetus, Ὁμιλίαι Ἐπικτήτου in twelve books. Upton thinks that this work is only another name for the Discourses, and that Photius has made the mistake of taking the Conversations to be a different work from the Discourses. Yet Photius has enumerated eight books of the Discourses and twelve books of the Conversations. Schweighaeuser observes that Photius had not seen these works of Arrian on Epictetus, for so he concludes from the brief notice of these works by Photius. The fact is that Photius does not say that he had read these books, as he generally does when he is speaking of the books, which he enumerates in his Bibliotheca. The conclusion is that we are not certain that there was a work of Arrian, entitled the Conversations of Epictetus.

The Discourses of Epictetus with the Encheiridion and Fragments were translated into English by the learned lady Mrs. Elizabeth Carter; who is said to have lived to the age of eighty-nine. The fourth edition (1807) contains the translator's last additions and alterations. There is an Introduction to this translation which contains a summary view of the Stoic philosophy for the purpose of explaining Epictetus; and also there are notes to the translation. The editor of this fourth edition says that "the Introduction and notes of the Christian translator of Epictetus are, in the estimation of most readers, not the least valuable parts of the work": and he adds "this was also the opinion of the late Archbishop Secker, who though he thought very highly of the philosophy of Epictetus, considered the Introduction and notes as admirably calculated to prevent any mistake concerning it, as well as to amend and instruct the world." The Introduction is certainly useful, though it is not free from errors. I do not think that the notes are valuable. I have used some of them without any remarks; and I have used others and made some remarks on them where I thought that Mrs. Carter was mistaken in her opinion of the original text, or on other matters.

The translation of Mrs. Carter is good; and perhaps no Englishman at that time would have made a better translation. I intended at first to revise Mrs. Carter's translation, and to correct any errors that I might discover. I had revised about half of it, when I found that I was not satisfied with my work; and I was advised by a learned friend to translate the whole myself. This was rather a great undertaking for an old man, who is now past seventy-six. I have however done the work with great care, and as well as I could. I have always compared my translation with the Latin version and with Mrs. Carter's; and I think that this is the best way of avoiding errors such as any translator may make. A man who has not attempted to translate a Greek or Latin author does not know the difficulty of the undertaking. That which may appear plain when he reads, often becomes very difficult when he tries to express it in another language. It is true that Epictetus is generally intelligible; but the style or manner of the author, or we may say of Arrian, who attempted to produce what he heard, is sometimes made obscure by the continual use of questions and answers to them, and for other reasons.

Upton remarks in a note on iii. 23 (p. 184 Trans.), that "there are many passages in these dissertations which are ambiguous or rather confused on account of the small questions, and because the matter is not expanded by oratorical copiousness, not to mention other causes." The discourses of Epictetus, it is supposed, were spoken extempore, and so one thing after another would come into the thoughts of the speaker (Wolf). Schweighaeuser also observes in a note (ii. 336 of his edition) that the connexion of the discourse is sometimes obscure through the omission of some words which are necessary to indicate the connexion of the thoughts. The reader then will find that he cannot always understand Epictetus, if he does not read him very carefully, and some passages more than once. He must also think and reflect, or he will miss the meaning. I do not say that the book is worth all this trouble. Every man must judge for himself. But I should not have translated the book, if I had not thought it worth study; and I think that all books of this kind require careful reading, if they are worth reading at all.

The text of Epictetus is sometimes corrupted, and this corruption causes a few difficulties. However, these difficulties are not numerous enough to cause or to admit much variety or diversity in the translations of the text. This remark will explain why many parts of my translation are the same or nearly the same as Mrs. Carter's. When this happened, I did not think it necessary to alter my translation in order that it might not be the same as hers. I made my translation first, and then compared it with Mrs. Carter's and the Latin version. I hope that I have not made many blunders. I do not suppose that I have made none.

The last and best edition of the Discourses, the Encheiridion, and the fragments is by J. Schweighaeuser in 6 vols. 8vo. This edition contains the commentary of Simplicius on the Encheiridion, and two volumes of useful notes on the Discourses. These notes are selected from those of Wolf, Upton, and a few from other commentators; but a large part are by Schweighaeuser himself, who was an excellent scholar and a very sensible man. I have read all these notes, and I have used them. Many of the notes to the translation are my own.

THE PHILOSOPHY OF EPICTETUS.

I HAVE made a large Index to this book; and any person, who has the necessary industry, may find in it almost every passage in the Discourses in which the opinions of the philosopher are stated; and thus he may acquire a general notion of the philosophical system of Epictetus. But few readers will have the time and the inclination for this labour, and therefore I shall attempt to do the work for them.

I have found two expositions of the system of Epictetus. One is by Dr. Heinrich Ritter in his Geschichte der Philosophie alter Zeit, Vierter Theil, 1839. The other is by Professor Christian A. Brandis.[1] Both of these expositions are useful; and I have used them. I do not think that either of them is complete, nor will mine be. I shall not make my exposition exactly in the same form as either of them; nor shall I begin it in the same way.

Ritter has prefixed a short sketch of C. Musonius Rufus, a Roman Stoic, to his exposition of the system of Epictetus. Rufus taught at Rome under the emperor Nero, who drove him from Rome; but Rufus returned after the tyrant's death, and lived to the times of Vespasian and his son Titus. He acquired great reputation as a teacher, but there is no evidence that he wrote anything, and all that we know of his doctrines is from a work of Pollio in

[1] Article EPICTETUS in the 'Dictionary of Greek and Roman Biography,' etc. edited by Doctor William Smith.

Greek, which was written after the model of Xenophon's Memorabilia of Socrates. Of this work there are many fragments.[2]

Rufus taught a practical philosophy, one that was useful for the purposes of life, and for the life of a philosopher who was not hindered by following the common occupations of mankind from philosophizing and aiding others to philosophize.[3] He urged young men especially to the study of philosophy, and even women, because without philosophy no person can be virtuous and do his duty. He asks, what hinders the scholar from working with his teacher and at the same time learning from him something about moderation (σωφροσύνη) and justice and endurance? His belief in the power of philosophy over men's minds was strong, and he was convinced that it was a perfect cure for the corruption of mankind. He showed the firmness of this conviction on an occasion which is recorded by Tacitus (Hist. iii. 81). He endeavoured to mediate between the partizans of Vitellius who were in Rome, and the army of Vespasian, which was before the gates: but he failed in his attempt. His behaviour was like that of a modern Christian, who should attempt to enforce the Christian doctrines of peace on men who are arrayed against one another with arms in their hands. Such a Christian would be called a fanatic now; and Tacitus, who was himself a philosopher, gives to the behaviour of Rufus the mild term of "intempestivam" or "unseasonable." The judgment of Tacitus was right: the behaviour of

[2] See the 'Fragments from Stobaeus,' cited by Ritter in his notes (Vierter Theil, p. 204). The notice of Πωλίων, as he is named, in Suidas, is not satisfactory. It speaks of the 'Απομνημονεύματα of Musonius by Polio or Pollio; and yet it states that Pollio taught at Rome in the time of Pompeius Magnus. See Clinton, Fasti, iii. p. 550.

[3] "It would be a strange thing indeed if the cultivation of the earth hindered a man from philosophizing or aiding others to philosophize." Stobaeus.

Rufus was unseasonable, as the result proved: but the attempt of Rufus was the act of a good man.

Rufus did not value Dialectic or Logic so highly as the old Stoics; but he did not undervalue it, and he taught that a man should learn how to deal with sophistical arguments, as we learn from Epictetus (I. c. 7 at the end).

In his teaching about the Gods he follows the general Stoic practice of maintaining the popular religion. He taught that nothing was unknown to the Gods: as Socrates (Xenophon, Mem. i. c. 1) taught that the Gods knew everything, what was said, what was done, and what men thought. He considered the souls of men to be akin to the Gods; but as they were mingled with the body, the soul must partake of the impurities of the body. The intelligent principle (*διάνοια*) is free from all necessity (compulsion) and self sufficient (*αὐτεξούσιος*). We can only conjecture that Rufus did not busy himself about either Dialectic or Physic; for he said that philosophizing was nothing else than an inquiry about what is becoming and conformable to duty; an inquiry which is conducted by reason, and the result is exhibited in practice.

The old Stoics considered virtue to be the property only of the wise man; and they even doubted whether such a man could be found. But Rufus said that it was not impossible for such a man to exist, for we cannot conceive such virtues as a wise man possesses otherwise than from the examples of human nature itself and by meeting with men such as those who are named divine and godlike. The Stoical doctrine that man should live according to nature is not pressed so hard by Rufus as by some Stoics, and he looks on a life which is conformable to nature as not very difficult; but he admits that those who attempt philosophy have been trained from youth in great corruption and filled with wickedness, and so when they seek after virtue they require more discipline or practice. Accordingly he views philosophy as a spiritual medicine, and gives more weight to the practice or exercise of virtue than the older Stoics did. The knowledge and the teaching of what is good, he says, should come first; but Rufus did not believe that the knowledge of the Good was strong enough without practice (discipline) to lead to moral conduct, and consequently he believed that practice has greater efficacy than teaching.[4] He makes two kinds of exercise, first, the exercise of the soul in thinking, in reflecting and in stamping on the mind sound rules of life; and second, in the enduring of bodily labours or pains, in which act of endurance the soul and the body act together.

"The sum of his several rules of life," says Ritter, may be thus briefly expressed: in his opinion a life according to Nature results in a social, philanthropic and contented state of mind, joined to the most simple satisfaction of our necessary wants. We see his social and philanthropic disposition in this that he opposes all selfishness (selbstsucht),

[4] I have followed the exposition of Ritter here. Perhaps a literal translation of the Greek is still better: "Reason which teaches how we should act co-operates with practice, and reason (or teaching) comes in order before custom (habit) or practice: for it is not possible to become habituated to any thing good if a person is not habituated by reason (by teaching); in power indeed the habit (practice) has the advantage over teaching, for habit (practice) is more efficacious in leading a man to act (properly) than reason is." I have given the meaning of the Greek as accurately as I can. In our modern education we begin with teaching general rules, or principles or beliefs; and there we stop. The result is what might be expected. Practice or the habit of doing what we ought to do is neglected. The teachers are teachers of words and no more. They are the men whom Epictetus (iii. 21, note 6) describes: "You have committed to memory the words only, and you say, Sacred are the words by themselves." See p. 245, note 3.

It is one of the greatest merits of Rufus that he laid down the principle which is expounded above; and it is the greatest demerit of our system of teaching that the principle is generally neglected: and most particularly by those teachers who proclaim ostentatiously that they give a religious education.

that he views marriage not only as the sole right and natural satisfaction of the sexual feelings, but also as the foundation of family, of a state, and of the continuation of the human race; and accordingly he declares himself against the exposure of children as an unnatural practice; and he often recommends beneficence."

Epictetus was a pupil of this noble Roman teacher, whose name occurs several times in the Discourses. Ritter conjectures that Epictetus also heard Euphrates, whom he highly commends. It has been justly said that, though Epictetus is named a Stoic, and that his principles are Stoical, he is not purely a Stoic. He learned from other teachers as well as the Stoic. He quotes the teaching and example of Socrates continually, and the example of Diogenes the Cynic, both of whom he mentions more frequently than Zeno the founder of the Stoic philosophy. He also valued Plato, who accepted from Socrates many of his principles, and developed and expanded them. So Epictetus learned that the beginning of philosophy is man's knowledge of himself (γνῶθι σεαυτόν), and the acknowledgment of his own ignorance and weakness. He teaches (i. c. 17; ii. c. 14; ii. c. 10) that the examination of names, the understanding of the notion, of the conception of a thing, is the beginning of education: he consistently teaches that we ought to pity those who do wrong, for they err in ignorance (i. c. 18; ii. c. 22, p. 181); and, as Plato says, every mind is deprived of truth unwillingly. Epictetus strongly opposes the doctrines of Epicurus, of the newer Academics, and of Pyrrho, the great leader of the Sceptical school (i. c. 5, c. 23; ii. c. 20). He has no taste for the subtle discussions of these men. He says (p. 81), "Let the followers of Pyrrho and the Academics come and make their objections. For I, as to my part, have no leisure for these disputes, nor am I able to undertake the defence of common consent (opinion)."

"How indeed perception is effected, whether through the whole body or any part, perhaps I cannot explain; for both opinions perplex me. But that you and I are not the same, I know with perfect certainty. How do you know it? When I intend to swallow anything, I never carry it to your mouth, but to my own. And you yourselves (the Pyrrhonists), who take away the evidence of the senses, do you act otherwise? Who among you, when he intended to enter a bath, ever went into a mill?" He also says (ii. c. 20) that "the propositions which are true and evident are of necessity used even by those who contradict them; and a man might perhaps consider it to be the greatest proof of a thing being evident that it is found to be necessary even for him who denies it to make use of it at the same time. For instance, if a man should deny that anything is universally true, it is plain that he must make the contradictory negation, that nothing is universally true."

Epictetus did not undervalue Dialectic or Logic, and the solution of what are called Sophistical and Hypothetical arguments (i. c. 7); but he considered the handling of all such arguments as a thing relating to the duties of life, and as a means towards Ethic, or the practice of morals. Rufus said, "for a man to use the appearances presented to him rashly and foolishly and carelessly, and not to understand argument nor demonstration nor sophism, nor, in a word, to see in questioning and answering what is consistent with that which we have granted or is not consistent: is there no error in this"? Accordingly Dialectic is not the object of our life, but it is a means for distinguishing between true and false appearances, and for ascertaining the validity of evidence, and it gives us security in our judgments. It is the application of these things to the purposes of life which is the first and necessary part of philosophy. So he says in the Encheiridion

(LI.): "The first and most necessary place in philosophy is the use of theorems (precepts), for instance, That we must not lie: the second is that of demonstration, for instance, How is it proved that we ought not to lie: the third is that which is confirmatory of these two and explanatory, for example, How is this a demonstration"? The philosophy of Epictetus is in fact only the way of living as a man ought to live, according to his nature.

Epictetus accordingly views that part of the Stoic teaching, named Physic or the Nature of things, also as subordinate to his philosophy, which is purely Ethical. We ought to live according to Nature, and therefore we must inquire what the Law of Nature is. The contemplation of the order of things is the duty of man, and to observe this wonderful system of which man is a part; but the purpose of the contemplation and the observation is that we may live a life such as we ought to live. He says (Frag. CLXXV., "What do I care whether all things are composed of atoms or of similar parts, or of fire and earth? for is it not enough to know the nature of the good and the evil, and the measures of the desires and aversions, and also the movements towards things and from them; and using these as rules to administer the affairs of life, but not to trouble ourselves about the things above us? For these things are perhaps incomprehensible to the human mind: and if any man should even suppose them to be in the highest degree comprehensible, what then is the profit of them, if they are comprehended? And must we not say that those men have needless trouble who assign these things as necessary to a philosopher's discourse?" Epictetus then did not value the inquiries of the Physical philosophers, or he had no taste for them. His Philosophy was Ethical, and his inquiry was, What is the rule of life?

"With respect to gods," says Epictetus (i. c. 12), "there are some who say that a divine being does not exist: others say that it exists, but is inactive and careless, and takes no forethought about anything; a third class say such a being exists and exercises forethought, but only about great things and heavenly things, and about nothing on the earth; a fourth class say that a divine being exercises forethought both about things on the earth and heavenly things, but in a general way only, and not about things severally. There is a fifth class to whom Ulysses and Socrates belong, who say, 'I move not without thy knowledge,'" (Iliad, x. 278). After a few remarks Epictetus concludes: "The wise and good man then after considering all these things, submits his own mind to him who administers the whole, as good citizens do to the law of the state."

The foundation of the Ethic of Epictetus is the doctrine which the Stoic Cleanthes proclaimed in his hymn to Zeus (God), "From thee our race comes." Epictetus speaks of Gods, whom we must venerate and make offerings to; and of God, from whom we all are sprung in an especial manner. "God is the father both of men and of Gods." This great descent ought to teach us to have no ignoble or mean thoughts about ourselves. He says, "Since these two things are mingled in the generation of man, body in common with the animals, and reason and intelligence in common with the Gods, many incline to this kinship, which is miserable and mortal; and some few to that which is divine and happy" (i. c. 3). In a chapter of Providence (i. c. 6) he attempts to prove the existence of God and his government of the world by everything which is or happens; but in order to understand these proofs, a man, he says, must have the faculty of seeing what belongs and happens to "all persons and things, and a grateful disposition" (also, i. c. 16). He argues from the very structure of things which have attained their completion, that we are accustomed to show that a work is certainly the act of some artificer, and that it has not been constructed without a purpose. "Does then each of these things demonstrate the workman, and do not visible things and the faculty of seeing and light demonstrate him"? He then considers the constitution of man's understanding and its operations; and he asks, if this is not sufficient to convince us, let people "explain to us what it is that makes each several thing, or how it is possible that things so wonderful and like the contrivances of art should exist by chance and from their own proper motion"?

It is enough for animals to do what their nature leads them to do without understanding why they do it. But it is not enough for us to whom God has given also the intellectual faculty; for unless we act conformably to the nature and constitution of each thing, we shall never attain our true end. God has introduced man into the world to be a spectator of God and his works; and not only a spectator of them, but an interpreter. For this reason, he says, "it is shameful for man to begin and to end where irrational animals do; but rather he ought to begin where they begin, and to end where nature ends in us; and nature ends in contemplation and understanding, and in a way of life conformable to nature" (p. 21). He examines in another chapter (i. c. 9), How from the fact that we are akin to God, a man may proceed to the consequences. Here he shows that a man who has observed with intelligence the administration of the world, and has learned that the greatest community is that which is composed of men and God, and that from God came all beings which are produced on the earth, and particularly rational beings who are by reason conjoined with him,—"why should not such a man call himself a citizen of the world, why not a son of God, and why should he be afraid of anything which happens among men?—when you have God for your maker, and father, and guardian, shall not this release us from sorrows and fears?"

In this chapter also is a supposed address of Epictetus to those people who on account of the bonds of the body and the troubles of this life intend to throw them off, "ar to depart to their kinsmen." Epictetus says, "Friend. wait for God: when He shall give the signal and release you from this service, then go to Him; but for the present endure to dwell in this place where He has put you—wai[illegible] then, do not depart without a reason." He gives the [illegible]xample of Socrates, who said that if God has put us in any place, we ought not to desert it. I think that Epictetus did not recommend suicide in any case, though he admitted that there were cases in which he would not condemn [illegible]; but a man ought to have good reasons for leaving his post.

The teaching of Epictetus, briefly expressed, is, that man ought to be thankful to God for all things, and always content with that which happens, for what God chooses is better than what man can choose (iv. c. 7). This is what Bishop Butler says, "Our resignation to the will of God may be said to be perfect when our will is lost and resolved up into his; when we rest in his will as our end, as being itself most just and right and good." (Sermon on the Love of God.)

I have not discovered any passage in which Epictetus gives any opinion of the mode of God's existence. He distinguishes God the maker and governor of the universe from the universe itself. His belief in the existence of this great power is as strong as any Christian's could be; and very much stronger than the belief of many who call themselves Christians, and who solemnly and publicly declare "I believe in God the Father Almighty, Maker of heaven and earth." Epictetus teaches us what our duty is towards God; and there is no doubt that he practised what he taught, as a sincere and honest man should do, or at least try to do with all his might. W[illegible]

that a man of his temper of mind[illegible]

did what he recommends (Fragments, cxviii., cxix.): "Let your talk of God be renewed every day rather than your food"; and "Think of God more frequently than you breathe." I see no other conclusion that such a man could come to than this, that God exists without doubt, and that He is incomprehensible to such feeble creatures as man who lives in so feeble a body. See p. 21, note 5.

We must now see what means God has given to His children for doing their duty. Epictetus begins by showing what things God has put in our power, and what things he has not (i. c. 1; Encheir. 1). "That which is best of all and supreme over all is the only thing which the gods have placed in our power, the right use of appearances; but all other things they have not placed in our power"; and the reason of this limitation of man's power is, "that as we exist on the earth and are bound to such a body and to such companions, how was it possible for us not to be hindered as to these things by externals?" He says again (Encheirid. 1): "Of things some are in our power, and others are not. In our power are opinion, movement towards a thing, desire, aversion (turning from a thing); and in a word, whatever are our own acts: not in our power are the body, property, reputation, offices (magisterial power), and in a word, whatever are not our own acts. And the things in our power are by nature free, not subject to restraint nor hindrance: but the things not in our power are weak, slavish, subject to restraint, in the power of others." This is his notion of man's freedom. On this notion all his system rests. He says (i. c. 17): "if God had made that part of himself, which he took from himself and gave to us, of such a nature as to be hindered or compelled either by himself or by another, he would not then be God nor would he be taking care of us as he ought."

He says (i. c. 1; iii. c. 3; and elsewhere) that the right

use of appearances is the only thing that the gods have placed in our power; and "that it is the business of the wise and good man to use appearances conformably to nature." For this purpose a man has what Epictetus names a ruling faculty (τὸ ἡγεμονικόν), of which he gives a definition or description (iv. c. 7). It is that faculty "which uses all other faculties and tries them, and selects and rejects;" a faculty by which we reflect and judge and determine, a faculty which no other animal has, a faculty which, as Bishop Butler says, "plainly bears upon it marks of authority over all the rest, and claims the absolute direction of them all, to allow or forbid their gratification" (Preface to the Sermons).

These appearances are named φαντασίαι by Epictetus; and the word is translated "Visa animi" by Gellius (Frag. clxxx.). This Phantasy (φαντασία) is not only the thing which is perceived by the eyes, but the impression which is made on the eyes, and generally it means any impression received by the senses; and also it is the power of the mind to represent things as if they were present, though they are only present in the mind and are really absent. This power of Phantasy exists also in animals in various degrees according to their several capacities: animals make use of appearances, but man only understands the use of appearances (i. c. 6).[5] If a man cannot or does not make a right use of appearances, he approaches the nature of an irrational animal; and he is not what God made him capable of being.

The nature of the Good is in the use of appearances,

[5] I suppose that this will be generally allowed to be true. Whatever an animal can do, we shall hardly admit that he understands the use of appearances, and uses them as a man can. However the powers of some animals, such as ants for example, are very wonderful; and it may be contended that they are not irrational in many of their acts, but quite rational.

and the nature of evil likewise; and things independent of the will do not admit either the nature of evil or of good (ii. c. 1). The good and the bad are in man's will, and in nothing external. The rational power therefore leads us to acknowledge as good only that which is conformable to reason, and to recognize as bad that which is not conformable to reason. The matter on which the good man labours is his rational faculty (τὸ ἴδιον ἡγεμονικόν): that is the business of the philosopher (iii. c. 3). A man who wishes to be what he is by nature, by his constitution, adapted for becoming, must "struggle against appearances" (ii. c. 18). This is not an easy thing, but it is the only way of obtaining true freedom, tranquillity of mind, and the dominion over the movements of the soul, in a word happiness, which is the true end and purpose of man's existence on earth. Every man carries in him his own enemy, whom he must carefully watch (Ench. xlviii.). There is danger that appearances, which powerfully resist reason, will carry you away: if you are conquered twice or even once, there is danger that a habit of yielding to them will be formed. "Generally, then, if you would make anything a habit, do it: if you would not make it a habit, do not do it; but accustom yourself to do something else in place of it" (ii. c. 18). As to pleasure Epictetus says (Ench. xxxiv.): "If you have received the impression (φαντασίαν) of any pleasure, guard yourself against being carried away by it; but let the thing wait for you, and allow yourself a certain delay on your own part. Then think of both times, of the time when you will enjoy the pleasure, and of the time after the enjoyment of the pleasure when you will repent and reproach yourself. And set against these things how you will rejoice, if you have abstained from the pleasure, and how you will commend yourself. But if it seem to you seasonable to undertake (do) the thing, take care that the charm of it, and the pleasure, and the attraction of it shall not conquer you: and set on the other side the consideration how much better it is to be conscious that you have gained this victory."

Hence the rule that a man must be careful and cautious in everything which is in the power of the will; but on the contrary, with respect to externals which are not in a man's power, he must be bold. "Confidence (courage) then ought to be employed against death, and caution against the fear of death: but now we do the contrary, and employ against death the attempt to escape; and to our opinion about it we employ carelessness, rashness and indifference" (ii. c. 1). For the purification of the soul and enabling it to employ its powers a man must root out of himself two things, arrogance (pride, οἴησις) and distrust. "Arrogance is the opinion that you want nothing (are deficient in nothing); but distrust is the opinion that you cannot be happy when so many circumstances surround you."[6]

The notion of Good and Bad should be firmly fixed in man's mind. There is in the opinion of Epictetus no difference among men on this matter. He says (ii. c. 11) on the beginning of Philosophy: As to good and evil, and what we ought to do and what we ought not to do, and the like, "whoever came into the world without having an idea (ἔμφυτος ἔννοια) of them?" These general notions he names προλήψεις, preconceptions, or praecognitions (ii. c. 2); and we need discipline "in order to learn how to adapt the preconception of the rational and the irrational to the several things conformably to nature." Why then do men differ in their opinions about particular things? The differences arise in the adaptation of the praecognitions to the particular cases. He says (iv. c. 1): "This is the

[6] Ritter, p. 227, has a wrong reading in his quotation of this passage, and he has misunderstood it.

cause to men of all their evils, the not being able to adapt the general preconceptions to the several things." It is so in everything. General principles are often very simple and intelligible; but when we come to the application of the principles, there arises difficulty and difference of opinions. "Education is the learning how to adapt the natural praecognitions to the particular things conformably to nature; and then to distinguish that of things some are in our power, but others are not." The Great Law of Life (i. c. 26) is that we must act conformably to nature. "In theory there is nothing which draws us away from following what is taught; but in the matters of life, many are the things which distract us." A man then must not begin with the matters of real life, for it is not easy to begin with the more difficult things. "This then is the beginning of philosophy, a man's perception of the state of his ruling faculty; for when a man knows that it is weak, then he will not employ it on things of the greatest difficulty"; and again (ii. 11), "the beginning of philosophy is a man's consciousness about his own weakness and inability about necessary things": and further, "this is the beginning of philosophy, a perception of the disagreement of men with one another, and an inquiry into the cause of the disagreement, and a condemnation and distrust of that which only 'seems,' and a certain investigation of that which 'seems,' whether it 'seems' rightly, and a discovery of some rule, as we have discovered a balance in the determination of weights, and a carpenter's rule (or square) in the case of straight and crooked things. This is the beginning of philosophy."

Epictetus urges the fact of a man assenting to or not assenting to a thing as a proof that man possesses something which is naturally free. He says (p. 253): "Who is able to compel you to assent to that which appears false? No man. And who can compel you not to assent to that which appears true? No man. By this then you see that there is something in you naturally free. But to desire or to be averse from, or to move towards an object or to move from it, or to prepare yourself, or to propose to do anything, which of you can do this, unless he has received an impression of the appearance of that which is profitable or a duty? No man. You have then in these things also something which is not hindered and is free. Wretched men, work out this, take care of this, seek for good here." (Compare iv. c. 1 p. 303, and note 20.)

Here the philosopher teaches that a man's opinion or his belief cannot be compelled by another, though we may conclude from what we see and hear and is done in the world, that a large part of mankind do not know this fact. A man cannot even think or believe as he chooses himself: if a thing is capable of demonstration, and if he understands demonstration, he must believe what is demonstrated. If the thing is a matter of probable evidence, he will follow that which seems the more probable, if he has any capacity for thinking. I say 'any capacity' for thinking, because the intellectual power in the minds of a great number of persons is very weak; and in all of us often very weak compared with the power of the necessities of our nature, of our desires, of our passions, in fact of all that is in this wonderful creature man, which is not pure reason or pure understanding or whatever name we give to the powers named intellectual.

The second part of this last quotation from Epictetus relates to the Will, by which I mean, and I suppose that he means, the wish and the intention and the attempt to do something particular, or to abstain from doing some particular thing. Much has been written about man's Will. Some persons think that he has none; that he moves as he is moved, and cannot help himself. Epictetus has no essay or dissertation on this matter; and it would have been contrary to his method of teaching to make a formal discussion of the Will, after the manner of modern philosophers. He does not touch on the question of man's will as dependent on the will of God, or as acting in opposition to it. God has made man as free as he could be in such a body, in which he must live on the earth. This body is not man's own, but it is clay finely tempered; and God has also given to man a small portion of himself, in a word, the faculty of using the appearances of things, of which faculty Epictetus says, "if you will take care of this faculty and consider it your only possession, you will never be hindered, never meet with impediments, you will not lament, you will not blame, you will not flatter any person" (i. c. 1). He says (iv. c. 12) that God "has placed me with myself, and has put my will in obedience to myself alone, and has given me rules for the right use of it."

The word of Epictetus which I have always translated by Will is προαίρεσις, which is literally a 'preference,' a choice of one thing before another, or before any other thing; a description which is sufficiently intelligible.[7]

[7] H. Stephanus in his Greek Lexicon (s. v. Αἱρέω) has a long discussion on the word προαίρεσις: which is not satisfactory. He objects to the translation by the old scholars of προαίρεσις by 'Electio,' 'choice, because προαίρεσις, he says, is not 'Electio,' but it is that which follows from the choice itself. "For," he adds, "Electio is the act of 'choosing, of selection,' and Electio can only be in the mind, when we have chosen this or that." This distinction is trifling. When he says that "προαίρεσις applies to him who out of several things selects one after deliberation and prefers it to others," he says right, and this is sufficient. He then discusses whether προαίρεσις should be rendered, when Aristotle uses it strictly, by 'Propositum' or 'Consilium,' and he decides in favour of 'Propositum.' At the beginning of Aristotle's Ethic he translates πᾶσα προαίρεσις by 'Propositum omne,' or 'Consilium omne:' but he prefers 'Propositum.' He objects to the Latin translation of προαίρεσις by 'Voluntas' in cases where Aristotle uses the word strictly, for Aristotle makes a distinction between προαίρεσις and βούλησις. A distinction between προαίρεσις and βούλησις is certain, and it is plain. But Stephanus does not seem to know that

Though Epictetus contends that man has power over his will, he well knew how weak this power sometimes is. An appearance, he says (p. 86), is presented, and straightway I act according to it; and, what is the name of those who follow every appearance? They are called madmen.—Such are a large part of mankind; and it is true, that many persons have no Will at all. They are deceived by appearances, perplexed, tossed about like a ship which has lost the helm: they have no steady, fixed, and rational purpose. Their perseverance or obstinacy is often nothing more than a perseverance in an irrational purpose. It is often so strong and so steady that the man himself and others too may view it as a strong will; and it is a strong will, if you choose, but it is a will in a wrong direction. "The nature of the Good is a certain Will: the nature of the Bad is a certain kind of Will" (i. c. 29).

Those who have been fortunate in their parents and in their education, who have acquired good habits, and are not greatly disturbed by the affects and the passions, may

---

the Latin word 'voluntas,' especially in the law writers, does represent a deliberate purpose or will, as when a man intends, designs, and uses the necessary means, for example, to kill another, in which case the Romans rightly viewed the will as equivalent to the deed. Cicero (Tuscul. iv. 6) says, "Quamobrem simul objecta species cujuspiam est, quod bonum videatur, ad id adipiscendum impellit ipsa natura. Id quum constanter prudenterque fit, ejusmodi appetitionem Stoici βούλησιν appellant, nos appellamus Voluntatem. Eam illi putant in solo esse sapiente, quam sic definiunt: Voluntas est quae quid cum ratione desiderat. Quae autem ratione adversa incitata est vehementius, ea libido est, vel cupiditas effrenata, quae in omnibus stultis invenitur."

In p. 183 Schweighaeuser has a note on the προαιρετικὴ δύναμις and προαίρεσις, which are generally, he says, translated by Voluntas; but, he adds, it has a wider meaning than is generally given to the Latin word, and it comprehends the intellect with the will, and all the active powers of the mind which we sometimes designate by the general name of Reason.

pass through life calmly and with little danger, even when the powers of the will are very weak, and hardly ever exercised. Life with them is fortunately a series of habits, generally good, or at least not bad. This is the condition of many men and women. They are good or seem to be good, because they are not tried above their power; but if a temptation should suddenly surprise them when they are not prepared for it, they are conquered and they fall. Even a man, who has trained himself to the exercise of his rational faculties and has for a long time passed a blameless life, may in a moment when his vigilance is relaxed, when he is off his guard, be defeated by the enemy whom he always carries about with him.

The difference between a man, who has within him the principles of reason and him who has not, appears from a story told by Gellius (xix. 1):—We were sailing, he says, from Cassiopa to Brundisium when a violent storm came on. In the ship there was a Stoic philosopher, a man of good repute. He who told the story says that he kept his eyes on the philosopher to see how he behaved under the circumstances. The philosopher did not weep and bewail like the rest, but his complexion and apparent perturbation did not much differ from those of the other passengers. When the danger was over, a wealthy Greek from Asia, went up to the Stoic, and in an insulting manner said, How is this, philosopher? when we were in danger, you were afraid and grew pale; but I was neither afraid nor was I pale. The philosopher after a little hesitation said, If I seemed to be a little afraid in so violent a tempest, you are not worthy to hear the reason of it. However he told the man a story about Aristippus [8], who on a like occasion was questioned by a man like this Greek; and so the philosopher got rid of the impertinent fellow. When they

[8] Or a follower of Aristippus. The text is not certain.

arrived at Brundisium, the narrator asked the philosopher for an explanation of his fear, which the philosopher readily gave. He took out of his bag a work of Epictetus, the fifth book of his discourses in which was the following passage (Frag. clxxx.): The affects of the mind (visa animi), which philosophers name φαντασίαι, by which a man's mind is struck by the first appearance of a thing which approaches, are not things which belong to the will nor in our power, but by a peculiar force they intrude themselves on men. But the assents, which they name συγκαταθέσεις (the assents of the judgment), by which the same affects (visa animi) are known and determined are from the will and are in the power of men to make. For this reason when some frightful sound in the heavens or from a fall, or some sudden news of danger comes, or any thing of the same kind happens, it is unavoidable that even the mind of the wise man must be moved somewhat and confounded, and that he must grow pale, not through an opinion which he has first conceived of any danger (or evil), but by certain rapid and inconsiderate emotions which anticipate (prevent) the exercise of the mind and the reason. In a short time however the wise man does not allow these emotions (visa animi) to remain, but he rejects them, and he sees nothing terrible in them. But this is the difference between the fool and the wise man: the fool, as the things at the first impulse appeared to be dangerous, such he thinks them to be; but the wise man, when he has been moved for a short time, recovers the former state and vigour of his mind, which he always had with reference to such appearances, that they are not objects of fear, but only terrify by a false show.[9]

This explanation may be applied to all the events, to all the thoughts and to all the emotions which disturb the mind

[9] This is the general sense of the passage. The translation is not easy.

and the reason, whatever be their cause or nature. If a man's mind has been long under proper discipline, after reflection he is able to recover from this disorder and to resume his former state. If he has not been under proper discipline when his powers of reason are thus assailed, he may do any thing however foolish or bad. A sound exercise of the faculty of the Will therefore requires discipline, in order that it may be corrected and maintained. A man must exercise his will and improve it by labour so as to make it conformable to nature and free. This exercise of the will and the improvement of it are a labour that never ends. A man should begin it as soon as he can. If the question is asked how a man must begin, who has never been trained by a parent or teacher to observe carefully his own conduct, to reflect, to determine, and then to act, I cannot tell. Perhaps a mere accident, some trifle which many persons would not notice, may be the beginning of a total change in a man's life, as in the case of Polemon, who was a dissolute youth, and as he was by chance passing the lecture room of Xenocrates, he and his drunken companions burst into the room. Polemon was so affected by the words of the excellent teacher, that he came out a different man, and at last succeeded Xenocrates in the school of the Academy (iii. c. 1). Folly and bad habits then may by reflection be altered into wisdom and a good course of life. If such a thing happens, and undoubtedly it has happened, it may be said that the origin of the change is not in a man's will, but in something external. Granted: a thing external has presented an appearance to a man, but the effect of the appearance would not be the same in all men, as we presume that it was not the same, as the story is told, in Polemon and his companions. One man in this case had a temper or disposition and a capacity to use his mental power and to profit by the words of Xenocrates. It may be said that this temper or disposition and capacity are not in the power of a man's Will; and this is true. But that matter is nothing to us. Men have various capacities, and, as Epictetus would say, they are the gift of God, who distributes them as he pleases. One man has the power of using an appearance in a way which is good for himself, and another has not. We can say no more. In whatever way then a man has been led to exercise his will towards a good end, he must practise the exercise of his will for such an end; he must make a habit of it, which habit will acquire strength; and he may then have a reasonable hope that he will not often fail in his good purpose. This I believe to be the meaning of Epictetus, as we may collect from the numerous passages in which he speaks of the will. I hope that no reader will think that I propose what I have said as a sufficient explanation of a difficult matter. I have only said what I think to be sufficient to explain Epictetus; and I have said what seems to me to be true.

Epicurus taught that we should not marry nor beget children nor engage in public affairs, because these things disturb our tranquillity. Epictetus and the Stoics taught that a man should marry, should beget children, and discharge all the duties of a citizen. In one of his best discourses (iii. c. 22; About Cynism), in which he describes what kind of person a Cynic (his ideal philosopher) should be, he says that he is a messenger from God (Zeus) to men about good and bad things, to show them that they have wandered and are seeking the substance of good and evil where it is not; but where it is, they never think. The Cynic is supposed to say, How is it possible that a man like himself, who is houseless and has nothing can live happily? The answer is, See, God has sent you a man to show you that it is possible. The man has no city, nor house, he has nothing; he has no wife, nor children; and yet he wants nothing. In reply to a question whether a

Cynic should marry and procreate children, Epictetus answers: "If you grant me a community of wise men, perhaps no man will readily apply himself to the Cynic practice." However, he says, if he does, nothing will prevent him from marrying and begetting children, for his wife will be another like himself. "But," he adds, "in the present state of things which is like that of an army placed in battle order, is it not fit that the Cynic should without any distraction be employed only on the ministration of God, able to go about among men, not tied down to the common duties of mankind, nor entangled in the ordinary relations of life, which if he neglects, he will not maintain the character of an honourable and good man? and if he observes them, he will lose the character of the messenger, and spy and herald of God." The conclusion is that it is better for a minister of God not to marry.[10]

Epictetus distinguishes the soul from the body in the chapter (iv. c. 11) about purity (cleanliness); but he wisely does not attempt to define the soul. He says, "We suppose that there is something superior in man and that we first receive it from the Gods: for since the Gods by their nature are pure and free from corruption, so far as men approach them by reason, so far do they cling to purity and to a love (habit) of purity." It is however impossible for man's nature to be altogether pure; but reason endeavours to make human nature love purity. "The first then and highest purity is that which is in the soul; and we say the same of impurity. But you could not discover the impurity of the soul as you could discover

[10] Dr. Farrar says in his 'Seekers after God' (Epictetus p. 213), "That Epictetus approves of celibacy as a 'counsel of perfection,' and indeed his views have a close and remarkable resemblance to those of St. Paul." I do not understand the first part of this sentence; and the reader of Epictetus will see that the second part is not true. There is a note on the matter (pp. 258, 316).

that of the body: but as to the soul, what else could you find in it than that which makes it filthy in respect to the acts which are her own? Now the acts of the soul are movement towards an object or movement from it, desire, aversion, preparation, design (purpose), assent. What then is it which in these acts makes the soul filthy and impure? Nothing else than her own bad judgments (κρίματα). Consequently the impurity of the soul is the soul's bad opinions; and the purification of the soul is the planting in it of proper opinions; and the soul is pure which has proper opinions, for the soul alone in her own acts is free from perturbation and pollution."

Epictetus says (iv. c. 7) that man is not "flesh nor bones nor sinews (νεῦρα), but he is that which makes use of these parts of the body and governs them and follows (understands) the appearances of things." This opinion seems to be the same or nearly the same as Bp. Butler's (iv. c. 7, note 10). If then Epictetus had any distinct notion of the soul, and he is a man whose notions are generally distinct, I think that his opinion of man's body and of man's soul are, that a man's body is not the man, but the body is that "finely tempered clay" in which the man dwells, and without the body he could not live this earthly life: and his notion of the soul is that which is stated above (iv. c. 11 and c. 7). As to the mode and nature of this connexion between the body and the soul, I can only suppose that he would have disclaimed all knowledge of it, as he does of the nature of perception (p. 82); and I do not suppose that any philosopher or theologian would venture to say what this connexion of soul and body is. In the life then which man lives on the earth I think that the opinions of Epictetus are the same or nearly the same as those of Swedenborg; but after the event, which comes to all men, and which we name Death, the opinions are very different.

And what is Death? (p. 280 in the chapter on Solitude). It is a going "to the place from which you came, to your friends and kinsmen, to the elements: what there was in you of fire goes to fire, of earth to earth; of air (spirit) to air; of water to water: no Hades, nor Acheron, nor Cocytus, nor Pyriphlegethon, but all is full of Gods and Daemons." He says (p. 282): "death is a greater change, not from the state which now is to that which is not, but to that which is not now. Shall I then no longer exist? You will not exist, but you will be something else, of which the world now has need: for you also came into existence not when you chose, but when the world had need of you." Death is the resolution of the matter of the body into the things out of which it is composed (p. 347). This is distinct and intelligible. Of the soul, which, as we have seen, he considers to be in some way different from the body during life, he does not speak so distinctly. I think that he means, if he means any thing, something like what I have said in p. 347, note 4.

The philosopher, who appears to have no belief in a future existence, as it is generally understood, teaches that we ought to live such a life in all our thoughts and in all our acts as a Christian would teach. He says (p. 285), "Then in the place of all other delights substitute this, that of being conscious that you are obeying God, that not in word, but in deed you are performing the acts of a wise and good man." He looks for no reward for doing what he ought to do. The virtuous man has his reward in his own acts. If he lives conformably to nature, he will do what is best in this short life, and will obtain all the happiness which he can obtain in no other way.

He says (p. 310): "Who are you and for what purpose did you come into the world? Did not God introduce you here, did he not show you the light, did he not give you fellow workers, and perception and reason? and as whom did he introduce you here? did he not introduce you as subject to death, and as one to live on the earth with a little flesh, and to observe his administration and to join with him in the spectacle and the festival for a short time? Will you not then, as long as you have been permitted, after seeing the spectacle and the solemnity, when he leads you out, go with adoration of him and thanks for what you have heard and seen"?

Perhaps we may say that the conclusion of Epictetus about the soul after the separation from the body is equivalent to a declaration that he knew nothing about it; as he disclaims sometimes the knowledge of other things. We cannot assume that in the books which are lost he expressed any opinions which are inconsistent with those contained in the books which exist. He must have known the opinion of Socrates about the immortality of the soul, or the opinion attributed to Socrates; but he has not said that he assents to it, nor does he express dissent from it. Bp. Butler in his Analogy of Religion Natural and Revealed (Part I. Of Natural Religion, Chap. I. of a Future Life) has examined the question of a Future Life with his usual modesty, good sense and sagacity. The inquiry is very difficult. He says at the end of the chapter: "The credibility of a future life, which has been here insisted on, how little soever it may satisfy our curiosity, seems to answer all the purposes of religion, in like manner as a demonstrative proof would. Indeed, a proof, even a demonstrative one, of a future life, would not be a proof of religion. For, that we are to live hereafter, is just as reconcileable with the scheme of atheism, and as well to be accounted for by it, as that we are now alive is; and therefore nothing can be more absurd than to argue from that scheme that there can be no future state. But as religion implies a future state, any presumption against such a state is a presumption against religion."

I conclude that Epictetus, who was a religious man, and who believed in the existence of God and his administration of all things, did not deny a future life; nor does he say that he believes it. I conclude that he did not understand it; that it was beyond his conception, as the nature of God also was. His great merit as a teacher is that he "attempted to show that there is in man's nature and in the constitution of things sufficient reason for living a virtuous life."[11] He knew well what man's nature is, and he endeavoured to teach us how we can secure happiness in this life as fàr as we are capable of attaining it.

More might be said; but this is enough. I will only add that the Stoics have been charged with arrogance; and the charge is just. Epictetus himself has been blamed for it even by modern theologians, who are not always free from this fault themselves. If there is any arrogance or apparent arrogance in Epictetus, he did not teach it, for he has especially warned us against this fault, as the reader will see in several passages.

[11] I am not sure that I rightly understood the Apostle Paul, when I wrote the note 22 in p. 283. The words "Let us eat and drink, for to-morrow we die," are said to be a quotation from a Greek writer. The words then may be taken not as Paul's, but as the conclusion of foolish persons. A friend who, as I understand his remarks, is of this opinion, also adds that as Paul was a learned man, and knew something about the Greek philosophers, he would certainly give them credit for better and more rational opinions. This may be the true meaning of the words. Paul is not always easy to understand, even by those who make a special study of his Epistles.

ARRIAN'S

DISCOURSES OF EPICTETUS.

ARRIAN *to* LUCIUS GELLIUS, *with wishes for his happiness.*

I NEITHER wrote these Discourses[1] of Epictetus in the way in which a man might write such things; nor did I make them public myself, inasmuch as I declare that I did not even write them. But whatever I heard him say, the same I attempted to write down in his own words as nearly as possible, for the purpose of preserving them as memorials to myself afterwards of the thoughts and the freedom of speech of Epictetus. Accordingly, the Discourses are naturally such as a man would address without preparation to another, not such as a man would write

[1] A. Gellius (i. 2 and xvii. 19) speaks of the Discourses of Epictetus being arranged by Arrian; and Gellius (xix. 1) speaks of a fifth book of these Discourses, but only four are extant and some fragments. The whole number of books was eight, as Photius (Cod. 58) says. There is also extant an Encheiridion or Manual, consisting of short pieces selected from the Discourses of Epictetus; and there is the valuable commentary on the Encheiridion written by Simplicius in the sixth century A.D. and in the reign of Justinian.

Arrian explains in a manner what he means by saying that he did not write these Discourses of Epictetus; but he does not explain his meaning when he says that he did not make them public. He tells us that he did attempt to write down in the words of Epictetus what the philosopher said; but how it happened that they were first published, without his knowledge or consent, Arrian does not say. It appears, however, that he did see the Discourses when they were published; and as Schweighaeuser remarks, he would naturally correct any errors that he detected, and so there would be an edition revised [illegible]. Schweighaeuser has a note (i. ch. 26, 13) on the difficulties [illegible] and in the Discourses.

with the view of others reading them. Now, being such, I do not know how they fell into the hands of the public, without either my consent or my knowledge. But it concerns me little if I shall be considered incompetent to write; and it concerns Epictetus not at all if any man shall despise his words; for at the time when he uttered them, it was plain that he had no other purpose than to move the minds of his hearers to the best things. If, indeed, these Discourses should produce this effect, they will have, I think, the result which the words of philosophers ought to have. But if they shall not, let those who read them know that, when Epictetus delivered them, the hearer could not avoid being affected in the way that Epictetus wished him to be. But if the Discourses themselves, as they are written, do not effect this result, it may be that the fault is mine, or, it may be, that the thing is unavoidable.

Farewell!

BOOK I.

CHAPTER I.

OF THE THINGS WHICH ARE IN OUR POWER, AND NOT IN OUR POWER.

Of all the faculties (except that which I shall soon mention), you will find not one which is capable of contemplating itself, and, consequently, not capable either of approving or disapproving.[1] How far does the grammatic art possess the contemplating power? As far as forming a judgment about what is written and spoken. And how far music? As far as judging about melody. Does either of them then contemplate itself? By no means. But when you must write something to your friend, grammar will tell you what words you should write; but whether you should write or not, grammar will not tell you. And so it is with music as to musical sounds; but whether you should sing at the present time and play on the lute, or do neither, music will not tell you. What faculty then will tell you? That which contemplates both itself and all other things. And what is this faculty? The rational faculty;[2] for this is the only faculty that we

[1] [illegible] is moral approving and disapproving faculty" is Bp. Butler's [illegible] of the δοκιμαστική and ἀποδοκιμαστική of Epictetus (i. 1, 1) [illegible]sertation, Of the Nature of Virtue. See his note.

[2] [illegible] rational faculty is the λογικὴ ψυχή of Epictetus and Antoninus, of which Antoninus says (xi. 1): "These are the properties of the rational soul: it sees itself, analyses itself, and makes itself such as it chooses; the fruit which it bears, itself enjoys."

have received which examines itself, what it is, and what power it has, and what is the value of this gift, and examines all other faculties: for what else is there which tells us that golden things are beautiful, for they do not say so themselves? Evidently it is the faculty which is capable of judging of appearances.[3] What else judges of music, grammar, and the other faculties, proves their uses, and points out the occasions for using them? Nothing else.

As then it was fit to be so, that which is best of all and supreme over all is the only thing which the gods have placed in our power, the right use of appearances; but all other things they have not placed in our power. Was it because they did not choose? I indeed think that, if they had been able, they would have put these other things also in our power, but they certainly could not.[4] For as we exist on the earth, and are bound to such a body and to such companions, how was it possible for us not to be hindered as to these things by externals?

But what says Zeus? Epictetus, if it were possible, I would have made both your little body and your little property free and not exposed to hindrance. But now be not ignorant of this: this body is not yours, but it is clay finely tempered. And since I was not able to do for you

[3] This is what he has just named the rational faculty. The Stoics gave the name of appearances (φαντασίαι) to all impressions received by the senses, and to all emotions caused by external things. Chrysippus said: φαντασία ἐστὶ πάθος ἐν τῇ ψυχῇ γινόμενον, ἐνδεικνύμενον ἑαυτό τε καὶ τὸ πεποιηκός (Plutarch, iv. c. 12, De Placit. Philosoph.)

[4] Compare Antoninus, ii. 3. Epictetus does not intend to limit the power of the gods, but he means that the constitution of things being what it is, they cannot do contradictories. They have so constituted things that man is hindered by externals. How then could they give to man a power of not being hindered by externals? Seneca (De Providentia, c. 6) says: "But it may be said, many things happen which cause sadness, fear, and are hard to bear. Because (God says) I could not save you from them, I have armed your minds against all." This is the answer to those who imagine that they have disproved the common assertion of the omnipotence of God, when they ask whether He can combine inherent contradictions, whether He can cause two and two to make five. This is indeed a very absurd way of talking.

what I have mentioned, I have given you a small portion of us,[5] this faculty of pursuing an object and avoiding it, and the faculty of desire and aversion, and, in a word, the faculty of using the appearances of things; and if you will take care of this faculty and consider it your only possession, you will never be hindered, never meet with impediments; you will not lament, you will not blame, you will not flatter any person.

Well, do these seem to you small matters? I hope not. Be content with them then and pray to the gods. But now when it is in our power to look after one thing, and to attach ourselves to it, we prefer to look after many things, and to be bound to many things, to the body and to property, and to brother and to friend, and to child and to slave. Since then we are bound to many things, we are depressed by them and dragged down. For this reason, when the weather is not fit for sailing, we sit down and torment ourselves, and continually look out to see what wind is blowing. It is north. What is that to us? When will the west wind blow? When it shall choose, my good man, or when it shall please Aeolus; for God has not made you the manager of the winds, but Aeolus.[6] What then? We must make the best use that we can of the things which are in our power, and use them according to their nature. What is their nature then? As God may please.

Must I then alone have my head cut off? What, would you have all men lose their heads that you may be con-

[5] Schweighaeuser observes that these faculties of pursuit and avoidance, and of desire and aversion, and even the faculty of using appearances, belong to animals as well as to man; but animals in using appearances are moved by passion only, and do not understand what they are doing, while in man these passions are under his control. Salmasius proposed to change ἡμέτερον into ὑμέτερον, to remove the difficulty about these animal passions being called "a small portion of us (the gods)." Schweighaeuser, however, though he sees the difficulty, does not accept the emendation. Perhaps Arrian has here imperfectly represented what his master said, and perhaps he did not.

[6] He alludes to the Odyssey, X. 21:

κεῖνον γὰρ ταμίην ἀνέμων ποίησε Κρονίων.

soled? Will you not stretch out your neck as Lateranus[7] did at Rome when Nero ordered him to be beheaded? For when he had stretched out his neck, and received a feeble blow, which made him draw it in for a moment, he stretched it out again. And a little before, when he was visited by Epaphroditus,[8] Nero's freedman, who asked him about the cause of offence which he had given, he said, "If I choose to tell anything, I will tell your master."

What then should a man have in readiness in such circumstances? What else than this? What is mine, and what is not mine; and what is permitted to me, and what is not permitted to me. I must die. Must I then die lamenting? I must be put in chains. Must I then also lament? I must go into exile. Does any man then hinder me from going with smiles and cheerfulness and contentment? Tell me the secret which you possess. I will not, for this is in my power. But I will put you in chains.[9] Man, what are you talking about? Me in chains? You may fetter my leg, but my will[10] not even Zeus himself can overpower. I will throw you into prison. My poor body, you mean. I will cut your head off. When then have I told you that my head alone cannot be cut off? These are the things which philosophers should meditate on, which they should write daily, in which they should exercise themselves.

Thrasea[11] used to say, I would rather be killed to-day

[7] Plautius Lateranus, consul-elect, was charged with being engaged in Piso's conspiracy against Nero. He was hurried to execution without being allowed to see his children; and though the tribune who executed him was privy to the plot, Lateranus said nothing. (Tacit. Ann. xv. 49, 60.)

[8] Epaphroditus was a freedman of Nero, and once the master of Epictetus. He was Nero's secretary. One good act is recorded of him: he helped Nero to kill himself, and for this act he was killed by Domitian (Suetonius, Domitian, c. 14).

[9] This is an imitation of a passage in the Bacchae of Euripides (v. 492, &c.), which is also imitated by Horace (Epp. i. 16).

[10] *ἡ προαίρεσις.* It is sometimes rendered by the Latin *propositum* or by *voluntas*, the will.

[11] Thrasea Paetus, a Stoic philosopher, who was ordered in Nero's time to put himself to death (Tacit. Ann. xvi. 21–35). He was the husband of Arria, whose mother Arria, the wife of Caecina Paetus

than banished to-morrow. What then did Rufus[12] s
him? If you choose death as the heavier misfo
how great is the folly of your choice? But if, a
lighter, who has given you the choice? Will yo
study to be content with that which has been giv
you? Stoic

What then did Agrippinus[13] say? He said, "I a
a hindrance to myself." When it was reported t
that his trial was going on in the Senate, he said, "
it may turn out well; but it is the fifth hour of the
—this was the time when he was used to exercise h
and then take the cold bath—"let us go and tak
exercise." After he had taken his exercise, one
and tells him, You have been condemned. To b
ment, he replies, or to death? To banishment.
about my property? It is not taken from you.
go to Aricia then,[14] he said, and dine.

This it is to have studied what a man ought to s
to have made desire, aversion, free from hindranc
free from all that a man would avoid. I must d
now, I am ready to die. If, after a short time, I no
because it is the dinner-hour; after this I will the
How? Like a man who gives up[15] what belo
another.

in the time of the Emperor Claudius, heroically showed her l
the way to die (Plinius, Letters, iii. 16.) Martial has immo
the elder Arria in a famous epigram (i. 14):—

> "When Arria to her Paetus gave the sword,
> Which her own hand from her chaste bosom drew,
> 'This wound,' she said, 'believe me, gives no pain,
> But that will pain me which thy hand will do.'"

[12] C. Musonius Rufus, a Tuscan by birth, of equestrian
philosopher and Stoic (Tacit. Hist. iii. 81).

[13] Paconius Agrippinus was condemned in Nero's time. The
against him was that he inherited his father's hatred of the
the Roman state (Tacit. Ann. xvi. 28). The father of Ag
had been put to death under Tiberius (Suetonius, Tib. c. 61).

[14] Aricia, about twenty Roman miles from Rome, on the Vi
(Horace, Sat. i. 5, 1):—

> "Egressum magna me excepit Aricia Roma."

[15] Epictetus, Encheiridion, c. 11: "Never say on the occ
anything, 'I have lost it,' but say, 'I have returned it.'"

CHAPTER II.

MAN ON EVERY OCCASION CAN MAINTAIN HIS PROPER CHARACTER.

rational animal only is the irrational intolerable; at which is rational is tolerable. Blows are not ly intolerable. How is that? See how the Lacedæiians[1] endure whipping when they have learned that ng is consistent with reason. To hang yourself is olerable. When then you have the opinion that it ›nal, you go and hang yourself. In short, if we ., we shall find that the animal man is pained by ; so much as by that which is irrational; and, on ıtrary, attracted to nothing so much as to that 's rational.

the rational and the irrational appear such in a ıt way to different persons, just as the good and the e profitable and the unprofitable. For this reason, larly, we need discipline, in order to learn how to he preconception[2] of the rational and the irrational everal things conformably to nature. But in order rmine the rational and the irrational, we use not e estimates of external things, but we consider also

[1] Spartan boys used to be whipped at the altar of Artemis ill blood flowed abundantly, and sometimes till death; but er uttered even a groan (Cicero, Tuscul. ii. 14; v. 27).

[2] preconception (πρόληψις) is thus defined by the Stoics: ἔστι ληψις ἔννοια φυσικὴ τῶν καθ' ὅλου (Diogenes Laert. vii.). "We ticipation all knowledge, by which I can *à priori* know and e that which belongs to empirical knowledge, and without is is the sense in which Epicurus used his expression πρό- Kant, Kritik der reinen Vernunft, p. 152, 7th ed.). He But since there is something in appearances which never nown *à priori*, and which consequently constitutes the differ- ween empirical knowledge and knowledge *à priori*, that is, (as the material of observation), it follows that this sen- specially that which cannot be anticipated (it cannot be a). On the other hand, we could name the pure determina- space and time, both in respect to form and magnitude, an- ns of the appearances, because these determinations represent whatever may be presented to us *à posteriori* in experience." p. 8, &c.

consistent with reason to hold a chamber pot for another, and to look to this only, that if he does not hold it, he will receive stripes, and he will not receive his food: but if he shall hold the pot, he will not suffer anything hard or disagreeable. But to another man not only does the holding of a chamber pot appear intolerable for himself, but intolerable also for him to allow another to do this office for him. If then you ask me whether you should hold the chamber pot or not, I shall say to you that the receiving of food is worth more than the not receiving of it, and the being scourged is a greater indignity than not being scourged; so that if you measure your interests by these things, go and hold the chamber pot. "But this," you say, "would not be worthy of me." Well then, it is you who must introduce this consideration into the inquiry, not I; for it is you who know yourself, how much you are worth to yourself, and at what price you sell yourself; for men sell themselves at various prices.

For this reason, when Florus was deliberating whether he should go down to Nero's[3] spectacles, and also perform in them himself, Agrippinus said to him, Go down: and when Florus asked Agrippinus, Why do not you go down? Agrippinus replied, Because I do not even deliberate about the matter. For he who has once brought himself to deliberate about such matters, and to calculate the value of external things, comes very near to those who have forgotten their own character. For why do you ask me the question, whether death is preferable or life? I say life. Pain or pleasure? I say pleasure. But if I do not take a part in the tragic acting, I shall have my head struck off. Go then and take a part, but I will not. Why? Because you consider yourself to be only one thread of those which are in the tunic. Well then it was fitting for you to take care how you should be like the rest of men, just as the thread has no design to be anything

[3] Nero was passionately fond of scenic representations, and used to induce the descendants of noble families, whose poverty made them consent, to appear on the stage (Tacitus, Annals, xiv. 14; Suetonius, Nero. c. 21).

superior to the other threads. But I wish to be purple,[4] that small part which is bright, and makes all the rest appear graceful and beautiful. Why then do you tell me to make myself like the many? and if I do, how shall I still be purple?

Priscus Helvidius[5] also saw this, and acted conformably. For when Vespasian sent and commanded him not to go into the senate, he replied, "It is in your power not to allow me to be a member of the senate, but so long as I am, I must go in." Well, go in then, says the emperor, but say nothing. Do not ask my opinion, and I will be silent. But I must ask your opinion. And I must say what I think right. But if you do, I shall put you to death. When then did I tell you that I am immortal? You will do your part, and I will do mine: it is your part to kill; it is mine to die, but not in fear: yours to banish me; mine to depart without sorrow.

What good then did Priscus do, who was only a single person? And what good does the purple do for the toga? Why, what else than this, that it is conspicuous in the toga as purple, and is displayed also as a fine example to all other things? But in such circumstances another would have replied to Caesar who forbade him to enter the senate, I thank you for sparing me. But such a man Vespasian would not even have forbidden to enter the senate, for he knew that he would either sit there like an earthen vessel, or, if he spoke, he would say what Caesar wished, and add even more.

[4] The "purple" is the broad purple border on the toga named the *toga praetexta*, worn by certain Roman magistrates and some others, and by senators, it is said, on certain days (Cic. Phil. ii. 43).

[5] Helvidius Priscus, a Roman senator and a philosopher, is commended by Tacitus (Hist. iv. 4, 5) as an honest man: "He followed the philosophers who considered those things only to be good which are virtuous, those only to be bad which are foul; and he reckoned power, rank, and all other things which are external to the mind as neither good nor bad." Vespasian, probably in a fit of passion, being provoked by Helvidius, ordered him to be put to death, and then revoked the order when it was too late (Suetonius, Vespasianus, [illegible]).

In this way an athlete also acted who was in danger of dying unless his private parts were amputated. His brother came to the athlete, who was a philosopher, and said, Come, brother, what are you going to do? Shall we amputate this member and return to the gymnasium? But the athlete persisted in his resolution and died. When some one asked Epictetus, How he did this, as an athlete or a philosopher? As a man, Epictetus replied, and a man who had been proclaimed among the athletes at the Olympic games and had contended in them, a man who had been familiar with such a place, and not merely anointed in Baton's school.[6] Another would have allowed even his head to be cut off, if he could have lived without it. Such is that regard to character which is so strong in those who have been accustomed to introduce it of themselves and conjoined with other things into their deliberations.

Come then, Epictetus, shave[7] yourself. If I am a philosopher, I answer, I will not shave myself. But I will take off your head? If that will do you any good, take it off.

Some person asked, how then shall every man among us perceive what is suitable to his character? How, he replied, does the bull alone, when the lion has attacked, discover his own powers and put himself forward in defence of the whole herd? It is plain that with the powers the perception of having them is immediately conjoined: and, therefore, whoever of us has such powers will not be ignorant of them. Now a bull is not made suddenly, nor a brave man; but we must discipline ourselves in the winter for the summer campaign, and not rashly run upon that which does not concern us.

Only consider at what price you sell your own will: if for no other reason, at least for this, that you sell it not for a small sum. But that which is great and superior per-

[6] Baton was elected for two years gymnasiarch or superintendent of a gymnasium in or about the time of M. Aurelius Antoninus. See Schweighaeuser's note.

[7] This is supposed, as Casaubon says, to refer to Domitian's order to the philosophers to go into exile; and some of them, in order to conceal their profession of philosophy, shaved their beards. Epictetus would not take off his beard.

haps belongs to Socrates and such as are like him. Why then, if we are naturally such, are not a very great number of us like him? Is it true then that all horses become swift, that all dogs are skilled in tracking footprints? What then, since I am naturally dull, shall I, for this reason, take no pains? I hope not. Epictetus is not superior to Socrates; but if he is not inferior,[8] this is enough for me; for I shall never be a Milo,[9] and yet I do not neglect my body; nor shall I be a Croesus, and yet I do not neglect my property; nor, in a word, do we neglect looking after anything because we despair of reaching the highest degree.

CHAPTER III.

HOW A MAN SHOULD PROCEED FROM THE PRINCIPLE OF GOD BEING THE FATHER OF ALL MEN TO THE REST.

If a man should be able to assent to this doctrine as ought, that we are all sprung from God[1] in an especi manner, and that God is the father both of men and gods, I suppose that he would never have any ignob or mean thoughts about himself. But if Caesar (t emperor) should adopt you, no one could endure yo arrogance; and if you know that you are the son of Ze will you not be elated? Yet we do not so; but sin

[8] The text is: εἰ δὲ μὴ οὐ χείρων. The sense seems to be: Ep tetus is not superior to Socrates, but if he is not worse, that is enou for me. On the different readings of the passage and on the sen see the notes in Schweig.'s edition. The difficulty, if there is an is in the negative μή.

[9] Milo of Croton, a great athlete. The conclusion is the same in Horace, Epp. i. 1, 28, &c.: "Est quodam prodire tenus, si non dat ultra."

[1] Epictetus speaks of God (ὁ θεός) and the gods. Also conformab to the practice of the people, he speaks of God under the name Zeus. The gods of the people were many, but his God was perha one. "Father of men and gods," says Homer of Zeus; and Virg says of Jupiter, "Father of gods and king of men." Salmasius pr posed ἀπὸ τοῦ θεοῦ. See Schweig.'s note.

these two things are mingled in the generation of man, body in common with the animals, and reason and intelligence in common with the gods, many incline to this kinship, which is miserable and mortal; and some few to that which is divine and happy. Since then it is of necessity that every man uses everything according to the opinion which he has about it, those, the few, who think that they are formed for fidelity and modesty and a sure use of appearances have no mean or ignoble thoughts about themselves; but with the many it is quite the contrary. For they say, What am I? A poor, miserable man, with my wretched bit of flesh. Wretched, indeed; but you possess something better than your bit of flesh. Why then do you neglect that which is better, and why do you attach yourself to this?

Through this kinship with the flesh, some of us inclining to it become like wolves, faithless and treacherous and mischievous: some become like lions, savage and bestial and untamed; but the greater part of us become foxes, and other worse animals. For what else is a slanderer and a malignant man than a fox, or some other more wretched and meaner animal? See[2] then and take care that you do not become some one of these miserable things.

CHAPTER IV.

OF PROGRESS OR IMPROVEMENT.

He who is making progress, having learned from philosophers that desire means the desire of good things, and aversion means aversion from bad things; having learned

[2] ὁρᾶτε καὶ προσέχετε μή τι τούτων ἀποβῆτε τῶν ἀτυχημάτων. Upton compares Matthew xvi. 6: ὁρᾶτε καὶ προσέχετε ἀπὸ τῆς ζύμης, &c. Upton remarks that many expressions in Epictetus are not unlike the style of the Gospels, which were written in the same period in which Epictetus was teaching. Schweighaeuser also refers to Wetstein's New Testament.

too that happiness[1] and tranquillity are not attainable by man otherwise than by not failing to obtain what he desires, and not falling into that which he would avoid; such a man takes from himself desire altogether and defers it,[2] but he employs his aversion only on things which are dependent on his will. For if he attempts to avoid anything independent of his will, he knows that sometimes he will fall in with something which he wishes to avoid, and he will be unhappy. Now if virtue promises good fortune and tranquillity and happiness, certainly also the progress towards virtue is progress towards each of these things. For it is always true that to whatever point the perfecting of anything leads us, progress is an approach towards this point.

How then do we admit that virtue is such as I have said, and yet seek progress in other things and make a display of it? What is the product of virtue? Tranquillity. Who then makes improvement? Is it he who has read many books of Chrysippus?[3] But does virtue consist in having understood Chrysippus? If this is so, progress is clearly nothing else than knowing a great deal of Chrysippus. But now we admit that virtue produces one thing, and we declare that approaching near to it is another thing, namely, progress or improvement. Such a person, says one, is already able to read Chrysippus by himself. Indeed, sir, you are making great progress. What kind of progress? But why do you mock the man? Why do you draw him away from the perception of his own misfortunes? Will you not show him the effect of virtue that he may learn where to look for improvement?

[1] τὸ εὔρουν or ἡ εὔροια is translated "happiness." The notion is that of "flowing easily," as Seneca (Epp. 120) explains it: "beata vita, secundo defluens cursu."

[2] ὑπερτέθειται. The Latin translation is: "in futurum tempus rejicit." Wolf says: "Significat id, quod in Enchiridio dictum est: philosophiae tironem non nimium tribuere sibi, sed quasi addubitantem expectare dum confirmetur judicium."

[3] Diogenes Laertius (Chrysippus, lib. vii.) states that Chrysippus wrote seven hundred and five books, or treatises, or whatever the word συγγράμματα means. He was born at Soli, in Cilicia, or at Tarsus, in B.C. 280, as it is reckoned, and on going to Athens he became a pupil of the Stoic Cleanthes.

Seek it there, wretch, where your work lies. And where is your work? In desire and in aversion, that you may not be disappointed in your desire, and that you may not fall into that which you would avoid; in your pursuit and avoiding, that you commit no error; in assent and suspension of assent, that you be not deceived. The first things, and the most necessary, are those which I have named.[4] But if with trembling and lamentation you seek not to fall into that which you avoid, tell me how you are improving.

Do you then show me your improvement in these things? If I were talking to an athlete, I should say, Show me your shoulders; and then he might say, Here are my Halteres. You and your Halteres[5] look to that. I should reply, I wish to see the effect of the Halteres. So, when you say: Take the treatise on the active powers (ὁρμή), and see how I have studied it. I reply, Slave, I am not inquiring about this, but how you exercise pursuit and avoidance, desire and aversion, how you design and purpose and prepare yourself, whether conformably to nature or not. If conformably, give me evidence of it, and I will say that you are making progress: but if not conformably, be gone, and not only expound your books, but write such books yourself; and

[4] Compare iii. c. 2. The word is τόποι.

[5] Halteres are gymnastic instruments (Galen. i. De Sanitate tuenda; Martial, xiv. 49; Juvenal, vi. 420, and the Scholiast. Upton). Halteres is a Greek word, literally "leapers." They are said to have been masses of lead, used for exercise and in making jumps. The effect of such weights in taking a jump is well known to boys who have used them. A couple of bricks will serve the purpose. Martial says (xiv. 49):—

> "Quid pereunt stulto fortes haltere lacerti?
> Exercet melius vinea fossa viros."

Juvenal (vi. 421) writes of a woman who uses dumb-bells till she sweats, and is then rubbed dry by a man,

> "Quum lassata gravi ceciderunt brachia massa."
> (Macleane's Juvenal.)

As to the expression, Ὄψει σὺ, καὶ οἱ ἁλτῆρες, see Upton's note. It is also a Latin form: "Epicurus hoc viderit," Cicero, Acad. ii. c. 7; "Haec fortuna viderit," Ad Attic. vi. 4. It occurs in M. Antoninus, iii. 41, v. 25; and in Acta Apostol. xviii. 15.

what will you gain by it? Do you not know that the whole book costs only five denarii? Does then the expounder seem to be worth more than five denarii? Never then look for the matter itself in one place, and progress towards it in another.

Where then is progress? If any of you, withdrawing himself from externals, turns to his own will (*προαίρεσις*) to exercise it and to improve it by labour, so as to make it conformable to nature, elevated, free, unrestrained, unimpeded, faithful, modest; and if he has learned that he who desires or avoids the things which are not in his power can neither be faithful nor free, but of necessity he must change with them and be tossed about with them as in a tempest,[6] and of necessity must subject himself to others who have the power to procure or prevent what he desires or would avoid; finally, when he rises in the morning, if he observes and keeps these rules, bathes as a man of fidelity, eats as a modest man; in like manner, if in every matter that occurs he works out his chief principles (*τὰ προηγούμενα*) as the runner does with reference to running, and the trainer of the voice with reference to the voice—this is the man who truly makes progress, and this is the man who has not travelled in vain. But if he has strained his efforts to the practice of reading books, and labours only at this, and has travelled for this, I tell him to return home immediately, and not to neglect his affairs there; for this for which he has travelled is nothing. But the other thing is something, to study how a man can rid his life of lamentation and groaning, and saying, Woe to me, and wretched that I am, and to rid it also of misfortune and disappointment, and to learn what death is, and exile, and prison, and poison, that he may be able to say when he is in fetters, Dear Crito,[7] if it is the will of the gods that it be so, let it be so; and not to say, Wretched am I, an old man; have I kept my grey hairs for this? Who is it that speaks thus? Do you think that I shall name some man of no repute and of low condition? Does

[6] *μεταρριπίζεσθαι.* Compare James, Ep. i. 6: *ὁ γὰρ διακρινόμενος ἔοικε κλύδωνι θαλάσσης ἀνεμιζομένῳ καὶ ῥιπιζομένῳ.*

[7] This is said in the Criton of Plato, 1; but not in exactly the same way.

not Priam say this? Does not Oedipus say this? Nay, all kings say it![8] For what else is tragedy than the perturbations (πάθη) of men who value externals exhibited in this kind of poetry? But if a man must learn by fiction that no external things which are independent of the will concern us, for my part I should like this fiction, by the aid of which I should live happily and undisturbed. But you must consider for yourselves what you wish.

What then does Chrysippus teach us? The reply is, to know that these things are not false, from which happiness comes and tranquillity arises. Take my books, and you will learn how true and conformable to nature are the things which make me free from perturbations. O great good fortune! O the great benefactor who points out the way! To Triptolemus all men have erected[9] temples and altars, because he gave us food by cultivation; but to him who discovered truth and brought it to light and communicated it to all, not the truth which shows us how to live, but how to live well, who of you for this reason has built an altar, or a temple, or has dedicated a statue, or who worships God for this? Because the gods have given the vine, or wheat, we sacrifice to them: but because they have produced in the human mind that fruit by which they designed to show us the truth which relates to happiness, shall we not thank God for this?

CHAPTER V.

AGAINST THE ACADEMICS.[1]

If a man, said Epictetus, opposes evident truths, it is not easy to find arguments by which we shall make him change his opinion. But this does not arise either from the

[8] So kings and such personages speak in the Greek tragedies. Compare what M. Antoninus (xi. 6) says of Tragedy.

[9] ἀνεστάκασιν. See the note of Schweig. on the use of this form of the verb.

[1] See Lecture V., The New Academy, Levin's Lectures Introductory to the Phoilsophical Writings of Cicero, Cambridge, 1871.

man's strength or the teacher's weakness; for when the man, though he has been confuted,[2] is hardened like a stone, how shall we then be able to deal with him by argument?

Now there are two kinds of hardening, one of the understanding, the other of the sense of shame, when a man is resolved not to assent to what is manifest nor to desist from contradictions. Most of us are afraid of mortification of the body, and would contrive all means to avoid such a thing, but we care not about the soul's mortification. And indeed with regard to the soul, if a man be in such a state as not to apprehend anything, or understand at all, we think that he is in a bad condition: but if the sense of shame and modesty are deadened, this we call even power (or strength).

Do you comprehend that you are awake? I do not, the man replies, for I do not even comprehend when in my sleep I imagine that I am awake. Does this appearance then not differ from the other? Not at all, he replies. Shall I still argue with this man?[3] And what fire or what iron shall I apply to him to make him feel that he is deadened? He does perceive, but he pretends that he does not. He is even worse than a dead man. He does not see the contradiction: he is in a bad condition. Another does see it, but he is not moved, and makes no improvement: he is even in a worse condition. His modesty is extirpated, and his sense of shame; and the rational faculty has not been cut off from him, but it is brutalised. Shall I name this strength of mind? Certainly not, unless we also name it such in catamites, through which they do and say in public whatever comes into their head.

[2] ἀπαχθείς. See the note in Schweig.'s edition.

[3] Compare Cicero, Academ. Prior. ii. 6.

CHAPTER VI.

OF PROVIDENCE.

FROM everything which is or happens in the world, it is easy to praise Providence, if a man possesses these two qualities, the faculty of seeing what belongs and happens to all persons and things, and a grateful disposition. If he does not possess these two qualities, one man will not see the use of things which are and which happen; another will not be thankful for them, even if he does know them. If God had made colours, but had not made the faculty of seeing them, what would have been their use? None at all. On the other hand, if He had made the faculty of vision, but had not made objects such as to fall under the faculty, what in that case also would have been the use of it? None at all. Well, suppose that He had made both, but had not made light? In that case, also, they would have been of no use. Who is it then who has fitted this to that and that to this? And who is it that has fitted the knife to the case and the case to the knife? Is it no one?[1] And, indeed, from the very structure of things which have attained their completion, we are accustomed to show that the work is certainly the act of some artificer, and that it has not been constructed without a purpose. Does then each of these things demonstrate the workman, and do not visible things and the faculty of seeing and light demonstrate Him? And the existence of male and female, and the desire of each for conjunction, and the power of using the parts which are constructed, do not even these declare the workman? If they do not, let us consider[2] the constitution of our understanding

[1] Goethe has a short poem, entitled Gleich und Gleich (Like and Like):

> "Ein Blumenglöckchen
> Vom Boden hervor
> War früh gesprosset
> In lieblichem Flor;
> Da kam ein Bienchen
> Und naschte fein:—
> Die müssen wohl beyde
> Für einander seyn."

[2] See Schweig.'s note. I have given the sense of the passage, I think.

according to which, when we meet with sensible objects, we do not simply receive impressions from them, but we also select[3] something from them, and subtract something, and add, and compound by means of them these things or those, and, in fact, pass from some to other things which, in a manner, resemble them: is not even this sufficient to move some men, and to induce them not to forget the workman? If not so, let them explain to us what it is that makes each several thing, or how it is possible that things so wonderful and like the contrivances of art should exist by chance and from their own proper motion?

What, then, are these things done in us only? Many, indeed, in us only, of which the rational animal had peculiarly need; but you will find many common to us with irrational animals. Do they then understand what is done? By no means. For use is one thing, and understanding is another: God had need of irrational animals to make use of appearances, but of us to understand the use of appearances.[4] It is therefore enough for them to eat and to drink, and to sleep and to copulate, and to do all the other things which they severally do. But for us, to whom He has given also the intellectual faculty, these things are not sufficient; for unless we act in a proper and orderly manner, and conformably to the nature and constitution of each thing, we shall never attain our true end. For where the constitutions of living beings are different, there also the acts and the ends are different. In those animals then whose constitution is adapted only to use, use alone is enough: but in an animal (man), which has also the power of understanding the use, unless there be the due exercise of the understanding, he will never attain his proper end. Well then God constitutes every animal, one to be eaten, another to serve for agriculture, another to supply cheese, and another for some like use; for which purposes what need is there to understand appearances and to be able to distinguish them? But God has introduced man to be a spectator of God[5] and of His

[3] Cicero, De Off. i. c. 4, on the difference between man and beast.

[4] See Schweig.'s note, tom. ii. p. 84.

[5] The original is *αὐτοῦ*, which I refer to God; but it may be ambiguous. Schweighaeuser refers it to man, and explains it t. . ean

works; and not only a spectator of them, but an interpreter. For this reason it is shameful for man to begin and to end where irrational animals do; but rather he ought to begin where they begin, and to end where nature ends in us; and nature ends in contemplation and understanding, and in a way of life conformable to nature. Take care then not to die without having been spectators of these things.

But you take a journey to Olympia to see the work of Phidias,[6] and all of you think it a misfortune to die without having seen such things. But when there is no need to take a journey, and where a man is, there he has the works (of God) before him, will you not desire to see and understand them? Will you not perceive either[7] what you are, or what you were born for, or what this is for which you have received the faculty of sight? But you may say, there are some things disagreeable and troublesome in life. And are there none at Olympia? Are you not scorched? Are you not pressed by a crowd? Are you not without comfortable means of bathing? Are you not wet when it rains? Have you not abundance of noise, clamour, and other disagreeable things? But I suppose that setting all these things off against the magnificence of the spectacle, you bear and endure. Well then and have

that man should be a spectator of himself, according to the maxim, Γνῶθι σεαυτόν. It is true that man can in a manner contemplate himself and his faculties as well as external objects; and as every man can be an object to every other man, so a man may be an object to himself when he examines his faculties and reflects on his own acts. Schweighaeuser asks how can a man be a spectator of God, except so far as he is a spectator of God's works? It is not enough, he says, to reply that God and the universe, whom and which man contemplates, are the same thing to the Stoics; for Epictetus always distinguishes God the maker and governor of the universe from the universe itself. But here lies the difficulty. The universe is an all-comprehensive term: it is all that we can in any way perceive and conceive as existing; and it may therefore comprehend God, not as something distinct from the universe, but as being the universe himself. This form of expression is an acknowledgment of the weakness of the human faculties, and contains the implicit assertion of Locke that the notion of God is beyond man's understanding (Essay, etc. ii. c. 17).

[6] This work was the colossal chryselephantine statue of Zeus (Jupiter) by Phidias, which was at Olympia. This wonderful work is described by Pausanias (Eliaca, A, 11).

[7] Compare Persius, Sat. iii. 66—

"Discite, io, miseri et causas cognoscite rerum,
Quid sumus aut quidnam victuri gignimur.

you not received faculties by which you will be able to bear all that happens? Have you not received greatness of soul? Have you not received manliness? Have you not received endurance? And why do I trouble myself about anything that can happen if I possess greatness of soul? What shall distract my mind or disturb me, or appear painful? Shall I not use the power for the purposes for which I received it, and shall I grieve and lament over what happens?

Yes, but my nose runs.[8] For what purpose then, slave, have you hands? Is it not that you may wipe your nose?—Is it then consistent with reason that there should be running of noses in the world?—Nay, how much better it is to wipe your nose than to find fault. What do you think that Hercules would have been if there had not been such a lion, and hydra, and stag, and boar, and certain unjust and bestial men, whom Hercules used to drive away and clear out? And what would he have been doing if there had been nothing of the kind? Is it not plain that he would have wrapped himself up and have slept? In the first place then he would not have been a Hercules, when he was dreaming away all his life in such luxury and ease; and even if he had been one, what would have been the use of him? and what the use of his arms, and of the strength of the other parts of his body, and his endurance and noble spirit, if such circumstances and occasions had not roused and exercised him? Well then must a man provide for himself such means of exercise, and seek to introduce a lion from some place into his country, and a boar, and a hydra? This would be folly and madness: but as they did exist, and were found, they were useful for showing what Hercules was and for exercising him. Come then do you also having observed these things look to the faculties which you have, and when you have looked at them, say: Bring now, O Zeus, any difficulty that thou pleasest, for I have means given to me by thee and powers [9]

[8] Compare Antoninus, viii. 50, and Epictetus, ii. 16, 13.

[9] ἀφορμὰς. This word in this passage has a different meaning from that which it has when it is opposed to ὁρμή. See Gataker, Antoninus, ix. 1 (Upton). Epictetus says that the powers which man has were given by God: Antoninus says, from nature. They mean the same thing. See Schweighaeuser's note.

for honouring myself through the things which happen You do not so: but you sit still, trembling for fear that some things will happen, and weeping, and lamenting, and groaning for what does happen: and then you blame the gods. For what is the consequence of such meanness of spirit but impiety?[10] And yet God has not only given us these faculties; by which we shall be able to bear everything that happens without being depressed or broken by it; but, like a good king and a true father, He has given us these faculties free from hindrance, subject to no compulsion, unimpeded, and has put them entirely in our own power, without even having reserved to Himself any power of hindering or impeding. You, who have received these powers free and as your own, use them not: you do not even see what you have received, and from whom; some of you being blinded to the giver, and not even acknowledging your benefactor, and others, through meanness of spirit, betaking yourselves to fault-finding and making charges against God. Yet I will show to you that you have powers and means for greatness of soul and manliness: but what powers you have for finding fault and making accusations, do you show me.

CHAPTER VII.

OF THE USE OF SOPHISTICAL ARGUMENTS AND HYPOTHETICAL AND THE LIKE.[1]

THE handling of sophistical and hypothetical arguments, and of those which derive their conclusions from questioning, and in a word the handling of all such arguments,

[10] Compare Antoninus, ix. 1.

[1] The title is *περὶ τῆς χρείας τῶν μεταπιπτόντων καὶ ὑποθετικῶν καὶ τῶν ὁμοίων*. Schweighaeuser has a big note on *μεταπίπτοντες λόγοι*, which he has collected from various critics. Mrs. Carter translates the title 'Of the Use of Convertible and Hypothetical Propositions and the like.' But "convertible" might be understood in the common logical sense, which is not the meaning of Epictetus. Schweighaeuser explains *μεταπίπτοντες λόγοι* to be sophistical arguments in which the meaning of propositions or of terms, which ought to remain the same, is dexterously changed and perverted to another meaning.

relates to the duties of life, though the many do not know this truth. For in every matter we inquire how the wise and good man shall discover the proper path and the proper method of dealing with the matter. Let then people either say that the grave man will not descend into the contest of question and answer, or, that if he does descend into the contest, he will take no care about not conducting himself rashly or carelessly in questioning and answering. But if they do not allow either the one or the other of these things, they must admit that some inquiry ought to be made into those topics (τόπων) on which particularly questioning and answering are employed. For what is the end proposed in reasoning? To establish true propositions, to remove the false, to withhold assent from those which are not plain. Is it enough then to have learned only this? It is enough, a man may reply. Is it then also enough for a man, who would not make a mistake in the use of coined money, to have heard this precept, that he should receive the genuine drachmae and reject the spurious? It is not enough. What then ought to be added to this precept? What else than the faculty which proves and distinguishes the genuine and the spurious drachmae? Consequently also in reasoning what has been said is not enough; but it is necessary that a man should acquire the faculty of examining and distinguishing the true and the false, and that which is not plain? It is necessary. Besides this, what is proposed in reasoning? That you should accept what follows from that which you have properly granted. Well, is it then enough in this case also to know this? It is not enough; but a man must learn how one thing is a consequence of other things, and when one thing follows from one thing, and when it follows from several collectively. Consider then if it be not necessary that this power should also be acquired by him, who purposes to conduct himself skilfully in reasoning, the power of demonstrating himself the several things which he has proposed,[2] and the power of understanding the demonstrations of others, and of not being deceived by sophists, as if they were demonstrating. Therefore there has arisen among us the practice and

[2] See Schweig.'s note on ἀποδείξειν ἕκαστα ἀποδόντα.

exercise of conclusive arguments[3] and figures, and it has been shown to be necessary.

But in fact in some cases we have properly granted the premises[4] or assumptions, and there results from them something; and though it is not true, yet none the less it does result. What then ought I to do? Ought I to admit the falsehood? And how is that possible? Well, should I say that I did not properly grant that which we agreed upon? But you are not allowed to do even this. Shall I then say that the consequence does not arise through what has been conceded? But neither is this allowed. What then must be done in this case? Consider if it is not this: as to have borrowed is not enough to make a man still a debtor, but to this must be added the fact that he continues to owe the money and that the debt is not paid, so it is not enough to compel you to admit the inference[5] that you have granted the premises (τὰ λήμματα), but you must abide by what you have granted. Indeed, if the premises continue to the end such as they were when they were granted, it is absolutely necessary for us to abide by what we have granted, and we must accept their consequences: but if the premises do not remain[6] such as they were when they

[3] These are syllogisms and figures, modes (τρόποι) by which the syllogism has its proper conclusion.

[4] Compare Aristotle, Topic. viii. 1, 22 (ed. J. Pac. 758). Afterwards Epictetus uses τὰ ὡμολογημένα as equivalent to λήμματα (premises or assumptions).

[5] "The inference," τὸ ἐπιφερόμενον. "'Επιφορά est 'illatio' quae assumptionem sequitur" (Upton).

[6] This, then, is a case of μεταπίπτοντες λόγοι (chap. vii. 1), where there has been a sophistical or dishonest change in the premises or in some term, by virtue of which change there appears to be a just conclusion, which, however, is false; and it is not a conclusion derived from the premises to which we assented. A ridiculous example is given by Seneca, Ep. 48: "Mus syllaba est: mus autem caseum rodit: syllaba ergo caseum rodit." Seneca laughs at this absurdity and says perhaps the following syllogism (*collectio*) may be a better example of acuteness: "Mus syllaba est: syllaba autem caseum non rodit: mus ergo caseum non rodit." One is as good as the other. We know that neither conclusion is true, and we see where the error is. Ménage says that though the Stoics particularly cultivated logic, some of them despised it, and he mentions Seneca, Epictetus, and Marcus Antoninus. Upton, however, observes that Epictetus and Marcus Antoninus did not despise logic (he says nothing about Seneca), but employed it for their own purposes.

It has been observed that if a man is asked whether, if every A is

were granted, it is absolutely necessary for us also to withdraw from what we granted, and from accepting what does not follow from the words in which our concessions were made. For the inference is now not our inference, nor does it result with our assent, since we have withdrawn from the premises which we granted. We ought then both to examine such kinds of premises, and such change and variation of them (from one meaning to another), by which in the course of questioning or answering, or in making the syllogistic conclusion, or in any other such way, the premises undergo variations, and give occasion to the foolish to be confounded, if they do not see what conclusions (consequences) are. For what reason ought we to examine? In order that we may not in this matter be employed in an improper manner nor in a confused way.

And the same in hypotheses and hypothetical arguments; for it is necessary sometimes to demand the granting of some hypothesis as a kind of passage to the argument which follows. Must we then allow every hypothesis that is proposed, or not allow every one? And if not every one, which should we allow? And if a man has allowed an hypothesis, must he in every case abide by allowing it? or must he sometimes withdraw from it, but admit the consequences and not admit contradictions? Yes; but suppose that a man says, If you admit the hypothesis of a possibility, I will draw you to an impossibility. With such a person shall a man of sense refuse to enter into a contest, and avoid discussion and conversation with him? But what other man than the man of sense can use argumentation and is skilful in questioning and answering, and

B, every B is also A, he might answer that it is. But if you put the conversion in this material form: "Every goose is an animal," he immediately perceives that he cannot say, "Every animal is a goose." What does this show? It shows that the man's comprehension of the proposition, every A is B, was not true, and that he took it to mean something different from what the person intended who put the question. He understood that A and B were coextensive. Whether we call this reasoning or something else, makes no matter. A man whose understanding is sound cannot in the nature of things reason wrong; but his understanding of the matter on which he reasons may be wrong somewhere, and he may not be able to discover where. A man who has been trained in the logical art may show him that his conclusion is just according to his understanding of the terms and the propositions employed, but yet it is not true.

incapable of being cheated and deceived by false reasoning? And shall he enter into the contest, and yet not take care whether he shall engage in argument not rashly and not carelessly? And if he does not take care, how can he be such a man as we conceive him to be? But without some such exercise and preparation, can he maintain a continuous and consistent argument? Let them show this; and all these speculations (θεωρήματα) become superfluous, and are absurd and inconsistent with our notion of a good and serious man.

Why are we still indolent and negligent and sluggish, and why do we seek pretences for not labouring and not being watchful in cultivating our reason? If then I shall make a mistake in these matters may I not have killed my father? Slave, where was there a father in this matter that you could kill him? What then have you done? The only fault that was possible here is the fault which you have committed. This is the very remark which I made to Rufus[7] when he blamed me for not having discovered the one thing omitted in a certain syllogism: I suppose, I said, that I have burnt the Capitol. Slave, he replied, was the thing omitted here the Capitol? Or are these the only crimes, to burn the Capitol and to kill your father? But for a man to use the appearances presented to him rashly and foolishly and carelessly, and not to understand argument, nor demonstration, nor sophism, nor, in a word, to see in questioning and answering what is consistent with that which we have granted or is not consistent; is there no error in this?

[7] Rufus is Musonius Rufus (i. 1). To kill a father and to burn the Roman Capitol are mentioned as instances of the greatest crimes Comp. Horace, Epode, iii.; Cicero, De Amicit. c. 11; Plutarch, Tib. Gracchus, c. 20.

CHAPTER VIII.

THAT THE FACULTIES[1] ARE NOT SAFE TO THE UNINSTRUCTED.

IN as many ways as we can change things[2] which are equivalent to one another, in just so many ways we can change the forms of arguments (ἐπιχειρήματα) and enthymemes[3] (ἐνθυμήματα) in argumentation. This is an instance: if you have borrowed and not repaid, you owe me the money: you have not borrowed and you have not repaid; then you do not owe me the money. To do this skilfully is suitable to no man more than to the philosopher; for if the enthymeme is an imperfect syllogism, it is plain that he who has been exercised in the perfect syllogism must be equally expert in the imperfect also.

Why then do we not exercise ourselves and one another in this manner? Because, I reply, at present, though we are not exercised in these things and not distracted from the study of morality, by me at least, still we make no progress in virtue. What then must we expect if we should add this occupation? and particularly as this would not only be an occupation which would withdraw us from more necessary things, but would also be a cause of self-conceit and arrogance, and no small cause. For great is the power of arguing and the faculty of persuasion, and particularly if it should be much exercised, and also receive additional ornament from language: and so universally, every faculty acquired by the uninstructed and weak brings with it the danger of these persons being elated

[1] The faculties, as Wolf says, are the faculties of speaking and arguing, which, as he also says, make men arrogant and careless who have no solid knowledge, according to Bion's maxim, ἡ γὰρ οἴησις ἐγκοπὴ τῆς προκοπῆς ἐστιν, "arrogance (self-conceit) is a hindrance to improvement." See viii. 8.

[2] Things mean "propositions" and "terms." See Aristot. Analyt. Prior. i. 39, δεῖ δὲ καὶ μεταλαμβάνειν, &c. 'Επιχειρήματα are arguments of any kind with which we attack (ἐπιχειρεῖν) an adversary.

[3] The Enthymeme is defined by Aristotle: ἐνθύμημα μὲν οὖν ἐστὶ συλλογισμὸς ἐξ εἰκότων ἢ σημείων (Anal. Prior. ii. c. 27). He has explained, in the first part of this chapter, what he means by εἰκός and σημεῖον. See also De Morgan's Formal Logic, p. 237; and P. C. Organon, p. 6, note.

and inflated by it. For by what means could one persuade a young man who excels in these matters, that he ought not to become an appendage[4] to them, but to make them an appendage to himself? Does he not trample on all such reasons, and strut before us elated and inflated, not enduring that any man should reprove him and remind him of what he has neglected and to what he has turned aside?

What then was not Plato a philosopher?[5] I reply, and was not Hippocrates a physician? but you see how Hippocrates speaks. Does Hippocrates then speak thus in respect of being a physician? Why do you mingle things which have been accidentally united in the same men? And if Plato was handsome and strong, ought I also to set to work and endeavour to become handsome or strong, as if this was necessary for philosophy, because a certain philosopher was at the same time handsome and a philosopher? Will you not choose to see and to distinguish in respect to what men become philosophers, and what things belong to them in other respects? And if I were a philosopher, ought you also to be made lame?[6] What then? Do I take away these faculties which you possess? By no means; for neither do I take away the faculty of seeing. But if you ask me what is the good of man, I cannot mention to you anything else than that it is a certain disposition of the will with respect to appearances.[7]

[4] A man, as Wolf explains it, should not make oratory, or the art of speaking, his chief excellence. He should use it to set off something which is superior.

[5] Plato was eloquent, and the adversary asks, if that is a reason for not allowing him to be a philosopher. To which the rejoinder is that Hippocrates was a physician, and eloquent too, but not as a physician.

[6] Epictetus was lame.

[7] In i. 20, 15, Epictetus defines the being (οὐσία) or nature of good to be a proper use of appearances; and he also says, i. 29, 1, that the nature of the good is a kind of will (προαίρεσις ποιά), and the nature of evil is a kind of will. But Schweighaeuser cannot understand how the "good of man" can be "a certain will with regard to appearances;" and he suggests that Arrian may have written, "a certain will which makes use of appearances."

CHAPTER IX.

HOW FROM THE FACT THAT WE ARE AKIN TO GOD A MAN MAY PROCEED TO THE CONSEQUENCES.

If the things are true which are said by the philosophers about the kinship between God and man, what else remains for men to do than what Socrates did? Never in reply to the question, to what country you belong, say that you are an Athenian or a Corinthian, but that you are a citizen of the world (κόσμιος).[1] For why do you say that you are an Athenian, and why do you not say that you belong to the small nook only into which your poor body was cast at birth? Is it not plain that you call yourself an Athenian or Corinthian from the place which has a greater authority and comprises not only that small nook itself and all your family, but even the whole country from which the stock of your progenitors is derived down to you? He then who has observed with intelligence the administration of the world, and has learned that the greatest and supreme and the most comprehensive community is that which is composed of men and God, and that from God have descended the seeds not only to my father and grandfather, but to all beings which are generated on the earth and are produced, and particularly to rational beings—for these only are by their nature formed to have communion with God, being by means of reason conjoined with him[2]—why

[1] Cicero, Tuscul. v. 37, has the same: "Socrates cum rogaretur, cujatem se esse diceret, Mundanum, inquit. Totius enim mundi se incolam et civem arbitrabatur." (Upton.)

[2] It is the possession of reason, he says, by which man has communion with God; it is not by any external means, or religious ceremonial. A modern expositor of Epictetus says, "Through reason our souls are as closely connected and mixed up with the deity as though they were part of him" (Epictet. i. 14, 6; ii. 8, 11, 17, 33). In the Epistle named from Peter (ii. 1, 4) it is written: "Whereby are given to us exceeding great and precious promises that by these (see v. 3) ye might be partakers of the divine nature (γένησθε θείας κοινωνοὶ φύσεως), having escaped the corruption that is in the world through lust." Mrs. Carter, Introduction, § 31, has some remarks on this Stoic doctrine, which are not a true explanation of the principles of Epictetus and Antoninus.

should not such a man call himself a citizen of the world, why not a son of God,[3] and why should he be afraid of anything which happens among men? Is kinship with Caesar (the emperor) or with any other of the powerful in Rome sufficient to enable us to live in safety, and above contempt and without any fear at all? and to have God for your maker (ποιητήν), and father and guardian, shall not this release us from sorrows and fears?

But a man may say, Whence shall I get bread to eat when I have nothing?

And how do slaves, and runaways, on what do they rely when they leave their masters? Do they rely on their lands or slaves, or their vessels of silver? They rely on nothing but themselves; and food does not fail them.[4] And shall it be necessary for one among us who is a philosopher to travel into foreign parts, and trust to and rely on others, and not to take care of himself, and shall he be inferior to irrational animals and more cowardly each of which being self-sufficient, neither fails to get its proper food, nor to find a suitable way of living, and one conformable to nature?

[3] So Jesus said, "Our Father which art in heaven." Cleanthes, in his hymn to Zeus, writes, ἐκ σοῦ γὰρ γένος ἐσμέν. Compare Acts of the Apostles, xvii. 28, where Paul quotes these words. It is not true then that the "conception of a parental deity," as it has been asserted, was unknown before the teaching of Jesus, and, after the time of Jesus, unknown to those Greeks who were unacquainted with His teaching.

[4] In our present society there are thousands who rise in the morning and know not how they shall find something to eat. Some find their food by fraud and theft, some receive it as a gift from others, and some look out for any work that they can find and get their pittance by honest labour. You may see such men everywhere, if you will keep your eyes open. Such men, who live by daily labour, live an heroic life, which puts to shame the well-fed philosopher and the wealthy Christian.

Epictetus has made a great misstatement about irrational animals. Millions die annually for want of sufficient food; and many human beings perish in the same way. We can hardly suppose that he did not know these facts.

Compare the passage in Matthew (vi. 25–34). It is said, v. 26: "Behold the fowls of the air: for they sow not, neither do they reap, nor gather into barns; yet your heavenly Father feedeth them. Are ye not much better than they?" The expositors of this passage may be consulted.

I indeed think that the old man[5] ought to be sitting here, not to contrive how you may have no mean thoughts nor mean and ignoble talk about yourselves, but to take care that there be not among us any young men of such a mind, that when they have recognised their kinship to God, and that we are fettered by these bonds, the body, I mean, and its possessions, and whatever else on account of them is necessary to us for the economy and commerce of life, they should intend to throw off these things as if they were burdens painful and intolerable, and to depart to their kinsmen. But this is the labour that your teacher and instructor ought to be employed upon, if he really were what he should be. You should come to him and say, "Epictetus, we can no longer endure being bound to this poor body, and feeding it and giving it drink, and rest, and cleaning it, and for the sake of the body complying with the wishes of these and of those.[6] Are not these things indifferent and nothing to us; and is not death no evil? And are we not in a manner kinsmen of God, and did we not come from him? Allow us to depart to the place from which we came; allow us to be released at last from these bonds by which we are bound and weighed down. Here there are robbers and thieves and courts of justice, and those who are named tyrants, and think that they have some power over us by means of the body and its possessions. Permit us to show them that they have no power over any man." And I on my part would say, "Friends, wait for God: when He shall give the signal[7] and release you from this service, then go to Him; but for the present endure to dwell in this place where He has put you: short indeed is this time of your dwelling here, and easy to bear for those who are so disposed: for what tyrant or what thief, or

[5] The old man is Epictetus.

[6] He means, as Wolf says, "on account of the necessities of the body seeking the favour of the more powerful by disagreeable compliances."

[7] Upton refers to Cicero, Tuscul. i. 30; Cato Major, c. 20; Somnium Scipionis, c. 3 (De Republica, iv. 15); the purport of which passages is that we must not depart from life without the command of God. See Marcus Antoninus, ii. 17; iii. 5; v. 33. But how shall a man know the signal for departure, of which Epictetus speaks?

what courts of justice, are formidable to those who have thus considered as things of no value the body and the possessions of the body? Wait then, do not depart without a reason."

Something like this ought to be said by the teacher to ingenuous youths. But now what happens? The teacher is a lifeless body, and you are lifeless bodies. When you have been well filled to-day, you sit down and lament about the morrow, how you shall get something to eat. Wretch, if you have it, you will have it; if you have it not, you will depart from life. The door is open.[8] Why do you grieve? where does there remain any room for tears? and where is there occasion for flattery? why shall one man envy another? why should a man admire the rich or the powerful, even if they be both very strong and of violent temper? for what will they do to us? We shall not care for that which they can do; and what we do care for, that they cannot do. How did Socrates behave with respect to these matters? Why, in what other way than a man ought to do who was convinced that he was a kinsman of the gods? "If you say to me now," said Socrates to his judges,[9] "we will acquit you on the condition that you no longer discourse in the way in which you have hitherto discoursed, nor trouble either our young or our old men, I shall answer, you make yourselves ridiculous by thinking that, if one of our commanders has appointed me to a certain post, it is my duty to keep and maintain it, and to resolve to die a thousand times rather than desert it; but if God has put us in any place and way of life, we ought to desert it." Socrates speaks like a

[8] Upton has referred to the passages of Epictetus in which this expression is used, i. 24, 20; i. 25, 18; ii. 1, 19, and others; to Seneca, De Provid. c. 6, Ep. 91; to Cicero, De Fin. iii. 18, where there is this conclusion: "e quo apparet et sapientis esse aliquando officium excedere e vita, quum beatus sit; et stulti manere in vita quum sit miser."

Compare Matthew vi. 31: "Therefore take no thought, saying, What shall we eat? or, What shall we drink? or, Wherewithal shall we be clothed? (For after all these things do the Gentiles seek:) for your heavenly Father knoweth that ye have need of all these things," &c.

[9] This passage is founded on and is in substance the same as that in Plato's Apology, c. 17.

D

man who is really a kinsman of the gods. But we think about ourselves, as if we were only stomachs, and intestines, and shameful parts; we fear, we desire; we flatter those who are able to help us in these matters, and we fear them also.

A man asked me to write to Rome about him, a man who, as most people thought, had been unfortunate, for formerly he was a man of rank and rich, but had been stripped of all, and was living here. I wrote on his behalf in a submissive manner; but when he had read the letter, he gave it back to me and said, "I wished for your help, not your pity: no evil has happened to me."

Thus also Musonius Rufus, in order to try me, used to say: This and this will befall you from your master; and when I replied that these were things which happen in the ordinary course of human affairs. Why then, said he, should I ask him for anything when I can obtain it from you? For, in fact, what a man has from himself, it is superfluous and foolish to receive from another?[10] Shall I then, who am able to receive from myself greatness of soul and a generous spirit, receive from you land and money or a magisterial office? I hope not: I will not be so ignorant about my own possessions. But when a man is cowardly and mean, what else must be done for him than to write letters as you would about a corpse.[11] Please to grant us the body of a certain person and a sextarius of poor blood. For such a person is, in fact, a carcase and a sextarius (a certain quantity) of blood, and nothing more. But if he were anything more, he would know that one man is not miserable through the means of another.

[10] Schweighaeuser has a long note on this passage, to "receive from another." I think that there is no difficulty about the meaning; and the careful reader will find none. Epictetus was once a slave.

[11] The meaning is obscure. Schweighaeuser thinks that the allusion is to a defeated enemy asking permission from the conqueror to bury the dead. Epictetus considers a man as a mere carcase who places his happiness in externals and in the favour of others.

CHAPTER X.

AGAINST THOSE WHO EAGERLY SEEK PREFERMENT AT ROME.

If we applied ourselves as busily to our own work as the old men at Rome do to those matters about which they are employed, perhaps we also might accomplish something. I am acquainted with a man older than myself, who is now superintendent of corn [1] at Rome, and I remember the time when he came here on his way back from exile, and what he said as he related the events of his former life, and how he declared that with respect to the future after his return he would look after nothing else than passing the rest of his life in quiet and tranquillity. For how little of life, he said, remains for me. I replied, you will not do it, but as soon as you smell Rome, you will forget all that you have said; and if admission is allowed even into the imperial palace, he [2] will gladly thrust himself in and thank God. If you find me, Epictetus, he answered, setting even one foot within the palace, think what you please. Well, what then did he do? Before he entered the city, he was met by letters from Caesar, and as soon as he received them, he forgot all, and ever after has added one piece of business to another. I wish that I were now by his side to remind him of what he said when he was passing this way, and to tell him how much better a seer I am than he is.

Well then do I say that man is an animal made for doing nothing? [3] Certainly not. But why are we not

[1] A "Præfectus Annonæ," or superintendent of the supply of corn at Rome is first mentioned by Livy (iv. 12) as appointed during a scarcity. At a later time this office was conferred on Cn. Pompeius for five years. Maecenas (Dion. 52, c. 24) advised Augustus to make a Praefectus Annonae or permanent officer over the corn market and all other markets (ἐπὶ τοῦ σίτου τῆς τε ἀγορᾶς τῆς λοιπῆς). He would thus have the office formerly exercised by the aediles.

[2] I cannot explain why the third person is used here instead of the second. See Schweig.'s note.

[3] The Stoics taught that man is adapted by his nature for action. He ought not therefore to withdraw from human affairs, and indulge in a lazy life, not even a life of contemplation and religious observances only. Upton refers to Antoninus, v. 1, viii. 19, and Cicero, De Fin. v. 20.

active?[4] (We are active.) For example, as to myself, as soon as day comes, in a few words I remind myself of what I must read over to my pupils;[5] then forthwith I say to myself, But what is it to me how a certain person shall read? the first thing for me is to sleep. And indeed what resemblance is there between what other persons do and what we do? If you observe what they do, you will understand. And what else do they do all day long than make up accounts, enquire among themselves, give and take advice about some small quantity of grain, a bit of land, and such kind of profits? Is it then the same thing to receive a petition and to read in it: I intreat you to permit me to export[6] a small quantity of corn; and one to this effect: "I intreat you to learn from Chrysippus what is the administration of the world, and what place in it the rational animal holds; consider also who you are, and what is the nature of your good and bad. Are these things like the other, do they require equal care, and is it equally base to neglect these and those? Well then are we the only persons who are lazy and love sleep? No; but much rather you young men are. For we old men when we see young men amusing themselves are eager to play with them; and if I saw you active and zealous, much more should I be eager myself to join you in your serious pursuits."

[4] Schweighaeuser proposes a small alteration in the Greek text, but I do not think it necessary. When Epictetus says, "Why are we not active?" He means, Why do some say that we are not active? And he intends to say that We are active, but not in the way in which some people are active. I have therefore added in ( ) what is necessary to make the text intelligible.

[5] This passage is rather obscure. The word ἐπαναγνῶναι signifies, it is said, to read over for the purpose of explaining as a teacher may do. The pupil also would read something to the teacher for the purpose of showing if he understood it. So Epictetus also says, "But what is it to me," &c.

[6] A plain allusion to restraints put on the exportation of grain.

CHAPTER XI.

OF NATURAL AFFECTION.

When he was visited by one of the magistrates, Epictetus inquired of him about several particulars, and asked if he had children and a wife. The man replied that he had; and Epictetus inquired further, how he felt under the circumstances. Miserable, the man said. Then Epictetus asked, In what respect, for men do not marry and beget children in order to be wretched, but rather to be happy. But I, the man replied, am so wretched about my children that lately, when my little daughter was sick and was supposed to be in danger, I could not endure to stay with her, but I left home till a person sent me news that she had recovered. Well then, said Epictetus, do you think that you acted right? I acted naturally, the man replied. But convince me of this that you acted naturally, and I will convince you that everything which takes place according to nature takes place rightly. This is the case, said the man, with all or at least most fathers. I do not deny that: but the matter about which we are inquiring is whether such behaviour is right; for in respect to this matter we must say that tumours also come for the good of the body, because they do come; and generally we must say that to do wrong is natural, because nearly all or at least most of us do wrong. Do you show me then how your behaviour is natural. I cannot, he said; but do you rather show me how it is not according to nature, and is not rightly done.

Well, said Epictetus, if we were inquiring about white and black, what criterion should we employ for distinguishing between them? The sight, he said. And if about hot and cold, and hard and soft, what criterion? The touch. Well then, since we are inquiring about things which are according to nature, and those which are done rightly or not rightly, what kind of criterion do you think that we should employ? I do not know, he said. And yet not to know the criterion of colours and smells, and also of tastes, is perhaps no great harm; but if a man do not know the criterion of good and bad, and of things according to nature and contrary to nature, does this seem to you a small harm? The greatest harm (I think). Come tell me, do all things which seem to some persons to be good and becoming, rightly appear such; and at present as to Jews and Syrians and Egyptians and Romans, is it possible that the opinions of all of them in respect to food are right? How is it possible? he said. Well, I suppose, it is absolutely necessary that, if the opinions of the Egyptians are right, the opinions of the rest must be wrong: if the opinions of the Jews are right, those of the rest cannot be right. Certainly. But where there is ignorance, there also there is want of learning and training in things which are necessary. He assented to this. You then, said Epictetus, since you know this, for the future will employ yourself seriously about nothing else, and will apply your mind to nothing else than to learn the criterion of things which are according to nature, and by using it also to determine each several thing. But in the present matter I have so much as this to aid you towards what you wish. Does affection to those of your family appear to you to be according to nature and to be good? Certainly. Well, is such affection natural and good, and is a thing consistent with reason not good? By no means. Is then that which is consistent with reason in contradiction with affection? I think not. You are right, for if it is otherwise, it is necessary that one of the contradictions being according to nature, the other must be contrary to nature. Is it not so? It is, he said. Whatever then we shall discover to be at the same time affectionate and also consistent with reason, this we confidently declare to be right and good. Agreed. Well then to leave your sick child and to go away is not reasonable, and I suppose that you will not say that it is; but it remains for us to inquire if it is consistent with affection. Yes, let us consider. Did you then, since you had an affectionate disposition to your child, do right when you ran off and left her; and has the mother no affection for the child? Certainly, she has. Ought then the mother also to have left her, or ought she not? She ought not. And the nurse, does she love her? She does. Ought then she also to have left her? By no means. And the paedagogue,[1] does he not love her? He does love her. Ought then he also to have deserted her? and so should the child have been left alone and without help on account of the great affection of you the parents and of those about her, or should she have died in the hands of those who neither loved her nor cared for her? Certainly not. Now this is unfair and unreasonable, not to allow those who have equal affection with yourself to do what you think to be proper for yourself to do because you have affection. It is absurd. Come then, if you were sick, would you wish your relations to be so affectionate, and all the rest, children and wife, as to leave you alone and deserted? By no means. And would you wish to be so loved by your own that through their excessive affection you would always be left alone in sickness? or for this reason would you rather pray, if it were possible, to be loved by your enemies and deserted by them? But if this is so, it results that your behaviour was not at all an affectionate act.

Well then, was it nothing which moved you and induced you to desert your child? and how is that possible? But it might be something of the kind which moved a man at Rome to wrap up his head while a horse was running which he favoured; and when contrary to expectation the horse won, he required sponges to recover from his fainting fit. What then is the thing which moved? The exact discussion of this does not belong to the present occasion perhaps; but it is enough to be convinced of this, if what the philosophers say is true, that we must not look for it anywhere without, but in all cases it is one and the same thing which is the cause of our doing or not doing something, of saying or not saying something, of being elated or depressed, of avoiding any thing or pursuing: the very thing which is now the cause to me and to you, to you of coming to me and sitting and hearing, and to me of saying what I do say. And what is this? Is it any other than our will to do so? No other. But

[1] "When we are children our parents put us in the hands of a paedagogue to see on all occasions that we take no harm."—Epictetus, Frag. 97.

if we had willed otherwise, what else should we have been doing than that which we willed to do? This then was the cause of Achilles' lamentation, not the death of Patroclus; for another man does not behave thus on the death of his companion; but it was because he chose to do so. And to you this was the very cause of your then running away, that you chose to do so; and on the other side, if you should (hereafter) stay with her, the reason will be the same. And now you are going to Rome because you choose; and if you should change your mind,[2] you will not go thither. And in a word, neither death nor exile nor pain nor anything of the kind is the cause of our doing anything or not doing; but our own opinions and our wills (δόγματα).

Do I convince you of this or not? You do convince me. Such then as the causes are in each case, such also are the effects. When then we are doing anything not rightly, from this day we shall impute it to nothing else than to the will (δόγμα or opinion) from which we have done it: and it is that which we shall endeavour to take away and to extirpate more than the tumours and abscesses out of the body. And in like manner we shall give the same account of the cause of the things which we do right; and we shall no longer allege as causes of any evil to us, either slave or neighbour, or wife or children, being persuaded, that if we do not think things to be what we do think them to be, we do not the acts which follow from such opinions; and as to thinking or not thinking, that is in our power and not in externals. It is so, he said. From this day then we shall inquire into and examine nothing else, what its quality is, or its state, neither land

[2] κἂν μεταδόξῃ, "if you should change your mind," as we say. So we may translate, in the previous part of this chapter, ἔδοξεν ἡμῖν, σοί, and the like, "we had a mind to such and such a thing." Below it is said that the causes of our actions are "our opinions and our wills," where the Greek for "wills" is δόγματα. If we translate ἔδοξεν ἡμῖν, "seemed right," as some persons would translate it, that is not the meaning, unless we understand "seemed right" in a sense in which it is often used, that is, a man's resolve to do so and so. See Schweig.'s note on ὑπόληψις and δόγμα. As Antoninus says (viii. 1): "How then shall a man do this (what his nature requires)? If he has principles (δόγματα) from which come his affects (ὅρμαι) and his acts (πράξεις)?"

nor slaves nor horses nor dogs, nothing else than opinions.[3] I hope so. You see then that you must become a Scholasticus,[4] an animal whom all ridicule, if you really intend to make an examination of your own opinions: and that this is not the work of one hour or day, you know yourself.

CHAPTER XII.

OF CONTENTMENT.

WITH respect to gods, there are some who say that a divine being does not exist: others say that it exists, but is inactive and careless, and takes no forethought about any thing; a third class say that such a being exists and exercises forethought, but only about great things and heavenly things, and about nothing on the earth; a fourth class say that a divine being exercises forethought both about things on the earth and heavenly things, but in a general way only, and not about things severally. There is a fifth class to whom Ulysses and Socrates belong, who say: "I move not without thy knowledge"[1] (Iliad, x. 278).

[3] He uses the word δόγματα, which contains the same element or root as δοκεῖ, ἔδοξε.

[4] A Scholasticus is one who frequents the schools; a studious and literary person, who does not engage in the business of active life.

[1] The line is from the prayer of Ulysses to Athena: "Hear me child of Zeus, thou who standest by me always in all dangers, nor do I even move without thy knowledge." Socrates said that the gods know everything, what is said and done and thought (Xenophon, Mem. i. 1, 19). Compare Cicero, De Nat. Deorum, i. 1, 2; and Dr. Price's Dissertation on Providence, sect. i. Epictetus enumerates the various opinions about the gods in antient times. The reader may consult the notes in Schweighaeuser's edition. The opinions about God among modern nations, who are called civilized, and are so more or less, do not seem to be so varied as in antient times; but the contrasts in modern opinions are striking. These modern opinions vary between denial of a God, though the number of those who deny is perhaps not large, and the superstitious notions about God and his administration of the world, which are taught by teachers, learned and ignorant, and exercise a great power over the minds of those who are unable or do not dare to exercise the faculty of reason.

Before all other things then it is necessary to inquire about each of these opinions, whether it is affirmed truly or not truly. For if there are no gods, how is it our proper end to follow them?[2] And if they exist, but take no care of anything, in this case also how will it be right to follow them? But if indeed they do exist and look after things, still if there is nothing communicated from them to men, nor in fact to myself, how even so is it right (to follow them)? The wise and good man then after considering all these things, submits his own mind to him who administers the whole, as good citizens do to the law of the state. He who is receiving instruction ought to come to be instructed with this intention, How shall I follow the gods in all things, how shall I be contented with the divine administration, and how can I become free? For he is free to whom every thing happens according to his will, and whom no man can hinder. What then is freedom madness? Certainly not: for madness and freedom do not consist. But, you say, I would have every thing result just as I like, and in whatever way I like. You are mad, you are beside yourself. Do you not know that freedom is a noble and valuable thing? But for me inconsiderately to wish for things to happen as I inconsiderately like, this appears to be not only not noble, but even most base. For how do we proceed in the matter of writing? Do I wish to write the name of Dion as I choose? No, but I am taught to choose to write it as it ought to be written. And how with respect to music? In the same manner. And what universally in every art or science? Just the same. If it were not so, it would be of no value to know anything, if knowledge were adapted to every man's whim. Is it then in this alone, in this which is the greatest and the chief thing, I mean freedom, that I am permitted to will inconsiderately? By no means; but to be instructed is this, to learn to wish that every thing may happen as it does.[3]

[2] "To follow God," is a Stoical expression. Antoninus, x. 11.

[3] This means that we ought to learn to be satisfied with everything that happens, in fact with the will of God. This is a part of education, according to Epictetus. But it does not appear in our systems of education so plainly as it does here. Antoninus (iv. 23): "Everything harmonizes with me, which is harmonious to thee, O universe. Nothing for me is too early nor too late, which is in due time for thee."

And how do things happen? As the disposer has disposed them? And he has appointed summer and winter, and abundance and scarcity, and virtue and vice, and all such opposites for the harmony of the whole;[4] and to each of us he has given a body, and parts of the body, and possessions, and companions.

Remembering then this disposition of things, we ought to go to be instructed, not that we may change the constitution[5] of things,—for we have not the power to do it, nor is it better that we should have the power,—but in order that, as the things around us are what they are and by nature exist, we may maintain our minds in harmony with the things which happen. For can we escape from men? and how is it possible? And if we associate with them, can we change them? Who gives us the power? What then remains, or what method is discovered of holding commerce with them? Is there such a method by which they shall do what seems fit to them, and we not the less shall be in a mood which is conformable to nature? But you are unwilling to endure and are discontented: and if you are alone, you call it solitude; and if you are with men, you call them knaves and robbers; and you find fault with your own parents and children, and brothers and neighbours. But you ought when you are alone to call this condition by the name of tranquillity and freedom,

[4] Upton has collected the passages in which this doctrine was mentioned. One passage is in Gellius (vi. 1), from the fourth book of Chrysippus on Providence, who says: "nothing is more foolish than the opinions of those who think that good could have existed without evil." Schweighaeuser wishes that Epictetus had discussed more fully the question on the nature and origin of Evil. He refers to the commentary of Simplicius on the Encheiridion of Epictetus, c. 13 (8), and 34 (27), for his treatment of this subject. Epictetus (Encheiridion, c. 27) says that "as a mark is not set up for the purpose of missing it, so neither does the nature of evil exist in the universe." Simplicius observes (p. 278, ed. Schweig.): "The Good is that which is according to each thing's nature, wherein each thing has its perfection: but the Bad is the disposition contrary to its nature of the thing which contains the bad, by which disposition it is deprived of that which is according to nature, namely, the good. For if the Bad as well as the Good were a disposition and perfection of the form (εἴδους) in which it is, the bad itself would also be good and would not then be called Bad."

[5] The word is ὑποθέσεις. It is explained by what follows.

and to think yourself like to the gods; and when you are with many, you ought not to call it crowd, nor trouble, nor uneasiness, but festival and assembly, and so accept all contentedly.

What then is the punishment of those who do not accept? It is to be what they are. Is any person dissatisfied with being alone? let him be alone. Is a man dissatisfied with his parents? let him be a bad son, and lament. Is he dissatisfied with his children? let him be a bad father. Cast him into prison. What prison? Where he is already, for he is there against his will; and where a man is against his will, there he is in prison. So Socrates was not in prison, for he was there willingly— Must my leg then be lamed? Wretch, do you then on account of one poor leg find fault with the world? Will you not willingly surrender it for the whole? Will you not withdraw from it? Will you not gladly part with it to him who gave it? And will you be vexed and discontented with the things established by Zeus, which he with the Moirae (fates) who were present and spinning the thread of your generation, defined and put in order? Know you not how small a part you are compared with the whole.[6] I mean with respect to the body, for as to intelligence you are not inferior to the gods nor less; for the magnitude of intelligence is not measured by length nor yet by height, but by thoughts.[7]

Will you not then choose to place your good in that in which you are equal to the gods?—Wretch that I am to have such a father and mother.—What then, was it permitted to you to come forth and to select and to say: Let such a man at this moment unite with such a woman that I may be produced? It was not permitted, but it was a

[6] "Et quota pars homo sit terrai totius unus." Lucret. vi. 652, and Antoninus, ii. 4.

[7] The original is δόγμασι, which the Latin translators render "decretis," and Mrs. Carter "principles." I don't understand either. I have rendered the word by "thoughts," which is vague, but I can do no better. It was the Stoic doctrine that the human intelligence is a particle of the divine. Mrs. Carter names this "one of the Stoic extravagancies, arising from the notion that human souls were literally parts of the Deity." But this is hardly a correct representation of the Stoic doctrine.

necessity for your parents to exist first, and then for you to be begotten. Of what kind of parents? Of such as they were. Well then, since they are such as they are, is there no remedy given to you? Now if you did not know for what purpose you possess the faculty of vision, you would be unfortunate and wretched if you closed your eyes when colours were brought before them; but in that you possess greatness of soul and nobility of spirit for every event that may happen, and you know not that you possess them, are you not more unfortunate and wretched? Things are brought close to you which are proportionate to the power which you possess, but you turn away this power most particularly at the very time when you ought to maintain it open and discerning. Do you not rather thank the gods that they have allowed you to be above these things which they have not placed in your power, and have made you accountable only for those which are in your power? As to your parents, the gods have left you free from responsibility; and so with respect to your brothers, and your body, and possessions, and death and life. For what then have they made you responsible? For that which alone is in your power, the proper use of appearances. Why then do you draw on yourself the things for which you are not responsible? It is, indeed, a giving of trouble to yourself.

CHAPTER XIII.

HOW EVERYTHING MAY BE DONE ACCEPTABLY TO THE GODS.

WHEN some one asked, how may a man eat acceptably to the gods, he answered: If he can eat justly and contentedly, and with equanimity, and temperately and orderly, will it not be also acceptably to the gods? But when you have asked for warm water and the slave has not heard, or if he did hear has brought only tepid water, or he is not even found to be in the house, then not to be vexed or to burst with passion, is not this acceptable to the gods?—How then shall a man endure such persons as this slave? Slave yourself, will you not bear with your own brother, who has Zeus for his progenitor, and is like a son from the same seeds and of the same descent from above? But if you have been put in any such higher place, will you immediately make yourself a tyrant? Will you not remember who you are, and whom you rule? that they are kinsmen, that they are brethren by nature, that they are the offspring of Zeus?[1]—But I have purchased them, and they have not purchased me. Do you see in what direction you are looking, that it is towards the earth, towards the pit, that it is towards these wretched laws of dead men?[2] but towards the laws of the gods you are not looking.

CHAPTER XIV.

THAT THE DEITY OVERSEES ALL THINGS.

When a person asked him how a man could be convinced that all his actions are under the inspection of God, he answered, Do you not think that all things are united in one?[1] I do, the person replied. Well, do you not think

[1] Mrs. Carter compares Job xxxi. 15: "Did not he that made me in the womb make him (my man-servant)? And did not one fashion us in the womb?"

[2] I suppose he means human laws, which have made one man a slave to another; and when he says "dead men," he may mean mortal men, as contrasted with the gods or God, who has made all men brothers.

[1] Things appear to be separate, but there is a bond by which they are united. "All this that you see, wherein things divine and human are contained, is One: we are members of one large body" (Seneca, Ep. 95). "The universe is either a confusion, a mutual involution of things and a dispersion; or it is unity and order and providence" (Antoninus, vi. 10): also vii. 9, "all things are implicated with one another, and the bond is holy; and there is hardly any thing unconnected with any other thing." See also Cicero, De Nat. Deorum, ii. 7; and De Oratore, iii. 5.

that earthly things have a natural agreement and union[2] with heavenly things? I do. And how else so regularly as if by God's command, when He bids the plants to flower, do they flower? when He bids them to send forth shoots, do they shoot? when He bids them to produce fruit, how else do they produce fruit? when He bids the fruit to ripen, does it ripen? when again He bids them to cast down the fruits, how else do they cast them down? and when to shed the leaves, do they shed the leaves? and when He bids them to fold themselves up and to remain quiet and rest, how else do they remain quiet and rest? And how else at the growth and the wane of the moon, and at the approach and recession of the sun, are so great an alteration and change to the contrary seen in earthly things?[3] But are plants and our bodies so bound up and united with the whole, and are not our souls much more? and our souls so bound up and in contact with God as parts of Him and portions of Him; and does not God perceive every motion of these parts as being his own motion connate with himself? Now are you able to think of the divine administration, and about all things divine, and at the same time also about human affairs, and to be moved by ten thousand things at the same time in your senses and in your understanding, and to assent to some, and to dissent from others, and again as to some things to suspend your judgment; and do you retain in your soul so many impressions from so many and various things, and being moved by them, do you fall upon notions similar to those first impressed, and do you retain numerous arts and the memories of ten thousand things; and is not God able to oversee all things, and to be present with all, and to receive from all a certain communication? And is the sun able to illuminate so large a part of the All, and to leave so little not illuminated, that part only which is occupied by the earth's shadow; and He who made the sun itself and makes it go round, being a small part of himself compared with the whole, cannot He perceive all things?

But I cannot, the man may reply, comprehend all these

[2] The word is *συμπαθεῖν*. Cicero (De Divin. ii. 69) translates *συμπάθειαν* by "continuatio conjunctioque naturae."

[3] Compare Swedenborg, Angelic Wisdom, 349–356.

things at once. But who tells you that you have equal power with Zeus? Nevertheless he has placed by every man a guardian, every man's Daemon,[4] to whom he has committed the care of the man, a guardian who never sleeps, is never deceived. For to what better and more careful guardian could He have intrusted each of us?[5] When then you have shut the doors and made darkness within, remember never to say that you are alone, for you are not; but God is within, and your Daemon is within, and what need have they of light to see what you are doing? To this God you ought to swear an oath just as the soldiers do to Caesar. But they who are hired for pay swear to regard the safety of Caesar before all things; and you who have received so many and such great favours, will you not swear, or when you have sworn, will you not abide by your oath? And what shall you swear? Never to be disobedient, never to make any charges, never to find fault with any thing that he has given, and never unwillingly to do or to suffer any thing that is necessary. Is this oath like the soldier's oath? The soldiers swear not to prefer any man to Cæsar: in this oath men swear to honour themselves before all.[6]

[4] Antoninus, v. 27: "Live with the gods. And he does live with the gods who constantly shows to them that his own soul is satisfied with that which is assigned to him, and that it does all that the Daemon wishes, which Zeus hath given to every man for his guardian and guide, a portion of himself. And this is every man's understanding and reason." Antoninus (iii. 5) names this Daemon "the god who is in thee." St. Paul (1 Cor. i. 3, 16) says, "Know ye not that ye are the temple of God, and that the spirit of God dwelleth in you?" Even the poets use this form of expression—

"Est Deus in nobis, agitante calescimus illo [ipso]:
Impetus hic sacrae semina mentis habet."—Ovid, 'Fasti.' vi. 5.

[5] See Schweig.'s note on παραδέδωκεν.

[6] See Schweig.'s note.

CHAPTER XV.

WHAT PHILOSOPHY PROMISES.

When a man was consulting him how he should persuade his brother to cease being angry with him, Epictetus replied, Philosophy does not propose to secure for a man any external thing. If it did (or, if it were not, as I say), philosophy would be allowing something which is not within its province. For as the carpenter's material is wood, and that of the statuary is copper, so the matter of the art of living is each man's life.—What then is my brother's?—That again belongs to his own art; but with respect to yours, it is one of the external things, like a piece of land, like health, like reputation. But Philosophy promises none of these. In every circumstance I will maintain, she says, the governing part[1] conformable to nature. Whose governing part? His in whom I am, she says.

How then shall my brother cease to be angry with me? Bring him to me and I will tell him. But I have nothing to say to you about his anger.

When the man, who was consulting him, said, I seek to know this, How, even if my brother is not reconciled to me, shall I maintain myself in a state conformable to nature? Nothing great, said Epictetus, is produced suddenly, since not even the grape or the fig is. If you say to me now that you want a fig, I will answer to you that it requires time: let it flower[2] first, then put forth fruit, and then ripen. Is then the fruit of a fig-tree not perfected suddenly and in one hour, and would you possess the fruit of a man's mind in so short a time and so easily? Do not expect it, even if I tell you.

[1] This is τὸ ἡγεμονικόν, a word often used by Antoninus, ii. 2; vi. 8.

[2] "The philosopher had forgot that fig-trees do not blossom" (Mrs. Carter). The flowers of a fig are inside the fleshy receptacle which becomes the fruit.

Schweig. prints μὴ δ' ἂν, ἐγώ σοι λέγω, προσδόκα: and in his Latin version he prints: "Id vero, ego tibi dico, ne expectes." I neither understand his pointing, nor his version. Wolf translates it, "Etsi ego tibi dixero (virtutem brevi parari posse), noli credere": which is right Wolf makes ἂν go with λέγω.

CHAPTER XVI.

OF PROVIDENCE.

Do not wonder if for other animals than man all things are provided for the body, not only food and drink, but beds also, and they have no need of shoes nor bed materials, nor clothing; but we require all these additional things. For animals not being made for themselves, but for service, it was not fit for them to be made so as to need other things. For consider what it would be for us to take care not only of ourselves, but also about cattle and asses, how they should be clothed, and how shod, and how they should eat and drink. Now as soldiers are ready for their commander, shod, clothed, and armed: but it would be a hard thing for the chiliarch (tribune) to go round and shoe or clothe his thousand men: so also nature has formed the animals which are made for service, all ready, prepared, and requiring no further care. So one little boy with only a stick drives the cattle.

But now we, instead of being thankful that we need not take the same care of animals as of ourselves, complain of God on our own account; and yet, in the name of Zeus and the gods, any one thing of those which exist would be enough to make a man perceive the providence of God, at least a man who is modest and grateful. And speak not to me now of the great things, but only of this, that milk is produced from grass, and cheese from milk, and wool from skins. Who made these things or devised them? No one, you say. O amazing shamelessness and stupidity!

Well, let us omit the works of nature, and contemplate her smaller (subordinate, πάρεργα) acts. Is there anything less useful than the hair on the chin? What then, has not nature used this hair also in the most suitable manner possible? Has she not by it distinguished the male and the female? does not the nature of every man forthwith proclaim from a distance, I am a man: as such approach me, as such speak to me; look for nothing else; see the signs? Again, in the case of women, as she has mingled something softer in the voice, so she has also deprived them of hair (on the chin). You say, not so: the human animal ought to have been left without marks of distinction, and each of us should have been obliged to proclaim, I am a man. But how is not the sign beautiful and becoming and venerable? how much more beautiful than the cock's comb, how much more becoming than the lion's mane? For this reason we ought to preserve the signs which God has given, we ought not to throw them away, nor to confound, as much as we can, the distinctions of the sexes.

Are these the only works of providence in us? And what words are sufficient to praise them and set them forth according to their worth? For if we had understanding, ought we to do any thing else both jointly and severally than to sing hymns and bless the deity, and to tell of his benefits?[1] Ought we not when we are digging and ploughing and eating to sing this hymn to God? "Great is God, who has given us such implements with which we shall cultivate the earth: great is God who has given us hands, the power of swallowing, a stomach, imperceptible growth, and the power of breathing while we sleep." This is what we ought to sing on every occasion, and to sing the greatest and most divine hymn for giving us the faculty of comprehending these things and using a proper way.[2] Well then, since most of you have become blind, ought there not to be some man to fill this office, and on behalf of all to sing[3] the hymn to God? For what else can I do, a lame old man, than sing hymns to God? If then I was a nightingale, I would do the part of a nightingale. if I were a swan, I would do like a swan. But now I am a rational creature, and I ought to praise God: this is my work; I do it, nor will I desert this post, so long as I am allowed to keep it; and I exhort you to join in this same song.

[1] Antoninus, v. 33.
[2] See Upton's note on ὁδῷ.
[3] ᾄδοντα is Schweighaeuser's probable emendation.

CHAPTER XVII.

THAT THE LOGICAL ART IS NECESSARY.

SINCE reason is the faculty which analyses[1] and perfects the rest, and it ought itself not to be unanalysed, by what should it be analysed? for it is plain that this should be done either by itself or by another thing. Either then this other thing also is reason, or something else superior to reason; which is impossible. But if it is reason, again who shall analyse that reason? For if that reason does this for itself, our reason also can do it. But if we shall require something else, the thing will go on to infinity and have no end.[2] Reason therefore is analysed by itself. Yes: but it is more urgent to cure (our opinions[3]) and the like. Will you then hear about those things? Hear. But if you should say, "I know not whether you are arguing truly or falsely," and if I should express myself in any way ambiguously, and you should say to me, "Distinguish," I will bear with you no longer, and I shall say to you, "It is more urgent."[4] This is the reason, I suppose, why they (the Stoic teachers) place the logical art first, as in the measuring of corn we place first the examination of the measure. But if we do not determine first what is a

[1] Λόγος ἐστὶν ὁ διαρθρῶν. Διαρθροῦν means "to divide a thing into its parts or members." The word "analyse" seems to be the nearest equivalent. See Schweig.'s note on ὑπὸ τίνος διαρθρωθῇ;

[2] This is obscure. The conclusion, "Reason therefore is analysed by itself" is not in Epictetus; but it is implied, as Schweighaeuser says (p. 197, notes). So Antoninus, xi. 1, writes: "These are the properties of the rational soul; it sees itself, analyses itself." If reason, our reason, requires another reason to analyse it, that other reason will require another reason to analyse that other reason; and so on to infinity. If reason then, our reason, can be analysed, it must be analysed by itself. The notes on the first part of this chapter in the edition of Schweighaeuser may be read by those who are inclined.

[3] "Our opinions." There is some defect in the text, as Wolf remarks. "The opponent," he says, "disparages Logic (Dialectic) as a thing which is not necessary to make men good, and he prefers moral teaching to Logic: but Epictetus informs him, that a man who is not a Dialectician will not have a sufficient perception of moral teaching."

[4] He repeats the words of the supposed opponent; and he means that his adversary's difficulty shows the necessity of Dialectic.

modius, and what is a balance, how shall we be able to measure or weigh anything?

In this case then if we have not fully learned and accurately examined the criterion of all other things, by which the other things are learned, shall we be able to examine accurately and to learn fully any thing else? How is this possible? Yes; but the modius is only wood, and a thing which produces no fruit.—But it is a thing which can measure corn.—Logic also produces no fruit.—As to this indeed we shall see: but then even if a man should grant this, it is enough that logic has the power of distinguishing and examining other things, and, as we may say, of measuring and weighing them. Who says this? Is it only Chrysippus, and Zeno, and Cleanthes? And does not Antisthenes say so?[5] And who is it that has written that the examination of names is the beginning of education? And does not Socrates say so? And of whom does Xenophon write, that he began with the examination of names, what each name signified?[6] Is this then the great and wondrous thing to understand or interpret Chrysippus? Who says this?—What then is the wondrous thing?—To understand the will of nature. Well then do you apprehend it yourself by your own power? and what more have you need of? For if it is true that all men err involuntarily, and you have learned the truth, of necessity you must act right.—But in truth I do not apprehend the will of nature. Who then tells us what it is?—They say that it is Chrysippus.—I proceed, and I inquire what this interpreter of nature says. I begin not to understand what he says: I seek an interpreter of Chrysippus.—Well, consider how this is said, just as if it were said in the

[5] Antisthenes, who professed the Cynic philosophy, rejected Logic and Physic (Schweig. note p. 201).

[6] Xenophon, Mem. iv. 5, 12, and iv. 6, 7. Epictetus knew what education ought to be. We learn language, and we ought to learn what it means. When children learn words, they should learn what the thing is which is signified by the word. In the case of children this can only be done imperfectly as to some words, but it may be done even then in some degree; and it must be done, or the word signifies nothing, or, what is equally bad, the word is misunderstood. All of us pass our lives in ignorance of many words which we use; some of us in greater ignorance than others, but all of us in ignorance to some degree.

Roman tongue.[7]—What then is this superciliousness of the interpreter?[8] There is no superciliousness which can justly be charged even to Chrysippus, if he only interprets the will of nature, but does not follow it himself; and much more is this so with his interpreter. For we have no need of Chrysippus for his own sake, but in order that we may understand nature. Nor do we need a diviner (sacrificer) on his own account, but because we think that through him we shall know the future and understand the signs given by the gods; nor do we need the viscera of animals for their own sake, but because through them signs are given; nor do we look with wonder on the crow or raven, but on God, who through them gives signs?[9]

I go then to the interpreter of these things and the sacrificer, and I say, Inspect the viscera for me, and tell me what signs they give. The man takes the viscera, opens them, and interprets: Man, he says, you have a will free by nature from hindrance and compulsion; this is written here in the viscera. I will show you this first in the matter of assent. Can any man hinder you from assenting to the truth? No man can. Can any man compel you to receive what is false? No man can. You see that in this matter you have the faculty of the will free from hindrance, free from compulsion, unimpeded. Well then, in the matter of desire and pursuit of an object, is it otherwise? And what can overcome pursuit except another pursuit? And what can overcome desire and aversion (ἔκκλισιν) except another desire and aversion? But, you object: "If you place before me the fear of death, you do compel me." No, it is not what is placed before you that compels, but your opinion that it is better to do so and so than to die. In this matter then it is your opinion that compelled you: that is, will compelled will.[10] For if God had made that part of himself,

[7] The supposed interpreter says this. When Epictetus says "the Roman tongue," perhaps he means that the supposed opponent is a Roman and does not know Greek well.

[8] Encheiridion, c. 49. "When a man gives himself great airs because he can understand and expound Chrysippus, say to yourself, If Chrysippus had not written obscurely, this man would have had nothing to be proud of." See the rest.

[9] Compare Xenophon, Mem. i. 1, 3.

[10] This is true. If you place before a man the fear of death, you threaten him with the fear of death. The man may yield to the

which he took from himself and gave to us, of such a nature as to be hindered or compelled either by himself or by another, he would not then be God nor would he be taking care of us as he ought. This, says the diviner, I find in the victims: these are the things which are signified to you. If you choose, you are free; if you choose, you will blame no one: you will charge no one. All will be at the same time according to your mind and the mind of God. For the sake of this divination I go to this diviner and to the philosopher, not admiring him for this interpretation, but admiring the things which he interprets.

CHAPTER XVIII.

THAT WE OUGHT NOT TO BE ANGRY WITH THE ERRORS (FAULTS) OF OTHERS.

If what philosophers say is true, that all men have one principle, as in the case of assent the persuasion[1] that a thing is so, and in the case of dissent the persuasion that a thing is not so, and in the case of a suspense of judgment the persuasion that a thing is uncertain, so also in the

threat and do what it is the object of the threat to make him do; or he may make resistance to him who attempts to enforce the threat; or he may refuse to yield, and so take the consequence of his refusal. If a man yields to the threat, he does so for the reason which Epictetus gives, and freedom of choice, and consequently freedom of will really exists in this case. The Roman law did not allow contracts or agreements made under the influence of threats to be valid; and the reason for declaring them invalid was not the want of free will in him who yielded to the threat, but the fact that threats are directly contrary to the purpose of all law, which purpose is to secure the independent action of every person in all things allowed by law. This matter is discussed by Savigny, Das heut. Römische Recht, iii. § 114. See the title 'Quod metus causa,' in the Digest, 4, 2. Compare also Epictetus, iv. 1, 68, etc.

[1] τὸ παθεῖν ὅτι, etc.: Schweighaeuser has a note on the distinction between τὸ ὀρέγεσθαι and τὸ ὁρμᾶν. Compare Epictetus, iii. 2, 1; iii. 3, 2; iii. 22, 43; and i. 4, 11. Schweig. says that ὀρέγεσθαι refers to the ἀγαθόν and συμφέρον, and ὁρμᾶν to the καθῆκον, and he concludes that there is a defect in the text, which he endeavours to supply.

case of a movement towards any thing the persuasion that a thing is for a man's advantage, and it is impossible to think that one thing is advantageous and to desire another, and to judge one thing to be proper and to move towards another, why then are we angry with the many?[2]

[2] Mrs. Carter says: "The most ignorant persons often practise what they know to be evil: and they, who voluntarily suffer, as many do, their inclinations to blind their judgment, are not justified by following it. (Perhaps she means "them," "their inclinations.") The doctrine of Epictetus therefore, here and elsewhere, on this head, contradicts the voice of reason and conscience: nor is it less pernicious than ill-grounded. It destroys all guilt and merit, all punishment and reward, all blame of ourselves or others, all sense of misbehaviour towards our fellow-creatures, or our Creator. No wonder that such philosophers did not teach repentance towards God."

Mrs. Carter has not understood Epictetus; and her censure is misplaced. It is true that "the most ignorant persons often practise what they know to be evil," as she truly says. But she might have said more. It is also true that persons, who are not ignorant, often do what they know to be evil, and even what they would condemn in another, at least before they had fallen into the same evil themselves; for when they have done what they know to be wrong, they have a fellow-feeling with others who are as bad as themselves. Nor does he say, as Mrs. Carter seems to imply that he does, for her words are ambiguous, that they who voluntarily suffer their inclinations to blind their judgment are justified by following them. He says that men will do as they do, so long as they think as they think. He only traces to their origin the bad acts which bad men do; and he says that we should pity them and try to mend them. Now the best man in the world, if he sees the origin and direct cause of bad acts in men, may pity them for their wickedness, and he will do right. He will pity, and still he will punish severely, if the interests of society require the guilty to be punished: but he will not punish in anger. Epictetus says nothing about legal penalties; and I assume that he would not say that the penalties are always unjust, if I understand his principles. His discourse is to this effect, as the title tells us, that we ought not to be angry with the errors of others: the matter of the discourse is the feeling and disposition which we ought to have towards those who do wrong, "because they are mistaken about good and evil."

He does not discuss the question of the origin of these men's mistake further than this: men think that a thing or act is advantageous; and it is impossible for them to think that one thing is advantageous and to desire another thing. Their error is in their opinion. Then he tells us to show them their error, and they will desist from their errors. He is not here examining the way of showing them their error; by which I suppose that he means convincing them of their error. He seems to admit that it may not be possible to convince

They are thieves and robbers, you may say. What do you mean by thieves and robbers? They are mistaken about good and evil. Ought we then to be angry with them, or to pity them? But show them their error, and you will see how they desist from their errors. If they do not see their errors, they have nothing superior to their present opinion.

Ought not then this robber and this adulterer to be destroyed? By no means say so, but speak rather in this way: This man who has been mistaken and deceived about the most important things, and blinded, not in the faculty of vision which distinguishes white and black, but in the faculty which distinguishes good and bad, should we not destroy him? If you speak thus, you will see how inhuman this is which you say, and that it is just as if you would say, Ought we not to destroy this blind and deaf man? But if the greatest harm is the privation of the greatest things, and the greatest thing in every man is the will or choice such as it ought to be, and a man is deprived of this will, why are you also angry with him? Man, you ought not to be affected contrary to nature by the bad things of another.[3] Pity him rather: drop this readiness to be offended and to hate, and these words which the many utter: "these accursed and odious fellows." How have you been made so wise at once? and how are you so peevish? Why then are we angry? Is it because we value so much the things of which these men rob us? Do not admire your clothes, and then you will not be angry with the thief. Do not admire the beauty of your wife, and you will not be angry with the adulterer. Learn that a thief and an adulterer have no place in the things which are yours, but in those which belong to others and which are not in your power. If you dismiss these things and consider them as nothing, with whom are you still angry? But so long as you value these things, be angry with yourself rather than with the thief and the adulterer.

them of their errors; for he says, "if they do not see their errors, they have nothing superior to their present opinion."

This is the plain and certain meaning of Epictetus which Mrs. Carter in her zeal has not seen.

[3] Here the text, 9, 10, 11 is defective. See Schweighaeuser's note.

Consider the matter thus: you have fine clothes; your neighbour has not: you have a window; you wish to air the clothes. The thief does not know wherein man's good consists, but he thinks that it consists in having fine clothes, the very thing which you also think. Must he not then come and take them away? When you show a cake to greedy persons, and swallow it all yourself, do you expect them not to snatch it from you? Do not provoke them: do not have a window: do not air your clothes. I also lately had an iron lamp placed by the side of my household gods: hearing a noise at the door, I ran down, and found that the lamp had been carried off. I reflected that he who had taken the lamp had done nothing strange. What then? To-morrow, I said, you will find an earthen lamp: for a man only loses that which he has. I have lost my garment. The reason is that you had a garment. I have pain in my head. Have you any pain in your horns? Why then are you troubled? for we only lose those things, we have only pains about those things which we possess.[4]

But the tyrant will chain—what? the leg. He will take away—what? the neck. What then will he not chain and not take away? the will. This is why the antients taught the maxim, Know thyself.[5] Therefore we ought to exercise ourselves in small[6] things, and beginning with them to proceed to the greater. I have pain in the head. Do not say, alas! I have pain in the ear. Do not say, alas! And I do not say, that you are not allowed to groan, but do not groan inwardly; and if your slave is slow in bringing a bandage, do not cry out and torment yourself, and say, "Every body hates me": for who would not hate such a man? For the

[4] The conclusion explains what precedes. A man can have no pain in his horns, because he has none. A man cannot be vexed about the loss of a thing if he does not possess it. Upton says that Epictetus alludes to the foolish quibble: "If you have not lost a thing, you have it: but you have not lost horns; therefore you have horns" (Seneca, Ep. 45). Epictetus says, "You do not lose a thing when you have it not." See Schweig.'s note.

[5] Compare what is said in Xenophon, Mem. iv. 2, 24, on the expression Know thyself.

[6] This ought to be the method in teaching children."

future, relying on these opinions, walk about upright, free; not trusting to the size of your body, as an athlete, for a man ought not to be invincible in the way that an ass is.[7]

Who then is the invincible? It is he whom none of the things disturb which are independent of the will. Then examining one circumstance after another I observe, as in the case of an athlete; he has come off victorious in the first contest: well then, as to the second? and what if there should be great heat? and what, if it should be at Olympia? And the same I say in this case: if you should throw money in his way, he will despise it. Well, suppose you put a young girl in his way, what then? and what, if it is in the dark?[8] what if it should be a little reputation, or abuse; and what, if it should be praise; and what if it should be death? He is able to overcome all. What then if it be in heat, and what if it is in the rain,[9] and what if he be in a melancholy (mad) mood, and what if he be asleep? He will still conquer. This is my invincible athlete.

[7] That is obstinate, as this animal is generally; and sometimes very obstinate. The meaning then is, as Schweighaeuser says: "a man should be invincible, not with a kind of stupid obstinacy or laziness and slowness in moving himself like an ass, but he should be invincible through reason, reflection, meditation, study, and diligence."

[8] "From the rustics came the old proverb, for when they commend a man's fidelity and goodness they say he is a man with whom you may play the game with the fingers in the dark." Cicero, De Officiis, iii. 19. See Forcellini, Micare.

[9] The MSS. have *ὑομένος* or *οἰόμενος*. Schweighaeuser has accepted Upton's emendation of *οἰνωμένος*, but I do not. The "sleep" refers to dreams. Aristotle, Ethic, i. 13, says: "better are the visions (dreams) of the good (*ἐπιεικῶν*) than those of the common sort;" and Zeno taught that "a man might from his dreams judge of the progress that he was making, if he observed that in his sleep he was not pleased with anything bad, nor desired or did anything unreasonable or unjust." Plutarch, *περὶ προκοπῆς*, ed. Wyttenbach, vol. i. c. 12.

CHAPTER XIX.

HOW WE SHOULD BEHAVE TO TYRANTS.

If a man possesses any superiority, or thinks that he does, when he does not, such a man, if he is uninstructed, will of necessity be puffed up through it. For instance, the tyrant says, "I am master of all?" And what can you do for me? Can you give me desire which shall have no hindrance? How can you? Have you the infallible power of avoiding what you would avoid? Have you the power of moving towards an object without error? And how do you possess this power? Come, when you are in a ship, do you trust to yourself or to the helmsman? And when you are in a chariot, to whom do you trust but to the driver? And how is it in all other arts? Just the same. In what then lies your power? All men pay respect [1] to me. Well, I also pay respect to my platter, and I wash it and wipe it; and for the sake of my oil flask, I drive a peg into the wall. Well then, are these things superior to me? No, but they supply some of my wants, and for this reason I take care of them. Well, do I not attend to my ass? Do I not wash his feet? Do I not clean him? Do you not know that every man has regard to himself, and to you just the same as he has regard to his ass? For who has regard to you as a man? Show me. Who wishes to become like you? Who imitates you, as he imitates Socrates?—But I can cut off your head.—You say right. I had forgotten that I must have regard to you, as I would to a fever [2] and the bile, and raise an altar to you, as there is at Rome an altar to fever.

What is it then that disturbs and terrifies the multitude? is it the tyrant and his guards? [By no means.] I hope that it is not so. It is not possible that what is by nature free can be disturbed by anything else, or

[1] θεραπεύουσι. Epictetus continues to use the same word.

[2] Febris, fever, was a goddess at Rome. Upton refers to an inscription in Gruter 97, which begins "Febri Divae." Compare Lactantius, De falsa religione, c. 20.

hindered by any other thing than by itself. But it is a man's own opinions which disturb him: for when the tyrant says to a man, "I will chain your leg," he who values his leg says, "Do not; have pity:" but he who values his own will says, "If it appears more advantageous to you, chain it." Do you not care? I do not care. I will show you that I am master. You cannot do that. Zeus has set me free: do you think that he intended to allow his own son[3] to be enslaved? But you are master of my carcase: take it.—So when you approach me, you have no regard to me? No, but I have regard to myself; and if you wish me to say that I have regard to you also, I tell you that I have the same regard to you that I have to my pipkin.

This is not a perverse self-regard,[4] for the animal is constituted so as to do all things for itself. For even the sun does all things for itself; nay, even Zeus himself. But when he chooses to be the Giver of rain and the Giver of fruits, and the Father of Gods and men, you see that he cannot obtain these functions and these names, if he is not useful to man; and, universally, he has made the nature of the rational animal such that it cannot obtain any one of its own proper interests, if it does not contribute something to the common interest.[5] In this manner and sense it is not unsociable for a man to do every thing for the sake of himself. For what do you expect? that a man should neglect himself and his own interest? And how in that case can there be one and the same principle in all animals, the principle of attachment (regard) to themselves?

What then? when absurd notions about things inde-

[3] Comp. i. c. 3.

[4] The word is φίλαυτον, self-love, but here it means self-regard, which implies no censure. See Aristotle, Ethic. Nicom. ix. c. 8: ὡς ἐν αἰσχρῷ φιλαύτους ἀποκαλοῦσι. His conclusion is: οὕτω μὲν οὖν δεῖ φίλαυτον εἶναι, καθάπερ εἴρηται· ὡς δ' οἱ πολλοί, οὐ χρή. See the note of Schweighaeuser. Epictetus, as usual, is right in his opinion of man's nature.

[5] This has been misunderstood by Wolf. Schweighaeuser, who always writes like a man of sense, says: "Epictetus means by 'our proper interests,' the interests proper to man, as a man, as a rational being; and this interest or good consists in the proper use of our powers, and so far from being repugnant to common interest or utility, it contains within itself the notion of general utility and cannot be separated from it."

pendent of our will, as if they were good and (or) bad, lie at the bottom of our opinions, we must of necessity pay regard to tyrants; for I wish that men would pay regard to tyrants only, and not also to the bedchamber men.[6] How is it that the man becomes all at once wise, when Caesar has made him superintendent of the close stool? How is it that we say immediately, "Felicion spoke sensibly to me." I wish he were ejected from the bedchamber, that he might again appear to you to be a fool.

Epaphroditus[7] had a shoemaker whom he sold because he was good for nothing. This fellow by some good luck was bought by one of Caesar's men, and became Caesar's shoemaker. You should have seen what respect Epaphroditus paid to him: "How does the good Felicion do, I pray?" Then if any of us asked, "What is master (Epaphroditus) doing?" the answer was, "He is consulting about something with Felicion." Had he not sold the man as good for nothing? Who then made him wise all at once? This is an instance of valuing something else than the things which depend on the will.

Has a man been exalted to the tribuneship? All who meet him offer their congratulations: one kisses his eyes, another the neck, and the slaves kiss his hands.[8] He goes to his house, he finds torches lighted. He ascends the Capitol: he offers a sacrifice on the occasion. Now who ever sacrificed for having had good desires? for having acted conformably to nature? For in fact we thank the gods for those things in which we place our good.[9]

[6] Such a man was named in Greek *κοιτωνίτης*; in Latin "cubicularius," a lord of the bedchamber, as we might say. Seneca, De Constantia Sapientis, c. 14, speaks "of the pride of the nomenclator (the announcer of the name), of the arrogance of the bedchamber man." Even the clerk of the close-stool was an important person. Slaves used to carry this useful domestic vessel on a journey. Horat. Sat. i. 6, 109 (Upton).

[7] Once the master of Epictetus (i. 1, 20).

[8] Hand-kissing was in those times of tyranny the duty of a slave, not of a free man. This servile practice still exists among men called free.

[9] Schweighaeuser says that he has introduced into the text Lord Shaftesbury's emendation, *ὅπου*. The emendation *ὅπου* is good, but Schweighaeuser has not put it in his text: he has *οἷ τὸ ἀγαθὸν τιθέμεθα*. Matthew vi. 21, "for where your treasure is, there will your heart be also." So these people show by thanking God, what it is for which they are thankful.

A person was talking to me to-day about the priesthood of Augustus.[10] I say to him: "Man, let the thing alone: you will spend much for no purpose." But he replies, "Those who draw up agreements will write my name." Do you then stand by those who read them, and say to such persons "It is I whose name is written there"? And if you can now be present on all such occasions, what will you do when you are dead? My name will remain.—Write it on a stone, and it will remain. But come, what remembrance of you will there be beyond Nicopolis?—But I shall wear a crown of gold.—If you desire a crown at all, take a crown of roses and put it on, for it will be more elegant in appearance.

CHAPTER XX.

ABOUT REASON, HOW IT CONTEMPLATES ITSELF.[1]

Every art and faculty contemplates certain things especially.[2] When then it is itself of the same kind with the objects which it contemplates, it must of necessity contemplate itself also: but when it is of an unlike kind, it cannot contemplate itself. For instance, the shoemaker's art is employed on skins, but itself is entirely distinct from the material of skins: for this reason it does not contemplate itself. Again, the grammarian's art is em-

[10] Casaubon, in a learned note on Suetonius, Augustus, c. 18, informs us that divine honours were paid to Augustus at Nicopolis, which town he founded after the victory at Actium. The priesthood of Augustus at Nicopolis was a high office, and the priest gave his name to the year; that is, when it was intended in any writing to fix the year, either in any writing which related to public matters, or in instruments used in private affairs, the name of the priest of Augustus was used, and this was also the practice in most Greek cities. In order to establish the sense of this passage, Casaubon changed the text from *τὰς φωνάς* into *τὰ σύμφωνα*, which emendation Schweighaeuser has admitted into his text.

[1] A comparison of lib. i. chap. 1, will help to explain this chapter. Compare also lib. i. chap. 17.

[2] Wolf suggests that we should read *προηγουμένως* instead of *προηγουμένων*.

ployed about articulate speech;[3] is then the art also articulate speech? By no means. For this reason it is not able to contemplate itself. Now reason, for what purpose has it been given by nature? For the right use of appearances. What is it then itself? A system (combination) of certain appearances. So by its nature it has the faculty of contemplating itself also. Again, sound sense, for the contemplation of what things does it belong to us? Good and evil, and things which are neither. What is it then itself? Good. And want of sense, what is it? Evil. Do you see then that good sense necessarily contemplates both itself and the opposite? For this reason it is the chief and the first work of a philosopher to examine appearances, and to distinguish them, and to admit none without examination. You see even in the matter of coin, in which our interest appears to be somewhat concerned, how we have invented an art, and how many means the assayer uses to try the value of coin, the sight, the touch, the smell, and lastly the hearing. He throws the coin (denarius) down, and observes the sound, and he is not content with its sounding once, but through his great attention he becomes a musician. In like manner, where we think that to be mistaken and not to be mistaken make a great difference, there we apply great attention to discovering the things which can deceive. But in the matter of our miserable ruling faculty, yawning and sleeping, we carelessly admit every appearance, for the harm is not noticed.

When then you would know how careless you are with respect to good and evil, and how active with respect to things which are indifferent[4] (neither good nor evil), observe how you feel with respect to being deprived of the sight of the eyes, and how with respect to being deceived, and you will discover that you are far from feeling as you ought to do in relation to good and evil. But this is a matter which requires much preparation, and much labour and study. Well then do you expect

[3] See Schweighaeuser's note.

[4] "We reckon death among the things which are indifferent (indifferentia), which the Greeks name ἀδιάφορα. But I name 'indifferent' the things which are neither good nor bad, as disease, pain, poverty, exile, death."—Seneca, Ep. 82.

to acquire the greatest of arts with small labour? And yet the chief doctrine of philosophers is very brief. If you would know, read Zeno's[5] writings and you will see For how few words it requires to say that man's end (or object) is to follow[6] the gods, and that the nature of good is a proper use of appearances. But if you say, What is God, what is appearance, and what is particular and what is universal[7] nature? then indeed many words are necessary. If then Epicurus should come and say, that the good must be in the body; in this case also many words become necessary, and we must be taught what is the leading principle in us, and the fundamental and the substantial; and as it is not probable that the good of a snail is in the shell, is it probable that the good of a man is in the body? But you yourself, Epicurus, possess something better than this. What is that in you which deliberates, what is that which examines every thing, what is that which forms a judgment about the body itself, that it is the principal part? and why do you light your lamp and labour for us, and write so many[8] books? is it that we may not be ignorant of the truth, who we are, and what we are with respect to you? Thus the discussion requires many words.

[5] Zeno, a native of Citium, in the island of Cyprus, is said to have come when he was young to Athens, where he spent the rest of a long life in the study and teaching of Philosophy. He was the founder of the Stoic sect, and a man respected for his ability and high character. He wrote many philosophical works. Zeno was succeeded in his school by Cleanthes.

[6] Follow. See i. 12, 5.

[7] "I now have what the universal nature wills me to have, and I do what my nature now wills me to do." M. Antoninus, v. 25, and xi. 5.

Epictetus never attempts to say what God is. He was too wise to attempt to do what man cannot do. But man does attempt to do it, and only shows the folly of his attempts, and, I think, his presumption also.

[8] Epicurus is said to have written more than any other person, as many as three hundred volumes (κύλινδροι, rolls). Chrysippus was his rival in this respect. For if Epicurus wrote anything, Chrysippus vied with him in writing as much; and for this reason he often repeated himself, because he did not read over what he had written, and he left his writings uncorrected in consequence of his hurry. Diogenes Laertius, x.—Upton. See i. 4.

CHAPTER XXI.

AGAINST THOSE WHO WISH TO BE ADMIRED.

When a man holds his proper station in life, he does not gape after things beyond it. Man, what do you wish to happen to you? I am satisfied if I desire and avoid conformably to nature, if I employ movements towards and from an object as I am by nature formed to do, and purpose and design and assent. Why then do you strut before us as if you had swallowed a spit? My wish has always been that those who meet me should admire me, and those who follow me should exclaim O the great philosopher. Who are they by whom you wish to be admired? Are they not those of whom you are used to say, that they are mad? Well then do you wish to be admired by madmen?

CHAPTER XXII.

ON PRAECOGNITIONS.[1]

Praecognitions are common to all men, and praecognition is not contradictory to praecognition. For who of us does not assume that Good is useful and eligible, and in all circumstances that we ought to follow and pursue it? And

[1] Praecognitions (προλήψεις) is translated Praecognita by John Smith, Select Discourses, p. 4. Cicero says (Topica, 7): "Notionem appello quod Graeci tum ἔννοιαν, tum πρόληψιν dicunt. Ea est insita et ante percepta cujusque formae cognitio, enodationis indigens." In the De Natura Deorum (i. 16) he says: "Quae est enim gens aut quod genus hominum, quod non habeat sine doctrina anticipationem quandam deorum, quam appellat πρόληψιν Epicurus? id est, anteceptam animo rei quandam informationem, sine qua nec intelligi quidquam nec quaeri nec disputari potest." Epicurus, as Cicero says in the following chapter (17), was the first who used πρόληψις in this sense, which Cicero applies to what he calls the ingrafted or rather innate cognitions of the existence of gods, and these cognitions he supposes to be universal; but whether this is so or not, I do not know. See i. c. 2; Tuscul. i. 24; De Fin. iii. 6, and πρόληψις in iv. 8. 6.

who of us does not assume that Justice is beautiful and becoming? When then does the contradiction arise? It arises in the adaptation of the praecognitions to the particular cases. When one man says, He has done well: he is a brave man, and another says, "Not so; but he has acted foolishly;" then the disputes arise among men. This is the dispute among the Jews and the Syrians and the Egyptians and the Romans; not whether holiness[2] should be preferred to all things and in all cases should be pursued, but whether it is holy to eat pig's flesh or not holy. You will find this dispute also between Agamemnon and Achilles;[3] for call them forth. What do you say, Agamemnon? ought not that to be done which is proper and right? Certainly. Well, what do you say, Achilles? do you not admit that what is good ought to be done? I do most certainly. Adapt your praecognitions then to the present matter. Here the dispute begins. Agamemnon says, I ought not to give up Chryseis to her father. Achilles says, You ought. It is certain that one of the two makes a wrong adaptation of the praecognition of "ought" or "duty." Further, Agamemnon says, Then if I ought to restore Chryseis, it is fit that I take his prize from some of you. Achilles replies, "Would you then take her whom I love?" Yes, her whom you love. Must I then be the only man who goes without a prize? and must I be the only man who has no prize? Thus the dispute begins.[4]

What then is education? Education is the learning how to adapt the natural praecognitions to the particular things conformably to nature; and then to distinguish that of things some are in our power, but others are not: in our power are will and all acts which depend on the will; things not in our power are the body, the parts of

[2] The word is ὅσιον, which is very difficult to translate. We may take an instance from ourselves. There is a general agreement about integrity, and about the worship of the supreme being, but a wondrous difference about certain acts or doings in trading, whether they are consistent with integrity or not; and a still more wondrous difference in forms of worship, whether they are conformable to religion or not.

[3] Horace, Epp. i. 2.

[4] Iliad, i. The quarrel of Achilles and Agamemnon about giving up Chryseis to her father.

the body, possessions, parents, brothers, children, country and generally, all with whom we live in society. In what then should we place the good? To what kind of things (οὐσίᾳ) shall we adapt it? To the things which are in our power? Is not health then a good thing, and soundness of limb, and life? and are not children and parents and country? Who will tolerate you if you deny this?

Let us then transfer the notion of good to these things. Is it possible then, when a man sustains damage and does not obtain good things, that he can be happy? It is not possible. And can he maintain towards society a proper behaviour? He can not. For I am naturally formed to look after my own interest. If it is my interest to have an estate in land, it is my interest also to take it from my neighbour. If it is my interest to have a garment, it is my interest also to steal it from the bath.[5] This is the origin of wars, civil commotions, tyrannies, conspiracies. And how shall I be still able to maintain my duty towards Zeus? for if I sustain damage and am unlucky, he takes no care of me; and what is he to me if he cannot help me; and further, what is he to me if he allows me to be in the condition in which I am? I now begin to hate him. Why then do we build temples, why set up statues to Zeus, as well as to evil daemons, such as to Fever;[6] and how is Zeus the Saviour, and how the giver of rain, and the giver of fruits? And in truth if we place the nature of Good in any such things, all this follows.

What should we do then? This is the inquiry of the true philosopher who is in labour.[7] Now I do not see

[5] The bath was a place of common resort, where a thief had the opportunity of carrying off a bather's clothes. From men's desires to have what they have not, and do not choose to labour for, spring the disorders of society, as it is said in the epistle of James, c. iv., v. 1, to which Mrs. Carter refers.

[6] See i. 19. 6, note 2.

[7] Upton refers to a passage in the Theaetetus (p. 150, Steph.), where Socrates professes that it is his art to discover whether a young man's mind is giving birth to an idol (an unreality) and a falsity, or to something productive and true; and he says (p. 151) that those who associate with him are like women in child-birth, for they are in labour and full of trouble nights and days much more than women, and his

what the Good is nor the Bad. Am I not mad? Yes. But suppose that I place the good somewhere among the things which depend on the will: all will laugh at me. There will come some greyhead wearing many gold rings on his fingers, and he will shake his head and say, Hear, my child. It is right that you should philosophize; but you ought to have some brains also: all this that you are doing is silly. You learn the syllogism from philosophers; but you know how to act better than philosophers do.—Man, why then do you blame me, if I know? What shall I say to this slave? If I am silent, he will burst. I must speak in this way: Excuse me, as you would excuse lovers: I am not my own master: I am mad.

CHAPTER XXIII.

AGAINST EPICURUS.

EVEN Epicurus perceives that we are by nature social, but having once placed our good in the husk[1] he is no longer able to say anything else. For on the other hand he strongly maintains this, that we ought not to admire nor to accept any thing which is detached from the nature of good; and he is right in maintaining this. How then are we [suspicious],[2] if we have no natural affection to our children? Why do you advise the wise man not to bring up children? Why are you afraid that he may thus fall into

art has the power of stirring up and putting to rest this labour of child-birth.

The conclusion in the chapter is not clear. The student is supposed to be addressed by some rich old man, who really does not know what to say; and the best way of getting rid of him and his idle talk is by dismissing him with a joke. See Schweighaeuser's note.

[1] That is in the body; see i. 20, 17. Compare ii. 20, at the beginning of the chapter.

[2] The word ὑπονοητικοί is not intelligible. Schweighaeuser suggests that it ought to be προνοητικοί, "how have we any care for others?" Epicurus taught that we should not marry nor beget children nor engage in public affairs, because these things disturb our tranquillity.

trouble? For does he fall into trouble on account of the mouse which is nurtured in the house? What does he care if a little mouse in the house makes lamentation to him? But Epicurus knows that if once a child is born, it is no longer in our power not to love it nor care about it. For this reason, Epicurus says, that a man who has any sense also does not engage in political matters; for he knows what a man must do who is engaged in such things; for indeed, if you intend to behave among men as you would among a swarm of flies, what hinders you? But Epicurus, who knows this, ventures to say that we should not bring up children. But a sheep does not desert its own offspring, nor yet a wolf; and shall a man desert his child? What do you mean? that we should be as silly as sheep? but not even do they desert their offspring: or as savage as wolves, but not even do wolves desert their young. Well, who would follow your advice, if he saw his child weeping after falling on the ground? For my part I think that even if your mother and your father had been told by an oracle, that you would say what you have said, they would not have cast you away.

CHAPTER XXIV.

HOW WE SHOULD STRUGGLE WITH CIRCUMSTANCES.

It is circumstances (difficulties) which show what men are.[1] Therefore when a difficulty falls upon you, remember that God, like a trainer of wrestlers, has matched you with a rough young man. For what purpose? you may say. Why that you may become an Olympic conqueror; but it is not accomplished without sweat. In my opinion no man has had a more profitable difficulty than you have had, if you choose to make use of it as an athlete would deal with a young antagonist. We are now

[1] So Ovid says, Trist. iv. 3, 79:—

> "Quae latet inque bonis cessat non cognita rebus,
> Apparet virtus arguiturque malis."

sending a scout to Rome;[2] but no man sends a cowardly scout, who, if he only hears a noise and sees a shadow anywhere, comes running back in terror and reports that the enemy is close at hand. So now if you should come and tell us, Fearful is the state of affairs at Rome, terrible is death, terrible is exile; terrible is calumny; terrible is poverty; fly, my friends; the enemy is near—we shall answer, Be gone, prophesy for yourself; we have committed only one fault, that we sent such a scout.

Diogenes,[3] who was sent as a scout before you, made a different report to us. He says that death is no evil, for neither is it base: he says that fame (reputation) is the noise of madmen. And what has this spy said about pain, about pleasure, and about poverty? He says that to be naked is better than any purple robe, and to sleep on the bare ground is the softest bed; and he gives as a proof of each thing that he affirms his own courage, his tranquillity, his freedom, and the healthy appearance and compactness of his body. There is no enemy near, he says; all is peace. How so, Diogenes? See, he replies, if I am struck, if I have been wounded, if I have fled from any man. This is what a scout ought to be. But you come to us and tell us one thing after another. Will you not go back, and you will see clearer when you have laid aside fear?

What then shall I do? What do you do when you leave a ship? Do you take away the helm or the oars? What then do you take away? You take what is your own, your bottle and your wallet; and now if you think of what is your own, you will never claim what belongs to others. The emperor (Domitian) says, Lay aside your lati-

[2] In the time of Domitian philosophers were banished from Rome and Italy by a Senatusconsultum (Sueton. Domitian, c. 10; Dion, 67, c. 13), and at that time Epictetus, as Gellius says (xv. 11), went from Rome to Nicopolis in Epirus, where he opened a school. We may suppose that Epictetus is here speaking of some person who had gone from Nicopolis to Rome to inquire about the state of affairs there under the cruel tyrant Domitian. (Schweighaeuser.)

[3] Diogenes was brought to king Philip after the battle of Chaeronea as a spy (iii. 22, 24). Plutarch in the treatise, Quomodo assentator ab amico dignoscatur, c. 30, states that when Philip asked Diogenes if he was a spy, he replied, Certainly I am a spy, Philip, of your want of judgment and of your folly, which lead you without any necessity to put to the hazard your kingdom and your life in one single hour.

clave.[4] See, I put on the angusticlave. Lay aside this also. See, I have only my toga. Lay aside your toga. See, I am now naked. But you still raise my envy. Take then all my poor body; when, at a man's command, I can throw away my poor body, do I still fear him?

But a certain person will not leave to me the succession to his estate. What then? had I forgotten that not one of these things was mine. How then do we call them mine? Just as we call the bed in the inn. If then the innkeeper at his death leaves you the beds; all well; but if he leaves them to another, he will have them, and you will seek another bed. If then you shall not find one, you will sleep on the ground: only sleep with a good will and snore, and remember that tragedies have their place among the rich and kings and tyrants, but no poor man fills a part in a tragedy, except as one of the Chorus. Kings indeed commence with prosperity: "ornament the palace with garlands": then about the third or fourth act they call out, "Oh Cithaeron,[5] why didst thou receive me"? Slave, where are the crowns, where the diadem? The guards help thee not at all. When then you approach any of these persons, remember this that you are approaching a tragedian, not the actor, but Oedipus himself. But you say, such a man is happy; for he walks about with many, and I also place myself with the many and walk about with many. In sum remember this: the door is open;[6] be not more timid than little children, but as they say, when the thing does not please them, "I will play no longer," so do you, when things seem to you of such a kind, say I will no longer play, and be gone: but if you stay, do not complain.

[4] The garment with the broad border, the laticlave, was the dress of a senator; the garment with the narrow border, the angusticlave, was the dress of a man of the equestrian order.

[5] The exclamation of Oedipus in the Oedipus Tyrannus of Sophocles, v. 1390.

[6] This means "you can die when you please." Comp. i. c. 9. The power of dying when you please is named by Plinius (N. H. ii. c. 7) the best thing that God has given to man amidst all the sufferings of life. Horace, Epp. ii. 2. 213,—

"Vivere si recte nescis, decede peritis:
Lusisti satis, edisti satis atque bibisti;
Tempus abire tibi."

CHAPTER XXV.

ON THE SAME.

If these things are true, and if we are not silly, and are not acting hypocritically when we say that the good of man is in the will, and the evil too, and that every thing else does not concern us, why are we still disturbed, why are we still afraid? The things about which we have been busied are in no man's power: and the things which are in the power of others, we care not for. What kind of trouble have we still?

But give me directions. Why should I give you directions? has not Zeus given you directions? Has he not given to you what is your own free from hindrance and free from impediment, and what is not your own subject to hindrance and impediment? What directions then, what kind of orders did you bring when you came from him? Keep by every means what is your own; do not desire what belongs to others. Fidelity (integrity) is your own, virtuous shame is your own; who then can take these things from you? who else than yourself will hinder you from using them? But how do you act? when you seek what is not your own, you lose that which is your own. Having such promptings and commands from Zeus, what kind do you still ask from me? Am I more powerful than he, am I more worthy of confidence? But if you observe these, do you want any others besides? Well, but he has not given these orders, you will say. Produce your praecognitions (προλήψεις), produce the proofs of philosophers, produce what you have often heard, and produce what you have said yourself, produce what you have read, produce what you have meditated on; and you will then see that all these things are from God.[1] How long then is

[1] The conclusion "and you will then see," is not in the text, but it is what Epictetus means. The argument is complete. If we admit the existence of God, and that he is our father, as Epictetus teaches, we have from him the intellectual powers which we possess; and those men in whom these powers have been roused to activity, and are exercised, require no other instructor. It is true that in a large part of mankind these powers are inactive and are not exercised, or if they

it fit to observe these precepts from God, and not to break up the play?[2] As long as the play is continued with propriety. In the Saturnalia[3] a king is chosen by lot, for it has been the custom to play at this game. The king commands: Do you drink, Do you mix the wine, Do you sing, Do you go, Do you come. I obey that the game may not be broken up through me.—But if he says, think that you are in evil plight: I answer, I do not think so; and who will compel me to think so? Further, we agreed to play Agamemnon and Achilles. He who is appointed to play Agamemnon says to me, Go to Achilles and tear from him Briseis. I go. He says, Come, and I come.

For as we behave in the matter of hypothetical arguments, so ought we to do in life. Suppose it to be night. I suppose that it is night. Well then; is it day? No, for I admitted the hypothesis that it was night. Suppose that you think that it is night? Suppose that I do. But also think that it is night. That is not consistent with the hypothesis. So in this case also: Suppose that you are unfortunate. Well, suppose so. Are you then unhappy? Yes. Well then are you troubled with an

are exercised, it is in a very imperfect way. But those who contemplate the improvement of the human race, hope that all men, or if not all men, a great number will be roused to the exercise of the powers which they have, and that human life will be made more conformable to Nature, that is, that man will use the powers which he has, and will not need advice and direction from other men, who professing that they are wise and that they can teach, prove by their teaching and often by their example that they are not wise, and are incapable of teaching.

This is equally true for those who may deny or doubt about the existence of God. They cannot deny that man has the intellectual powers which he does possess; and they are certainly not the persons who will proclaim their own want of these powers. If man has them and can exercise them, the fact is sufficient; and we need not dispute about the source of these powers which are in man Naturally, that is, according to the constitution of his Nature.

[2] See the end of the preceding chapter. Upton compares Horace's "Incidere ludum" (Epp. i. 14, 36). Compare also Epictetus, ii. 16, 37.

[3] A festival at Rome in December, a season of jollity and license (Livy, xxii. 1). Compare the passage in Tacitus, Ann. xiii. 15, in which Nero is chosen by lot to be king: and Seneca, De Constant. Sapient. c. 12, "Illi (pueri) inter ipsos magistratus gerunt, et praetextam fascesque ac tribunal imitantur."

unfavourable daemon (fortune)? Yes. But think also that you are in misery. This is not consistent with the hypothesis; and another (Zeus) forbids me to think so.

How long then must we obey such orders? As long as it is profitable; and this means as long as I maintain that which is becoming and consistent. Further, some men are sour and of bad temper, and they say, "I cannot sup with this man to be obliged to hear him telling daily how he fought in Mysia": "I told you, brother, how I ascended the hill: then I began to be besieged again." But another says, "I prefer to get my supper and to hear him talk as much as he likes." And do you compare these estimates (judgments): only do nothing in a depressed mood, nor as one afflicted, nor as thinking that you are in misery, for no man compels you to that.—Has it smoked in the chamber? If the smoke is moderate, I will stay; if it is excessive, I go out: for you must always remember this and hold it fast, that the door is open.—Well, but you say to me, Do not live in Nicopolis. I will not live there.—Nor in Athens.—I will not live in Athens.—Nor in Rome.—I will not live in Rome.—Live in Gyarus.[4]—I will live in Gyarus, but it seems like a great smoke to live in Gyarus; and I depart to the place where no man will hinder me from living, for that dwelling place is open to all; and as to the last garment,[5] that is the poor body, no one has any power over me beyond this. This was the reason why Demetrius[6] said to Nero, "You threaten me with death, but nature threatens you." If I set my admiration on the poor body, I have given myself up to be a slave: if on my little possessions, I also make myself a slave: for I immediately make it plain with what I may be caught; as if the snake

[4] Gyarus or Gyara a wretched island in the Aegean sea, to which criminals were sent under the empire at Rome. Juvenal, Sat. i. 73.

[5] See Schweighaeuser's note.

[6] Demetrius was a Cynic philosopher, of whom Seneca (De Benef. vii. 1) says: "He was in my opinion a great man, even if he is compared with the greatest." One of his sayings was; "You gain more by possessing a few precepts of philosophy, if you have them ready and use them, than by learning many, if you have them not at hand." Seneca often mentions Demetrius. The saying in the text is also attributed to Anaxagoras (Life by Diogenes Laertius) and to Socrates by Xenophon (Apologia, 27).

draws in his head, I tell you to strike that part of him which he guards; and do you be assured that whatever part you choose to guard, that part your master will attack. Remembering this whom will you still flatter or fear?

But I should like to sit where the Senators sit.[7]—Do you see that you are putting yourself in straits, you are squeezing yourself.—How then shall I see well in any other way in the amphitheatre? Man, do not be a spectator at all; and you will not be squeezed. Why do you give yourself trouble? Or wait a little, and when the spectacle is over, seat yourself in the place reserved for the Senators and sun yourself. For remember this general truth, that it is we who squeeze ourselves, who put ourselves in straits; that is our opinions squeeze us and put us in straits. For what is it to be reviled? Stand by a stone and revile it; and what will you gain? If then a man listens like a stone, what profit is there to the reviler? But if the reviler has as a stepping-stone (or ladder) the weakness of him who is reviled, then he accomplishes something.—Strip him.—What do you mean by him?[8]—Lay hold of his garment, strip it off. I have insulted you. Much good may it do you.

This was the practice of Socrates: this was the reason why he always had one face. But we choose to practise and study any thing rather than the means by which we shall be unimpeded and free. You say, Philosophers talk paradoxes.[9] But are there no paradoxes in the other arts? and what is more paradoxical than to puncture a man's eye in order that he may see? If any one said this to a man ignorant of the surgical art, would he not ridicule the speaker? Where is the wonder then if in philosophy also many things which are true appear paradoxical to the inexperienced?

[7] At Rome, and probably in other towns, there were seats reserved for the different classes of men at the public spectacles.

[8] See Schweighaeuser's note.

[9] Paradoxes (παράδοξα), "things contrary to opinion," are contrasted with paralogies (παράλογα), "things contrary to reason" (iv. 1. 173). Cicero says (Prooemium to his Paradoxes), that paradoxes are "something which cause surprise and contradict common opinion;" and in another place he says that the Romans gave the name of "admirabilia" to the Stoic paradoxes.—The puncture of the eye is the operation for cataract.

CHAPTER XXVI.

WHAT IS THE LAW OF LIFE.

When a person was reading hypothetical arguments, Epictetus said, This also is an hypothetical law that we must accept what follows from the hypothesis. But much before this law is the law of life, that we must act conformably to nature. For if in every matter and circumstance we wish to observe what is natural, it is plain that in every thing we ought to make it our aim that neither that which is consequent shall escape us, and that we do not admit the contradictory. First then philosophers exercise us in theory[1] (contemplation of things), which is easier; and then next they lead us to the more difficult things; for in theory, there is nothing which draws us away from following what is taught; but in the matters of life, many are the things which distract us. He is ridiculous then who says that he wishes to begin with the matters of real life, for it is not easy to begin with the more difficult things; and we ought to employ this fact as an argument to those parents who are vexed at their children learning philosophy: Am I doing wrong then

[1] ἐπὶ τῆς θεωρίας. "Intelligere quid verum rectumque sit, prius est et facilius. Id vero exsequi et observare, posterius et difficilius."—Wolf.

This is a profound and useful remark of Epictetus. General principles are most easily understood and accepted. The difficulty is in the application of them. What is more easy, for example, than to understand general principles of law which are true and good? But in practice cases are presented to us which as Bacon says, are "immersed in matter;" and it is this matter which makes the difficulty of applying the principles, and requires the ability and study of an experienced man. It is easy, and it is right, to teach the young the general principles of the rules of life; but the difficulty of applying them is that in which the young and the old too often fail. So if you ask whether virtue can be taught, the answer is that the rules for a virtuous life can be delivered; but the application of the rules is the difficulty, as teachers of religion and morality know well, if they are fit to teach. If they do not know this truth, they are neither fit to teach the rules, nor to lead the way to the practice of them by the only method which is possible; and this method is by their own example, assisted by the example of those who direct the education of youth, and of those with whom young persons live.

my father, and do I not know what is suitable to me and becoming? If indeed this can neither be learned nor taught, why do you blame me? but if it can be taught, teach me; and if you can not, allow me to learn from those who say that they know how to teach. For what do you think? do you suppose that I voluntarily fall into evil and miss the good? I hope that it may not be so. What is then the cause of my doing wrong? Ignorance. Do you not choose then that I should get rid of my ignorance? Who was ever taught by anger the art of a pilot or music? Do you think then that by means of your anger I shall learn the art of life? He only is allowed to speak in this way who has shown such an intention.[2] But if a man only intending to make a display at a banquet and to show that he is acquainted with hypothetical arguments reads them and attends the philosophers, what other object has he than that some man of senatorian rank who sits by him may admire? For there (at Rome) are the really great materials (opportunities), and the riches here (at Nicopolis) appear to be trifles there. This is the reason why it is difficult for a man to be master of the appearances, where the things which disturb the judgment are great.[3] I know a certain person who complained, as he embraced the knees of Epaphroditus, that he had only one hundred and fifty times ten thousand denarii[4] remaining. What then did Epaphroditus do? Did he laugh at him, as we slaves of Epaphroditus did? No, but he cried out with amazement, "Poor man, how then did you keep silence, how did you endure it?"

When Epictetus had reproved[5] (called) the person who

[2] "Such an intention" appears to mean "the intention of learning." "The son alone can say this to his father, when the son studies philosophy for the purpose of living a good life, and not for the purpose of display."—Wolf.

[3] I have followed Schweighaeuser's explanation of this difficult passage, and I have accepted his emendation ἐκσείοντα, in place of the MSS. reading ἐκεῖ ὄντα.

[4] This was a large sum. He is speaking of drachmae, or of the Roman equivalents denarii. In Roman language the amount would be briefly expressed by "sexagies centena millia H.S.," or simply by "sexagies."

[5] See Schweighaeuser's note; and all his notes on this chapter, which is rather difficult.

was reading the hypothetical arguments, and the teacher who had suggested the reading was laughing at the reader, Epictetus said to the teacher, "You are laughing at yourself: you did not prepare the young man nor did you ascertain whether he was able to understand these matters; but perhaps, you are only employing him as a reader." Well then said Epictetus, if a man has not ability enough to understand a complex (syllogism), do we trust him in giving praise, do we trust him in giving blame, do we allow that he is able to form a judgment about good or bad? and if such a man blames any one, does the man care for the blame? and if he praises any one, is the man elated, when in such small matters as an hypothetical syllogism he who praises cannot see what is consequent on the hypothesis?

This then is the beginning of philosophy,[6] a man's perception of the state of his ruling faculty; for when a man knows that it is weak, then he will not employ it on things of the greatest difficulty. But at present, if men cannot swallow even a morsel, they buy whole volumes and attempt to devour them; and this is the reason why they vomit them up or suffer indigestion: and then come gripings, defluxes, and fevers.[7] Such men ought to consider what their ability is. In theory it is easy to convince an ignorant person; but in the affairs of real life no one offers himself to be convinced, and we hate the man who has convinced us. But Socrates advised us not to live a life which is not subjected to examination.[8]

[6] See ii. c. 11.

[7] Seneca, De Tranquillitate animi, c. 9, says: "What is the use of countless books and libraries, when the owner scarcely reads in his whole life the tables of contents? The number only confuses a learner, does not instruct him. It is much better to give yourself up to a few authors than to wander through many."

[8] See Plato's Apology, c. 28; and Antoninus, iii. 5.

CHAPTER XXVII.

IN HOW MANY WAYS APPEARANCES EXIST, AND WHAT AIDS WE SHOULD PROVIDE AGAINST THEM.

Appearances are to us in four ways: for either things appear as they are; or they are not, and do not even appear to be; or they are, and do not appear to be; or they are not, and yet appear to be. Further, in all these cases to form a right judgment (to hit the mark) is the office of an educated man. But whatever it is that annoys (troubles) us, to that we ought to apply a remedy. If the sophisms of Pyrrho[1] and of the Academics are what annoys (troubles), we must apply the remedy to them. If it is the persuasion of appearances, by which some things appear to be good, when they are not good, let us seek a remedy for this. If it is habit which annoys us, we must try to seek aid against habit. What aid then can we find against habit? The contrary habit. You hear the ignorant say: "That unfortunate person is dead: his father and mother are overpowered with sorrow;[2] he was cut off by an untimely death and in a foreign land." Hear the contrary way of speaking: Tear yourself from these expressions: oppose to one habit the contrary habit; to sophistry oppose reason, and the exercise and discipline of reason; against persuasive (deceitful) appearances we ought to have manifest praecognitions (προλήψεις), cleared of all impurities and ready to hand.

When death appears an evil, we ought to have this rule in readiness, that it is fit to avoid evil things, and that

[1] Pyrrho was a native of Elis, in the Peloponnesus. He is said to have accompanied Alexander the Great in his Asiatic expedition (Diogenes Laertius, ix. 61). The time of his birth is not stated, but it is said that he lived to the age of ninety.

See Levin's Six Lectures, 1871. Lecture II., On the Pyrrhonian Ethic; Lecture III., On the grounds of Scepticism.

[2] ἀπώλετο does not mean that the father is dead, and that the mother is dead. They survive and lament. Compare Euripides, Alcestis, v. 825:

ἀπωλόμεσθα πάντες, οὐ κείνη μόνη.

death is a necessary thing. For what shall I do, and where shall I escape it? Suppose that I am not Sarpedon,[3] the son of Zeus, nor able to speak in this noble way: I will go and I am resolved either to behave bravely myself or to give to another the opportunity of doing so; if I cannot succeed in doing any thing myself, I will not grudge another the doing of something noble.—Suppose that it is above our power to act thus; is it not in our power to reason thus? Tell me where I can escape death: discover for me the country, show me the men to whom I must go, whom death does not visit. Discover to me a charm against death. If I have not one, what do you wish me to do? I cannot escape from death. Shall I not escape from the fear of death, but shall I die lamenting and trembling? For the origin of perturbation is this, to wish for something, and that this should not happen. Therefore if I am able to change externals according to my wish, I change them; but if I can not, I am ready to tear out the eyes of him who hinders me. For the nature of man is not to endure to be deprived of the good, and not to endure the falling into the evil. Then at last, when I am neither able to change circumstances nor to tear out the eyes of him who hinders me, I sit down and groan, and abuse whom I can, Zeus and the rest of the gods. For if they do not care for me, what are they to me?—Yes, but you will be an impious man.—In what respect then will it be worse for me than it is now?—To sum up, remember this that unless piety and your interest be in the same thing, piety cannot be maintained in any man. Do not these things seem necessary (true)?

Let the followers of Pyrrho and the Academics come and make their objections. For I, as to my part, have no leisure for these disputes, nor am I able to undertake the defence of common consent (opinion).[4] If I had a suit even about a bit of land, I would call in another to defend my

[3] Homer, Iliad, xii. v. 328: *ἴομεν, ἠὲ τῳ εὖχος ὀρέξομεν ἦέ τις ἡμῖν.*

[4] "This means, the received opinion about the knowledge and certainty of things, which knowledge and certainty the Sceptic philosophers attack by taking away general assent or consent" (Wolf). Lord Shaftesbury accepts this explanation. See also Schweig.'s note.

interests. With what evidence then am I satisfied? With that which belongs to the matter in hand.[5] How indeed perception is effected, whether through the whole body or any part, perhaps I cannot explain: for both opinions perplex me. But that you and I are not the same, I know with perfect certainty. How do you know it? When I intend to swallow any thing, I never carry it to your mouth, but to my own. When I intend to take bread, I never lay hold of a broom, but I always go to the bread as to a mark.[6] And you yourselves (the Pyrrhonists), who take away the evidence of the senses, do you act otherwise? Who among you, when he intended to enter a bath, ever went into a mill?

What then? Ought we not with all our power to hold to this also, the maintaining of general opinion,[7] and fortifying ourselves against the arguments which are directed against it? Who denies that we ought to do this? Well, he should do it who is able, who has leisure for it; but as to him who trembles and is perturbed and is inwardly broken in heart (spirit), he must employ his time better on something else.

[5] "The chief question which was debated between the Pyrrhonists and the Academics on one side, and the Stoics on the other, was this, whether there is a criterion of truth; and in the first place, the question is about the evidence of the senses, or the certainty of truth in those things which are perceived by the senses."—Schweighaeuser.

The strength of the Stoic system was that "it furnishes a groundwork of common sense, and the universal belief of mankind, on which to found sufficient certitude for the requirements of life: on the other hand, the real question of knowledge, in the philosophical sense of the word, was abandoned." Levin's Six Lectures, p. 70.

[6] *ὡς πρὸς σκοπόν*, Schweighaeuser's emendation in place of *ὡς προκόπτων*.

[7] For the word *συνήθειαν*, which occurs in s. 20, Schweighaeuser suggests *ἀλήθειαν* here, and translates it by "veritas." See his notes on this chapter, s. 15 and s. 20.

CHAPTER XXVIII.

THAT WE OUGHT NOT TO BE ANGRY WITH MEN; AND WHAT ARE THE SMALL AND THE GREAT THINGS AMONG MEN.[1]

What is the cause of assenting to any thing? The fact that it appears to be true. It is not possible then to assent to that which appears not to be true. Why? Because this is the nature of the understanding, to incline to the true, to be dissatisfied with the false, and in matters uncertain to withhold assent. What is the proof of this? Imagine (persuade yourself), if you can, that it is now night. It is not possible. Take away your persuasion that it is day. It is not possible. Persuade yourself or take away your persuasion that the stars are even in number.[2] It is impossible. When then any man assents to that which is false, be assured that he did not intend to assent to it as false, for every soul is unwillingly deprived of the truth, as Plato says; but the falsity seemed to him to be true. Well, in acts what have we of the like kind as we have here truth or falsehood? We have the fit and the not fit (duty and not duty), the profitable and the unprofitable, that which is suitable to a person and that which is not, and whatever is like these. Can then a man think that a thing is useful to him and not choose it? He cannot. How says Medea?[3]—

> "'Tis true I know what evil I shall do,
> But passion overpowers the better counsel."

She thought that to indulge her passion and take vengeance on her husband was more profitable than to spare her children. It was so; but she was deceived. Show her plainly that she is deceived, and she will not do it; but so long as you do not show it, what can she follow except

[1] See c. 18 of this book.

[2] We cannot conceive that the number of stars is either even or odd. The construction of the word ἀποπάσχειν is uncertain, for, says Schweighaeuser, the word is found only here.

[3] The Medea of Euripides, 1079, "where, instead of δρᾶν μέλλω of Epictetus, the reading is τολμήσω" (Upton). "τολμήσω (Kirchoff), with the best MSS., for δρᾶν μέλλω, which, however is the reading cited by several antient authors." Paley's Euripides, note.

that which appears to herself (her opinion)? Nothing else. Why then are you angry with the unhappy woman that she has been bewildered about the most important things, and is become a viper instead of a human creature? And why not, if it is possible, rather pity, as we pity the blind and the lame, so those who are blinded and maimed in the faculties which are supreme?

Whoever then clearly remembers this, that to man the measure of every act is the appearance (the opinion),—whether the thing appears good or bad: if good, he is free from blame; if bad, himself suffers the penalty, for it is impossible that he who is deceived can be one person, and he who suffers another person—whoever remembers this will not be angry with any man, will not be vexed at any man, will not revile or blame any man, nor hate nor quarrel with any man.

So then all these great and dreadful deeds have this origin, in the appearance (opinion)? Yes, this origin and no other. The Iliad is nothing else than appearance and the use of appearances. It appeared[4] to Alexander to carry off the wife of Menelaus: it appeared to Helene to follow him. If then it had appeared to Menelaus to feel that it was a gain to be deprived of such a wife, what would have happened? Not only would the Iliad have been lost, but the Odyssey also. On so small a matter then did such great things depend? But what do you mean by such great things? Wars and civil commotions, and the destruction of many men and cities. And what great matter is this? Is it nothing?—But what great matter is the death of many oxen, and many sheep, and many nests of swallows or storks being burnt or destroyed? Are these things then like those? Very like. Bodies of men are destroyed, and the bodies of oxen and sheep; the dwellings of men are burnt, and the nests of storks. What is there in this great or dreadful? Or show me what is the difference between a man's house and a stork's nest, as far

[4] This is the literal version. It does not mean "that it appeared right," as Mrs. Carter translates it. Alexander never thought whether it was right or wrong. All that appeared to him was the possessing of Helene, and he used the means for getting possession of her, as a dog who spies and pursues some wild animal.

as each is a dwelling; except that man builds his little houses of beams and tiles and bricks, and the stork builds them of sticks and mud. Are a stork and a man then like things? What say you?—In body they are very much alike.

Does a man then differ in no respect from a stork? Don't suppose that I say so; but there is no difference in these matters (which I have mentioned). In what then is the difference? Seek and you will find that there is a difference in another matter. See whether it is not in a man the understanding of what he does, see if it is not in social community, in fidelity, in modesty, in steadfastness, in intelligence. Where then is the great good and evil in men? It is where the difference is. If the difference is preserved and remains fenced round, and neither modesty is destroyed, nor fidelity, nor intelligence, then the man also is preserved; but if any of these things is destroyed and stormed like a city, then the man too perishes; and in this consist the great things. Alexander, you say, sustained great damage then when the Hellenes invaded and when they ravaged Troy, and when his brothers perished. By no means; for no man is damaged by an action which is not his own; but what happened at that time was only the destruction of storks' nests: now the ruin of Alexander was when he lost the character of modesty, fidelity, regard to hospitality, and to decency. When was Achilles ruined? Was it when Patroclus died? Not so. But it happened when he began to be angry, when he wept for a girl, when he forgot that he was at Troy not to get mistresses, but to fight. These things are the ruin of men, this is being besieged, this is the destruction of cities, when right opinions are destroyed, when they are corrupted.

When then women are carried off, when children are made captives, and when the men are killed, are these not evils? How is it then that you add to the facts these opinions? Explain this to me also.—I shall not do that; but how is it that you say that these are not evils?—Let us come to the rules: produce the praecognitions (προλήψεις): for it is because this is neglected that we can not sufficiently wonder at what men do. When we intend to judge of weights, we do not judge by guess: where we intend to judge of straight and crooked, we do not judge by guess. In all cases where it is our interest to know what is true in any matter, never will any man among us do anything by guess. But in things which depend on the first and on the only cause of doing right or wrong, of happiness or unhappiness, of being unfortunate or fortunate, there only we are inconsiderate and rash. There is then nothing like scales (balance), nothing like a rule: but some appearance is presented, and straightway I act according to it. Must I then suppose that I am superior to Achilles or Agamemnon, so that they by following appearances do and suffer so many evils: and shall not the appearance be sufficient for me?[5]—And what tragedy has any other beginning? The Atreus of Euripides, what is it? An appearance.[6] The Oedipus of Sophocles, what is it? An appearance. The Phœnix? An appearance. The Hippolytus? An appearance. What kind of a man then do you suppose him to be who pays no regard to this matter? And what is the name of those who follow every appearance? They are called madmen. Do we then act at all differently?

[5] Schweighaeuser proposes to erase μὴ from the text, but it is, I suppose, in all the MSS.: and it is easy to explain the passage without erasing the μὴ.

[6] The expression τὸ φαινόμενον often occurs in this chapter, and it is sometimes translated by the Latin "sententia" or "opinio": and so it may be, and I have translated it by "opinion." But Epictetus says (s. 30) ἀλλὰ τί ἐφάνη, καὶ εὐθὺς ποιῶ τὸ φανέν: which means that there was an appearance, which was followed by the act. The word generally used by Epictetus is φαντασία, which occurs very often. In the Encheiridion (i. 5) there is some difference between φαντασία and τὸ φαινόμενον, for they are contrasted: τὸ φαινόμενον is the phenomenon, the bare appearance: φαντασία in this passage may be the mental state consequent on the φαινόμενον: or as Diogenes Laertius says, Φαντασία ἐστι τύπωσις ἐν ψυχῇ.

CHAPTER XXIX.

ON CONSTANCY (OR FIRMNESS).

THE being[1] (nature) of the Good is a certain Will; the being of the Bad is a certain kind of Will. What then are externals? Materials for the Will, about which the will being conversant shall obtain its own good or evil. How shall it obtain the good. If it does not admire[2] (overvalue) the materials; for the opinions about the materials, if the opinions are right, make the will good: but perverse and distorted opinions make the will bad. God has fixed this law, and says, "If you would have any thing good, receive it from yourself." You say, No, but I will have it from another.—Do not so: but receive it from yourself. Therefore when the tyrant threatens and calls me, I say, Whom do you threaten? If he says, I will put you in chains, I say, You threaten my hands and my feet. If he says, I will cut off your head, I reply, You threaten my head. If he says, I will throw you into prison, I say, You threaten the whole of this poor body. If he threatens me with banishment, I say the same. Does he then not threaten you at all? If I feel that all these things do not concern me, he does not threaten me at all; but if I fear any of them, it is I whom he threatens. Whom then do I fear? the master of what? The master of things which are in my own power? There is no such master. Do I fear the

[1] The word is οὐσία. The corresponding Latin word which Cicero introduced is "essentia" (Seneca, Epist. 58). The English word "essence" has obtained a somewhat different sense. The proper translation of οὐσία is "being" or "nature."

[2] This is the maxim of Horace, Epp. i. 6; and Macleane's note,—

> "Nil admirari prope res est una, Numici,
> Solaque quae possit facere et servare beatum."

on which Upton remarks that this maxim is explained very philosophically and learnedly by Lord Shaftesbury (the author of the Characteristics), vol. iii. p. 202. Compare M. Antoninus, xii. 1 Seneca, De Vita Beata, c. 3, writes, "Aliarum rerum quae vitam instruunt diligens, sine admiratione cujusquam." Antoninus (i. 15) expresses the "sine admiratione" by τὸ ἀθαύμαστον.

master of things which are not in my power? And what are these things to me?

Do you philosophers then teach us to despise kings? I hope not. Who among us teaches to claim against them the power over things which they possess? Take my poor body, take my property, take my reputation, take those who are about me. If I advise any persons to claim these things, they may truly accuse me.—Yes, but I intend to command your opinions also.—And who has given you this power? How can you conquer the opinion of another man? By applying terror to it, he replies, I will conquer it. Do you not know that opinion conquers itself,[3] and is not conquered by another? But nothing else can conquer Will except the Will itself. For this reason too the law of God is most powerful and most just, which is this: Let the stronger always be superior to the weaker. Ten are stronger than one. For what? For putting in chains, for killing, for dragging whither they choose, for taking away what a man has. The ten therefore conquer the one in this in which they are stronger. In what then are the ten weaker? If the one possesses right opinions and the others do not. Well then, can the ten conquer in this matter? How is it possible? If we were placed in the scales, must not the heavier draw down the scale in which it is.

How strange then that Socrates should have been so treated by the Athenians. Slave, why do you say Socrates? Speak of the thing as it is: how strange that the poor body of Socrates should have been carried off and dragged to prison by stronger men, and that any one should have given hemlock to the poor body of Socrates, and that it should breathe out the life. Do these things seem strange, do they seem unjust, do you on account of these things blame God? Had Socrates then no equivalent for these things? Where then for him was the nature of good? Whom shall we listen to, you or him? And what does Socrates say? Anytus and Melitus[4] can kill me, but they

[3] This is explained by what follows. Opinion does not really conquer itself; but one opinion can conquer another, and nothing else can.

[4] The two chief prosecutors of Socrates (Plato, Apology, c. 18; Epictetus, ii. 2, 15).

cannot hurt me: and further, he says, "If it so pleases God, so let it be."

But show me that he who has the inferior principles overpowers him who is superior in principles. You will never show this, nor come near showing it; for this is the law of nature and of God that the superior shall always overpower the inferior. In what? In that in which it is superior. One body is stronger than another: many are stronger than one: the thief is stronger than he who is not a thief. This is the reason why I also lost my lamp,[5] because in wakefulness the thief was superior to me. But the man bought the lamp at this price: for a lamp he became a thief, a faithless fellow, and like a wild beast. This seemed to him a good bargain. Be it so. But a man has seized me by the cloak, and is drawing me to the public place: then others bawl out, Philosopher, what has been the use of your opinions? see you are dragged to prison, you are going to be beheaded. And what system of philosophy (εἰσαγωγήν) could I have made so that, if a stronger man should have laid hold of my cloak, I should not be dragged off; that if ten men should have laid hold of me and cast me into prison, I should not be cast in? Have I learned nothing else then? I have learned to see that every thing which happens, if it be independent of my will, is nothing to me. I may ask, if you have not gained by this.[6] Why then do you seek advantage in any thing else than in that in which you have learned that advantage is?

Then sitting in prison I say: The man who cries out in this way[7] neither hears what words mean, nor understands what is said, nor does he care at all to know what philosophers say or what they do. Let him alone.

But now he says to the prisoner, Come out from your prison.—If you have no further need of me in prison, I come out: if you should have need of me again, I will enter the prison.—How long will you act thus?—So long as reason requires me to be with the body: but when reason does not require this, take away the body, and fare

[5] See i. 18, 15, p. 58.

[6] ὠφέλησαι. See Schweighaeuser's note.

[7] One of those who cry out "Philosopher," &c.

you well.[8] Only we must not do it inconsiderately, nor weakly, nor for any slight reason; for, on the other hand, God does not wish it to be done, and he has need of such a world and such inhabitants in it.[9] But if he sounds the signal for retreat, as he did to Socrates, we must obey him who gives the signal, as if he were a general.[10]

Well then, ought we to say such things to the many? Why should we? Is it not enough for a man to be persuaded himself? When children come clapping their hands and crying out, "To-day is the good Saturnalia,"[11] do we say, "The Saturnalia are not good"? By no means, but we clap our hands also. Do you also then, when you are not able to make a man change his mind, be assured that he is a child, and clap your hands with him; and if you do not choose[12] to do this, keep silent.

A man must keep this in mind; and when he is called to any such difficulty, he should know that the time is come for showing if he has been instructed. For he who is come into a difficulty is like a young man from a school who has practised the resolution of syllogisms; and if any person proposes to him an easy syllogism, he says, rather propose to me a syllogism which is skilfully complicated that I may exercise myself on it. Even athletes are dissatisfied with slight young men, and say, "He cannot lift me."—"This is a youth of noble disposition."[13] [You do not so]; but when the time of trial is come, one of you must weep and say, "I wish that I had learned more." A little more of what? If you did not learn these things in order to show them in practice, why did you learn them?

[8] See i. 9. 20.

[9] See i. 6. 13.

[10] Socrates was condemned by the Athenians to die, and he was content to die, and thought that it was a good thing; and this was the reason why he made such a defence as he did, which brought on him condemnation; and he preferred condemnation to escaping it by entreating the dicasts (judges), and lamenting, and saying and doing things unworthy of himself, as others did.—Plato, Apology, cc. 29–33. Compare Epict. i. 9, 16.

[11] See i. 25, 8.

[12] Read θέλῃς instead of θέλῃ. See Schweighaeuser's note.

[13] See Schweighaeuser's note. This appears to be the remark of Epictetus. If it is so, what follows is not clear. Schweighaeuser explains it, "But most of you act otherwise."

I think that there is some one among you who are sitting here, who is suffering like a woman in labour, and saying, "Oh, that such a difficulty does not present itself to me as that which has come to this man; oh, that I should be wasting my life in a corner, when I might be crowned at Olympia. When will any one announce to me such a contest?" Such ought to be the disposition of all of you. Even among the gladiators of Caesar (the Emperor) there are some who complain grievously that they are not brought forward and matched, and they offer up prayers to God and address themselves to their superintendents intreating that they may fight.[14] And will no one among you show himself such? I would willingly take a voyage [to Rome] for this purpose and see what my athlete is doing, how he is studying his subject.[15]—I do not choose such a subject, he says. Why, is it in your power to take what subject you choose? There has been given to you such a body as you have, such parents, such brethren, such a country, such a place in your country: —then you come to me and say, Change my subject. Have you not abilities which enable you to manage the subject which has been given to you? [You ought to say]: It is your business to propose; it is mine to exercise myself well. However, you do not say so, but you say, Do not propose to me such a tropic;[16] but such [as I would

[14] The Roman emperors kept gladiators for their own amusement and that of the people (Lipsius, Saturnalia, ii. 16). Seneca says (De Provid. c. 4), "I have heard a mirmillo (a kind of gladiator) in the time of C. Caesar (Caligula) complaining of the rarity of gladiatorial exhibitions: "What a glorious period of life is wasting." "Virtue," says Seneca, "is eager after dangers; and it considers only what it seeks, not what it may suffer."—Upton.

[15] The word is Hypothesis (ὑπόθεσις), which in this passage means "matter to work on," "material," "subject," as in ii. 5, 11, where it means the "business of the pilot." In i. 7 hypothesis has the sense of a proposition supposed for the present to be true, and used as the foundation of an argument.

[16] Tropic (τροπικόν), a logical term used by Stoics, which Schweighaeuser translates "propositio connexa in syllogismo hypothetico."

The meaning of the whole is this. You do not like the work which is set before you: as we say, you are not content "to do your duty in that state of life unto which it shall please God to call you." Now this is as foolish, says Wolf, as for a man in any discussion to require that his adversary should raise no objection except such as may serve the man's own case.

choose]: do not urge against me such an objection, but such [as I would choose]." There will be a time perhaps when tragic actors will suppose that they are [only] masks and buskins and the long cloak.[17] I say, these things, man, are your material and subject. Utter something that we may know whether you are a tragic actor or a buffoon; for both of you have all the rest in common. If any one then should take away the tragic actor's buskins and his mask, and introduce him on the stage as a phantom, is the tragic actor lost, or does he still remain? If he has voice, he still remains.

An example of another kind. "Assume the governorship of a province." I assume it, and when I have assumed it, I show how an instructed man behaves. "Lay aside the laticlave (the mark of senatorial rank), and clothing yourself in rags, come forward in this character." What then have I not the power of displaying a good voice (that is, of doing something that I ought to do)? How then do you now appear (on the stage of life)? As a witness summoned by God. "Come forward,[18] you, and bear testimony for me, for you are worthy to be brought forward as a witness by me: is any thing external to the will good or bad? do I hurt any man? have I made every man's interest dependent on any man except himself? What testimony do you give for God?"—I am in a wretched condition, Master [19] (Lord), and I am unfortunate; no man

[17] There will be a time when Tragic actors shall not know what their business is, but will think that it is all show. So, says Wolf, philosophers will be only beard and cloak, and will not show by their life and morals what they really are; or they will be like false monks, who only wear the cowl, and do not show a life of piety and sanctity.

[18] God is introduced as speaking.—Schweighaeuser.

[19] The word is Κύριος, the name by which a slave in Epictetus addresses his master (dominus), a physician is addressed by his patient, and in other cases also it is used. It is also used by the Evangelists. They speak of the angel of the Lord (Matt. i. 24); and Jesus is addressed by the same term (Matt. viii. 2), Lord or master.

Mrs. Carter has the following note: "It hath been observed that this manner of expression is not to be met with in the Heathen authors before Christianity, and therefore it is one instance of Scripture language coming early into common use."

But the word (κύριος) is used by early Greek writers to indicate one who has power or authority, and in a sense like the Roman "dominus,"

cares for me, no man gives me anything; all blame me, all speak ill of me.—Is this the evidence that you are going to give, and disgrace his summons, who has conferred so much honour on you, and thought you worthy of being called to bear such testimony?

But suppose that he who has the power has declared, "I judge you to be impious and profane." What has happened to you? I have been judged to be impious and profane? Nothing else? Nothing else. But if the same person had passed judgment on an hypothetical syllogism (συνημμένου), and had made a declaration, "the conclusion that, if it is day, it is light, I declare to be false," what has happened to the hypothetical syllogism? who is judged in this case? who has been condemned? the hypothetical syllogism, or the man who has been deceived by it? Does he then who has the power of making any declaration about you know what is pious or impious? Has he studied it, and has he learned it? Where? From whom? Then is it the fact that a musician pays no regard to him who declares that the lowest[20] chord in the lyre is the highest; nor yet a geometrician, if he declares that the lines from the centre of a circle to the circumference are

as by Sophocles for instance. The use of the word then by Epictetus was not new, and it may have been used by the Stoic writers long before his time. The language of the Stoics was formed at least two centuries before the Christian aera, and the New Testament writers would use the Greek which was current in their age. The notion of "Scripture language coming early into common use" is entirely unfounded, and is even absurd. Mrs. Carter's remark implies that Epictetus used the Scripture language, whereas he used the particular language of the Stoics, and the general language of his age, and the New Testament writers would do the same. There are resemblances between the language of Epictetus and the New Testament writers, such as the expression μὴ γένοιτο of Paul, which Epictetus often uses; but this is a slight matter. The words of Peter (Ep. ii. 1, 4), "that by these ye might be partakers of the divine nature," are a Stoic expression, and the writer of this Epistle, I think, took them from the language of the Stoics.

[20] The words in the text are: περὶ τῆς νήτης (νεάτης) εἶναι ὑπάτην. "When ὑπάτη is translated 'the lowest chord or note,' it must be remembered that the names employed in the Greek musical terminology are precisely the opposite to ours. Compare νεάτη 'the highest note,' though the word in itself means lowest."—Key's Philological Essays, p. 42, note 1.

not equal; and shall he who is really instructed pay any regard to the uninstructed man when he pronounces judgment on what is pious and what is impious, on what is just and unjust? Oh, the signal wrong done by the instructed. Did they learn this here?[21]

Will you not leave the small arguments (λογάρια)[22] about these matters to others, to lazy fellows, that they may sit in a corner and receive their sorry pay, or grumble that no one gives them any thing; and will you not come forward and make use of what you have learned? For it is not these small arguments that are wanted now: the writings of the Stoics are full of them. What then is the thing which is wanted? A man who shall apply them, one who by his acts shall bear testimony to his words.[23] Assume, I intreat you, this character, that we may no longer use in the schools the examples of the antients, but may have some example of our own.

To whom then does the contemplation of these matters (philosophical inquiries) belong? To him who has leisure, for man is an animal that loves contemplation. But it is shameful to contemplate these things as runaway slaves do: we should sit, as in a theatre, free from distraction, and listen at one time to the tragic actor, at another time to the lute-player; and not do as slaves do. As soon as the slave has taken his station he praises the actor[24] and at the same time looks round: then if any one calls out his master's name, the slave is immediately frightened and disturbed. It is shameful for philosophers thus to contemplate the works of nature. For what is a master? Man is not the master of man; but death is, and life and plea-

[21] I think that Schweighaeuser's interpretation is right, that "the instructed" are those who think that they are instructed but are not, as they show by their opinion that they accept in moral matters the judgment of an ignorant man, whose judgment in music or geometry they would not accept.

[22] He names these "small arguments" λογάρια, which Cicero (Tusc. Disput. ii. 12) names "ratiunculae."

[23] "What is the profit, my brethren, if any one should say that he hath faith and have not works?......Thus also faith, if it hath not works, is dead in itself. But a man may say, Thou hast faith, and I have works: shew me thy faith without thy works, and I will shew thee my faith by my works."—Epistle of James, ii. 14–18.

[24] See Schweighaeuser's note on ἐπέστη.

sure and pain; for if he comes without these things, bring Caesar to me and you will see how firm I am.[25] But when he shall come with these things, thundering and lightning,[26] and when I am afraid of them, what do I do then except to recognize my master like the runaway slave? But so long as I have any respite from these terrors, as a runaway slave stands in the theatre, so do I: I bathe, I drink, I sing: but all this I do with terror and uneasiness. But if I shall release myself from my masters, that is from those things by means of which masters are formidable, what further trouble have I, what master have I still?

What then, ought we to publish these things to all men? No, but we ought to accommodate ourselves to the ignorant[27] (τοῖς ἰδιώταις) and to say: "This man recommends to me that which he thinks good for himself: I excuse him." For Socrates also excused the jailor, who had the charge of him in prison and was weeping when Socrates was going to drink the poison, and said, How generously he laments over us.[28] Does he then say to the jailor that for this reason we have sent away the women? No, but he says it to his friends who were able to hear (understand) it; and he treats the jailor as a child.

[25] The word is εὐσταθῶ. The corresponding noun is εὐστάθεια, which is the title of this chapter.

[26] Upton supposes that Epictetus is alluding to the verse of Aristophanes (Acharn. 531), where it is said of Pericles:

"He flashed, he thundered, and confounded Hellas."

[27] He calls the uninstructed and ignorant by the Greek word "Idiotae," "idiots," which we now use in a peculiar sense. An Idiota was a private individual as opposed to one who filled some public office; and thence it had generally the sense of one who was ignorant of any particular art, as, for instance, one who had not studied philosophy.

[28] Compare the Phaedon of Plato (p. 116). The children of Socrates were brought in to see him before he took the poison by which he died; and also the wives of the friends of Socrates who attended him to his death. Socrates had ordered his wife Xanthippe to be led home before he had his last conversation with his friends, and she was taken away lamenting and bewailing.

CHAPTER XXX.

WHAT WE OUGHT TO HAVE READY IN DIFFICULT CIRCUMSTANCES.[1]

When you are going in to any great personage, remember that another also from above sees what is going on, and that you ought to please him rather than the other. He then who sees from above asks you: In the schools what used you to say about exile and bonds and death and disgrace? I used to say that they are things indifferent (neither good nor bad). What then do you say of them now? Are they changed at all? No. Are you changed then? No. Tell me then what things are indifferent? The things which are independent of the will. Tell me, also, what follows from this. The things which are independent of the will are nothing to me. Tell me also about the Good, what was your opinion? A will such as we ought to have and also such a use of appearances. And the end (purpose), what is it? To follow thee. Do you say this now also? I say the same now also.

Then go in to the great personage boldly and remember these things; and you will see what a youth is who has studied these things when he is among men who have not studied them. I indeed imagine that you will have such thoughts as these: Why do we make so great and so many preparations for nothing? Is this the thing which men name power? Is this the antechamber? this the men of the bedchamber? this the armed guards? Is it for this that I listened to so many discourses? All this is nothing: but I have been preparing myself as for something great.

[1] The reader may understand why Epictetus gave such a lesson as this, if he will remember the tyranny under which men at that time lived.

BOOK II.

CHAPTER I.

THAT CONFIDENCE (COURAGE) IS NOT INCONSISTENT WITH CAUTION.

The opinion of the philosophers perhaps seems to some to be a paradox; but still let us examine as well as we can, if it is true that it is possible to do every thing both with caution and with confidence. For caution seems to be in a manner contrary to confidence, and contraries are in no way consistent. That which seems to many to be a paradox in the matter under consideration in my opinion is of this kind: if we asserted that we ought to employ caution and confidence in the same things, men might justly accuse us of bringing together things which cannot be united. But now where is the difficulty in what is said? for if these things are true, which have been often said and often proved, that the nature of good is in the use of appearances, and the nature of evil likewise, and that things independent of our will do not admit either the nature of evil nor of good, what paradox do the philosophers assert if they say that where things are not dependent on the will, there you should employ confidence, but where they are dependent on the will, there you should employ caution? For if the bad consists in a bad exercise of the will, caution ought only to be used where things are dependent on the will. But if things independent of the will and not in our power are nothing to us, with respect to these we must employ confidence; and thus we shall both be cautious and confident, and indeed confident because of our caution. For by employing caution towards things which are really bad, it will result that we shall have confidence with respect to things which are not so.

We are then in the condition of deer;[1] when they flee from the huntsmen's feathers in fright, whither do they turn and in what do they seek refuge as safe? They turn to the nets, and thus they perish by confounding things which are objects of fear with things that they ought not to fear. Thus we also act: in what cases do we fear? In things which are independent of the will. In what cases on the contrary do we behave with confidence, as if there were no danger? In things dependent on the will. To be deceived then, or to act rashly, or shamelessly or with base desire to seek something, does not concern us at all, if we only hit the mark in things which are independent of our will. But where there is death, or exile or pain or infamy, there we attempt to run away, there we are struck with terror. Therefore as we may expect it to happen with those who err in the greatest matters, we convert natural confidence (that is, according to nature) into audacity, desperation, rashness, shamelessness; and we convert natural caution and modesty into cowardice and meanness, which are full of fear and confusion. For if a man should transfer caution to those things in which the will may be exercised and the acts of the will, he will immediately by willing to be cautious have also the power of avoiding what he chooses: but if he transfer it to the things which are not in his power and will, and attempt to avoid the things which are in the power of others, he will of necessity fear, he will be unstable, he will be disturbed. For death or pain is not formidable, but the fear of pain or death. For this reason we commend the poet[2] who said

Not death is evil, but a shameful death.

---

[1] It was the fashion of hunters to frighten deer by displaying feathers of various colours on ropes or strings and thus frightening them towards the nets. Virgil, Georg. iii. 372—

Puniceaeve agitant pavidos formidine pennae.

[2] Euripides, fragments.

Confidence (courage) then ought to be employed against death, and caution against the fear of death. But now we do the contrary, and employ against death the attempt to escape; and to our opinion about it we employ carelessness, rashness and indifference. These things Socrates[3] properly used to call tragic masks; for as to children masks appear terrible and fearful from inexperience, we also are affected in like manner by events (the things which happen in life) for no other reason than children are by masks. For what is a child? Ignorance. What is a child? Want of knowledge. For when a child knows these things, he is in no way inferior to us. What is death? A tragic mask. Turn it and examine it. See, it does not bite. The poor body must be separated[4] from the spirit either now or later as it was separated from it before. Why then are you troubled, if it be separated now? for if it is not separated now, it will be separated afterwards. Why? That the period of the universe may be completed,[5] for it has need of the present, and of the future, and of the past. What is pain? A mask. Turn it and examine it. The poor flesh is moved roughly, then on the contrary smoothly. If this does not satisfy (please) you, the door is open:[6] if it

[3] In the Phaedon, c. 24, or p. 78.

[4] It was the opinion of some philosophers that the soul was a portion of the divinity sent down into human bodies.

[5] This was a doctrine of Heraclitus and of Zeno. Zeno (Diog. Laert. vii. 137) speaks of God as "in certain periods or revolutions of time exhausting into himself the universal substance (οὐσία) and again generating it out of himself." Antoninus (xi. 1) speaks of the periodical renovation of all things. For man, whose existence is so short, the doctrine of all existing things perishing in the course of time and then being renewed, is of no practical value. The present is enough for most men. But for the few who are able to embrace in thought the past, the present and the future, the contemplation of the perishable nature of all existing things may have a certain value by elevating their minds above the paltry things which others prize above their worth.

[6] Sec. i. 9, note 7. Schweighaeuser says that he does not quite see what is the meaning of 'ought to be open'; and he suggests that Epictetus intended to say 'we ought to consider that the door is open for all occasions'; but the occasions, he says, ought to be when things are such that a man can in no way bear them or cannot honourably endure them, and such occasions the wise man considers to be the voice of God giving to him the signal to retire.

does, bear (with things). For the door ought to be open for all occasions; and so we have no trouble.

What then is the fruit of these opinions? It is that which ought to be the most noble and the most becoming to those who are really educated, release from perturbation, release from fear, freedom. For in these matters we must not believe the many, who say that free persons only ought to be educated, but we should rather believe the philosophers who say that the educated only are free. How is this? In this manner. Is freedom any thing else than the power of living as we choose? Nothing else. Tell me then, ye men, do you wish to live in error? We do not. No one then who lives in error is free. Do you wish to live in fear? Do you wish to live in sorrow? Do you wish to live in perturbation? By no means. No one then who is in a state of fear or sorrow or perturbation is free; but whoever is delivered from sorrows and fears and perturbations, he is at the same time also delivered from servitude. How then can we continue to believe you, most dear legislators, when you say, We only allow free persons to be educated? For philosophers say we allow none to be free except the educated; that is, God does not allow it. When then a man has turned[7] round before the praetor his own slave, has he done nothing? He has done something. What? He has turned round his own slave before the praetor. Has he done nothing more? Yes: he is also bound to pay for him the tax called the twentieth. Well then, is not the man who has gone through this ceremony become free? No more than he is become free from perturbations. Have you who are able to turn round (free) others no

[7] This is an allusion to one of the Roman modes of manumitting a slave before the praetor. Compare, Persius, Sat. V. 75—

> —Heu steriles veri, quibus una Quiritem
> Vertigo facit;

and again

> Verterit hunc dominus, momento turbinis exit
> Marcus Dama.

The sum paid on manumission was a tax of five per cent., established in B.C. 356 (Livy, vii. 16), and paid by the slave. Epictetus here speaks of the tax being paid by the master; but in iii. 26, he speaks of it as paid by the enfranchised slave. See Dureau de la Malle, Économie Politique des Romains, i. 290, ii. 469.

master? is not money your master, or a girl or a boy, or some tyrant, or some friend of the tyrant? why do you tremble then when you are going off to any trial (danger) of this kind? It is for this reason that I often say, study and hold in readiness these principles by which you may determine what those things are with reference to which you ought to have confidence (courage), and those things with reference to which you ought to be cautious: courageous in that which does not depend on your will; cautious in that which does depend on it.

Well have I not read to you,[8] and do you not know what I was doing? In what? In my little dissertations —Show me how you are with respect to desire and aversion (ἔκκλισιν); and show me if you do not fail in getting what you wish, and if you do not fall into the things which you would avoid: but as to these long and labored sentences [9] you will take them and blot them out.

What then did not Socrates write? And who wrote so much?[10]—But how? As he could not always have at hand one to argue against his principles or to be argued against in turn, he used to argue with and examine himself, and he was always treating at least some one subject in a practical way. These are the things which a philosopher writes. But little dissertations and that method, which I speak of, he leaves to others, to the stupid, or to those happy men who being free from perturbations[11] have

[8] These are the words of some pupil who is boasting of what he has written.

[9] The word is περιόδια. I am not sure about the exact meaning of περιόδια: see the notes of Wolf and Schweig.

[10] No other author speaks of Socrates having written any thing. It is therefore very difficult to explain this passage in which Arrian, who took down the words of Epictetus, represents him as saying that Socrates wrote so much. Socrates talked much, and Epictetus may have spoken of talking as if it were writing; for he must have known that Socrates was not a writer. See Schweig.'s note.

[11] The word is ὑπὸ ἀταραξίας. Mrs. Carter thinks that the true reading is ὑπὸ ἀπραξίας, 'through idleness' or 'having nothing to do'; and she remarks that 'freedom from perturbations' is the very thing that Epictetus had been recommending through the whole chapter and is the subject of the next chapter, and therefore cannot be well supposed to be the true reading in a place where it is mentioned with contempt. It is probable that Mrs. Carter is right. Upton thinks that Epictetus is alluding to the Sophists, and that we should understand him as speaking ironically: and this may also be right. Schweighaeuser

leisure, or to such as are too foolish to reckon consequences.

And will you now, when the opportunity invites, go and display those things which you possess, and recite them, and make an idle show,[12] and say, See how I make dialogues? Do not so, my man; but rather say; See how I am not disappointed of that which I desire: See how I do not fall into that which I would avoid. Set death before me, and you will see. Set before me pain, prison, disgrace and condemnation. This is the proper display of a young man who is come out of the schools. But leave the rest to others, and let no one ever hear you say a word about these things; and if any man commends you for them, do not allow it; but think that you are nobody and know nothing. Only show that you know this, how never to be disappointed in your desire and how never to fall into that which you would avoid. Let others labour at forensic causes, problems and syllogisms: do you labour at thinking about death,[13] chains, the rack, exile;[14] and do all this with confidence and reliance on him who has called you to these sufferings, who has judged you worthy of the place in which being stationed you will show what things the rational governing power can do when it takes its stand against the forces which are not within the power of our will. And thus this paradox will no longer appear either impossible or a paradox,

attempts to explain the passage by taking 'free from perturbations' in the ordinary simple sense; but I doubt if he has succeeded.

[12] ἐμπερπερεύσῃ. Epictetus (iii. 2. 14) uses the adjective πέρπερος to signify a vain man. Antoninus (v. 5) uses the verb περπέρευεσθαι: and Paul (Corinthians i. c. 13, 4), where our version is, 'charity (love) vaunteth not itself.' Cicero (ad Attic. i. 14, 4) uses ἐνεπερπερευσάμην, to express a rhetorical display.

[13] 'The whole life of philosophers,' says Cicero (Tusc. i. 30), following Plato, 'is a reflection upon death.'

[14] "Some English readers, too happy to comprehend how chains, torture, exile and sudden executions, can be ranked among the common accidents of life, may be surprised to find Epictetus so frequently endeavouring to prepare his hearers for them. But it must be recollected that he addressed himself to persons who lived under the Roman emperors, from whose tyranny the very best of men were perpetually liable to such kind of dangers."—Mrs. Carter. All men even now are exposed to accidents and misfortunes against which there is no security, and even the most fortunate of men must die at last. The lessons of Epictetus may be as useful now as they were in his time. See i. 30.

that a man ought to be at the same time cautious and courageous: courageous towards the things which do not depend on the will, and cautious in things which are within the power of the will.

CHAPTER II.

OF TRANQUILLITY (FREEDOM FROM PERTURBATION).

CONSIDER, you who are going into court, what you wish to maintain and what you wish to succeed in. For if you wish to maintain a will conformable to nature, you have every security, every facility, you have no troubles. For if you wish to maintain what is in your own power and is naturally free, and if you are content with these, what else do you care for? For who is the master of such things? Who can take them away? If you choose to be modest and faithful, who shall not allow you to be so? If you choose not to be restrained or compelled, who shall compel you to desire what you think that you ought not to desire? who shall compel you to avoid what you do not think fit to avoid? But what do you say? The judge will determine against you something that appears formidable; but that you should also suffer in trying to avoid it, how can he do that? When then the pursuit of objects and the avoiding of them are in your power, what else do you care for? Let this be your preface,[1] this your narrative, this your confirmation, this your victory, this your peroration, this your applause (or the approbation which you will receive).

Therefore Socrates said to one who was reminding him to prepare for his trial,[2] Do you not think then that I have been preparing for it all my life? By what kind of preparation? I have maintained that which was in my own power. How then? I have never done anything unjust either in my private or in my public life.

[1] Epictetus refers to the rhetorical divisions of a speech.

[2] Xenophon (Mem. iv. c. 8, 4) has reported this saying of Socrates on the authority of Hermogenes. Compare the Apology of Xenophon near the beginning.

But if you wish to maintain externals also, your poor body, your little property and your little estimation, I advise you to make from this moment all possible preparation, and then consider both the nature of your judge and your adversary. If it is necessary to embrace his knees, embrace his knees; if to weep, weep; if to groan, groan. For when you have subjected to externals what is your own, then be a slave and do not resist, and do not sometimes choose to be a slave, and sometimes not choose, but with all your mind be one or the other, either free or a slave, either instructed or uninstructed, either a well bred cock or a mean one, either endure to be beaten until you die or yield at once; and let it not happen to you to receive many stripes and then to yield. But if these things are base, determine immediately. Where is the nature of evil and good? It is where truth is: where truth is and where nature is, there is caution: where truth is, there is courage where nature is.[3]

For what do you think? do you think that, if Socrates had wished to preserve externals, he would have come forward and said: Anytus and Melitus can certainly kill me, but to harm me they are not able? Was he so foolish as not to see that this way leads not to the preservation of life and fortune, but to another end? What is the reason then that he takes no account of his adversaries, and even irritates them?[4] Just in the same way my friend Heraclitus, who had a little suit in Rhodes about a bit of land, and had proved to the judges (δικασταῖς) that his case was just, said when he had come to the peroration of his speech, I will neither intreat you nor do I care what judgment you will give, and it is you rather than I who are on your trial. And thus he ended the business.[5] What need was there of this? Only do not intreat; but do not also say, 'I do not intreat;' unless there is a fit occasion to irritate purposely the judges, as was the case with Socrates. And you, if you are preparing such a peroration, why do you wait, why do you obey the order

[3] Schweighaeuser says that he can extract no sense out of this passage. I leave it as it is.

[4] There is some difficulty here in the original. See Schweig.'s note.

[5] The words may mean either what I have written in the text, or 'and so he lost his suit.'

to submit to trial? For if you wish to be crucified, wait and the cross will come: but if you choose to submit and to plead your cause as well as you can, you must do what is consistent with this object, provided you maintain what is your own (your proper character).

For this reason also it is ridiculous to say, Suggest something to me[6] (tell me what to do). What should I suggest to you? Well, form my mind so as to accommodate itself to any event. Why that is just the same as if a man who is ignorant of letters should say, Tell me what to write when any name is proposed to me. For if I should tell him to write Dion, and then another should come and propose to him not the name of Dion but that of Theon, what will be done? what will he write? But if you have practised writing, you are also prepared to write (or to do) any thing that is required. If[7] you are not, what can I now suggest? For if circumstances require something else, what will you say, or what will you do? Remember then this general precept and you will need no suggestion. But if you gape after externals, you must of necessity ramble up and down in obedience to the will of your master. And who is the master? He who has the power over the things which you seek to gain or try to avoid.[8]

6 "The meaning is, You must not ask for advice when you are come into a difficulty, but every man ought to have such principles as to be ready on all occasions to act as he ought; just as he who knows how to write can write any name which is proposed to him."—Wolf.

7 "The reader must know that these dissertations were spoken extempore, and that one thing after another would come into the thoughts of the speaker. So the reader will not be surprised that when the discourse is on the maintenance of firmness or freedom from perturbations, Epictetus should now speak of philosophical preparation, which is most efficient for the maintenance of firmness."—Wolf. See also Schweig.'s note on section 21, "Suggest something to me:" and ii. 24.

8 In the Encheiridion or Manual (c. 14) it is written, 'Every man's master is he who has the power to give to a man or take away that which he would have or not have: whoever then wishes to be free, let him neither seek any thing or avoid any thing which is in the power of others: if he does not act thus, he will be a slave.'

CHAPTER III.

TO THOSE WHO RECOMMEND PERSONS TO PHILOSOPHERS.

DIOGENES said well to one who asked from him letters of recommendation, "That you are a man, he said, he will know as soon as he sees you; and he will know whether you are good or bad, if he is by experience skilful to distinguish the good and the bad; but if he is without experience, he will never know, if I write to him ten thousand times."[1] For it is just the same as if a drachma (a piece of silver money) asked to be recommended to a person to be tested. If he is skilful in testing silver, he will know what you are, for you (the drachma) will recommend yourself. We ought then in life also to have some skill as in the case of silver coin that a man may be able to say like the judge of silver, Bring me any drachma and I will test it. But in the case of syllogisms, I would say, Bring any man that you please, and I will distinguish for you the man who knows how to resolve syllogisms and the man who does not. Why? Because I know how to resolve syllogisms. I have the power, which a man must have who is able to discover those who have the power of resolving syllogisms. But in life how do I act? At one time I call a thing good, and at another time bad. What is the reason? The contrary to that which is in the case of syllogisms, ignorance and inexperience.

[1] Mrs. Carter says 'This is one of the many extravagant refinements of the philosophers; and might lead persons into very dangerous mistakes, if it was laid down as a maxim in ordinary life.' I think that Mrs. Carter has not seen the meaning of Epictetus. The philosopher will discover the man's character by trying him, as the assayer tries the silver by a test.

Cicero (De legibus, i. 9) says that the face expresses the hidden character. Euripides (Medea, 518) says better, that no mark is impressed on the body by which we can distinguish the good man from the bad. Shakspere says

> There 's no art
> To find the mind's construction in the face.
> Macbeth, act i. sc. 4.

CHAPTER IV.

AGAINST A PERSON WHO HAD ONCE BEEN DETECTED IN ADULTERY.

As Epictetus was saying that man is formed for fidelity and that he who subverts fidelity subverts the peculiar characteristic of men, there entered one of those who are considered to be men of letters, who had once been detected in adultery in the city. Then Epictetus continued, But if we lay aside this fidelity for which we are formed and make designs against our neighbour's wife, what are we doing? What else but destroying and overthrowing? Whom, the man of fidelity, the man of modesty, the man of sanctity. Is this all? And are we not overthrowing neighbourhood, and friendship, and the community; and in what place are we putting ourselves? How shall I consider you, man? As a neighbour, as a friend? What kind of one? As a citizen? Wherein shall I trust you? So if you were an utensil so worthless that a man could not use you, you would be pitched out on the dung heaps, and no man would pick you up. But if being a man you are unable to fill any place which befits a man, what shall we do with you? For suppose that you cannot hold the place of a friend, can you hold the place of a slave? And who will trust you? Are you not then content that you also should be pitched somewhere on a dung heap, as a useless utensil, and a bit of dung? Then will you say, no man cares for me, a man of letters? They do not, because you are bad and useless. It is just as if the wasps complained because no man cares for them, but all fly from them, and if a man can, he strikes them and knocks them down. You have such a sting that you throw into trouble and pain any man that you wound with it. What would you have us do with you? You have no place where you can be put.

What then, are not women common by nature?[1] So I

[1] It is not clear what is meant by women being common by nature in any rational sense. Zeno and his school said (Diogenes Laertius, vii.; Zeno, p. 195. London, 1664): 'it is their opinion also that the women

say also; for a little pig is common to all the invited guests, but when the portions have been distributed, go, if you think it right, and snatch up the portion of him who reclines next to you, or slily steal it, or place your hand down by it and lay hold of it, and if you can not tear away a bit of the meat, grease your fingers and lick them. A fine companion over cups, and Socratic guest indeed! Well, is not the theatre common to the citizens? When then they have taken their seats, come, if you think proper, and eject one of them. In this way women also are common by nature. When then the legislator, like the master of a feast, has distributed them, will you not also look for your own portion and not filch and handle what belongs to another. But I am a man of letters and understand Archedemus.[2]—Understand Archedemus then, and be an adulterer, and faithless, and instead of a man, be a wolf or an ape: for what is the difference?[3]

CHAPTER V.

HOW MAGNANIMITY IS CONSISTENT WITH CARE.

THINGS themselves (materials) are indifferent;[1] but the use of them is not indifferent. How then shall a man preserve firmness and tranquillity, and at the same time

should be common among the wise, so that any man should use any woman, as Zeno says in his Polity, and Chrysippus in the book on Polity, and Diogenes the Cynic and Plato; and we shall love all the children equally like fathers, and the jealousy about adultery will be removed.' These wise men knew little about human nature, if they taught such doctrines.

[2] Archedemus was a Stoic philosopher of Tarsus. We know little about him.

[3] A man may be a philosopher or pretend to be; and at the same time he may be a beast.

[1] The materials (ὕλαι) on which man works are neither good nor bad, and so they are, as Epictetus names them, indifferent. But the use of things, or of material, is not indifferent. They may be used well or ill, conformably to nature or not.

be careful and neither rash nor negligent? If he imitates those who play at dice. The counters are indifferent; the dice are indifferent. How do I know what the cast will be? But to use carefully and dexterously the cast of the dice, this is my business.[2] Thus then in life also the chief business is this: distinguish and separate things, and say, Externals are not in my power: will is in my power. Where shall I seek the good and the bad? Within, in the things which are my own. But in what does not belong to you call nothing either good or bad, or profit or damage or any thing of the kind.

What then? Should we use such things carelessly? In no way: for this on the other hand is bad for the faculty of the will, and consequently against nature; but we should act carefully because the use is not indifferent, and we should also act with firmness and freedom from perturbations because the material is indifferent. For where the material is not indifferent, there no man can hinder me nor compel me. Where I can be hindered and compelled, the obtaining of those things is not in my power, nor is it good or bad; but the use is either bad or good, and the use is in my power. But it is difficult to mingle and to bring together these two things, the carefulness of him who is affected by the matter (or things about him) and the firmness of him who has no regard for it; but it is not impossible: and if it is, happiness is impossible. But we should act as we do in the case of a voyage. What can I do? I can choose the master of the ship, the sailors, the day, the opportunity. Then comes a storm. What more have I to care for? for my part is done. The business belongs to another, the master.—But the ship is sinking—what then have I to do? I do the only thing that I can, not to be drowned full of fear, nor screaming nor blaming God, but knowing that what has been produced must also perish: for I am not an immortal being, but a man, a part of the whole, as an hour is a part of the day:

[2] Terence says (Adelphi, iv. 7)—

> Si illud, quod est maxime opus, jactu non cadit,
> Illud quod cecidit forte, id arte ut corrigas.

'Dexterously' is 'arte,' τεχνικῶς in Epictetus.—Upton.

I must be present like the hour, and past like the hour. What difference then does it make to me, how I pass away, whether by being suffocated or by a fever, for I must pass through some such means?

This is just what you will see those doing who play at ball skilfully. No one cares about the ball[3] as being good or bad, but about throwing and catching it. In this therefore is the skill, in this the art, the quickness, the judgment, so that even if I spread out my lap I may not be able to catch it, and another, if I throw, may catch the ball. But if with perturbation and fear we receive or throw the ball, what kind of play is it then, and wherein shall a man be steady, and how shall a man see the order in the game? But one will say, Throw; or Do not throw; and another will say, You have thrown once. This is quarrelling, not play.

Socrates then knew how to play at ball. How? By using pleasantry in the court where he was tried. Tell me, he says, Anytus, how do you say that I do not believe in God. The Daemons (δαίμονες), who are they, think you? Are they not sons of Gods, or compounded of gods and men? When Anytus admitted this, Socrates said, Who then, think you, can believe that there are mules (half asses), but not asses; and this he said as if he were playing at ball.[4] And what was the ball in that case? Life, chains, banishment, a draught of poison, separation from wife and leaving children orphans. These were the things with which he was playing; but still he did play and threw the ball skilfully. So we should do: we must employ all the care of the players, but show the same indifference about the ball. For we ought by all means

[3] The word is ἁρπαστόν, which was also used by the Romans. One threw the ball and the other caught it. Chrysippus used this simile of a ball in speaking of giving and receiving (Seneca, De Beneficiis, ii. 17). Martial has the word (Epig. iv. 19) 'Sive harpasta manu pulverulenta rapis'; and elsewhere.

[4] In Plato's Apology c. 15, Socrates addresses Meletus; and he says, it would be equally absurd if a man should believe that there are foals of horses and asses, and should not believe that there are horses and asses. But Socrates says nothing of mules, for the word mules in some texts of the Apology is manifestly wrong

to apply our art to some external material, not as valuing the material, but, whatever it may be, showing our art in it. Thus too the weaver does not make wool, but exercises his art upon such as he receives. Another gives you food and property and is able to take them away and your poor body also. When then you have received the material, work on it. If then you come out (of the trial) without having suffered any thing, all who meet you will congratulate you on your escape; but he who knows how to look at such things, if he shall see that you have behaved properly in the matter, will commend you and be pleased with you; and if he shall find that you owe your escape to any want of proper behaviour, he will do the contrary. For where rejoicing is reasonable, there also is congratulation reasonable.

How then is it said that some external things are according to nature and others contrary to nature? It is said as it might be said if we were separated from union (or society): for to the foot I shall say that it is according to nature for it to be clean; but if you take it as a foot and as a thing not detached (independent), it will befit it both to step into the mud and tread on thorns, and sometimes to be cut off for the good of the whole body; otherwise it is no longer a foot. We should think in some such way about ourselves also. What are you? A man. If you consider yourself as detached from other men, it is according to nature to live to old age, to be rich, to be healthy. But if you consider yourself as a man and a part of a certain whole, it is for the sake of that whole that at one time you should be sick, at another time take a voyage and run into danger, and at another time be in want, and in some cases die prematurely. Why then are you troubled? Do you not know, that as a foot is no longer a foot if it is detached from the body, so you are no longer a man if you are separated from other men. For what is a man?[6] A part of a state, of that first which consists of Gods and of men; then of that which is called

[5] ἀπόλυτοι. Compare Antoninus, x. 24, viii. 34.

[6] Compare Antoninus, ii. 16, iii. 11, vi. 44, xii. 36; and Seneca, de Otio Sap. c. 31; and Cicero, De Fin. iii. 19.

next to it, which is a small image of the universal state. What then must I be brought to trial; must another have a fever, another sail on the sea, another die, and another be condemned? Yes, for it is impossible in such a body, in such a universe of things, among so many living together, that such things should not happen, some to one and others to others. It is your duty then since you are come here, to say what you ought, to arrange these things as it is fit.[7] Then some one says, "I shall charge you with doing me wrong." Much good may it do you: I have done my part; but whether you also have done yours, you must look to that; for there is some danger of this too, that it may escape your notice.

CHAPTER VI.

OF INDIFFERENCE.[1]

THE hypothetical proposition[2] is indifferent: the judgment about it is not indifferent, but it is either knowledge or opinion or error. Thus life is indifferent: the use is not indifferent. When any man then tells you that these things also are indifferent, do not become negligent; and when a man invites you to be careful (about such things), do not become abject and struck with admiration of material things. And it is good for you to know your own preparation and power, that in those matters where you have not been prepared, you may keep quiet, and not be

[7] He tells some imaginary person, who hears him, that since he is come into the world, he must do his duty in it.

[1] This discussion is with a young philosopher who, intending to return from Nicopolis to Rome, feared the tyranny of Domitian, who was particularly severe towards philosophers. See also the note on i. 24. 3. Schweig. Compare Plin. Epp. i. 12, and the expression of Corellius Rufus about the detestable villain, the emperor Domitian.

The title 'of Indifference' means 'of the indifference of things;' of the things which are neither good nor bad.

[2] τὸ συνημμένον, p. 93.

vexed, if others have the advantage over you. For you too in syllogisms will claim to have the advantage over them; and if others should be vexed at this, you will console them by saying, 'I have learned them, and you have not.' Thus also where there is need of any practice, seek not that which is acquired from the need (of such practice), but yield in that matter to those who have had practice, and be yourself content with firmness of mind.

Go and salute a certain person. How? Not meanly.—But I have been shut out, for I have not learned to make my way through the window; and when I have found the door shut, I must either come back or enter through the window.—But still speak to him.—In what way? Not meanly. But suppose that you have not got what you wanted. Was this your business, and not his? Why then do you claim that which belongs to another? Always remember what is your own, and what belongs to another; and you will not be disturbed. Chrysippus therefore said well, So long as future things are uncertain, I always cling to those which are more adapted to the conservation of that which is according to nature; for God himself has given me the faculty of such choice. But if I knew that it was fated (in the order of things) for me to be sick, I would even move towards it; for the foot also, if it had intelligence, would move to go into the mud.[3] For why are ears of corn produced? Is it not that they may become dry? And do they not become dry that they may be reaped?[4] for they are not separated from communion with other things. If then they had perception, ought they to wish never to be reaped? But this is a curse upon ears of corn, to be never reaped. So we must know that in the case of men too it is a curse not to die, just the same as not to be ripened and not to be reaped. But since we must be reaped, and we also know that we are reaped,

[3] Sec. ii. 5, 24.

[4] Epictetus alludes to the verses from the Hypsipyle of Euripides. Compare Antoninus (vii. 40): 'Life must be reaped like the ripe ears of corn: one man is born; another dies.' Cicero (Tuscul. Disp. iii. 25) has translated six verses from Euripides, and among them are these two:

tum vita omnibus
Metenda ut fruges: sic jubet necessitas.

we are vexed at it; for we neither know what we are nor have we studied what belongs to man, as those who have studied horses know what belongs to horses. But Chrysantas[5] when he was going to strike the enemy checked himself when he heard the trumpet sounding a retreat: so it seemed better to him to obey the general's command than to follow his own inclination. But not one of us chooses, even when necessity summons, readily to obey it, but weeping and groaning we suffer what we do suffer, and we call them 'circumstances.' What kind of circumstances, man? If you give the name of circumstances to the things which are around you, all things are circumstances; but if you call hardships by this name, what hardship is there in the dying of that which has been produced? But that which destroys is either a sword, or a wheel, or the sea, or a tile, or a tyrant. Why do you care about the way of going down to Hades? All ways are equal.[6] But if you will listen to the truth, the way which the tyrant sends you is shorter. A tyrant never killed a man in six months: but a fever is often a year about it. All these things are only sound and the noise of empty names.

I am in danger of my life from Caesar.[7] And am not I in danger who dwell in Nicopolis, where there are so many earthquakes: and when you are crossing the Hadriatic, what hazard do you run? Is it not the hazard of your life? But I am in danger also as to opinion. Do you mean your own? how? For who can compel you to have any opinion which you do not choose? But is it as to another man's opinion? and what kind of danger is

[5] The story is in Xenophon's Cyropaedia (IV. near the beginning) where Cyrus says that he called Chrysantas by name. Epictetus, as Upton remarks, quotes from memory.

[6] So Anaxagoras said that the road to the other world (ad inferos) is the same from all places. (Cicero, Tusc. Disp. i. 43). What follows is one of the examples of extravagant assertion in Epictetus. A tyrant may kill by a slow death as a fever does. I suppose that Epictetus would have some answer to that. Except to a Stoic the ways to death are not indifferent: some ways of dying are painful, and even he who can endure with fortitude, would prefer an easy death.

[7] The text has ἐπὶ Καίσαρος; but ἐπὶ perhaps ought to be ὑπό or ἀπό.

yours, if others have false opinions? But I am in danger of being banished. What is it to be banished? To be somewhere else than at Rome? Yes: what then if I should be sent to Gyara?[8] If that suits you, you will go there; but if it does not, you can go to another place instead of Gyara, whither he also will go, who sends you to Gyara, whether he choose or not. Why then do you go up to Rome as if it were something great? It is not worth all this preparation, that an ingenuous youth should say, It was not worth while to have heard so much and to have written so much and to have sat so long by the side of an old man who is not worth much. Only remember that division by which your own and not your own are distinguished: never claim any thing which belongs to others. A tribunal and a prison are each a place, one high and the other low; but the will can be maintained equal, if you choose to maintain it equal in each. And we shall then be imitators of Socrates, when we are able to write paeans in prison.[9] But in our present disposition, consider if we could endure in prison another person saying to us, Would you like me to read Paeans to you?—Why do you trouble me? do you not know the evils which hold me? Can I in such circumstances (listen to paeans)?—What circumstances?—I am going to die.—And will other men be immortal?

[8] See i. 25, note 4.

[9] Diogenes Laertius reports in his life of Socrates that he wrote in prison a Paean, and he gives the first line which contains an address to Apollo and Artemis.

CHAPTER VII.

HOW WE OUGHT TO USE DIVINATION.

THROUGH an unreasonable regard to divination many of us omit many duties.[1] For what more can the diviner see than death or danger or disease, or generally things of that kind? If then I must expose myself to danger for a friend, and if it is my duty even to die for him, what need have I then for divination? Have I not within me a diviner who has told me the nature of good and of evil, and has explained to me the signs (or marks) of both? What need have I then to consult the viscera of victims or the flight of birds, and why do I submit when he says, It is for your interest? For does he know what is for my interest, does he know what is good; and as he has learned the signs of the viscera, has he also learned the signs of good and evil? For if he knows the signs of these, he knows the signs both of the beautiful and of the ugly, and of the just and of the unjust. Do you tell me, man, what is the thing which is signified for me: is it life or death, poverty or wealth? But whether these things are for my interest or whether they are not, I do not intend to ask you. Why don't you give your opinion on matters of grammar, and why do you give it here about things on which we are all in error and disputing with one another?[2] The woman therefore, who intended to

[1] Divination was a great part of antient religion, and, as Epictetus says, it led men 'to omit many duties.' In a certain sense there was some meaning in it. If it is true that those who believe in God can see certain signs in the administration of the world by which they can judge what their behaviour ought to be, they can learn what their duties are. If these signs are misunderstood, or if they are not seen right, men may be governed by an abject superstition. So the external forms of any religion may become the means of corruption and of human debasement, and the true indications of God's will may be neglected. Upton compares Lucan (ix. 572), who sometimes said a few good things.

[2] A man who gives his opinion on grammar gives an opinion on a thing of which many know something. A man who gives his opinion on divination or on future events, gives an opinion on things of which we all know nothing. When then a man affects to instruct on things unknown, we may ask him to give his opinion on things which are known, and so we may learn what kind of man he is.

send by a vessel a month's provisions to Gratilla[3] in her banishment, made a good answer to him who said that Domitian would seize what she sent, I would rather, she replied, that Domitian should seize all than that I should not send it.

What then leads us to frequent use of divination? Cowardice, the dread of what will happen. This is the reason why we flatter the diviners. Pray, master, shall I succeed to the property of my father? Let us see: let us sacrifice on the occasion.—Yes, master, as fortune chooses. —When he has said, You shall succeed to the inheritance, we thank him as if we received the inheritance from him. The consequence is that they play upon us.[4]

What then should we do? We ought to come (to divination) without desire or aversion, as the wayfarer asks of the man whom he meets which of two roads leads (to his journey's end), without any desire for that which leads to the right rather than to the left, for he has no wish to go by any road except the road which leads (to his end). In the same way ought we to come to God also as a guide; as we use our eyes, not asking them to show us rather such things as we wish, but receiving the appearances of things such as the eyes present them to us. But now we trembling take the augur (bird interpreter)[5] by the hand, and while we invoke God we intreat the augur, and say Master have mercy on me;[6] suffer me to come safe out of this difficulty. Wretch, would you have then any thing other than what is best? Is there then any thing better than what pleases God? Why do you, as far as is in your power, corrupt your judge and lead astray your adviser?

[3] Gratilla was a lady of rank, who was banished from Rome and Italy by Domitian. Pliny, Epp. iii. 11. See the note in Schweig.'s ed. on ἐπιμήνια.

[4] As knavish priests have often played on the fears and hopes of the superstitious.

[5] Schweighaeuser reads τὸν ὀρνιθάριον. See his note.

[6] 'Κύριε ἐλέησον, Domine miserere. Notissima formula in Christiana ecclesia jam usque a primis temporibus usurpata.' Upton.

CHAPTER VIII.

WHAT IS THE NATURE (ἡ οὐσία) OF THE GOOD?[1]

God is beneficial. But the Good also is beneficial.[2] It is consistent then that where the nature of God is, there also the nature of the good should be. What then is the nature of God?[3] Flesh? Certainly not. An estate in land? By no means. Fame? No. Is it intelligence, knowledge, right reason? Yes. Herein then simply seek the nature of the good; for I suppose that you do not seek it in a plant. No. Do you seek it in an irrational animal? No. If then you seek it in a rational animal, why do you still seek it any where except in the superiority of rational over irrational animals?[4] Now plants have not even the power of using appearances, and for this reason you do not apply the term good to them. The good then requires the use of appearances. Does it require this use only? For if you say that it requires this use only, say that the good, and that happiness and unhappiness are in irrational animals also. But you do not say this, and you do right; for if they possess even in the highest degree the use of appearances, yet they have not the faculty of understanding the use of appearances; and there is good reason for this, for they exist for the purpose of serving others, and they exercise no superiority. For the ass, I suppose, does not exist for any superiority over others. No; but because we had need of a back which is able to bear something; and in truth we had need also of his being able to walk, and for this reason he received also the faculty of making use of appearances, for other

[1] Schweighaeuser observes that the title of this chapter would more correctly be ὁ Θεὸς ἐν ὑμῖν, God in man. There is no better chapter in the book.

[2] Socrates (Xenophon, Mem. iv. 6, 8) concludes 'that the useful is good to him to whom it is useful.'

[3] I do not remember that Epictetus has attempted any other description of the nature of God. He has done more wisely than some who have attempted to answer a question which cannot be answered. But see ii. 14, 11–13.

[4] Compare Cicero, de Offic. i. 27.

wise he would not have been able to walk. And here then the matter stopped. For if he had also received the faculty of comprehending the use of appearances, it is plain that consistently with reason he would not then have been subjected to us, nor would he have done us these services, but he would have been equal to us and like to us.

Will you not then seek the nature of good in the rational animal? for if it is not there, you will not choose to say that it exists in any other thing (plant or animal). What then? are not plants and animals also the works of God? They are; but they are not superior things, nor yet parts of the Gods. But you are a superior thing; you are a portion separated from the deity; you have in yourself a certain portion of him. Why then are you ignorant of your own noble descent?[5] Why do you not know whence you came? will you not remember when you are eating, who you are who eat and whom you feed? When you are in conjunction with a woman, will you not remember who you are who do this thing? When you are in social intercourse, when you are exercising yourself, when you are engaged in discussion, know you not that you are nourishing a god, that you are exercising a god? Wretch, you are carrying about a god with you, and you know it not.[6] Do you think that I mean some God of

[5] Noble descent. See i. c. 9.

The doctrine that God is in man is an old doctrine. Euripides said (Apud Theon. Soph. Progym.):—

'Ο νοῦς γὰρ ἡμῖν ἐστιν ἐν ἑκάστῳ Θεός.

The doctrine became a common place of the poets (Ovid, Fast. vi.), 'Est deus in nobis, agitante calescimus illo;' and Horace, Sat. ii. 6, 79, 'Atque affigit humo divinae particulam aurae.' See i. 14, note 4.

[6] Mrs. Carter has a note here. 'See 1 Cor. vi. 19, 2 Cor. vi. 16, 2 Tim. i. 14, 1 John iii. 24, iv. 12, 13. But though the simple expression of carrying God about with us may seem to have some nearly parallel to it in the New Testament, yet those represent the Almighty in a more venerable manner, as taking the hearts of good men for a temple to dwell in. But the other expressions here of feeding and exercising God, and the whole of the paragraph, and indeed of the Stoic system, show the real sense of even its more decent phrases to be vastly different from that of Scripture.'

The passage in 1 Cor. vi. 19 is, 'What? know ye not that your body is the temple of the Holy Ghost which is in you, which ye have of God and ye are not your own'? This follows v. 18, which is an exhortation to 'flee fornication.' The passage in 2 Cor. vi. 16 is 'And

silver or of gold, and external? You carry him within yourself, and you perceive not that you are polluting him

what agreement hath the temple of God with idols? for ye are the temple of the living God; as God hath said, I will dwell in them and walk in them,' etc. Mrs. Carter has not correctly stated the sense of these two passages.

It is certain that Epictetus knew nothing of the writers of the Epistles in the New Testament; but whence did these writers learn such forms of expression as we find in the passages cited by Mrs. Carter? I believe that they drew them from the Stoic philosophers who wrote before Epictetus and that they applied them to the new religion which they were teaching. The teaching of Paul and of Epictetus does not differ: the spirit of God is in man.

Swedenborg says, 'In these two faculties (rationality and liberty) the Lord resides with every man, whether he be good or evil, they being the Lord's mansions in the human race. But the mansion of the Lord is nearer with a man, in proportion as the man opens the superior degrees by these faculties; for by the opening thereof he comes into superior degrees of love and wisdom, and consequently nearer to the Lord. Hence it may appear that as these degrees are opened, so a man is in the Lord and the Lord in him.' Swedenborg, Angelic Wisdom, 240. Again, 'the faculty of thinking rationally, viewed in itself, is not man's, but God's in man.'

I am not quite sure in what sense the administration of the Eucharist ought to be understood in the church of England service. Some English divines formerly understood, and perhaps some now understand, the ceremony as a commemoration of the blood of Christ shed for us and of his body which was broken; as we see in T. Burnet's Posthumous work (de Fide et Officiis Christianorum, p. 80). It was a commemoration of the last supper of Jesus and the Apostles. But this does not appear to be the sense in which the ceremony is now understood by some priests and by some members of the church of England, whose notions approach near to the doctrine of the Catholic mass. Nor does it appear to be the sense of the prayer made before delivering the bread and wine to the Communicants, for the prayer is 'Grant us, gracious Lord, so to eat the flesh of thy dear son Jesus Christ and to drink his blood that our sinful bodies may be made clean by his body and our souls washed through his most precious blood and that we may evermore dwell in him and he in us.' This is a different thing from Epictetus' notion of God being in man, and also different, as I understand it, from the notion contained in the two passages of Paul; for it is there said generally that the Holy Ghost is in man or God in man, not that God is in man by virtue of a particular ceremony. It should not be omitted that there is after the end of the Communion service an admonition that the sacramental bread and wine remain what they were, 'and that the natural body and blood of our Saviour Christ are in heaven and not here; it being against the truth of Christ's natural body to be at one time in more places than one.' It was affirmed by the Reformers and the best writers of the English church that the presence of Christ in the Eucharist is a spiritual

by impure thoughts and dirty deeds. And if an image of God were present, you would not dare to do any of the things which you are doing: but when God himself is present within and sees all and hears all, you are not ashamed of thinking such things and doing such things, ignorant as you are of your own nature and subject to the anger of God. Then why do we fear when we are sending a young man from the school into active life, lest he should do anything improperly, eat improperly, have improper intercourse with women; and lest the rags in which he is wrapped should debase him, lest fine garments should make him proud? This youth (if he acts thus) does not know his own God: he knows not with whom he sets out (into the world). But can we endure when he says 'I wish I had you (God) with me.' Have you not God with you? and do you seek for any other, when you have him? or will God tell you any thing else than this? If you were a statue of Phidias, either Athena or Zeus, you would think both of yourself and of the artist, and if you had any understanding (power of perception) you would try to do nothing unworthy of him who made you or of yourself, and try not to appear in an unbecoming dress (attitude) to those who look on you. But now because Zeus has made you, for this reason do you care not how you shall appear? And yet is the artist (in the one case) like the artist in the other? or the work in the one case like the other? And what work of an artist, for instance, has in itself the faculties, which the artist shows in making it? Is it not marble or bronze, or gold or ivory? and the Athena of Phidias when she has once extended the hand and received in it the figure of Victory[7] stands in that

presence, and in this opinion they followed Calvin and the Swiss divines: and yet in the Prayer book we have the language that I have quoted; and even Calvin, who only maintained a spiritual presence, said, 'that the verity is nevertheless joined to the signs, and that in the sacrament we have "true Communion in Christ's body and blood"' (Contemporary Review, p. 464, August 1874). What would Epictetus have thought of the subtleties of our days?

[7] The Athena of Phidias was in the Parthenon on the Athenian Acropolis, a colossal chryselephantine statue, that is, a frame work of wood, covered with ivory and gold (Pausanias, i. 24). The figure of

attitude for ever. But the works of God have power of motion, they breathe, they have the faculty of using the appearances of things, and the power of examining them. Being the work of such an artist do you dishonour him? And what shall I say, not only that he made you, but also entrusted you to yourself and made you a deposit to yourself? Will you not think of this too, but do you also dishonour your guardianship? But if God had entrusted an orphan to you, would you thus neglect him? He has delivered yourself to your own care, and says, I had no one fitter to intrust him to than yourself: keep him for me such as he is by nature, modest, faithful, erect, unterrified, free from passion and perturbation. And then you do not keep him such.

But some will say, whence has this fellow got the arrogance which he displays and these supercilious looks?—I have not yet so much gravity as befits a philosopher; for I do not yet feel confidence in what I have learned and in what I have assented to: I still fear my own weakness. Let me get confidence and then you shall see a countenance such as I ought to have and an attitude such as I ought to have: then I will show to you the statue, when it is perfected, when it is polished. What do you expect? a supercilious countenance? Does the Zeus at Olympia[8] lift up his brow? No, his look is fixed as becomes him who is ready to say

> Irrevocable is my word and shall not fail.—Iliad, i. 526.

Such will I show myself to you, faithful, modest, noble, free from perturbation—What, and immortal too, exempt from old age, and from sickness? No, but dying as becomes a god, sickening as becomes a god. This power I possess; this I can do. But the rest I do not possess, nor can I do. I will show the nerves (strength) of a philosopher. What

Victory stood on the hand of the goddess, as we frequently see in coins. See. i. 6, 23, and the note in Schweig.'s edition. Cicero, de Natura Deorum, iii. 34.

[8] The great statue at Olympia was the work of Phidias (Pausanias, v. 11). It was a seated colossal chryselephantine statue, and held a Victory in the right hand.

nerves[9] are these? A desire never disappointed, an aversion[10] which never falls on that which it would avoid, a proper pursuit (ὁρμήν), a diligent purpose, an assent which is not rash. These you shall see.

CHAPTER IX.

THAT WHEN WE CANNOT FULFIL THAT WHICH THE CHARACTER OF A MAN PROMISES, WE ASSUME THE CHARACTER OF A PHILOSOPHER.

It is no common (easy) thing to do this only, to fulfil the promise of a man's nature. For what is a man? The answer is, a rational and mortal being. Then by the rational faculty from whom are we separated?[1] From wild beasts. And from what others? From sheep and like animals. Take care then to do nothing like a wild beast; but if you do, you have lost the character of a man; you have not fulfilled your promise. See that you do nothing like a sheep; but if you do, in this case also the man is lost. What then do we do as sheep? When we act gluttonously, when we act lewdly, when we act rashly, filthily, inconsiderately, to what have we declined? To sheep. What have we lost? The rational faculty. When we act contentiously and harmfully and passionately, and violently, to what have we declined? To wild beasts. Consequently some of us are great wild beasts, and others little beasts, of a bad disposition and

[9] An allusion to the combatants in the public exercises, who used to show their shoulders, muscles and sinews as a proof of their strength. See i. 4, ii. 18, iii. 22 (Mrs. Carter).

[10] ἔκκλισιν. See Book iii. c. 2.

[1] 'The abuse of the faculties, which are proper to man, called rationality and liberty, is the origin of evil. By rationality is meant the faculty of understanding truths and thence falses, and goods and then evils; and by liberty is meant the faculty of thinking, willing and acting freely—and these faculties distinguish man from beasts.' Swedenborg, Angelic Wisdom, 264 and also 240. See Epictetus, ii. c. 8,

small, whence we may say, Let me be eaten by a lion.[2] But in all these ways the promise of a man acting as a man is destroyed. For when is a conjunctive (complex) proposition maintained?[3] When it fulfils what its nature promises; so that the preservation of a complex proposition is when it is a conjunction of truths. When is a disjunctive maintained? When it fulfils what it promises. When are flutes, a lyre, a horse, a dog, preserved? (when they severally keep their promise). What is the wonder then if man also in like manner is preserved, and in like manner is lost? Each man is improved and preserved by corresponding acts, the carpenter by acts of carpentry, the grammarian by acts of grammar. But if a man accustoms himself to write ungrammatically, of necessity his art will be corrupted and destroyed. Thus modest actions preserve the modest man, and immodest actions destroy him: and actions of fidelity preserve the faithful man, and the contrary actions destroy him. And on the other hand contrary actions strengthen contrary characters: shamelessness strengthens the shameless man, faithlessness the faithless man, abusive words the abusive man, anger the man of an angry temper, and unequal receiving and giving make the avaricious man more avaricious.

For this reason philosophers admonish us not to be satisfied with learning only, but also to add study, and then practice.[4] For we have long been accustomed to do

[2] This seems to be a proverb. If I am eaten, let me be eaten by the nobler animal.

[3] A conjunctive or complex (συμπεπλεγμένον) axiom or lemma. Gellius (xvi. 8) gives an example: 'P. Scipio, the son of Paulus, was both twice consul and triumphed, and exercised the censorship and was the colleague of L. Mummius in his censorship.' Gellius adds, 'in every conjunctive if there is one falsehood, though the other parts are true, the whole is said to be false.' For the whole is proposed as true: therefore if one part is false, the whole is not true. The disjunctive (διεζευγμένον) is of this kind: 'pleasure is either bad or good, or neither good nor bad.'

[4] We often say a man learns a particular thing; and there are men who profess to teach certain things, such as a language, or an art; and they mean by teaching that the taught shall learn; and learning means that they shall be able to do what they learn. He who teaches an art professes that the scholar shall be able to practise the art, the art of

contrary things, and we put in practice opinions which are contrary to true opinions. If then we shall not also put in practice right opinions, we shall be nothing more than the expositors of the opinions of others. For now who among us is not able to discourse according to the rules of art about good and evil things (in this fashion)? That of things some are good, and some are bad, and some are indifferent: the good then are virtues, and the things which participate in virtues; and the bad are the contrary; and the indifferent are wealth, health, reputation.—Then, if in the midst of our talk there should happen some greater noise than usual, or some of those who are present should laugh at us, we are disturbed. Philosopher, where are the things which you were talking about? Whence did you produce and utter them. From the lips, and thence only. Why then do you corrupt the aids provided by others? Why do you treat the weightiest matters as if you were playing a game of dice? For it is one thing to lay up bread and wine as in a storehouse, and another thing to eat. That which has been eaten, is digested, distributed, and is become sinews, flesh, bones, blood, healthy colour, healthy breath. Whatever is stored up, when you choose you can readily take and show it; but you have no other advantage from it except so far as to appear to possess it. For what is the difference between explaining these doctrines and those of men who have different opinions? Sit down now and explain according to the rules of art the opinions of Epicurus, and perhaps you will explain his opinions in a more useful manner than Epicurus himself.[5] Why then do you call yourself a

making shoes for example, or other useful things. There are men who profess to teach religion, and morality, and virtue generally. These men may tell us what they conceive to be religion, and morality, and virtue; and those who are said to be taught may know what their teachers have told them. But the learning of religion, and of morality and of virtue, mean that the learner will do the acts of religion and of morality and of virtue; which is a very different thing from knowing what the acts of religion, of morality, and of virtue are. The teacher's teaching is in fact only made efficient by his example, by his doing that which he teaches.

[5] 'He is not a Stoic philosopher, who can only explain in a subtle and proper manner the Stoic principles: for the same person can explain the principles of Epicurus, of course for the purpose of refuting

Stoic? Why do you deceive the many? Why do you act the part of a Jew,[6] when you are a Greek? Do you not see how (why) each is called a Jew, or a Syrian or an Egyptian? and when we see a man inclining to two sides, we are accustomed to say, This man is not a Jew, but he acts as one. But when he has assumed the affects of one who has been imbued with Jewish doctrine and has adopted that sect, then he is in fact and he is named a Jew.[7] Thus we too being falsely imbued (baptized), are in name Jews, but in fact we are something else. Our affects (feelings) are inconsistent with our words; we are far from practising what we say, and that of which we are proud, as if we knew it. Thus being unable to fulfil even what the character of a man promises, we even add to it the profession of a philosopher, which is as heavy a burden, as if a man who is unable to bear ten pounds should attempt to raise the stone which Ajax[8] lifted.

them, and perhaps he can explain them better than Epicurus himself. Consequently he might be at the same time a Stoic and an Epicurean; which is absurd.'—Schweig. He means that the mere knowledge of Stoic opinions does not make a man a Stoic, or any other philosopher. A man must according to Stoic principles practise them in order to be a Stoic philosopher. So if we say that a man is a religious man, he must do the acts which his religion teaches; for it is by his acts only that we can know him to be a religious man. What he says and professes may be false; and no man knows except himself whether his words and professions are true. The uniformity, regularity, and consistency of his acts are evidence which cannot be mistaken.

[6] It has been suggested that Epictetus confounded under the name of Jews those who were Jews and those who were Christians. We know that some Jews became Christians. But see Schweig.'s note 1 and note 7.

[7] It is possible, as I have said, that by Jews Epictetus means Christians, for Christians and Jews are evidently confounded by some writers, as the first Christians were of the Jewish nation. In book iv. c. 7, Epictetus gives the name of Galilaeans to the Jews. The term Galilaeans points to the country of the great teacher. Paul says (Romans, ii. 28), 'For he is not a Jew, which is one outwardly—but he is a Jew which is one inwardly,' etc. His remarks (ii. 17–29) on the man 'who is called a Jew, and rests in the law and makes his boast of God' may be compared with what Epictetus says of a man who is called a philosopher, and does not practise that which he professes.

[8] See ii. 24, 26; Iliad, vii. 264, etc.; Juvenal, xv. 65,

Nec hunc lapidem, quales et Turnus et Ajax
Vel quo Tydides percussit pondere coxam
Aeneae.—Upton.

CHAPTER X.

HOW WE MAY DISCOVER THE DUTIES OF LIFE FROM NAMES.

CONSIDER who you are. In the first place, you are a man;[1] and this is one who has nothing superior to the faculty of the will, but all other things subjected to it; and the faculty itself he possesses unenslaved and free from subjection. Consider then from what things you have been separated by reason. You have been separated from wild beasts: you have been separated from domestic animals (προβάτων). Further, you are a citizen of the world,[2] and a part of it, not one of the subservient (serving), but one of the principal (ruling) parts, for you are capable of comprehending the divine administration and of considering the connexion of things. What then does the character of a citizen promise (profess)? To hold nothing as profitable to himself; to deliberate about nothing as if he were detached from the community, but to act as the hand or foot would do, if they had reason and understood the constitution of nature, for they would never put themselves in motion nor desire any thing otherwise than with reference to the whole. Therefore the philosophers say well, that if the good man had foreknowledge of what would happen, he would co-operate towards his own sickness and death and mutilation, since he knows[3] that these things are assigned to him according to the universal

[1] Cicero (de Fin. iv. 10); Seneca, Ep. 95.

[2] See i. 9. M. Antoninus, vi. 44: 'But my nature is rational and social; and my city and country, so far as I am Antoninus, is Rome, but so far as I am a man, it is the world.'

I have here translated προβάτων by 'domestic animals;' I suppose that the bovine species, and sheep and goats are meant.

[3] This may appear extravagant; but it is possible to explain it, and even to assent to it. If a man believes that all is wisely arranged in the course of human events, he would not even try to resist that which he knows it is appointed for him to suffer: he would submit and he would endure. If Epictetus means that the man would actively promote the end or purpose which he foreknew, in order that his acts may be consistent with what he foreknows and with his duty, perhaps the philosopher's saying is too hard to deal with; and as it rests on an impossible assumption of foreknowledge, we may be here wiser than the philosophers, if we say no more about it. Compare Seneca, de Provid. c. 5.

arrangement, and that the whole is superior to the part, and the state to the citizen.[4] But now because we do not know the future, it is our duty to stick to the things which are in their nature more suitable for our choice, for we were made among other things for this.

After this remember that you are a son. What does this character promise? To consider that every thing which is the son's belongs to the father, to obey him in all things, never to blame him to another, nor to say or do any thing which does him injury, to yield to him in all things and give way, co-operating with him as far as you can. After this know that you are a brother also, and that to this character it is due to make concessions; to be easily persuaded, to speak good of your brother, never to claim in opposition to him any of the things which are independent of the will, but readily to give them up, that you may have the larger share in what is dependent on the will. For see what a thing it is, in place of a lettuce, if it should so happen, or a seat, to gain for yourself goodness of disposition. How great is the advantage.[5]

Next to this, if you are a senator of any state, remember that you are a senator: if a youth, that you are a youth: if an old man, that you are an old man; for each of such names, if it comes to be examined, marks out the proper duties. But if you go and blame your brother, I say to you, You have forgotten who you are and what is your name. In the next place, if you were a smith and made a wrong use of the hammer, you would have forgotten the smith; and if you have forgotten the brother and instead of a brother have become an enemy, would you appear not to have changed one thing for another in that case? And if instead of a man, who is a tame animal and social, you are become a mischievous wild beast, treacherous, and biting, have you lost nothing? But, (I suppose) you must lose a bit of money that you may suffer damage? And does the loss of nothing else do a man damage? If you

[4] Antoninus, vi. 42: 'We are all working together to one end, some with knowledge and design, and others without knowing what they do.'

[5] A lettuce is an example of the most trifling thing. A seat probably means a seat of superiority, a magistrate's seat, a Roman sella curulis.

had lost the art of grammar or music, would you think the loss of it a damage? and if you shall lose modesty, moderation (καταστολήν) and gentleness, do you think the loss nothing? And yet the things first mentioned are lost by some cause external and independent of the will, and the second by our own fault; and as to the first neither to have them nor to lose them is shameful; but as to the second, not to have them and to lose them is shameful and matter of reproach and a misfortune. What does the pathic lose? He loses the (character of) man. What does he lose who makes the pathic what he is? Many other things; and he also loses the man no less than the other. What does he lose who commits adultery? He loses the (character of the) modest, the temperate, the decent, the citizen, the neighbour. What does he lose who is angry? Something else. What does the coward lose? Something else. No man is bad without suffering some loss and damage. If then you look for the damage in the loss of money only, all these men receive no harm or damage; it may be, they have even profit and gain, when they acquire a bit of money by any of these deeds. But consider that if you refer every thing to a small coin, not even he who loses his nose is in your opinion damaged. Yes, you say, for he is mutilated in his body. Well; but does he who has lost his smell only lose nothing? Is there then no energy of the soul which is an advantage to him who possesses it, and a damage to him who has lost it?—Tell me what sort (of energy) you mean.—Have we not a natural modesty?—We have.—Does he who loses this sustain no damage? is he deprived of nothing, does he part with nothing of the things which belong to him? Have we not naturally fidelity? natural affection, a natural disposition to help others, a natural disposition to forbearance? The man then who allows himself to be damaged in these matters, can he be free from harm and uninjured[6] What then? shall I not hurt him, who has hurt me?[7] In the

[6] οὗτος ἢ ἀβλαβής. See Schweig.'s note.

[7] Socrates. We must by no means then do an act of injustice. Crito. Certainly not. Socrates. Nor yet when you are wronged must you do wrong in return, as most people think, since you must in no way do an unjust act. Plato, Crito, c. 10.

first place consider what hurt (βλάβη) is, and remember what you have heard from the philosophers. For if the good consists in the will (purpose, intention, προαιρέσει), and the evil also in the will,[8] see if what you say is not this: What then, since that man has hurt himself by doing an unjust act to me, shall I not hurt myself by doing some unjust act to him? Why do we not imagine to ourselves (mentally think of) something of this kind? But where there is any detriment to the body or to our possession, there is harm there; and where the same thing happens to the faculty of the will, there is (you suppose) no harm; for he who has been deceived or he who has done an unjust act neither suffers in the head nor in the eye nor in the hip, nor does he lose his estate; and we wish for nothing else than (security to) these things. But whether we shall have the will modest and faithful or shameless and faithless, we care not the least, except only in the school so far as a few words are concerned. Therefore our proficiency is limited to these few words; but beyond them it does not exist even in the slightest degree.[9]

CHAPTER XI.

WHAT THE BEGINNING OF PHILOSOPHY IS.

The beginning of philosophy to him at least who enters on it in the right way and by the door, is a consciousness of his own weakness and inability about necessary things. For we come into the world with no natural notion of a right angled triangle, or of a diesis (a quarter tone), or of a half tone; but we learn each of these things by a certain transmission according to art; and for this reason

[8] See the beginning of ii. 16.

[9] The same remark will apply to most dissertations spoken or written on moral subjects: they are exercises of skill for him who delivers or writes them, or matter for criticism and perhaps a way of spending an idle hour for him who listens; and that is all. Epictetus blames our indolence and indifference as to acts, and the trifling of the schools of philosophy in disputation.

those who do not know them, do not think that they know them. But as to good and evil, and beautiful and ugly, and becoming and unbecoming, and happiness and misfortune, and proper and improper, and what we ought to do and what we ought not to do, who ever came into the world without having an innate idea of them? Wherefore we all use these names, and we endeavour to fit the preconceptions[1] to the several cases (things) thus: he has done well, he has not done well; he has done as he ought not as he ought; he has been unfortunate, he has been fortunate; he is unjust, he is just: who does not use these names? who among us defers the use of them till he has learned them, as he defers the use of the words about lines (geometrical figures) or sounds? And the cause of this is that we come into the world already taught as it were by nature some things on this matter (τόπον), and proceeding from these we have added to them self-conceit (οἴησιν).[2] For why, a man says, do I not know the beautiful and the ugly? Have I not the notion of it? You have. Do I not adapt it to particulars? You do. Do I not then adapt it properly? In that lies the whole question; and conceit is added here. For beginning from these things which are admitted men proceed to that which is matter of dispute by means of unsuitable adaptation; for if they possessed this power of adaptation in addition to those things, what would hinder them from being perfect? But now since you think that you properly adapt the preconceptions to the particulars, tell me whence you derive this (assume that you do so). Because I think so. But it does not seem so to another, and he thinks that he also makes a proper adaptation; or does he not think so? He does think so. Is it possible then that both of you can properly apply the preconceptions to things about which you have contrary opinions? It is not possible. Can you then show us anything better towards adapting the preconceptions beyond your thinking that you do? Does the madman do any other things than the things which seem to him right? Is then this criterion sufficient for him also? It is not sufficient.

[1] See i. c. 2.

[2] See Cicero's use of 'opinatio' (Tusc. iv. 11).

Come then to something which is superior to seeming (τοῦ δοκεῖν). What is this?

Observe, this is the beginning of philosophy, a perception of the disagreement of men with one another, and an inquiry into the cause of the disagreement, and a condemnation and distrust of that which only 'seems,' and a certain investigation of that which 'seems' whether it 'seems' rightly, and a discovery of some rule (κανόνος), as we have discovered a balance in the determination of weights, and a carpenter's rule (or square) in the case of straight and crooked things.—This is the beginning of philosophy. Must we say that all things are right which seem so to all?[3] And how is it possible that contradictions can be right?—Not all then, but all which seem to us to be right.—How more to you than those which seem right to the Syrians? why more than what seem right to the Egyptians? why more than what seems right to me or to any other man? Not at all more. What then 'seems' to every man is not sufficient for determining what 'is;' for neither in the case of weights or measures are we satisfied with the bare appearance, but in each case we have discovered a certain rule. In this matter then is there no rule superior to what 'seems'? And how is it possible that the most necessary things among men should have no sign (mark), and be incapable of being discovered? There is then some rule. And why then do we not seek the rule and discover it, and afterwards use it without varying from it, not even stretching out the finger without it?[4] For this, I think, is that which when it is discovered cures of their madness those who use mere 'seeming' as a measure, and misuse it; so that for the future proceeding from certain things (principles) known and made clear we may use in the case of particular things the preconceptions which are distinctly fixed.

What is the matter presented to us about which we are inquiring? Pleasure (for example). Subject it to the rule, throw it into the balance. Ought the good to be

[3] See Schweig.'s note.

[4] Doing nothing without the rule. This is a Greek proverb, used also by Persius, Sat. v. 119; compare Cicero, de Fin. iii. 17; and Antoninus, ii. 16.

such a thing that it is fit that we have confidence in it? Yes. And in which we ought to confide? It ought to be. Is it fit to trust to any thing which is insecure? No. Is then pleasure any thing secure? No. Take it then and throw it out of the scale, and drive it far away from the place of good things. But if you are not sharp-sighted, and one balance is not enough for you, bring another. Is it fit to be elated over what is good? Yes. Is it proper then to be elated over present pleasure? See that you do not say that it is proper; but if you do, I shall then not think you worthy even of the balance.[5] Thus things are tested and weighed when the rules are ready. And to philosophize is this, to examine and confirm the rules; and then to use them when they are known is the act of a wise and good man.[6]

CHAPTER XII.

OF DISPUTATION OR DISCUSSION.

WHAT things a man must learn in order to be able to apply the art of disputation, has been accurately shown by our philosophers (the Stoics); but with respect to the proper use of the things, we are entirely without practice. Only give to any of us, whom you please, an illiterate man to discuss with, and he can not discover how to deal with the man. But when he has moved the man a little, if he answers beside the purpose, he does not know how to treat him, but he then either abuses or ridicules him, and says, He is an illiterate man; it is not possible to do any thing

[5] That is, so far shall I consider you from being able to judge rightly of things without a balance that I shall understand that not even with the aid of a balance can you do it, that you cannot even use a balance, and consequently that you are not worth a single word from me. Schweig.

[6] This is a just conclusion. We must fix the canons or rules by which things are tried; and then the rules may be applied by the wise and good to all cases.

with him. Now a guide, when he has found a man out of the road leads him into the right way: he does not ridicule or abuse him and then leave him. Do you also show the illiterate man the truth, and you will see that he follows. But so long as you do not show him the truth, do not ridicule him, but rather feel your own incapacity.

How then did Socrates act? He used to compel his adversary in disputation to bear testimony to him, and he wanted no other witness.[1] Therefore he could say, 'I care not for other witnesses, but I am always satisfied with the evidence (testimony) of my adversary, and I do not ask the opinion of others, but only the opinion of him who is disputing with me.' For he used to make the conclusions drawn from natural notions[2] so plain that every man saw the contradiction (if it existed) and withdrew from it (thus): Does the envious[3] man rejoice? By no means, but he is rather pained.[4] Well, Do you think that envy is pain over evils? and what envy is there of evils? Therefore he made his adversary say that envy is pain over good things. Well then, would any man envy those who are nothing to him? By no means. Thus having completed the notion and distinctly fixed it he

[1] This is what is said in the Gorgias of Plato, p. 472, 474.

[2] The word is ἔννοιαι, which Cicero explains to be the same as προλήψεις. Acad. Pr. ii. 10.

[3] Socrates' notion of envy is stated by Xenophon (Mem. iii. 9, 8), to be this: 'it is the pain or vexation which men have at the prosperity of their friends, and that such are the only envious persons.' Bishop Butler gives a better definition; at least a more complete description of the thing. 'Emulation is merely the desire and hope of equality with or superiority over others, with whom we may compare ourselves. There does not appear to be any *other grief* in the natural passion, but only *that want* which is implied in desire. However this may be so strong as to be the occasion of great *grief*. To desire the attainment of this equality or superiority, by the *particular means* of others being brought down to our level, or below it, is, I think, the distinct notion of envy. From whence it is easy to see, that the real end which the natural passion, emulation, and which the unlawful one, envy, aims at is the same; namely, that equality or superiority: and consequently that to do mischief is not the end of envy, but merely the means it makes use of to attain its end.'—Sermons upon Human Nature, I.

[4] I have omitted the words ἀπὸ τοῦ ἐναντίου ἐκίνησε τὸν πλήσιον. I see no sense in them; and the text is plain without them.

would go away without saying to his adversary, Define to me envy; and if the adversary had defined envy, he did not say, You have defined it badly, for the terms of the definition do not correspond to the thing defined—These are technical terms, and for this reason disagreeable and hardly intelligible to illiterate men, which terms we (philosophers) cannot lay aside. But that the illiterate man himself, who follows the appearances presented to him, should be able to concede any thing or reject it, we can never by the use of these terms move him to do.[5] Accordingly being conscious of our own inability, we do not attempt the thing; at least such of us as have any caution do not. But the greater part and the rash, when they enter into such disputations, confuse themselves and confuse others; and finally abusing their adversaries and abused by them, they walk away.

Now this was the first and chief peculiarity of Socrates, never to be irritated in argument, never to utter any thing abusive, any thing insulting, but to bear with abusive persons and to put an end to the quarrel. If you would know what great power he had in this way, read the Symposium of Xenophon,[6] and you will see how many quarrels he put an end to. Hence with good reason in the poets also this power is most highly praised,

> Quickly with skill he settles great disputes.
>
> Hesiod, Theogony, v. 87.

Well then; the matter is not now very safe, and particularly at Rome; for he who attempts to do it, must not do it in a corner, you may be sure, but must go to a man of consular rank, if it so happen, or to a rich man, and ask him, Can you tell me, Sir, to whose care you have entrusted your horses? I can tell you. Have you entrusted them to any person indifferently and to one who has no experience of horses?—By no means.—Well then; can you tell me to whom you entrust your gold or silver things or your vestments? I don't entrust even these to

[5] I am not sure that I have understood rightly ἐξ ὧν δὲ αὐτός at the beginning of this sentence.

[6] The Symposium or Banquet of Xenophon is extant. Compare Epictetus, iii. 16, 5, and iv. c. 5, the beginning.

any one indifferently. Well; your own body, have you already considered about entrusting the care of it to any person?—Certainly.—To a man of experience, I suppose, and one acquainted with the aliptic,[7] or with the healing art?—Without doubt.—Are these the best things that you have, or do you also possess something else which is better than all these?—What kind of a thing do you mean?—That I mean which makes use of these things, and tests each of them, and deliberates.—Is it the soul that you mean?—You think right, for it is the soul that I mean.—In truth I do think that the soul is a much better thing than all the others which I possess.—Can you then show us in what way you have taken care of the soul? for it is not likely that you, who are so wise a man and have a reputation in the city, inconsiderately and carelessly allow the most valuable thing that you possess to be neglected and to perish.—Certainly not.—But have you taken care of the soul yourself; and have you learned from another to do this, or have you discovered the means yourself?—Here comes the danger that in the first place he may say, What is this to you, my good man, who are you? Next, if you persist in troubling him, there is danger that he may raise his hands and give you blows. I was once myself also an admirer of this mode of instruction until I fell into these dangers.[8]

CHAPTER XIII.

ON ANXIETY (SOLICITUDE).

When I see a man anxious, I say, What does this man want? If he did not want some thing which is not in his power, how could he be anxious? For this reason a lute

[7] The aliptic art is the art of anointing and rubbing, one of the best means of maintaining a body in health. The iatric or healing art is the art of restoring to health a diseased body. The aliptic art is also equivalent to the gymnastic art, or the art of preparing for gymnastic exercises, which are also a means of preserving the body's health, when the exercises are good and moderate.

[8] Epictetus in speaking of himself and of his experience at Rome.

player when he is singing by himself has no anxiety, but when he enters the theatre, he is anxious even if he has a good voice and plays well on the lute; for he not only wishes to sing well, but also to obtain applause: but this is not in his power. Accordingly, where he has skill, there he has confidence. Bring any single person who knows nothing of music, and the musician does not care for him. But in the matter where a man knows nothing and has not been practised, there he is anxious. What matter is this? He knows not what a crowd is or what the praise of a crowd is. However he has learned to strike the lowest chord and the highest;[1] but what the praise of the many is, and what power it has in life he neither knows nor has he thought about it. Hence he must of necessity tremble and grow pale. I cannot then say that a man is not a lute player when I see him afraid, but I can say something else, and not one thing, but many. And first of all I call him a stranger and say, This man does not know in what part of the world he is, but though he has been here so long, he is ignorant of the laws of the State and the customs, and what is permitted and what is not; and he has never employed any lawyer to tell him and to explain the laws. But a man does not write a will, if he does not know how it ought to be written, or he employs a person who does know; nor does he rashly seal a bond or write a security. But he uses his desire without a lawyer's advice, and aversion, and pursuit (movement), and attempt and purpose. How do you mean without a lawyer? He does not know that he wills what is not allowed, and does not will that which is of necessity; and he does not know either what is his own or what is another man's; but if he did know, he would never be impeded, he would never be hindered, he would not be anxious. How so?—Is any man then afraid about things which are not evils?—No.—Is he afraid about things which are evils, but still so far within his power that they may not happen?—Certainly he is not.—If then the things which are independent of the will are neither good nor bad, and all things which do depend on

[1] See i. 29, note 20.

the will are within our power, and no man can either take them from us or give them to us, if we do not choose, where is room left for anxiety? But we are anxious about our poor body, our little property, about the will of Caesar; but not anxious about things internal. Are we anxious about not forming a false opinion?—No, for this is in my power.—About not exerting our movements contrary to nature?—No, not even about this.—When then you see a man pale, as the physician says, judging from the complexion, this man's spleen is disordered, that man's liver; so also say, this man's desire and aversion are disordered, he is not in the right way, he is in a fever. For nothing else changes the colour, or causes trembling or chattering of the teeth, or causes a man to

> Sink in his knees and shift from foot to foot.—Iliad, xiii. 281.

For this reason when Zeno was going to meet Antigonus,[2] he was not anxious, for Antigonus had no power over any of the things which Zeno admired; and Zeno did not care for those things over which Antigonus had power. But Antigonus was anxious when he was going to meet Zeno, for he wished to please Zeno; but this was a thing external (out of his power). But Zeno did not want to please Antigonus; for no man who is skilled in any art wishes to please one who has no such skill.

Should I try to please you? Why? I suppose, you know the measure by which one man is estimated by another. Have you taken pains to learn what is a good man and what is a bad man, and how a man becomes one or the other? Why then are you not good yourself?—How, he replies, am I not good?—Because no good man laments or groans or weeps, no good man is pale and trembles, or says, How will he receive me, how will he listen to me?—Slave, just as it pleases him. Why do you care about what belongs to others? Is it now his fault if he receives badly what proceeds from you?—Certainly.—

[2] In Diogenes Laertius (Zeno, vii.) there is a letter from Antigonus to Zeno and Zeno's answer. Simplicius (note on the Encheiridion, c. 51) supposes this Antigonus to be the King of Syria; but Upton remarks that it is Antigonus Gonatas, king of Macedonia.

And is it possible that a fault should be one man's, and the evil in another?—No.—Why then are you anxious about that which belongs to others?—Your question is reasonable; but I am anxious how I shall speak to him. Cannot you then speak to him as you choose?—But I fear that I may be disconcerted?—If you are going to write the name of Dion, are you afraid that you would be disconcerted?—By no means.—Why? is it not because you have practised writing the name?—Certainly.—Well, if you were going to read the name, would you not feel the same? and why? Because every art has a certain strength and confidence in the things which belong to it. —Have you then not practised speaking? and what else did you learn in the school? Syllogisms and sophistical propositions?[3] For what purpose? was it not for the purpose of discoursing skilfully? and is not discoursing skilfully the same as discoursing seasonably and cautiously and with intelligence, and also without making mistakes and without hindrance, and besides all this with confidence?—Yes.—When then you are mounted on a horse and go into a plain, are you anxious at being matched against a man who is on foot, and anxious in a matter in which you are practised, and he is not?—Yes, but that person (to whom I am going to speak) has power to kill me.[4] Speak the truth then, unhappy man, and do not brag, nor claim to be a philosopher, nor refuse to acknowledge your masters, but so long as you present this handle in your body, follow every man who is stronger than yourself. Socrates used to practise speaking, he who talked as he did to the tyrants,[5] to the dicasts (judges), he who talked in his prison. Diogenes had practised speaking, he who spoke as he did to Alexander, to the pirates, to the person

[3] See i. c. 7.

[4] The original is 'but that person (ἐκεῖνος) has power to kill me.' 'That person' must be the person already mentioned, and Mrs. Carter has done right in adding this explanation.

[5] The Thirty tyrants of Athens, as they were named (Xenophon, Hellenica, ii.). The talk of Socrates with Critias and Charicles two of the Thirty is reported in Xenophon's Memorabilia (i. 2, 33). The defence of Socrates before those who tried him and his conversation in prison are reported in Plato's Apology, and in the Phaedon and Crito. Diogenes was captured by some pirates and sold (iv. 1, 115).

who bought him. These men were confident in the things which they practised.[6] But do you walk off to your own affairs and never leave them: go and sit in a corner, and weave syllogisms, and propose them to another. There is not in you the man who can rule a state.

CHAPTER XIV.

TO NASO.

When a certain Roman entered with his son and listened to one reading, Epictetus said, This is the method of instruction; and he stopped. When the Roman asked him to go on, Epictetus said, Every art when it is taught causes labour to him who is unacquainted with it and is unskilled in it, and indeed the things which proceed from the arts immediately show their use in the purpose for which they were made; and most of them contain something attractive and pleasing. For indeed to be present and to observe how a shoemaker learns is not a pleasant thing; but the shoe is useful and also not disagreeable to look at. And the discipline of a smith when he is learning is very disagreeable to one who chances to be present and is a stranger to the art: but the work shows the use of the art. But you will see this much more in music; for if you are present while a person is learning, the discipline will appear most disagreeable; and yet the results of music are pleasing and delightful to those who know nothing of music. And here we conceive the work of a philosopher to be something of this kind: he must adapt his wish (*βούλησιν*) to what is going on,[1] so that neither any of the things which are taking place shall take place contrary to our wish, nor any of the things which do not take place shall not take place when we wish that they

[6] There is some corruption here.

[1] Encheiridion, c. 8: 'Do not seek (wish) that things which take place shall take place as you desire, but desire that things which take place shall take place as they do, and you will live a tranquil life.'

should. From this the result is to those who have so arranged the work of philosophy, not to fail in the desire, nor to fall in with that which they would avoid; without uneasiness, without fear, without perturbation to pass through life themselves, together with their associates maintaining the relations both natural and acquired,[2] as the relation of son, of father, of brother, of citizen, of man, of wife, of neighbour, of fellow traveller, of ruler, of ruled. The work of a philosopher we conceive to be something like this. It remains next to inquire how this must be accomplished.

We see then that the carpenter (*τέκτων*) when he has learned certain things becomes a carpenter; the pilot by learning certain things becomes a pilot. May it not then in philosophy also not be sufficient to wish to be wise and good, and that there is also a necessity to learn certain things? We inquire then what these things are. The philosophers say that we ought first to learn that there is a God and that he provides for all things; also that it is not possible to conceal from him our acts, or even our intentions and thoughts.[3] The next thing is to learn what is the nature

[2] Compare iii. 2. 4, iv. 8. 20. Antoninus (viii. 27) writes: 'There are three relations [between thee and other things]: the one to the body which surrounds thee; the second to the divine cause from which all things come to all; and the third to those who live with thee.' This is precise, true and practical. Those who object to 'the divine cause,' may write in place of it 'the nature and constitution of things;' for there is a constitution of things, which the philosopher attempts to discover; and for most practical purposes, it is immaterial whether we say that it is of divine origin or has some other origin, or no origin can be discovered. The fact remains that a constitution of things exists; or, if that expression be not accepted, we may say that we conceive that it exists and we cannot help thinking so.

[3] See i. 14. 13, ii. 8. 14. Socrates (Xen. Mem. i. 1. 19) said the same. That man should make himself like the Gods is said also by Antoninus, x. 8.—See Plato, De Legg. i. 4. (Upton.)

When God is said to provide for all things, this is what the Greeks called *πρόνοια*, providence. (Epictetus, i. 16, iii. 17.) In the second of these passages there is a short answer to some objections made to Providence.

Epictetus could only know or believe what God is by the observation of phaenomena; and he could only know what he supposed to be God's providence by observing his administration of the world and all that happens in it. Among other works of God is man, who possesses

of the Gods; for such as they are discovered to be, he, who would please and obey them, must try with all his power to be like them. If the divine is faithful, man also must be faithful; if it is free, man also must be free; if beneficent, man also must be beneficent; if magnanimous, man also must be magnanimous; as being then an imitator of God he must do and say every thing consistently with this fact.

With what then must we begin? If you will enter on the discussion, I will tell you that you must first understand names[4] (words).—So then you say that I do not now understand names.—You do not understand them.—How then do I use them?—Just as the illiterate use written language, as cattle use appearances: for use is one thing, understanding is another. But if you think that you understand them, produce whatever word you please, and let us try whether we understand it.—But it is a disagreeable thing for a man to be confuted who is now old, and, it may be, has now served his three campaigns.—I too know this: for now you are come to me as if you were in want of nothing: and what could you even imagine to be wanting to you? You are rich, you have children and a wife perhaps, and many slaves: Caesar

certain intellectual powers which enable him to form a judgment of God's works, and a judgment of man himself. Man has or is supposed to have certain moral sentiments, or a capacity of acquiring them in some way. On the supposition that all man's powers are the gift of God, man's power of judging what happens in the world under God's providence is the gift of God; and if he should not be satisfied with God's administration, we have the conclusion that man, whose powers are from God, condemns that administration which is also from God. Thus God and man, who is God's work, are in opposition to one another.

If a man rejects the belief in a deity and in a providence, because of the contradictions and difficulties involved in this belief or supposed to be involved in it, and if he finds the contradictions and difficulties such as he cannot reconcile with his moral sentiments and judgments, he will be consistent in rejecting the notion of a deity and of providence. But he must also consistently admit that his moral sentiments and judgments are his own, and that he cannot say how he acquired them, or how he has any of the corporeal or intellectual powers which he is daily using. By the hypothesis they are not from God. All then that a man can say is that he has such powers.

[4] See ii. 10, i. 17. 12, ii. 11. 4, etc. M. Antoninus, x. 8.

knows you, in Rome you have many friends, you render their dues to all, you know how to requite him who does you a favour, and to repay in the same kind him who does you a wrong. What do you lack? If then I shall shew you that you lack the things most necessary and the chief things for happiness, and that hitherto you have looked after every thing rather than what you ought, and, to crown all,[5] that you neither know what God is nor what man is, nor what is good nor what is bad; and as to what I have said about your ignorance of other matters, that may perhaps be endured, but if I say that you know nothing about yourself, how is it possible that you should endure me and bear the proof and stay here? It is not possible; but you immediately go off in bad humour. And yet what harm have I done you? unless the mirror also injures the ugly man because it shows him to himself such as he is; unless the physician also is supposed to insult the sick man, when he says to him, Man, do you think that you ail nothing? But you have a fever: go without food to-day; drink water. And no one says, what an insult! But if you say to a man, Your desires are inflamed, your aversions are low, your intentions are inconsistent, your pursuits (movements) are not conformable to nature, your opinions are rash and false, the man immediately goes away and says, He has insulted me.

Our way of dealing is like that of a crowded assembly.[6] Beasts are brought to be sold and oxen; and the greater part of the men come to buy and sell, and there are some few who come to look at the market and to inquire how it is carried on, and why, and who fixes the meeting and for what purpose. So it is here also in this assembly (of life): some like cattle trouble themselves about nothing except their fodder. For to all of you who are busy about possessions and lands and slaves and magisterial offices, these are nothing except fodder. But there are a few who attend the assembly, men who love to look on and consider what is the world, who governs it.

[5] The original is 'to add the colophon,' which is a proverbial expression and signifies to give the last touch to a thing.

[6] See the fragments of Menander quoted by Upton.

Has it no governor?[7] And how is it possible that a city or a family cannot continue to exist, not even the shortest time without an administrator and guardian, and that so great and beautiful a system should be administered with such order and yet without a purpose and by chance?[8] There is then an administrator. What kind of administrator and how does he govern? And who are we, who were produced by him, and for what purpose? Have we some connexion with him and some relation towards him, or none? This is the way in which these few are affected, and then they apply themselves only to this one thing, to examine the meeting and then to go away. What then? They are ridiculed by the many, as the spectators at the fair are by the traders; and if the beasts had any understanding, they would ridicule those who admired anything else than fodder.

CHAPTER XV.

TO OR AGAINST THOSE WHO OBSTINATELY PERSIST IN WHAT THEY HAVE DETERMINED.

When some persons have heard these words, that a man ought to be constant (firm), and that the will is naturally free and not subject to compulsion, but that all other things are subject to hindrance, to slavery, and are in the power of others, they suppose that they ought without deviation to abide by every thing which they have determined. But in the first place that which has been determined ought to be sound (true). I require tone (sinews) in the body, but such as exists in a healthy body, in an athletic body; but if it is plain to me that you have the

[7] Sunt in Fortunae qui casibus omnia ponunt,
Et mundum credunt nullo rectore moveri.
Juvenal, xiii. 86.

[8] From the fact that man has some intelligence Voltaire concludes that we must admit that there is a greater intelligence. (Letter to Mde. Necker. Vol. 67, ed. Kehl. p, 278.)

tone of a phrensied man and you boast of it, I shall say to you, man, seek the physician: this is not tone, but atony (deficiency in right tone). In a different way something of the same kind is felt by those who listen to these discourses in a wrong manner; which was the case with one of my companions who for no reason resolved to starve himself to death.[1] I heard of it when it was the third day of his abstinence from food and I went to inquire what had happened. I have resolved, he said.—But still tell me what it was which induced you to resolve; for if you have resolved rightly, we shall sit with you and assist you to depart; but if you have made an unreasonable resolution, change your mind.—We ought to keep to our determinations. —What are you doing, man? We ought to keep not to all our determinations, but to those which are right; for if you are now persuaded that it is night, do not change your mind, if you think fit, but persist and say, we ought to abide by our determinations. Will you not make the beginning and lay the foundation in an inquiry whether the determination is sound or not sound, and so then build on it firmness and security? But if you lay a rotten and ruinous foundation, will not your miserable little building fall down the sooner, the more and the stronger are the materials which you shall lay on it? Without any reason would you withdraw from us out of life a man who is a friend, and a companion, a citizen of the same city, both the great and the small city?[2] Then while you are committing murder and destroying a man who has done no wrong, do you say that you ought to abide by your determinations? And if it ever in any way came into your head to kill me, ought you to abide by your determinations?

Now this man was with difficulty persuaded to change his mind. But it is impossible to convince some persons at present; so that I seem now to know, what I did not know before, the meaning of the common saying, That

[1] The word is ἀποκαρτερεῖν, which Cicero (Tusc. i. 34) renders 'per inediam vita discedere.' The words 'I have resolved' are in Epictetus, κέκρικα. Pliny (Epp. i. 12) says that Corellius Rufus, when he determined to end his great sufferings by starvation made the same answer, κέκρικα, to the physician who offered him food.

[2] The great city is the world.

you can neither persuade nor break a fool.[3] May it never be my lot to have a wise fool for my friend: nothing is more untractable. 'I am determined,' the man says. Madmen are also; but the more firmly they form a judgment on things which do not exist, the more ellebore[4] they require. Will you not act like a sick man and call in the physician?—I am sick, master, help me; consider what I must do: it is my duty to obey you. So it is here also: I know not what I ought to do, but I am come to learn.—Not so; but speak to me about other things: upon this I have determined.—What other things? for what is greater and more useful than for you to be persuaded that it is not sufficient to have made your determination and not to change it. This is the tone (energy) of madness, not of health.—I will die, if you compel me to this.—Why, man? What has happened?—I have determined—I have had a lucky escape that you have not determined to kill me—I take no money.[5] Why?—I have determined—Be assured that with the very tone (energy) which you now use in refusing to take, there is nothing to hinder you at some time from inclining without reason to take money and then saying, I have determined. As in a distempered body, subject to defluxions, the humour inclines sometimes to these parts, and then to those, so too a sickly soul knows not which way to incline: but if to this inclination and movement there is added a tone (obstinate resolution), then the evil becomes past help and cure.

[3] The meaning is that you cannot lead a fool from his purpose either by words or force. 'A wise fool' must mean a fool who thinks himself wise; and such we sometimes see. 'Though thou shouldst bray a fool in the mortar among wheat with a pestle, yet will not his foolishness depart from him.' Proverbs, xxvii. 22.

[4] Ellebore was a medicine used in madness. Horace says, Sat. ii. 3. 82—

Danda est ellebori multo pars maxima avaris.

[5] 'Epictetus seems in this discussion to be referring to some professor, who had declared that he would not take money from his hearers, and then, indirectly at least, had blamed our philosopher for receiving some fee from his hearers.' Schweig.

CHAPTER XVI.

THAT WE DO NOT STRIVE TO USE OUR OPINIONS ABOUT GOOD AND EVIL.

WHERE is the good? In the will.[1] Where is the evil? In the will. Where is neither of them? In those things which are independent of the will. Well then? Does any one among us think of these lessons out of the schools? Does any one meditate (strive) by himself to give an answer to things[2] as in the case of questions? Is it day?—Yes.—Is it night?—No.—Well, is the number of stars even?[3]—I cannot say.—When money is shown (offered) to you, have you studied to make the proper answer, that money is not a good thing? Have you practised yourself in these answers, or only against sophisms? Why do you wonder then if in the cases which you have studied, in those you have improved; but in those which you have not studied, in those you remain the same? When the rhetorician knows that he has written well, that he has committed to memory what he has written, and brings an agreeable voice, why is he still anxious? Because he is not satisfied with having studied. What then does he want? To be praised by the audience? For the purpose then of being able to practise declamation he has been disciplined; but with respect to praise and blame he has not been disciplined. For when did he hear from any one what praise is, what blame is, what the nature of each is, what kind of praise should be sought, or what kind of blame should be shunned? And when did he practise this discipline which follows these words (things)?[4] Why then do you still wonder, if in the matters which a man has learned, there he surpasses others, and in those in

[1] See ii. 10. 25.

[2] 'To answer to things' means to act in a way suitable to circumstances, to be a match for them. So Horace says (Sat. ii. 7. 85)—

> Responsare cupidinibus, contemnere honores
> Fortis.

[3] Perhaps this was a common puzzle. The man answers right; he cannot say.

[4] That is which follows praise or blame. He seems to mean making the proper use of praise or of blame.

which he has not been disciplined, there he is the same with the many. So the lute player knows how to play, sings well, and has a fine dress, and yet he trembles when he enters on the stage; for these matters he understands, but he does not know what a crowd is, nor the shouts of a crowd, nor what ridicule is. Neither does he know what anxiety is, whether it is our work or the work of another, whether it is possible to stop it or not. For this reason if he has been praised, he leaves the theatre puffed up, but if he has been ridiculed, the swollen bladder has been punctured and subsides.

This is the case also with ourselves. What do we admire? Externals. About what things are we busy? Externals. And have we any doubt then why we fear or why we are anxious? What then happens when we think the things, which are coming on us, to be evils? It is not in our power not to be afraid, it is not in our power not to be anxious. Then we say, Lord God, how shall I not be anxious? Fool, have you not hands, did not God make them for you? Sit down now and pray that your nose may not run.[5] Wipe yourself rather and do not blame him. Well then, has he given to you nothing in the present case? Has he not given to you endurance? has he not given to you magnanimity? has he not given to you manliness? When you have such hands, do you still look for one who shall wipe your nose? But we neither study these things nor care for them. Give me a man who cares how he shall do any thing, not for the obtaining of a thing, but who cares about his own energy. What man, when he is walking about, cares for his own energy? who, when he is deliberating, cares about his own deliberation, and not about obtaining that about which he deliberates? And if he succeeds, he is elated and says, How well we have deliberated; did I not tell you, brother, that it is impossible, when we have thought about any thing, that it should not turn out thus? But if the thing should turn out otherwise, the wretched man is humbled; he knows not even what to say about what has taken place. Who

[5] By the words 'Sit down' Epictetus indicates the man's baseness and indolence, who wishes God to do for him that which he can do himself and ought to do. Schweig.

among us for the sake of this matter has consulted a seer? Who among us as to his actions has not slept in indifference?[6] Who? Give (name) to me one that I may see the man whom I have long been looking for, who is truly noble and ingenuous, whether young or old; name him.[7]

Why then are we still surprised, if we are well practised in thinking about matters (any given subject), but in our acts are low, without decency, worthless, cowardly impatient of labour, altogether bad? For we do not care about these things nor do we study them. But if we had feared not death or banishment, but fear itself,[8] we should have studied not to fall into those things which appear to us evils. Now in the school we are irritable and wordy; and if any little question arises about any of these things, we are able to examine them fully. But drag us to practice, and you will find us miserably shipwrecked. Let some disturbing appearance come on us, and you will know what we have been studying and in what we have been exercising ourselves. Consequently through want of discipline we are always adding something to the appearance and representing things to be greater than what they

[6] So Schweighaeuser explains this difficult passage. Perhaps he is right. This part of the chapter is obscure.

[7] 'It is observable, that this most practical of all the philosophers owns his endeavours met with little or no success among his scholars. The Apostles speak a very different language in their epistles to the first converts of Christianity: and the Acts of the Apostles, and all the monuments of the primitive ages bear testimony to the reformation of manners produced by the Gospel. This difference of success might indeed justly be expected from the difference of the two systems.' Mrs. Carter.—I have not quoted this note of Mrs. Carter, because I think that it is true. We do not know what was the effect of the teaching of Epictetus, unless this passage informs us, if Mrs. Carter has drawn a right inference from it. The language of Paul to the Corinthians is not very different from that of Epictetus, and he speaks very unfavourably of some of his Corinthian converts. We may allow that "a reformation of manners was produced by the Gospel" in many of the converts to Christianity, but there is no evidence that this reformation was produced in all; and there is evidence that it was not. The corruptions in the early Christian church and in subsequent ages are a proof that the reforms made by the Gospel were neither universal nor permanent; and this is the result which our knowledge of human nature would lead us to expect.

[8] See ii. 1. 13.

are. For instance as to myself, when I am on a voyage and look down on the deep sea, or look round on it and see no land, I am out of my mind and imagine that I must drink up all this water if I am wrecked, and it does not occur to me that three pints are enough. What then disturbs me? The sea? No, but my opinion. Again, when an earthquake shall happen, I imagine that the city is going to fall on me; but is not one little stone enough to knock my brains out?

What then are the things which are heavy on us and disturb us? What else than opinions? What else than opinions lies heavy upon him who goes away and leaves his companions and friends and places and habits of life? Now little children, for instance, when they cry on the nurse leaving them for a short time, forget their sorrow if they receive a small cake. Do you choose then that we should compare you to little children?—No, by Zeus, for I do not wish to be pacified by a small cake, but by right opinions.—And what are these? Such as a man ought to study all day, and not to be affected by any thing that is not his own, neither by companion nor place nor gymnasia, and not even by his own body, but to remember the law and to have it before his eyes. And what is the divine law? To keep a man's own, not to claim that which belongs to others, but to use what is given, and when it is not given, not to desire it; and when a thing is taken away, to give it up readily and immediately, and to be thankful for the time that a man has had the use of it, if you would not cry for your nurse and mamma. For what matter does it make by what thing a man is subdued, and on what he depends? In what respect are you better than he who cries for a girl, if you grieve for a little gymnasium, and little porticoes and young men and such places of amusement? Another comes and laments that he shall no longer drink the water of Dirce. Is the Marcian water worse than that of Dirce? But I was used to the water of Dirce.[9] And you in turn will be used to the other. Then if you become attached to this also, cry

[9] Dirce a pure stream in Boeotia, which flows into the Ismenus. The Marcian water is the Marcian aqueduct at Rome, which was constructed B.C. 144, and was the best water that Rome had. Some of the

for this too, and try to make a verse like the verse of Euripides,

The hot baths of Nero and the Marcian water.

See how tragedy is made when common things happen to silly men.

When then shall I see Athens again and the Acropolis? Wretch, are you not content with what you see daily? have you any thing better or greater to see than the sun, the moon, the stars, the whole earth, the sea? But if indeed you comprehend him who administers the Whole, and carry him about in yourself, do you still desire small stones, and a beautiful rock?[10] When then you are going to leave the sun itself and the moon, what will you do? will you sit and weep like children? Well, what have you been doing in the school? what did you hear, what did you learn? why did you write yourself a philosopher, when you might have written the truth; as, "I made certain introductions,[11] and I read Chrysippus, but I did not even approach the door of a philosopher." For how should I[12] possess any thing of the kind which Socrates possessed, who died as he did, who lived as he did, or any thing such as Diogenes possessed? Do you think that any one of such men wept or grieved, because he was not going to see a certain man, or a certain woman, nor to be in Athens or in Corinth, but, if it should so happen, in Susa or in Ecbatana? For if a man can quit the banquet when he chooses, and no longer amuse himself, does he still stay and complain, and does he not stay, as at any amusement, only so long as he is pleased? Such a man, I suppose, would endure perpetual exile or to be condemned to death. Will you not be weaned now, like children, and

arches of this aqueduct exist. The 'bright stream of Dirce' is spoken of in the Hercules Furens of Euripides (v. 573). The verse in the text which we may suppose that Epictetus made, has a spondee in the fourth place, which is contrary to the rule.

[10] The 'small stones' are supposed to be the marbles which decorated Athens, and the rock to be the Acropolis.

[11] In the original it is Εἰσαγωγαί. It was a name used for short commentaries on the principles of any art; such as we now call Introductions, Compendiums, Elements. Gellius, xvi. 8.

[12] See Schweig.'s note.

take more solid food, and not cry after mammas and nurses, which are the lamentations of old women?—But if I go away, I shall cause them sorrow.—You cause them sorrow? By no means; but that will cause them sorrow which also causes you sorrow, opinion. What have you to do then? Take away your own opinion, and if these women are wise, they will take away their own: if they do not, they will lament through their own fault.

My man, as the proverb says, make a desperate effort on behalf of tranquillity of mind, freedom and magnanimity. Lift up your head at last as released from slavery. Dare to look up to God and say, Deal with me for the future as thou wilt; I am of the same mind as thou art; I am thine:[13] I refuse nothing that pleases thee: lead me where thou wilt: clothe me in any dress thou choosest: is it thy will that I should hold the office of a magistrate, that I should be in the condition of a private man, stay here or be an exile, be poor, be rich? I will make thy defence to men in behalf of all these conditions:[14] I will shew the nature of each thing what it is.—You will not do so; but sit in an ox's belly[15] and wait for your mamma till she shall feed you. Who would Hercules have been, if he had sat at home? He would have been Eurystheus and not Hercules. Well, and in his travels through the world how many intimates and how many friends had he? But nothing more dear to him than God. For this reason it was believed that he was the son of God, and he was. In obedience to God then he went about purging away injustice and lawlessness. But you are not Hercules and you are not able to purge away the wickedness of others; nor yet are you Theseus, able to purge away the evil

[13] The MSS. have ἴσος εἰμί: but the emendation of Salmasius, σός εἰμι, is certain.

[14] "There are innumerable passages in St. Paul, which, in reality, bear that noble testimony which Epictetus here requires in his imaginary character. Such are those in which he glories in tribulation; speaks with an heroic contempt of life, when set in competition with the performance of his duty; rejoices in bonds and imprisonments, and the view of his approaching martyrdom; and represents afflictions as a proof of God's love. See Acts xx. 23, 24; Rom. v. 3, viii. 38–39; 2 Tim. iv. 6."—Mrs. Carter.

[15] The meaning is uncertain. See Schweighaeuser's note.

things of Attica. Clear away your own. From yourself, from your thoughts cast away instead of Procrustes and Sciron,[16] sadness, fear, desire, envy, malèvolence, avarice, effeminacy, intemperance. But it is not possible to eject these things otherwise than by looking to God only, by fixing your affections on him only, by being consecrated to his commands. But if you choose any thing else, you will with sighs and groans be compelled to follow[17] what is stronger than yourself, always seeking tranquillity and never able to find it; for you seek tranquillity there where it is not, and you neglect to seek it where it is.

CHAPTER XVII.

HOW WE MUST ADAPT PRECONCEPTIONS TO PARTICULAR CASES.

What is the first business of him who philosophizes? To throw away self-conceit (οἴησις).[1] For it is impossible for a man to begin to learn that which he thinks that he knows. As to things then which ought to be done and ought not to be done, and good and bad, and beautiful and ugly, all of us talking of them at random go to the philosophers; and on these matters we praise, we censure, we accuse, we blame, we judge and determine about principles honourable and dishonourable. But why do we go to the philosophers? Because we wish to learn what we do not think that we know. And what is this? Theorems.[2] For we wish to learn what philosophers say as being something elegant and acute; and some wish to learn that

[16] Procrustes and Sciron, two robbers who infested Attica and were destroyed by Theseus, as Plutarch tells in his life of Theseus.

[17] Antoninus x. 28, "only to the rational animal is it given to follow voluntarily what happens; but simply to follow is a necessity imposed on all." Compare Seneca, Quaest. Nat. ii. 59.

[1] See ii. 11. 1, and iii. 14. 8.

[2] Theorems are defined by Cicero, de Fato, c. 6, 'Percepta appello quae dicuntur Graece θεωρήματα.'

they may get profit from what they learn. It is ridiculous then to think that a person wishes to learn one thing, and will learn another; or further, that a man will make proficiency in that which he does not learn. But the many are deceived by this which deceived also the rhetorician Theopompus,[3] when he blames even Plato for wishing everything to be defined. For what does he say? Did none of us before you use the words Good or Just, or do we utter the sounds in an unmeaning and empty way without understanding what they severally signify? Now who tells you, Theopompus, that we had not natural notions of each of these things and preconceptions (*προλήψεις*)? But it is not possible to adapt preconceptions to their correspondent objects if we have not distinguished (analyzed) them, and inquired what object must be subjected to each preconception. You may make the same charge against physicians also. For who among us did not use the words healthy and unhealthy before Hippocrates lived, or did we utter these words as empty sounds? For we have also a certain preconception of health,[4] but we are not able to adapt it. For this reason one says, abstain from food; another says, give food; another says, bleed; and another says, use cupping. What is the reason? is it any other than that a man cannot properly adapt the preconception of health to particulars?

So it is in this matter also, in the things which concern life. Who among us does not speak of good and bad, of useful and not useful; for who among us has not a preconception of each of these things? Is it then a distinct and perfect preconception? Show this. How shall I show this? Adapt the preconception properly to the particular things. Plato, for instance, subjects definitions to the preconception of the useful, but you to the preconception of the useless. Is it possible then that both of you are

[3] This rhetorician or orator, as Epictetus names him, appears to be the same person as Theopompus of Chios, the historian.

[4] 'That Epictetus does not quite correctly compare the notion of what is wholesome to the human body with the preconceived notion (anticipata notione) of moral good and bad, will be apparent to those who have carefully inquired into the various origin and principles of our notions.' Schweigh. Also see his note on *ἀνάτεινον*.

right? How is it possible? Does not one man adapt the preconception of good to the matter of wealth, and another not to wealth, but to the matter of pleasure and to that of health? For, generally, if all of us who use those words know sufficiently each of them, and need no diligence in resolving (making distinct) the notions of the preconceptions, why do we differ, why do we quarrel, why do we blame one another?

And why do I now allege this contention with one another and speak of it? If you yourself properly adapt your preconceptions, why are you unhappy, why are you hindered? Let us omit at present the second topic about the pursuits (ὅρμας) and the study of the duties which relate to them. Let us omit also the third topic, which relates to the assents (συγκαταθέσεις): I give up to you these two topics. Let us insist upon the first, which presents an almost obvious demonstration that we do not properly adapt the preconceptions.[5] Do you now desire that which is possible and that which is possible to you? Why then are you hindered? why are you unhappy? Do you not now try to avoid the unavoidable? Why then do you fall in with any thing which you would avoid? Why are you unfortunate? Why, when you desire a thing, does it not happen, and, when you do not desire it, does it happen? For this is the greatest proof of unhappiness and misery: I wish for something, and it does not happen. And what is more wretched than I?[6]

It was because she could not endure this that Medea came to murder her children: an act of a noble spirit in this view at least, for she had a just opinion what it is for a thing not to succeed which a person wishes. Then she says, 'Thus I shall be avenged on him (my husband) who has wronged and insulted me; and what shall I gain if he is punished thus? how then shall it be done? I shall kill my children, but I shall punish myself also: and what do I care?'[7] This is the aberration of soul which possesses great energy. For she did not know

[5] The topic of the desires and aversions. Sec. iii. c. 2.

[6] Compare i. c. 27, 10.

[7] This is the meaning of what Medea says in the Medea of Euripides. Epictetus does not give the words of the poet.

wherein lies the doing of that which we wish; that you cannot get this from without, nor yet by the alteration and new adaptation of things. Do not desire the man (Jason, Medea's husband), and nothing which you desire will fail to happen: do not obstinately desire that he shall live with you: do not desire to remain in Corinth; and in a word desire nothing than that which God wills.—And who shall hinder you? who shall compel you? No man shall compel you any more than he shall compel Zeus.

When you have such a guide[8] and your wishes and desires are the same as his, why do you still fear disappointment? Give up your desire to wealth and your aversion to poverty, and you will be disappointed in the one, you will fall into the other. Well give them up to health, and you will be unfortunate: give them up to magistracies, honours, country, friends, children, in a word to any of the things which are not in man's power (and you will be unfortunate). But give them up to Zeus and to the rest of the gods; surrender them to the gods, let the gods govern, let your desire and aversion be ranged on the side of the gods, and wherein will you be any longer unhappy?[9] But if, lazy wretch, you envy, and complain, and are jealous, and fear, and never cease for a single day complaining both of yourself and of the gods, why do you still speak of being educated? What kind of an education, man? Do you mean that you have been employed about sophistical syllogisms (*συλλογισμοὺς μεταπίπτοντας*)?[10] Will you not, if it is possible, unlearn all these things and begin from the beginning, and see at the same time that hitherto you have not even touched the matter; and then commencing from this foundation, will you not build up all that comes after, so that nothing may happen which you do not choose, and nothing shall fail to happen which you do choose?

Give me one young man who has come to the school with this intention, who is become a champion for this matter and says, 'I give up every thing else, and it is

[8] Compare iv. 7. 20.

[9] 'If you would subject all things to yourself, subject yourself to reason.' Seneca, Ep. 37.

[10] See i. 7. 1.

enough for me if it shall ever be in my power to pass my life free from hindrance and free from trouble, and to stretch out (present) my neck to all things like a free man, and to look up to heaven as a friend of God and fear nothing that can happen.' Let any of you point out such a man that I may say, 'Come, young man, into the possession of that which is your own, for it is your destiny to adorn philosophy: yours are these possessions, yours these books, yours these discourses.' Then when he shall have laboured sufficiently and exercised himself in this part of the matter (τόπον), let him come to me again and say, 'I desire to be free from passion and free from perturbation; and I wish as a pious man and a philosopher and a diligent person to know what is my duty to the gods, what to my parents, what to my brothers, what to my country, what to strangers.' (I say) 'Come also to the second matter (τόπον): this also is yours.'—'But I have now sufficiently studied the second part (τόπον) also, and I would gladly be secure and unshaken, and not only when I am awake, but also when I am asleep, and when I am filled with wine, and when I am melancholy.' Man, you are a god, you have great designs.

No: but I wish to understand what Chrysippus says in his treatise of the Pseudomenos[11] (the Liar).—Will you not hang yourself, wretch, with such your intention? And what good will it do you? You will read the whole with sorrow, and you will speak to others trembling. Thus you also do. "Do you wish me,[12] brother, to read to you, and you to me"?—You write excellently, my man; and you also excellently in the style of Xenophon, and you

[11] The Pseudomenos was a treatise by Chrysippus (Diog. Laert. vii. Chrysippus). "The Pseudomenos was a famous problem among the Stoics, and it is this. When a person says, I lie; doth he lie, or doth he not? If he lies, he speaks truth: if he speaks truth, he lies. The philosophers composed many books on this difficulty. Chrysippus wrote six. Philetas wasted himself in studying to answer it." Mrs. Carter.

[12] Epictetus is ridiculing the men who compliment one another on their writings. Upton compares Horace, Epp. ii. 2. 87.

ut alter
Alterius sermone meros audiret honores—
Discedo Alcaeus puncto illius? ille meo quis?
Quis nisi Callimachus?

in the style of Plato, and you in the style of Antisthenes. Then having told your dreams to one another you return to the same things: your desires are the same, your aversions the same, your pursuits are the same, and your designs and purposes, you wish for the same things and work for the same. In the next place you do not even seek for one to give you advice, but you are vexed if you hear such things (as I say). Then you say, "An ill-natured old fellow: when I was going away, he did not weep nor did he say, Into what danger you are going: if you come off safe, my child, I will burn lights.[13] This is what a good natured man would do." It will be a great thing for you if you do return safe, and it will be worth while to burn lights for such a person: for you ought to be immortal and exempt from disease.

Casting away then, as I say, this conceit of thinking that we know something useful, we must come to philosophy as we apply to geometry, and to music: but if we do not, we shall not even approach to proficiency though we read all the collections[14] and commentaries of Chrysippus and those of Antipater and Archedemus.[15]

CHAPTER XVIII.

HOW WE SHOULD STRUGGLE AGAINST APPEARANCES.

EVERY habit and faculty[1] is maintained and increased by the corresponding actions: the habit of walking by walking, the habit of running by running. If you would be a good reader, read; if a writer, write. But when you shall not have read for thirty days in succession, but have done something else, you will know the consequence. In the same way, if you shall have lain down ten days, get up

[13] Compare i. 19. 4.

[14] Schweighaeuser has no doubt that we ought instead of συναγωγάς, 'collections,' to read εἰσαγωγάς, 'introductions.'

[15] As to Archedemus, see ii. 4, 11; and Antipater, ii. 19, 2.

[1] See iv. c. 12.

and attempt to make a long walk, and you will see how your legs are weakened. Generally then if you would make any thing a habit, do it; if you would not make it a habit, do not do it, but accustom yourself to do something else in place of it.

So it is with respect to the affections of the soul: when you have been angry, you must know that not only has this evil befallen you, but that you have also increased the habit, and in a manner thrown fuel upon fire. When you have been overcome in sexual intercourse with a person, do not reckon this single defeat only, but reckon that you have also nurtured, increased your incontinence. For it is impossible for habits and faculties, some of them not to be produced, when they did not exist before, and others not be increased and strengthened by corresponding acts.

In this manner certainly, as philosophers say, also diseases of the mind grow up.[2] For when you have once desired money, if reason be applied to lead to a perception of the evil, the desire is stopped, and the ruling faculty of our mind is restored to the original authority. But if you apply no means of cure, it no longer returns to the same state, but being again excited by the corresponding appearance, it is inflamed to desire quicker than before: and when this takes place continually, it is henceforth hardened (made callous), and the disease of the mind confirms the love of money. For he who has had a fever, and has been relieved from it, is not in the same state that he was before, unless he has been completely cured. Something of the kind happens also in diseases of the soul. Certain traces and blisters are left in it, and unless a man shall completely efface them, when he is again lashed on the same places, the lash will produce not blisters (weals) but sores. If then you wish not to be of an angry temper, do not feed the habit: throw nothing on it which will increase it: at first keep quiet, and count the days on which you have not been angry. I used to be in passion every day; now every second day; then every third, then every fourth. But if you have intermitted thirty days, make a sacrifice to God. For the habit at first begins to

[2] ἀῤῥωστήματα. 'Aegrotationes quae appellantur a Stoicis ἀῤῥωστήματα.' Cicero, Tusc. iv. 10.

be weakened, and then is completely destroyed. "I have not been vexed to-day, nor the day after, nor yet on any succeeding day during two or three months; but I took care when some exciting things happened." Be assured that you are in a good way.[3] To-day when I saw a handsome person, I did not say to myself, I wish I could lie with her, and Happy is her husband; for he who says this says, Happy is her adulterer also. Nor do I picture the rest to my mind; the woman present, and stripping herself and lying down by my side. I stroke my head and say, Well done, Epictetus, you have solved a fine little sophism, much finer than that which is called the master sophism. And if even the woman is willing, and gives signs, and sends messages, and if she also fondle me and come close to me, and I should abstain and be victorious, that would be a sophism beyond that which is named the Liar, and the Quiescent.[4] Over such a victory as this a man may justly be proud; not for proposing the master sophism.

How then shall this be done? Be willing at length to be approved by yourself, be willing to appear beautiful to God, desire to be in purity with your own pure self and with God. Then when any such appearance visits you, Plato says,[5] Have recourse to expiations, go a suppliant to the temples of the averting deities. It is even sufficient if you resort to the society of noble and just men, and compare yourself with them, whether you find one who is living or dead. Go to Socrates and see him lying down with Alcibiades, and mocking his beauty:

[3] *κομψῶς σοί ἐστι.* Compare the Gospel of St. John iv. 52, *ἐπύθετο οὖν παρ' αὐτῶν τὴν ὥραν ἐν ᾗ κομψότερον ἔσχε.*

[4] Placet enim Chrysippo cum gradatim interrogetur, verbi causa, tria pauca sint anne multa, aliquanto prius quam ad multa perveniat quiescere; id est quod ab iis dicitur *ἡσυχάζειν.* Cicero, Acad. ii. Pr. 29. Compare Persius, Sat. vi. 80:

Depinge ubi sistam,
Inventus, Chrysippe, tui finitor acervi.

[5] The passage is in Plato, Laws, ix. p. 854, *ὅταν σοι προσπίπτῃ τι τῶν τοιούτων δογμάτων,* etc. The conclusion is, 'if you cannot be cured of your (mental) disease, seek death which is better and depart from life.' This bears some resemblance to the precept in Matthew vi. 29 'And if thy right eye offend thee, pluck it out and cast it from thee,' etc.

consider what a victory he at last found that he had gained over himself; what an Olympian victory; in what number he stood from Hercules;[6] so that, by the Gods, one may justly salute him, Hail, wondrous man, you who have conquered not these sorry boxers[7] and pancratiasts, nor yet those who are like them, the gladiators. By placing these objects on the other side you will conquer the appearance: you will not be drawn away by it. But in the first place be not hurried away by the rapidity of the appearance, but say, Appearances, wait for me a little: let me see who you are, and what you are about:[8] let me put you to the test. And then do not allow the appearance to lead you on and draw lively pictures of the things which will follow; for if you do, it will carry you off wherever it pleases. But rather bring in to oppose it some other beautiful and noble appearance and cast out this base appearance. And if you are accustomed to be exercised in this way, you will see what shoulders, what sinews, what strength you have. But now it is only trifling words, and nothing more.

This is the true athlete, the man who exercises himself against such appearances. Stay, wretch, do not be carried away. Great is the combat, divine is the work; it is for kingship, for freedom, for happiness, for freedom from perturbation. Remember God: call on him as a helper and protector, as men at sea call on the Dioscuri[9] in a storm. For what is a greater storm than that which comes from appearances which are violent and drive away the reason?[10] For the storm itself, what else is it but an appearance? For take away the fear of death, and suppose

[6] Hercules is said to have established gymnastic contests and to have been the first victor. Those who gained the victory both in wrestling and in the pancratium were reckoned in the list of victors as coming in the second or third place after him, and so on.

[7] I have followed Wolff's conjecture *πύκτας* instead of the old reading *παίκτας*.

[8] Compare iii. 12. 15.

[9] Castor and Pollux. Horace, Carm. i. 12:—

> Quorum simul alba nautis
> Stella refulsit, etc.

[10] Gellius, xix. c. 1, 'visa quae vi quadam sua sese inferunt noscitanda hominibus.'

as many thunders and lightnings as you please, and you will know what calm[11] and serenity there is in the ruling faculty. But if you have once been defeated and say that you will conquer hereafter, and then say the same again, be assured that you will at last be in so wretched a condition and so weak that you will not even know afterwards that you are doing wrong, but you will even begin to make apologies (defences) for your wrong doing, and then you will confirm the saying of Hesiod[12] to be true,

With constant ills the dilatory strives.

CHAPTER XIX.

AGAINST THOSE WHO EMBRACE PHILOSOPHICAL OPINIONS ONLY IN WORDS.[1]

The argument called the ruling argument (ὁ κυριεύων λόγος)[2] appears to have been proposed from such principles as these: there is in fact a common contradiction between one another in these three propositions, each two being in contradiction to the third. The propositions are, that every thing past must of necessity be true; that an impossibility does not follow a possibility; and that a thing is possible which neither is nor will be true. Diodorus[3] observing this contradiction employed the probative force of the first two for the demonstration of this proposition, That nothing is possible which is not true and never will

[11] 'Consider that every thing is opinion, and opinion is in thy power. Take away then, when thou choosest, thy opinion, and like a mariner, who has doubled the promontory, thou wilt find calm, every thing stable, and a waveless bay.' Antoninus, xii. 22.

[12] Hesiod, Works and Days, v. 411.

[1] Compare Gellius xvii. c. 19.

[2] See the long note communicated to Upton by James Harris; and Schweighaeuser's note.

[3] Diodorus, surnamed Cronus, lived at Alexandria in the time of Ptolemaeus Soter. He was of the school named the Megaric, and distinguished in dialectic.

be. Now another will hold these two: That something is possible, which is neither true nor ever will be: and That an impossibility does not follow a possibility. But he will not allow that every thing which is past is necessarily true, as the followers of Cleanthes seem to think, and Antipater copiously defended them. But others maintain the other two propositions, That a thing is possible which is neither true nor will be true: and That everything which is past is necessarily true; but then they will maintain that an impossibility can follow a possibility. But it is impossible to maintain these three propositions, because of their common contradiction.[4]

If then any man should ask me, which of these propositions do you maintain? I will answer him, that I do not know; but I have received this story, that Diodorus maintained one opinion, the followers of Panthoides, I think, and Cleanthes maintained another opinion, and those of Chrysippus a third. What then is your opinion? I was not made for this purpose, to examine the appearances that occur to me, and to compare what others say and to form an opinion of my own on the thing. Therefore I differ not at all from the grammarian. Who was Hector's father? Priam. Who were his brothers? Alexander and Deiphobus. Who was their mother? Hecuba.—I have heard this story. From whom? From Homer. And Hellanicus also, I think, writes about the same things, and perhaps others like him. And what further have I about the ruling argument? Nothing. But, if I am a vain man, especially at a banquet I surprise the guests by enumerating those who have written on these matters. Both Chrysippus has written wonderfully in his first book about Possibilities, and Cleanthes has written specially on the subject, and Archedemus. Antipater also has written not only in his work about Possibilities, but also separately in his work on the ruling argument. Have you not read the work? I have not read it. Read. And what profit will a man have from it? he will be more trifling and impertinent than he is now; for what else have you gained by reading it? What opinion have you formed on

[4] If you assume any two of these three, they must be in contradiction to the third and destroy it.

this subject? none; but you will tell us of Helen and Priam, and the island of Calypso which never was and never will be. And in this matter indeed it is of no great importance if you retain the story, but have formed no opinion of your own. But in matters of morality (Ethic) this happens to us much more than in these things of which we are speaking.

Speak to me about good and evil. Listen:

> The wind from Ilium to Ciconian shores
> Brought me.[5]—Odyssey, ix. 39.

Of things some are good, some are bad, and others are indifferent. The good then are the virtues and the things which partake of the virtues: the bad are the vices, and the things which partake of them; and the indifferent are the things which lie between the virtues and the vices, wealth, health, life, death, pleasure, pain. Whence do you know this? Hellanicus says it in his Egyptian history; for what difference does it make to say this, or to say that Diogenes has it in his Ethic, or Chrysippus or Cleanthes? Have you then examined any of these things and formed an opinion of your own? Show how you are used to behave in a storm on shipboard? Do you remember this division (distinction of things), when the sail rattles and a man, who knows nothing of times and seasons, stands by you when you are screaming and says, Tell me, I ask you by the Gods, what you were saying just now, Is it a vice to suffer shipwreck: does it participate in vice? Will you not take up a stick and lay it on his head? What have we to do with you, man? we are perishing and you come

[5] 'Speak to me,' etc. may be supposed to be said to Epictetus, who has been ridiculing logical subtleties and the grammarians' learning. When he is told to speak of good and evil, he takes a verse of the Odyssey, the first which occurs to him, and says, Listen. There is nothing to listen to, but it is as good for the hearer as any thing else. Then he utters some philosophical principles, and being asked where he learned them, he says, from Hellanicus, who was an historian, not a philosopher. He is bantering the hearer: it makes no matter from what author I learned them; it is all the same. The real question is, have you examined what Good and Evil are, and have you formed an opinion yourself?

to mock us? But if Caesar send for you to answer a charge, do you remember the distinction? If when you are going in pale and trembling, a person should come up to you and say, Why do you tremble, man? what is the matter about which you are engaged? Does Caesar who sits within give virtue and vice to those who go in to him? You reply, Why do you also mock me and add to my present sorrows?—Still tell me, philosopher, tell me why you tremble? Is it not death of which you run the risk, or a prison, or pain of the body, or banishment, or disgrace? What else is there? Is there any vice or anything which partakes of vice? What then did you use to say of these things?—'What have you to do with me, man? my own evils are enough for me.' And you say right. Your own evils are enough for you, your baseness, your cowardice, your boasting which you showed when you sat in the school. Why did you decorate yourself with what belonged to others? Why did you call yourself a Stoic?

Observe yourselves thus in your actions, and you will find to what sect you belong. You will find that most of you are Epicureans, a few Peripatetics,[6] and those feeble. For wherein will you show that you really consider virtue equal to everything else or even superior? But show me a Stoic, if you can. Where or how? But you can show me an endless number who utter small arguments of the Stoics. For do the same persons repeat the Epicurean opinions any worse? And the Peripatetic, do they not handle them also with equal accuracy? who then is a Stoic? As we call a statue Phidiac, which is fashioned according to the art of Phidias; so show me a man who is fashioned according to the doctrines which he utters. Show me a man who is sick and happy, in danger and happy, dying and happy, in exile and happy, in disgracé and happy. Show him: I desire, by the gods, to see a Stoic. You cannot show me one fashioned so; but show me at least one who is forming, who has shown a tendency to be a Stoic. Do me this favour: do not grudge

[6] The Peripatetics allowed many things to be good which contributed to a happy life; but still they contended that the smallest mental excellence was superior to all other things. Cicero, De Fin. v. 5. 31.

an old man seeing a sight which I have not seen yet. Do you think that you must show me the Zeus of Phidias or the Athena, a work of ivory and gold?[7] Let any of you show me a human soul ready to think as God does, and not to blame[8] either God or man, ready not to be disappointed about any thing, not to consider himself damaged by any thing, not to be angry, not to be envious, not to be jealous; and why should I not say it direct? desirous from a man to become a god, and in this poor mortal body thinking of his fellowship with Zeus.[9] Show me the man. But you cannot. Why then do you delude yourselves and cheat others? and why do you put on a guise which does not belong to you, and walk about being thieves and pilferers of these names and things which do not belong to you?

And now I am your teacher, and you are instructed in my school. And I have this purpose, to make you free from restraint, compulsion, hindrance, to make you free, prosperous, happy, looking to God in everything small and great. And you are here to learn and practise these things. Why then do you not finish the work, if you also have such a purpose as you ought to have, and if I in addition to the purpose also have such qualification as I ought to have? What is that which is wanting? When I see an artificer and material lying by him, I expect the work. Here then is the artificer, here the material; what is it that we want? Is not the thing one that can be taught? It is. Is it not then in our power? The only thing of all

[7] See ii. c. 8. 20.

[8] 'to blame God' means to blame the constitution and order of things, for to do this appeared to Epictetus to be absurd and wicked; as absurd as for the potter's vessel to blame the potter, if that can be imagined, for making it liable to wear out and to break.

[9] 'Our fellowship is with the Father and with his son Jesus Christ,' 1 John i. 3. The attentive reader will observe several passages besides those which have been noticed, in which there is a striking conformity between Epictetus and the Scriptures; and will perceive from them, either that the Stoics had learnt a good deal of the Christian language or that treating a subject practically and in earnest leads men to such strong expressions as we often find in Scripture and sometimes in the philosophers, especially Epictetus.' Mrs. Carter.

The word 'fellowship' in the passage of John and of Epictetus is *κοινωνία*. See i. 29. note 19.

that is in our power. Neither wealth is in our power, nor health, nor reputation, nor in a word any thing else except the right use of appearances. This (right use) is by nature free from restraint, this alone is free from impediment. Why then do you not finish the work? Tell me the reason. For it is either through my fault that you do not finish it, or through your own fault, or through the nature of the thing. The thing itself is possible, and the only thing in our power. It remains then that the fault is either in me or in you, or, what is nearer the truth, in both. Well then, are you willing that we begin at last to bring such a purpose into this school, and to take no notice of the past? Let us only make a beginning. Trust to me, and you will see.

CHAPTER XX.

AGAINST THE EPICUREANS AND ACADEMICS.

The propositions which are true and evident are of necessity used even by those who contradict them: and a man might perhaps consider it to be the greatest proof of a thing being evident that it is found to be necessary even for him who denies it to make use of it at the same time. For instance, if a man should deny that there is anything universally true, it is plain that he must make the contradictory negation, that nothing is universally true. What, wretch, do you not admit even this? For what else is this than to affirm that whatever is universally affirmed is false? Again if a man should come forward and say: Know that there is nothing that can be known,[1] but all things are incapable of sure evidence; or if another say, Believe me and you will be the better for it, that a man

[1] 'Itaque Arcesilas negabat esse quidquam quod sciri posset, ne illud quidem ipsum, quod Socrates sibi reliquisset. Sic omnia latere censebat in occulto, neque esse quidquam quod cerni aut intelligi possit. Quibus de causis nihil oportere neque profiteri neque adfirmare quemquam neque adsensione adprobare.' Cicero, Academ. Post. 1. 12, Diog. Laert. ix. 90 of the Pyrrhonists.

ought not to believe any thing; or again, if another should say, Learn from me, man, that it is not possible to learn any thing; I tell you this and will teach you, if you choose. Now in what respect do these differ from those? Whom shall I name? Those who call themselves Academics? 'Men, agree [with us] that no man agrees [with another]: believe us that no man believes anybody.'

Thus Epicurus[2] also, when he designs to destroy the natural fellowship of mankind, at the same time makes use of that which he destroys. For what does he say? 'Be not deceived, men, nor be led astray, nor be mistaken: there is no natural fellowship among rational animals; believe me. But those who say otherwise, deceive you and seduce you by false reasons.'—What is this to you? Permit us to be deceived. Will you fare worse, if all the rest of us are persuaded that there is a natural fellowship among us, and that it ought by all means to be preserved? Nay, it will be much better and safer for you. Man, why do you trouble yourself about us? Why do you keep awake for us? Why do you light your lamp? Why do you rise early? Why do you write so many books, that no one of us may be deceived about the gods and believe that they take care of men; or that no one may suppose the nature of good to be other than pleasure? For if this is so, lie down and sleep, and lead the life of a worm, of which you judged yourself worthy: eat and drink, and enjoy women, and ease yourself, and snore.[3] And what is it to you, how the rest shall think about these things, whether right or wrong? For what have we to do with you? You take care of sheep because they supply us with wool and milk, and last of all with their flesh. Would it not be a desirable

[2] Cicero, de Fin. ii. 30. 31, speaking of the letter, which Epicurus wrote to Hermarchus when he was dying, says 'that the actions of Epicurus were inconsistent with his sayings,' and 'his writings were confuted by his probity and morality.'

[3] Paul says, Cor. i. 15. 32: 'If after the manner of men I have fought with beasts at Ephesus, what advantageth it me, if the dead rise not? let us eat and drink, for to-morrow we die.' The words 'let us eat and drink, etc.' are said to be a quotation from the Thais of Menander. The meaning seems to be, that if I do not believe in the resurrection of the dead, why should I not enjoy the sensual pleasures of life only? This is not the doctrine of Epictetus, as we see in the text.

thing if men could be lulled and enchanted by the Stoics, and sleep and present themselves to you and to those like you to be shorn and milked? For this you ought to say to your brother Epicureans: but ought you not to conceal it from others, and particularly before every thing to persuade them, that we are by nature adapted for fellowship, that temperance is a good thing; in order that all things may be secured for you?[4] Or ought we to maintain this fellowship with some and not with others? With whom then ought we to maintain it? With such as on their part also maintain it, or with such as violate this fellowship? And who violate it more than you who establish such doctrines?

What then was it that waked Epicurus from his sleepiness, and compelled him to write what he did write? What else was it than that which is the strongest thing in men, nature, which draws a man to her own will though he be unwilling and complaining? For since, she says, you think that there is no community among mankind, write this opinion and leave it for others, and break your sleep to do this, and by your own practice condemn your own opinions. Shall we then say that Orestes was agitated by the Erinyes (Furies) and roused from his deep sleep, and did not more savage Erinyes and Pains rouse Epicurus from his sleep and not allow him to rest, but compelled him to make known his own evils, as madness and wine did the Galli (the priests of Cybele)? So strong and invincible is man's nature, For how can a vine be moved not in the manner of a vine, but in the manner of an olive tree? or on the other hand how can an olive tree be moved not in the manner of an olive tree, but in the manner of a vine? It is impossible: it cannot be conceived. Neither then is it possible for a man completely to lose the movements (affects) of a man; and even those who are deprived of their genital members are not able to deprive themselves of man's desires.[5] Thus Epicurus also mutilated all the offices of a man, and of a father of a family, and of a citizen and of a friend, but he did not

[4] It would give security to the Epicureans, that they would enjoy all that they value, if other men should be persuaded that we are all made for fellowship, and that temperance is a good thing.

[5] See Upton's note.

mutilate human desires, for he could not; not more than the lazy Academics can cast away or blind their own senses, though they have tried with all their might to do it. What a shame is this? when a man has received from nature measures and rules for the knowing of truth, and does not strive to add to these measures and rules and to improve [6] them, but just the contrary, endeavours to take away and destroy whatever enables us to discern the truth?

What say you philosopher? piety and sanctity, what do you think that they are? If you like, I will demonstrate that they are good things. Well, demonstrate it, that our citizens may be turned and honour the deity and may no longer be negligent about things of the highest value. Have you then the demonstrations?—I have, and I am thankful.—Since then you are well pleased with them, hear the contrary: That there are no Gods, and, if there are, they take no care of men, nor is there any fellowship between us and them; and that this piety and sanctity which is talked of among most men is the lying of boasters and sophists, or certainly of legislators for the purpose of terrifying and checking wrong doers.[7]—Well done, philosopher, you have done something for our citizens, you have brought back all the young men to contempt of things divine.—What then, does not this satisfy you? Learn now, that justice is nothing, that modesty is folly, that a father is nothing, a son nothing.—Well done, philosopher, persist, persuade the young men, that we may have more with the same opinions as you and who say the same as you. From such principles as these have grown our well constituted states; by these was Sparta founded: Lycurgus fixed these opinions in the Spartans by his laws and education, that neither is the servile condition more base than honourable, nor the condition of free men more honourable

[6] I have followed Schweighaeuser who suggests προσεξεργάσασθαι in place of the MSS. προσεργάσασθαι.

[7] Polybius (vi. 56), when he is speaking of the Roman state, commends the men of old time, who established in the minds of the multitude the opinions about the gods and Hades, wherein, he says, they acted more wisely than those in his time who would destroy such opinions.

than base, and that those who died at Thermopylae[8] died from these opinions; and through what other opinions did the Athenians leave their city?[9] Then those who talk thus, marry and beget children, and employ themselves in public affairs and make themselves priests and interpreters. Of whom? of gods who do not exist: and they consult the Pythian priestess that they may hear lies, and they report the oracles to others. Monstrous impudence and imposture.

Man what are you doing?[10] are you refuting yourself every day; and will you not give up these frigid attempts? When you eat, where do you carry your hand to? to your mouth or to your eye? when you wash yourself, what do you go into? do you ever call a pot a dish, or a ladle a spit? If I were a slave of any of these men, even if I must be flayed by him daily, I would rack him. If he said, 'Boy, throw some olive oil into the bath,' I would take pickle sauce and pour it down on his head. What is this? he would say—An appearance was presented to me, I swear by your genius, which could not be distinguished from oil and was exactly like it—Here give me the barley-drink (tisane), he says—I would fill and carry him a dish of sharp sauce—Did I not ask for the barley drink? Yes, master: this is the barley drink? Take it and smell; take it and taste. How do you know then if our senses deceive us?—If I had three or four fellow-slaves of the same opinion, I should force him to hang himself through passion or to change his mind. But now they mock us by using all the things which nature gives, and in words destroying them.

Grateful indeed are men and modest, who, if they do

[8] Epictetus alludes to the Spartans who fought at Thermopylae B.C. 480 against Xerxes and his army. Herodotus (vii. 228) has recorded the inscription placed over the Spartans:—

> Stranger, go tell the Spartans, Here we lie
> Obedient to those who bade us die.

The inscription is translated by Cicero, Tusc. Disp. i. 42.

[9] When Xerxes was advancing on Athens, the Athenians left the city and embarked on their vessels before the battle of Salamis, B.C. 480. See Cicero, De Officiis, iii. 11.

[10] He is now attacking the Academics, who asserted that we can know nothing.

nothing else, are daily eating bread and yet are shameless enough to say, we do not know if there is a Demeter or her daughter Persephone or a Pluto;[11] not to mention that they are enjoying the night and the day, the seasons of the year, and the stars, and the sea and the land and the co-operation of mankind, and yet they are not moved in any degree by these things to turn their attention to them; but they only seek to belch out their little problem (matter for discussion), and when they have exercised their stomach to go off to the bath. But what they shall say, and about what things or to what persons, and what their hearers shall learn from this talk, they care not even in the least degree, nor do they care if any generous youth after hearing such talk should suffer any harm from it, nor after he has suffered harm should lose all the seeds of his generous nature; nor if we[12] should give an adulterer help towards being shameless in his acts; nor if a public peculator should lay hold of some cunning excuse from these doctrines; nor if another who neglects his parents should be confirmed in his audacity by this teaching.—What then in your opinion is good or bad? This or that?—Why then should a man say any more in reply to such persons as these, or give them any reason or listen to any reason from them, or try to convince them? By Zeus one might much sooner expect to make catamites change their mind than those who are become so deaf and blind to their own evils.[13]

[11] Epictetus is speaking according to the popular notions. To deny Demeter and to eat the bread which she gives is the same thing in the common notions of the Greeks, as it would be for Epictetus to deny the existence of God and to eat the bread which he gives.

[12] The MSS. have παράσχωμεν. Παράσχωσι would be in conformity with the rest of the passage. But this change of persons is common in Epictetus.

[13] 'This resembles what our Saviour said to the Jewish rulers: Verily I say unto you, that the publicans and the harlots go into the kingdom of God before you.' Matthew, xxi. 31. Mrs. Carter.

To an Academic who said he comprehended nothing, the Stoic Ariston replied, 'Do you not see even the person who is sitting near you?' When the Academic denied it, Ariston said, 'Who made you blind? who stole your power of sight?' (Diog. Laert. vii. 163. Upton.)

CHAPTER XXI.

OF INCONSISTENCY.[1]

Some things men readily confess, and other things they do not. No one then will confess that he is a fool or without understanding; but quite the contrary you will hear all men saying, I wish that I had fortune equal to my understanding. But men readily confess that they are timid, and they say: I am rather timid, I confess; but as to other respects you will not find me to be foolish. A man will not readily confess that he is intemperate; and that he is unjust, he will not confess at all. He will by no means confess that he is envious or a busy body. Most men will confess that they are compassionate. What then is the reason?—The chief thing (the ruling thing) is inconsistency and confusion in the things which relate to good and evil. But different men have different reasons; and generally what they imagine to be base, they do not confess at all. But they suppose timidity to be a characteristic of a good disposition, and compassion also; but silliness to be the absolute characteristic of a slave. And they do not at all admit (confess) the things which are offences against society. But in the case of most errors for this reason chiefly they are induced to confess them, because they imagine that there is something involuntary in them as in timidity and compassion; and if a man confess that he is in any respect intemperate, he alleges love (or passion) as an excuse for what is involuntary. But men do not imagine injustice to be at all involuntary. There is also in jealousy, as they suppose, something involuntary; and for this reason they confess to jealousy also.

Living then among such men, who are so confused, so ignorant of what they say, and of the evils which they have or have not, and why they have them, or how they shall be relieved of them, I think it is worth the trouble

[1] Schweig. has some remarks on the title of this chapter. He says 'that this discourse does not keep to the same subject, but proceeds from that with which it began to other things.'

for a man to watch constantly (and to ask) whether I also am one of them, what imagination I have about myself, how I conduct myself, whether I conduct myself as a prudent man, whether I conduct myself as a temperate man, whether I ever say this, that I have been taught to be prepared for every thing that may happen. Have I the consciousness, which a man who knows nothing ought to have, that I know nothing? Do I go to my teacher as men go to oracles, prepared to obey? or do I like a snivelling boy go to my school to learn history and understand the books which I did not understand before, and, if it should happen so, to explain them also to others?—Man, you have had a fight in the house with a poor slave, you have turned the family upside down, you have frightened the neighbours, and you come to me [2] as if you were a wise man, and you take your seat and judge how I have explained some word, and how I have babbled whatever came into my head. You come full of envy, and humbled, because you bring nothing from home; [3] and you sit during the discussion thinking of nothing else than how your father is disposed towards you and your brother. 'What are they saying about me there? now they think that I am improving, and are saying, He will return with all knowledge. I wish I could learn every thing before I return: but much labour is necessary, and no one sends me any thing, and the baths at Nicopolis are dirty; every thing is bad at home, and bad here.'

Then they say, no one gains any profit from the school.—Why, who comes to the school? who comes for the purpose of being improved? who comes to present his opinions to be purified? who comes to learn what he is in want of? Why do you wonder then if you carry back from the school the very things which you bring into it? For you come not to lay aside (your principles) or to correct

[2] *καταστολὰς ποιήσας.* I have omitted these words because I don't understand them; nor do the commentators. The word *καταστολή* occurs in ii. 10. 15, where it is intelligible.

[3] Literally, 'because to you or for you nothing is brought from home.' Perhaps the meaning is explained by what follows. The man has no comfort at home; he brings nothing by the thought of which he is comforted.

them or to receive other principles in place of them. By no means, nor any thing like it. You rather look to this, whether you possess already that for which you come. You wish to prattle about theorems? What then? Do you not become greater triflers? Do not your little theorems give you some opportunity of display? You solve sophistical syllogisms.[4] Do you not examine the assumptions of the syllogism named the Liar?[5] Do you not examine hypothetical syllogisms? Why then are you still vexed if you receive the things for which you come to the school? Yes; but if my child die or my brother, or if I must die or be racked, what good will these things do me[6]?—Well, did you come for this? for this do you sit by my side? did you ever for this light your lamp or keep awake? or, when you went out to the walking place, did you ever propose any appearance that had been presented to you instead of a syllogism, and did you and your friends discuss it together? Where and when? Then you say, Theorems are useless. To whom? To such as make a bad use of them. For eye-salves are not useless to those who use them as they ought and when they ought. Fomentations are not useless. Dum-bells[7] are not useless; but they are useless to some, useful to others. If you ask me now if syllogisms are useful, I will tell you that they are useful, and if you choose, I will prove it.[8]—How then will they in any way be useful to me? Man, did you ask if they are useful to you, or did you ask generally? Let him who is suffering from dysentery, ask me if vinegar is useful; I will say that it is useful.—Will it then be useful to me?—I will say, no. Seek first for the discharge to be stopped and the ulcers to be closed. And do you, O men, first cure the ulcers and stop the discharge; be tranquil in your mind, bring it free from distraction into the school, and you will know what power reason has.

[4] See i. 7.

[5] See ii. 17. 34.

[6] τί με ταῦτα ὠφελήσει; Schweig. in his note says that he has written the text thus; but he has not. He has written τί μετὰ ταῦτα ὠφελήσει; The με appears to be necessary, and he has rendered the passage accordingly; and rightly, I think.

[7] See i. 4, note 5 on Halteres.

[8] See ii. 25.

CHAPTER XXII.

ON FRIENDSHIP.[1]

What a man applies himself to earnestly, that he naturally loves. Do men then apply themselves earnestly to the things which are bad? By no means. Well, do they apply themselves to things which in no way concern themselves? not to these either. It remains then that they employ themselves earnestly only about things which are good; and if they are earnestly employed about things, they love such things also. Whoever then understands what is good, can also know how to love: but he who cannot distinguish good from bad, and things which are neither good nor bad from both, how can he possess the power of loving? To love then is only in the power of the wise.

How is this? a man may say; I am foolish, and yet I love my child.—I am surprised indeed that you have begun by making the admission that you are foolish. For what are you deficient in? Can you not make use of your senses? do you not distinguish appearances? do you not use food which is suitable for your body, and clothing and habitation? Why then do you admit that you are foolish? It is in truth because you are often disturbed by appearances and perplexed, and their power of persuasion often conquers you; and sometimes you think these things to be good, and then the same things to be bad, and lastly neither good nor bad; and in short you grieve, fear, envy, are disturbed, you are changed. This is the reason why you confess that you are foolish. And are you not changeable in love? But wealth, and pleasure and in a word

[1] 'In this dissertation is expounded the Stoic principle that friendship is only possible between the good.' Schweig. He also says that there was another discourse by Epictetus on this subject, in which he expressed some of the opinions of Musonius Rufus (i. 1. note 12). Schweig. draws this conclusion from certain words of Stobaeus; and he supposes that this dissertation of Epictetus was in one of the last four books of Epictetus' discourses by Arrian, which have been lost.

Cicero (de Amicit. c. 5) says 'nisi in bonis amicitiam esse non posse,' and c. 18.

things themselves, do you sometimes think them to be good, and sometimes bad? and do you not think the same men at one time to be good, at another time bad? and have you not at one time a friendly feeling towards them, and at another time the feeling of an enemy? and do you not at one time praise them, and at another time blame them? Yes; I have these feelings also. Well then, do you think that he who has been deceived about a man is his friend? Certainly not. And he who has selected a man as his friend and is of a changeable disposition, has he good will towards him? He has not. And he who now abuses a man, and afterwards admires him? This man also has no good will to the other. Well then, did you never see little dogs caressing and playing with one another, so that you might say, there is nothing more friendly? but that you may know what friendship is; throw a bit of flesh among them, and you will learn. Throw between yourself and your son a little estate, and you will know how soon he will wish to bury you and how soon you wish your son to die. Then you will change your tone and say, what a son I have brought up! He has long been wishing to bury me. Throw a smart girl between you; and do you the old man love her, and the young one will love her too. If a little fame intervene or dangers, it will be just the same. You will utter the words of the father of Admetus!

Life gives you pleasure: and why not your father?[2]

Do you think that Admetus did not love his own child when he was little? that he was not in agony when the child had a fever? that he did not often say, I wish I had the fever instead of the child? then when the test (the thing) came and was near, see what words they utter. Were not Eteocles and Polynices from the same mother and from the same father? Were they not brought up together, had they not lived together, drunk together, slept together, and often kissed one another? So that, if

[2] The first verse is from the Alcestis of Euripides, v. 691. The second in Epictetus is not in Euripides. Schweighaeuser thinks that it has been intruded into the text from a trivial scholium.

any man, I think, had seen them, he would have ridiculed the philosophers for the paradoxes which they utter about friendship. But when a quarrel rose between them about the royal power, as between dogs about a bit of meat, see what they say

Polynices. Where will you take your station before the towers?
Eteocles. Why do you ask me this?
Pol. I will place myself opposite and try to kill you.
Et. I also wish to do the same.[3]

Such are the wishes that they utter.

For universally, be not deceived, every animal is attached to nothing so much as to its own interest.[4] Whatever then appears to it an impediment to this interest, whether this be a brother, or a father, or a child, or beloved, or lover, it hates, spurns, curses: for its nature is to love nothing so much as its own interest; this is father, and brother and kinsman, and country, and God. When then the gods appear to us to be an impediment to this, we abuse them and throw down their statues and burn their temples, as Alexander ordered the temples of Aesculapius to be burned when his dear friend died.[5]

For this reason if a man put in the same place his interest, sanctity, goodness, and country, and parents, and friends, all these are secured: but if he puts in one place his interest, in another his friends, and his country and his kinsmen and justice itself, all these give way being borne down by the weight of interest. For where the I and the Mine are placed, to that place of necessity the animal inclines: if in the flesh, there is the ruling power: if in the will, it is there: and if it is in externals, it is

[3] From the Phoenissae of Euripides, v. 723, etc.

[4] Compare Euripides, Hecuba, v. 846, etc.:—

δεινόν γε θνητοῖς ὡς ἅπαντα συμπίτνει·
καὶ τὰς ἀνάγκας ὡς νόμοι διώρισαν,
φίλους τιθέντες τούς γε πολεμιωτάτους
ἐχθρούς τε τοὺς πρὶν εὐμενεῖς ποιούμενοι.

[5] Alexander did this when Hephaestion died. Arrian. Expedition of Alexander, vii. 14.

there.[6] If then I am there where my will is, then only shall I be a friend such as I ought to be, and son, and father; for this will be my interest, to maintain the character of fidelity, of modesty, of patience, of abstinence, of active co-operation, of observing my relations (towards all). But if I put myself in one place, and honesty in another, then the doctrine of Epicurus becomes strong, which asserts either that there is no honesty or it is that which opinion holds to be honest (virtuous).[7]

It was through this ignorance that the Athenians and the Lacedaemonians quarrelled, and the Thebans with both; and the great king quarrelled with Hellas, and the Macedonians with both; and the Romans with the Getae.[8] And still earlier the Trojan war happened for these reasons. Alexander was the guest of Menelaus; and if any man had seen their friendly disposition, he would not have believed any one who said that they were not friends. But there was cast between them (as between dogs) a bit of meat, a handsome woman, and about her war arose. And now when you see brothers to be friends appearing to have one mind, do not conclude from this any thing about their friendship, not even if they swear it and say that it is impossible for them to be separated from one another. For

[6] Matthew vi. 21, 'for where your treasure is, there will your heart be also.'

[7] 'By "self" is here meant the proper Good, or, as Solomon expresses it, Eccl. xii. 13, "the whole of man." The Stoic proves excellently the inconvenience of placing this in any thing but a right choice (a right disposition and behaviour): but how it is the interest of each individual in every case to make that choice in preference to present pleasure and in defiance of present sufferings, appears only from the doctrine of a future recompense.' Mrs. Carter. Compare Cicero, De Fin. ii. 15, where he is speaking of Epicurus, and translates the words ἀποφαίνειν ἢ μηδὲν εἶναι τὸ καλὸν ἢ ἄρα τὸ ἔνδοξον, "ut enim consuetudo loquitur, id solum dicitur Honestum quod est populari fama gloriosum (ἔνδοξον)." See Schweig.'s note.

[8] The quarrels of the Athenians with the Lacedaemonians appear chiefly in the history of the Peloponnesian war. (Thucydides, i. 1). The quarrel of the great king, the king of Persia, is the subject of the history of Herodotus (i. 1). The great quarrel of the Macedonians with the Persians is the subject of Arrian's expedition of Alexander. The Romans were at war with the Getae or Daci in the time of Trajan, and we may assume that Epictetus was still living then.

the ruling principle of a bad man cannot be trusted, it is insecure, has no certain rule by which it is directed, and is overpowered at different times by different appearances.[9] But examine, not what other men examine, if they are born of the same parents and brought up together, and under the same paedagogue; but examine this only, wherein they place their interest, whether in externals or in the will. If in externals, do not name them friends, no more than name them trustworthy or constant, or brave or free: do not name them even men, if you have any judgment. For that is not a principle of human nature which makes them bite one another, and abuse one another, and occupy deserted places or public places, as if they were mountains,[10] and in the courts of justice display the acts of robbers; nor yet that which makes them intemperate and adulterers and corrupters, nor that which makes them do whatever else men do against one another through this one opinion only, that of placing themselves and their interests in the things which are not within the power of their will. But if you hear that in truth these men think the good to be only there, where will is, and where there is a right use of appearances, no longer trouble yourself whether they are father or son, or brothers, or have associated a long time and are companions, but when you have ascertained this only, confidently declare that they are friends, as you declare that they are faithful, that they are just. For where else is friendship than where there is fidelity, and modesty, where there is a communion[11] of honest things and of nothing else?

But you may say, such a one treated me with regard so long; and did he not love me? How do you know, slave, if he did not regard you in the same way as he wipes his

[9] Aristotle, Eth. viii. c. 8. Mrs. Carter.

[10] Schweig. thinks that this is the plain meaning: 'as wild beasts in the mountains lie in wait for men, so men lie in wait for men, not only in deserted places, but even in the forum.'

[11] *ὅπου δόσις τοῦ καλοῦ.* Lord Shaftesbury suggested *δόσις καὶ λῆψις τοῦ καλοῦ*: which Upton approved, and he refers to ii. 9. 12, *αἱ ἀκατάλληλοι λήψεις καὶ δόσεις.* Schweighaeuser suggests *διαδόσις* which I have followed in the version. Schweig. refers to i. 12. 6, i. 14. 9. The MSS. give no help.

shoes with a sponge, or as he takes care of his beast? How do you know, when you have ceased to be useful as a vessel, he will not throw you away like a broken platter? But this woman is my wife, and we have lived together so long. And how long did Eriphyle live with Amphiaraus, and was the mother of children and of many? But a necklace[12] came between them: and what is a necklace? It is the opinion about such things. That was the bestial principle, that was the thing which broke asunder the friendship between husband and wife, that which did not allow the woman to be a wife nor the mother to be a mother. And let every man among you who has seriously resolved either to be a friend himself or to have another for his friend, cut out these opinions, hate them, drive them from his soul. And thus first of all he will not reproach himself, he will not be at variance with himself, he will not change his mind, he will not torture himself. In the next place, to another also, who is like himself, he will be altogether and completely a friend.[13] But he will bear with the man who is unlike himself, he will be kind to him, gentle, ready to pardon on account of his ignorance, on account of his being mistaken in things of the greatest importance; but he will be harsh to no man, being well convinced of Plato's doctrine that every mind is deprived of truth unwillingly. If you cannot do this, yet you can do in all other respects as friends do, drink together, and lodge together, and sail together, and you may be born of the same parents; for snakes also are: but neither will they be friends nor you, so long as you retain these bestial and cursed opinions.

[12] The old story about Eriphyle who betrayed her husband for a necklace.

[13] See Schweig.'s note

CHAPTER XXIII.

ON THE POWER OF SPEAKING.

Every man will read a book with more pleasure or even with more ease, if it is written in fairer characters. Therefore every man will also listen more readily to what is spoken, if it is signified by appropriate and becoming words. We must not say then that there is no faculty of expression: for this affirmation is the characteristic of an impious and also of a timid man. Of an impious man, because he undervalues the gifts which come from God, just as if he would take away the commodity of the power of vision, or of hearing, or of seeing. Has then God given you eyes to no purpose? and to no purpose has he infused into them a spirit[1] so strong and of such skilful contrivance as to reach a long way and to fashion the forms of things which are seen? What messenger is so swift and vigilant? And to no purpose has he made the interjacent atmosphere so efficacious and elastic that the vision penetrates through the atmosphere which is in a manner moved?[2] And to no purpose has he made light, without the presence of which there would be no use in any other thing?

Man, be neither ungrateful for these gifts nor yet forget the things which are superior to them. But indeed for the power of seeing and hearing, and indeed for life itself, and for the things which contribute to support it, for the fruits which are dry, and for wine and oil give thanks to God: but remember that he has given you something else better than all these, I mean the power of using them, proving them and estimating the value of each. For what is that

[1] The word for 'spirit' is πνεῦμα, a vital spirit, an animal spirit, a nervous fluid, as Schweighaeuser explains it, or as Plutarch says (De Placit. Philosoph. iv. 15), 'the spirit which has the power of vision, which permeates from the chief faculty of the mind to the pupil of the eye;' and in another passage of the same treatise (iv. 8), 'the instruments of perception are said to be intelligent spirits (πνεύματα νοερά) which have a motion from the chief faculty of the mind to the organs.'

[2] See Schweig.'s note.

which gives information about each of these powers, what each of them is worth?[3] Is it each faculty itself? Did you ever hear the faculty of vision saying any thing about itself? or the faculty of hearing? or wheat, or barley, or a horse or a dog? No; but they are appointed as ministers and slaves to serve the faculty which has the power of making use of the appearances of things. And if you inquire what is the value of each thing, of whom do you inquire? who answers you? How then can any other faculty be more powerful than this, which uses the rest as ministers and itself proves each and pronounces about them? for which of them knows what itself is, and what is its own value? which of them knows when it ought to employ itself and when not? what faculty is it which opens and closes the eyes, and turns them away from objects to which it ought not to apply them and does apply them to other objects? Is it the faculty of vision? No; but it is the faculty of the will. What is that faculty which closes and opens the ears? what is that by which they are curious and inquisitive, or on the contrary unmoved by what is said? is it the faculty of hearing? It is no other than the faculty of the will.[4] Will this faculty then, seeing that it is amidst all the other faculties which are blind and dumb and unable to see any thing else except the very acts for which they are appointed in order to minister to this (faculty) and serve it, but this faculty alone sees sharp and sees what is the value of each of the rest; will this faculty declare to us that any thing else is the best, or that itself is? And what else does the eye do when it is opened than see? But whether we ought to look on the wife of a certain person, and in what manner, who tells us? The faculty of the will. And whether we ought to believe what is said or not to believe it, and if we do believe, whether we ought to be moved by it or not, who tells us? Is it not the faculty of the will?

[3] See i. 1.

[4] Schweighaeuser has this note: 'That which Epictetus names the προαιρετικὴ δυναμίς and afterwards frequently προαίρεσις, is generally translated by 'voluntas' (will); but it has a wider meaning than is generally given to the Latin word, and it comprehends the intellect with the will, and all the active power of the mind which we sometimes designate by the general name Reason.'

But this faculty of speaking and of ornamenting words, if there is indeed any such peculiar faculty, what else does it do, when there happens to be discourse about a thing, than to ornament the words and arrange them as hairdressers do the hair? But whether it is better to speak or to be silent, and better to speak in this way or that way, and whether this is becoming or not becoming, and the season for each and the use, what else tells us than the faculty of the will? Would you have it then to come forward and condemn itself?

What then? it (the will) says,[5] if the fact is so, can that which ministers be superior to that to which it ministers, can the horse be superior to the rider, or the dog to the huntsman, or the instrument to the musician, or the servants to the king? What is that which makes use of the rest? The will. What takes care of all? The will. What destroys the whole man, at one time by hunger, at another time by hanging, and at another time by a precipice? The will. Then is any thing stronger in men than this? and how is it possible that the things which are subject to restraint are stronger than that which is not? What things are naturally formed to hinder the faculty of vision? Both will and things which do not depend on the faculty of the will.[6] It is the same with the faculty of hearing, with the faculty of speaking in like manner. But what has a natural power of hindering the will? Nothing which is independent of the will; but only the will itself, when it is perverted. Therefore this (the will) is alone vice or alone virtue.

Then being so great a faculty and set over all the rest, let it (the will) come forward and tell us that the most excellent of all things is the flesh. Not even if the flesh itself declared that it is the most excellent, would any person bear that it should say this. But what is it, Epicurus, which pronounces this, which wrote about the End

[5] On the Greek text Upton remarks that, 'there are many passages in these dissertations which are ambiguous or rather confused on account of the small questions, and because the matter is not expanded by oratorical copiousness, not to mention other causes.'

[6] The general reading is *καὶ προαιρετά*. Salmasius proposes *καὶ ἀπροαίρετα*, which Schweig. says in a note that he accepts, and so he translates it in the Latin; but in his text he has *καὶ προαιρετά*.

(purpose) of our Being,[7] which wrote on the Nature of Things, which wrote about the Canon (rule of truth), which led you to wear a beard, which wrote when it was dying that it was spending the last and a happy day?[8] Was this the flesh or the will? Then do you admit that you possess any thing superior to this (the will)? and are you not mad? are you in fact so blind and deaf?

What then? does any man despise the other faculties? I hope not. Does any man say that there is no use or excellence in the speaking faculty?[9] I hope not. That would be foolish, impious, ungrateful towards God. But a man renders to each thing its due value. For there is some use even in an ass, but not so much as in an ox: there is also use in a dog, but not so much as in a slave: there is also some use in a slave, but not so much as in citizens: there is also some use in citizens, but not so much as in magistrates. Not indeed because some things are superior, must we undervalue the use which other things have. There is a certain value in the power of speaking, but it is not so great as the power of the will. When then I speak thus, let no man think that I ask you to neglect the power of speaking, for neither do I ask you to neglect the eyes, nor the ears nor the hands nor the feet, nor clothing nor shoes. But if you ask me what then is the most excellent of all things, what must I say? I cannot say the power of speaking, but the power of the will, when it is right (ὀρθὴ). For it is this which uses the other (the power of speaking), and all the other faculties both small and great. For when this faculty of the will is set right, a man who is not good becomes good:

[7] This appears to be the book which Cicero (Tuscul. iii. 18) entitles on the 'supreme good' (de summo bono), which, as Cicero says, contains all the doctrine of Epicurus. The book on the Canon or Rule is mentioned by Velleius in Cicero de Nat. Deorum i. c. 16, as 'that celestial volume of Epicurus on the Rule and Judgment.' See also De Fin. i. 19.

[8] This is said in a letter written by Epicurus, when he was dying in great pain (Diog. Laert. x. 22); Cicero (De Fin. ii. c. 30) quotes this letter.

[9] The MSS. have προαιρετικῆς δυνάμεως. Lord Shaftesbury suggested φραστικῆς and Salmasius also. Schweig. has put φραστικῆς in the text, and he has done right.

but when it fails, a man becomes bad. It is through this that we are unfortunate, that we are fortunate, that we blame one another, are pleased with one another. In a word, it is this which if we neglect it makes unhappiness, and if we carefully look after it, makes happiness.

But to take away the faculty of speaking and to say that there is no such faculty in reality, is the act not only of an ungrateful man towards those who gave it, but also of a cowardly man: for such a person seems to me to fear, if there is any faculty of this kind, that we shall not be able to despise it. Such also are those who say that there is no difference between beauty and ugliness. Then it would happen that a man would be affected in the same way if he saw Thersites and if he saw Achilles; in the same way, if he saw Helen and any other woman. But these are foolish and clownish notions, and the notions of men who know not the nature of each thing, but are afraid, if a man shall see the difference, that he shall immediately be seized and carried off vanquished. But this is the great matter; to leave to each thing the power (faculty) which it has, and leaving to it this power to see what is the worth of the power, and to learn what is the most excellent of all things, and to pursue this always, to be diligent about this, considering all other things of secondary value compared with this, but yet, as far as we can, not neglecting all those other things. For we must take care of the eyes also, not as if they were the most excellent thing, but we must take care of them on account of the most excellent thing, because it will not be in its true natural condition, if it does not rightly use the other faculties, and prefer some things to others.

What then is usually done? Men generally act as a traveller would do on his way to his own country, when he enters a good inn, and being pleased with it should remain there. Man, you have forgotten your purpose: you were not travelling to this inn, but you were passing through it.—But this is a pleasant inn.—And how many other inns are pleasant? and how many meadows are pleasant? yet only for passing through. But your purpose is this, to return to your country, to relieve your kinsmen of anxiety, to discharge the duties of a citizen, to marry, to beget children, to fill the usual magistracies.[10] For you are not come to select more pleasant places, but to live in these where you were born and of which you were made a citizen. Something of the kind takes place in the matter which we are considering. Since by the aid of speech and such communication as you receive here you must advance to perfection, and purge your will and correct the faculty which makes use of the appearances of things; and since it is necessary also for the teaching (delivery) of theorems to be effected by a certain mode of expression and with a certain variety and sharpness, some persons captivated by these very things abide in them, one captivated by the expression, another by syllogisms, another again by sophisms, and still another by some other inn (πανδοκείου) of the kind; and there they stay and waste away as if they were among Sirens.

Man, your purpose (business) was to make yourself capable of using comformably to nature the appearances presented to you, in your desires not to be frustrated, in your aversion from things not to fall into that which you would avoid, never to have no luck (as one may say), nor ever to have bad luck, to be free, not hindered, not compelled, conforming yourself to the administration of Zeus, obeying it, well satisfied with this, blaming no one, charging no one with fault, able from your whole soul to utter these verses

Lead me, O Zeus, and thou too Destiny.[11]

Then having this purpose before you, if some little form of expression pleases you, if some theorems please you, do

[10] The Stoics taught that a man should lead an active life. Horace (Ep. i. 1. 16) represents himself as sometimes following the Stoic principles:

'Nunc agilis fio et mersor civilibus undis.'

but this was only talk. The Stoic should discharge all the duties of a citizen, says Epictetus; he should even marry and beget children. But the marrying may be done without any sense of duty; and the continuance of the human race is secured by the naturel love of the male and of the female for conjunction. Still it is good advice, which the Roman censor Metellus gave to his fellow citizens, that, as they could not live without women, they should make the best of this business of marriage. (Gellius, i. 6.)

[11] The rest of the verses are quoted in the Encheiridion, s. 52.

you abide among them and choose to dwell there, forgetting the things at home, and do you say, These things are fine? Who says that they are not fine? but only as being a way home, as inns are. For what hinders you from being an unfortunate man, even if you speak like Demosthenes? and what prevents you, if you can resolve syllogisms like Chrysippus,[12] from being wretched, from sorrowing, from envying, in a word, from being disturbed, from being unhappy? Nothing. You see then that these were inns, worth nothing; and that the purpose before you was something else. When I speak thus to some persons, they think that I am rejecting care about speaking or care about theorems. But I am not rejecting this care, but I am rejecting the abiding about these things incessantly [13] and putting our hopes in them. If a man by this teaching does harm to those who listen to him, reckon me too among those who do this harm: for I am not able, when I see one thing which is most excellent and supreme, to say that another is so, in order to please you.

CHAPTER XXIV.

TO (OR AGAINST) A PERSON WHO WAS ONE OF THOSE WHO WERE NOT VALUED (ESTEEMED) BY HIM.

A CERTAIN person said to him (Epictetus): Frequently I desired to hear you and came to you, and you never gave me any answer: and now, if it is possible, I intreat you to say something to me. Do you think, said Epictetus, that as there is an art in any thing else, so there is also an art in speaking, and that he who has the art, will speak skilfully, and he who has not, will speak unskilfully?— I do think so.—He then who by speaking receives benefit

[12] Chrysippus wrote a book on the resolution of Syllogisms. Diogenes Laertius (vii.) says of Chrysippus that he was so famous among Dialecticians that most persons thought, if there was Dialectic among the Gods, it would not be any other than that of Chrysippus.

[13] See Schweig.'s note on ἀκαταληκτικῶς.

himself, and is able to benefit others, will speak skilfully: but he who is rather damaged by speaking and does damage to others, will he be unskilled in this art of speaking? And you may find that some are damaged and others benefited by speaking. And are all who hear benefited by what they hear? Or will you find that among them also some are benefited and some damaged?—There are both among these also, he said.—In this case also then those who hear skilfully are benefited, and those who hear unskilfully are damaged? He admitted this. Is there then a skill in hearing also, as there is in speaking?—It seems so.—If you choose, consider the matter in this way also. The practice of music, to whom does it belong? To a musician. And the proper making of a statue, to whom do you think that it belongs? To a statuary. And the looking at a statue skilfully, does this appear to you to require the aid of no art?—This also requires the aid of art.—Then if speaking properly is the business of the skilful man, do you see that to hear also with benefit is the business of the skilful man? Now as to speaking and hearing perfectly, and usefully,[1] let us for the present, if you please, say no more, for both of us are a long way from every thing of the kind. But I think that every man will allow this, that he who is going to hear philosophers requires some amount of practice in hearing. Is it not so?

Tell me then about what I should talk to you: about what matter are you able to listen?—About good and evil. —Good and evil in what? In a horse? No. Well, in an ox? No. What then? In a man? Yes. Do we know then what a man is, what the notion is which we have of him, or have we our ears in any degree practised about this matter? But do you understand what nature is? or can you even in any degree understand me when I say, I shall use demonstration to you? How? Do you understand this very thing, what demonstration is, or how any thing is demonstrated, or by what means; or what things are

[1] 'That is, let us not now consider whether I am perfect in the art of speaking, and you have a mind well prepared to derive real advantage from philosophical talk. Let us consider this only, whether your ears are sufficiently prepared for listening, whether you can understand a philosophical discussion.' Schweig.

like demonstration, but are not demonstration? Do you know what is true or what is false? What is consequent on a thing, what is repugnant to a thing, or not consistent, or inconsistent?[2] But must I excite you to philosophy, and how? Shall I show to you the repugnance in the opinions of most men, through which they differ about things good and evil, and about things which are profitable and unprofitable, when you know not this very thing, what repugnance (contradiction) is? Show me then what I shall accomplish by discoursing with you: excite my inclination to do this. As the grass which is suitable, when it is presented to a sheep, moves its inclination to eat, but if you present to it a stone or bread, it will not be moved to eat; so there are in us certain natural inclinations also to speak, when the hearer shall appear to be somebody, when he himself shall excite us: but when he shall sit by us like a stone or like grass, how can he excite a man's desire (to speak)? Does the vine say to the husbandman, Take care of me? No, but the vine by showing in itself that it will be profitable to the husbandman, if he does take care of it, invites him to exercise care. When children are attractive and lively, whom do they not invite to play with them, and crawl with them, and lisp with them? But who is eager to play with an ass or to bray with it? for though it is small, it is still a little ass.

Why then do you say nothing to me? I can only say this to you, that he who knows not who he is, and for what purpose he exists, and what is this world, and with whom he is associated, and what things are the good and the bad, and the beautiful and the ugly, and who neither understands discourse nor demonstration, nor what is true nor what is false, and who is not able to distinguish them, will neither desire according to nature nor turn away nor move towards, nor intend (to act), nor assent, nor dissent nor suspend his judgment: to say all in a few words, he will go about dumb and blind, thinking that he is somebody, but being nobody. Is this so now for the first time? Is it not the fact that ever since the human race existed, all errors and misfortunes have arisen through this igno-

[2] See Schweig.'s note.

rance? Why did Agamemnon and Achilles quarrel with one another? Was it not through not knowing what things are profitable and not profitable? Does not the one say it is profitable to restore Chryseis to her father, and does not the other say that it is not profitable? does not the one say that he ought to take the prize of another, and does not the other say that he ought not? Did they not for these reasons forget, both who they were and for what purpose they had come there? Oh, man, for what purpose did you come? to gain mistresses or to fight? To fight. With whom? the Trojans or the Hellenes? With the Trojans. Do you then leave Hector alone and draw your sword against your own king? And do you, most excellent Sir, neglect the duties of the king, you who are the people's guardian and have such cares; and are you quarrelling about a little girl with the most warlike of your allies, whom you ought by every means to take care of and protect? and do you become worse than (inferior to) a well behaved priest who treats you these fine gladiators with all respect? Do you see what kind of things ignorance of what is profitable does?

But I also am rich. Are you then richer than Agamemnon? But I am also handsome. Are you then more handsome than Achilles? But I have also beautiful hair. But had not Achilles more beautiful hair and gold coloured? and he did not comb it elegantly nor dress it. But I am also strong. Can you then lift so great a stone as Hector or Ajax? But I am also of noble birth. Are you the son of a goddess mother? are you the son of a father sprung from Zeus? What good then do these things do to him, when he sits and weeps for a girl? But I am an orator. And was he not? Do you not see how he handled the most skilful of the Hellenes in oratory, Odysseus and Phoenix? how he stopped their mouths?[3]

This is all that I have to say to you; and I say even this not willingly. Why? Because you have not roused me. For what must I look to in order to be roused, as men who are expert in riding are roused by generous

[3] In the ninth book of the Iliad, where Achilles answers the messengers sent to him by Agamemnon. The reply of Achilles is a wonderful example of eloquence.

horses? Must I look to your body? You treat it disgracefully. To your dress? That is luxurious. To your behaviour, to your look? That is the same as nothing. When you would listen to a philosopher, do not say to him, You tell me nothing; but only show yourself worthy of hearing or fit for hearing; and you will see how you will move the speaker.

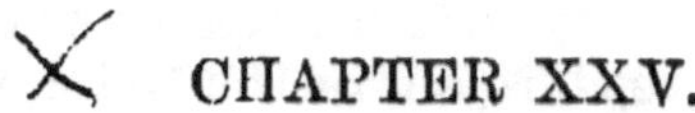

CHAPTER XXV.

THAT LOGIC IS NECESSARY.[1]

When one of those who were present said, Persuade me that logic is necessary, he replied, Do you wish me to prove this to you? The answer was—Yes.—Then I must use a demonstrative form of speech.—This was granted.—How then will you know if I am cheating you by my argument? The man was silent. Do you see, said Epictetus, that you yourself are admitting that logic is necessary, if without it you cannot know so much as this, whether logic is necessary or not necessary?

CHAPTER XXVI.

WHAT IS THE PROPERTY OF ERROR.

Every error comprehends contradiction: for since he who errs does not wish to err, but to be right, it is plain that he does not do what he wishes. For what does the thief wish to do? That which is for his own interest.[1] If then the theft is not for his interest, he does not do that which he wishes. But every rational soul is by nature offended at contradiction, and so long as it does not understand this contradiction, it is not hindered from doing contradictory

[1] See i. 17.

[1] Compare Xenophon, Mem. iii. 9. 4.

things: but when it does understand the contradiction, it must of necessity avoid the contradiction and avoid it as much as a man must dissent from the false when he sees that a thing is false; but so long as this falsehood does not appear to him, he assents to it as to truth.

He then is strong in argument and has the faculty of exhorting and confuting, who is able to show to each man the contradiction through which he errs and clearly to prove how he does not do that which he wishes and does that which he does not wish. For if any one shall show this, a man will himself withdraw from that which he does; but so long as you do not show this, do not be surprised if a man persists in his practice; for having the appearance of doing right, he does what he does. For this reason Socrates also trusting to this power used to say, I am used to call no other witness of what I say, but I am always satisfied with him with whom I am discussing, and I ask him to give his opinion and call him as a witness, and though he is only one, he is sufficient in the place of all. For Socrates knew by what the rational soul is moved, just like a pair of scales, and then it must incline, whether it chooses or not.[2] Show the rational governing faculty a contradiction, and it will withdraw from it; but if you do not show it, rather blame yourself than him who is not persuaded.[3]

[2] There is some deficiency in the text. Cicero (Acad. Prior. i. 12), 'ut enim necesse est lancem in libra ponderibus impositis deprimi; sic animum perspicuis cedere,' appears to supply the deficiency.

[3] M. Antoninus, v. 28; x. 4.

BOOK III.

CHAPTER I.

OF FINERY IN DRESS.

A CERTAIN young man a rhetorician came to see Epictetus, with his hair dressed more carefully than was usual and his attire in an ornamental style; whereupon Epictetus said, Tell me if you do not think that some dogs are beautiful and some horses, and so of all other animals. I do think so, the youth replied. Are not then some men also beautiful and others ugly? Certainly. Do we then for the same reason call each of them in the same kind beautiful, or each beautiful for something peculiar? And you will judge of this matter thus. Since we see a dog naturally formed for one thing, and a horse for another, and for another still, as an example, a nightingale, we may generally and not improperly declare each of them to be beautiful then when it is most excellent according to its nature; but since the nature of each is different, each of them seems to me to be beautiful in a different way. Is it not so? He admitted that it was. That then which makes a dog beautiful, makes a horse ugly; and that which makes a horse beautiful, makes a dog ugly, if it is true that their natures are different. It seems to be so. For I think that what makes a Pancratiast beautiful, makes a wrestler to be not good, and a runner to be most ridiculous; and he who is beautiful for the Pentathlon, is very ugly for wrestling.[1] It is so said he. What then makes

[1] A Pancratiast is a man who is trained for the Pancratium, that is, both for boxing and wrestling. The Pentathlon comprised five exercises, which are expressed by one Greek line,

Leaping, running, the quoit, throwing the javelin, wrestling.

Compare Aristotle, Rhet. i. 5.

a man beautiful? Is it that which in its kind makes both a dog and a horse beautiful? It is, he said. What then makes a dog beautiful? The possession of the excellence of a dog. And what makes a horse beautiful? The possession of the excellence of a horse. What then makes a man beautiful? Is it not the possession of the excellence of a man? And do you then, if you wish to be beautiful, young man, labour at this, the acquisition of human excellence. But what is this? Observe whom you yourself praise, when you praise many persons without partiality: do you praise the just or the unjust? The just. Whether do you praise the moderate or the immoderate? The moderate. And the temperate or the intemperate? The temperate. If then you make yourself such a person, you will know that you will make yourself beautiful: but so long as you neglect these things, you must be ugly (αἰσχρόν), even though you contrive all you can to appear beautiful.

Further I do not know what to say to you: for if I say to you what I think, I shall offend you, and you will perhaps leave the school and not return to it: and if I do not say what I think, see how I shall be acting, if you come to me to be improved, and I shall not improve you at all, and if you come to me as to a philosopher, and I shall say nothing to you as a philosopher. And how cruel it is to you to leave you uncorrected. If at any time afterwards you shall acquire sense, you will with good reason blame me and say, What did Epictetus observe in me that when he saw me in such a plight coming to him in such a scandalous condition, he neglected me and never said a word? did he so much despair of me? was I not young? was I not able to listen to reason? and how many other young men at this age commit many like errors? I hear that a certain Polemon from being a most dissolute youth underwent such a great change. Well, suppose that he did not think that I should be a Polemon;[2] yet he

[2] Comp. Horace, Sat. ii. 3, v. 253.

Quaero, faciasne quod olim
Mutatus Polemon? etc.

The story of Polemon is told by Diogenes Laertius. He was a dissolute youth. As he was passing one day the place where Xenocrates

might have set my hair right, he might have stripped off my decorations, he might have stopped me from plucking the hair out of my body; but when he saw me dressed like—what shall I say?—he kept silent. I do not say like what; but you will say when you come to your senses, and shall know what it is, and what persons use such a dress.

If you bring this charge against me hereafter, what defence shall I make? Why, shall I say that the man will not be persuaded by me? Was Laius persuaded by Apollo? Did he not go away and get drunk and show no care for the oracle?[3] Well then for this reason did Apollo refuse to tell him the truth? I indeed do not know, whether you will be persuaded by me or not; but Apollo knew most certainly that Laius would not be persuaded and yet he spoke. But why did he speak? I say in reply, But why is he Apollo, and why does he deliver oracles, and why has he fixed himself in this place as a prophet and source of truth and for the inhabitants of the world to resort to him? and why are the words Know yourself written in front of the temple, though no person takes any notice of them?

Did Socrates persuade all his hearers to take care of themselves? Not the thousandth part. But however, after he had been placed in this position by the deity, as he himself says, he never left it. But what does he say even to his judges? "If you acquit me on these conditions that I no longer do that which I do now, I will not consent and I will not desist; but I will go up both to young and to old, and, to speak plainly, to every man whom I meet, and I will ask the questions which I ask now; and most particularly will I do this to you my fellow citizens, because you are more nearly related to me."[4]—Are you so

was lecturing, he and his drunken companions burst into the school, but Polemon was so affected by the words of the excellent teacher that he came out quite a different man, and ultimately succeeded Xenocrates in the school of the Academy. See Epict. iv. 11. 30.

[3] Laius consulted the oracle at Delphi how he should have children. The oracle told him not to beget children, and even to expose them if he did. Laius was so foolish as to disobey the god in both respects, for he begot children and brought them up. He did indeed order his child Oedipus to be exposed, but the boy was saved and became the murderer of Laius.

[4] Plato, Apology, i. 9, etc. and c. 17.

curious, Socrates, and such a busy-body? and how does it concern you how we act? and what is it that you say? Being of the same community and of the same kin, you neglect yourself, and show yourself a bad citizen to the state, and a bad kinsman to your kinsmen, and a bad neighbour to your neighbours. Who then are you?—Here it is a great thing to say, "I am he whose duty it is to take care of men; for it is not every little heifer which dares to resist a lion; but if the bull comes up and resists him, say to the bull, if you choose, 'and who are you, and what business have you here?'" Man, in every kind there is produced something which excels; in oxen, in dogs, in bees, in horses. Do not then say to that which excels, Who then are you? If you do, it will find a voice in some way and say, I am such a thing as the purple in a garment:[5] do not expect me to be like the others, or blame my nature that it has made me different from the rest of men.

What then? am I such a man? Certainly not. And are you such a man as can listen to the truth? I wish you were. But however since in a manner I have been condemned to wear a white beard and a cloak, and you come to me as to a philosopher, I will not treat you in a cruel way nor yet as if I despaired of you, but I will say, Young man, whom do you wish to make beautiful? In the first place, know who you are and then adorn yourself appropriately. You are a human being; and this is a mortal animal which has the power of using appearances rationally. But what is meant by 'rationally'? Conformably to nature[6] and completely. What then do you possess which is peculiar? Is it the animal part? No. Is it the condition of mortality? No. Is it the power of using appearances?[7] No. You possess the rational faculty as a peculiar thing: adorn and beautify this; but leave

[5] i. 2. note 4.

[6] Cicero, de Fin. ii. 11: Horace, Epp. i. 10, 12. This was the great principle of Zeno, to live according to nature. Bishop Butler in the Preface to his Sermons says of this philosophical principle, that virtue consisted in following nature, that it is "a manner of speaking not loose and undeterminate, but clear and distinct, strictly just and true."

[7] The bare use of objects (appearances) belongs to all animals; a rational use of them is peculiar to man. Mrs. Carter, Introd. § 7.

your hair to him who made it as he chose. Come, what other appellations have you? Are you man or woman? Man. Adorn yourself then as man, not as woman. Woman is naturally smooth and delicate; and if she has much hair (on her body), she is a monster and is exhibited at Rome among monsters. And in a man it is monstrous not to have hair; and if he has no hair, he is a monster: but if he cuts off his hairs and plucks them out, what shall we do with him? where shall we exhibit him? and under what name shall we show him? I will exhibit to you a man who chooses to be a woman rather than a man. What a terrible sight! There is no man who will not wonder at such a notice. Indeed I think that the men who pluck out their hairs do what they do without knowing what they do. Man what fault have you to find with your nature? That it made you a man? What then? was it fit that nature should make all human creatures women? and what advantage in that case would you have had in being adorned? for whom would you have adorned yourself, if all human creatures were women? But you are not pleased with the matter: set to work then upon the whole business.[8] Take away—what is its name?—that which is the cause of the hairs: make yourself a woman in all respects, that we may not be mistaken: do not make one half man, and the other half woman. Whom do you wish to please? The women? Please them as a man. Well; but they like smooth men. Will you not hang yourself? and if women took delight in catamites, would you become one? Is this your business? were you born for this purpose, that dissolute women should delight in you? Shall we make such a one as you a citizen of Corinth and perchance a praefect of the city, or chief of the youth, or general or superintendent of the games? Well, and when you have taken a wife, do you intend to have your hairs plucked out? To please whom and for what purpose? And when you have begotten children, will you introduce them also into the state with the habit of plucking their hairs? A beautiful citizen, and senator

[8] ὅλον δι' ὅλων αὐτὸ ποίησον. Wolf proposed an emendation which Schweighaeuser does not put in his text, but he has expressed it in the Latin version. The Greek is intelligible, if we look to what follows.

and rhetorician. We ought to pray that such young men be born among us and brought up.

Do not so, I intreat you by the Gods, young man: but when you have once heard these words, go away and say to yourself, 'Epictetus has not said this to me; for how could he? but some propitious God through him: for it would never have come into his thoughts to say this, since he is not accustomed to talk thus with any person. Come then let us obey God, that we may not be subject to his anger.' You say, No. But (I say), if a crow by his croaking signifies any thing to you, it is not the crow which signifies, but God through the crow; and if he signifies any thing through a human voice, will he not cause the man to say this to you, that you may know the power of the divinity, that he signifies to some in this way, and to others in that way, and concerning the greatest things and the chief he signifies through the noblest messenger? What else is it which the poet says:

For we ourselves have warned him, and have sent
Hermes the careful watcher, Argus' slayer,
The husband not to kill nor wed the wife.[9]

Was Hermes going to descend from heaven to say this to him (Aegisthus)? And now the Gods say this to you and send the messenger, the slayer of Argus, to warn you not to pervert that which is well arranged, nor to busy yourself about it, but to allow a man to be a man, and a woman to be a woman, a beautiful man to be as a beautiful man, and an ugly man as an ugly man, for you are not flesh and hair, but you are will (*προαίρεσις*); and if your will is beautiful, then you will be beautiful. But up to the present time I dare not tell you that you are ugly, for I think that you are readier to hear anything than this. But see what Socrates says to the most beautiful and blooming of men Alcibiades: Try then to be beautiful. What does he say to him? Dress your hair and pluck the hairs from your legs? Nothing of that kind. But adorn your will, take away bad opinions. How with

[9] From the Odyssey, i. 37, where Zeus is speaking of Aegisthus.

the body? Leave it as it is by nature. Another has looked after these things: intrust them to him. What then, must a man be uncleaned? Certainly not; but what you are and are made by nature, cleanse this. A man should be cleanly as a man, a woman as a woman, a child as a child. You say no: but let us also pluck out the lion's mane, that he may not be uncleaned, and the cock's comb for he also ought to be cleaned. Granted, but as a cock, and the lion as a lion, and the hunting dog as a hunting dog.

CHAPTER II.

IN WHAT A MAN OUGHT TO BE EXERCISED WHO HAS MADE PROFICIENCY;[1] AND THAT WE NEGLECT THE CHIEF THINGS.

THERE are three things (topics, τόποι) in which a man ought to exercise himself who would be wise and good.[2] The first concerns the desires and the aversions, that a man may not fail to get what he desires, and that he may not fall into that which he does not desire.[3] The second concerns the movements (towards an object) and the movements from an object, and generally in doing what a man ought to do, that he may act according to order, to reason, and not carelessly. The third thing concerns freedom from deception and rashness in judgment, and generally it concerns the assents (συγκαταθέσεις). Of these

[1] In place of προκόψαντα Schweig. suggests that we should read προκόψοντα: and this is probable.

[2] καλὸς καὶ ἀγαθός is the usual Greek expression to signify a perfect man. The Stoics, according to Stobaeus, absurdly called 'virtue,' καλόν (beautiful), because it naturally 'calls' (καλεῖ) to itself those who desire it. The Stoics also said that every thing good was beautiful (καλός), and that the good and the beautiful were equivalent. The Roman expression is Vir bonus et sapiens. (Hor. Epp., i. 7, 22 and 16, 20). Perhaps the phrase καλὸς καὶ ἀγαθός arose from the notion of beauty and goodness being the combination of a perfect human being.

[3] Antoninus, xi. 37, 'as to sensual desire he should altogether keep away from it; and as to avoidance [aversion] he should not show it with respect to any of the things which are not in our power.'

topics the chief and the most urgent is that which relates to the affects (τὰ πάθη, perturbations); for an affect is produced in no other way than by a failing to obtain that which a man desires or falling into that which a man would wish to avoid. This is that which brings in perturbations, disorders, bad fortune, misfortunes, sorrows, lamentations, and envy; that which makes men envious and jealous; and by these causes we are unable even to listen to the precepts of reason. The second topic concerns the duties of a man; for I ought not to be free from affects (ἀπαθῆ) like a statue, but I ought to maintain the relations (σχέσεις) natural and acquired, as a pious man, as a son, as a father, as a citizen.

The third topic is that which immediately concerns those who are making proficiency, that which concerns the security of the other two, so that not even in sleep any appearance unexamined may surprise us, nor in intoxication, nor in melancholy. This, it may be said, is above our power. But the present philosophers neglecting the first topic and the second (the affects and duties), employ themselves on the third, using sophistical arguments (μεταπίπτοντας), making conclusions from questioning, employing hypotheses, lying. For a man must, as it is said, when employed on these matters, take care that he is not deceived. Who must? The wise and good man. This then is all that is wanting to you. Have you successfully worked out the rest? Are you free from deception in the matter of money? If you see a beautiful girl, do you resist the appearance? If your neighbour obtains an estate by will, are you not vexed? Now is there nothing else wanting to you except unchangeable firmness of mind (ἀμεταπτωσία)? Wretch, you hear these very things with fear and anxiety that some person may despise you, and with inquiries about what any person may say about you. And if a man come and tell you that in a certain conversation in which the question was, Who is the best philosopher, a man who was present said that a certain person was the chief philosopher, your little soul which was only a finger's length stretches out to two cubits. But if another who is present says, You are mistaken; it is not worth while to listen to a certain person, for what does he know? he has only the first principles, and no more? then you are confounded, you grow pale, you cry out immediately, I will show him who I am, that I am a great philosopher.—It is seen by these very things: why do you wish to show it by others? Do you not know that Diogenes pointed out one of the sophists in this way by stretching out his middle finger?[4] And then when the man was wild with rage, This, he said, is the certain person: I have pointed him out to you. For a man is not shown by the finger, as a stone or a piece of wood; but when any person shows the man's principles, then he shows him as a man.

Let us look at your principles also. For is it not plain that you value not at all your own will (προαίρεσις), but you look externally to things which are independent of your will? For instance, what will a certain person say? and what will people think of you? will you be considered a man of learning; have you read Chrysippus or Antipater? for if you have read Archedemus[5] also, you have every thing [that you can desire]. Why are you still uneasy lest you should not show us who you are? Would you let me tell you what manner of man you have shown us that you are? You have exhibited yourself to us as a mean fellow, querulous, passionate, cowardly, finding fault with every thing, blaming every body, never quiet, vain: this is what you have exhibited to us. Go away now and read Archedemus; then if a mouse should leap down and make a noise, you are a dead man. For such a death awaits you as it did[6]—what was the man's name?—Crinis; and he too was proud, because he understood Archedemus.

Wretch, will you not dismiss these things that do not concern you at all? These things are suitable to those who are able to learn them without perturbation, to those who can say: "I am not subject to anger, to grief, to envy: I am not hindered, I am not restrained. What

[4] To point out a man with the middle finger was a way of showing the greatest contempt for him.

[5] As to Archedemus, see ii. 4, 11. Ἀπέχεις ἅπαντα: this expression is compared by Upton with Matthew vi. 2, ἀπέχουσι μισθόν.

[6] Wolf suggests οἷος. Crinis was a Stoic philosopher mentioned by Diogenes Laertius. We may suppose that he was no real philosopher, and that he died of fright.

remains for me? I have leisure, I am tranquil: let us see how we must deal with sophistical arguments;[7] let us see how when a man has accepted an hypothesis he shall not be led away to any thing absurd." To them such things belong. To those who are happy it is appropriate to light a fire, to dine; if they choose, both to sing and to dance. But when the vessel is sinking, you come to me and hoist the sails.[8]

CHAPTER III.

WHAT IS THE MATTER ON WHICH A GOOD MAN SHOULD BE EMPLOYED, AND IN WHAT WE OUGHT CHIEFLY TO PRACTISE OURSELVES.

THE material for the wise and good man is his own ruling faculty: and the body is the material for the physician and the aliptes (the man who oils persons); the land is the matter for the husbandman. The business of the wise and good man is to use appearances conformably to nature: and as it is the nature of every soul to assent to the truth, to dissent from the false, and to remain in suspense as to that which is uncertain; so it is its nature to be moved towards the desire of the good, and to aversion from the evil; and with respect to that which is neither good nor bad it feels indifferent. For as the money-changer (banker) is not allowed to reject Caesar's coin, nor the seller of herbs, but if you show the coin, whether he chooses or not, he must give up what is sold for the coin; so it is also in the matter of the soul. When the good appears, it immediately

[7] See this chapter above.

[8] τοὺς σιφάρους. On this reading the student may consult the note in Schweighaeuser's edition. The word σιφάρους, if it is the right reading, is not clear; nor the meaning of this conclusion.

The philosopher is represented as being full of anxiety about things which do not concern him, and which are proper subjects for those only who are free from disturbing passions and are quite happy, which is not the philosopher's condition. He is compared to a sinking ship, and at this very time he is supposed to be employed in the useless labour of hoisting the sails.

attracts to itself; the evil repels from itself. But the soul will never reject the manifest appearance of the good, any more than persons will reject Caesar's coin. On this principle depends every movement both of man and God.[1]

For this reason the good is preferred to every intimate relationship (obligation). There is no intimate relationship between me and my father, but there is between me and the good. Are you so hard-hearted? Yes, for such is my nature; and this is the coin which God has given me. For this reason if the good is something different from the beautiful and the just, both father is gone (neglected), and brother and country, and every thing. But shall I overlook my own good, in order that you may have it, and shall I give it up to you? Why? I am your father. But you are not my good. I am your brother. But you are not my good. But if we place the good in a right determination of the will, the very observance of the relations of life is good, and accordingly he who gives up any external things, obtains that which is good. Your father takes away your property. But he does not injure you. Your brother will have the greater part of the estate in land. Let him have as much as he chooses. Will he then have a greater share of modesty, of fidelity, of brotherly affection? For who will eject you from this possession? Not even Zeus, for neither has he chosen to do so; but he has made this in my own power, and he has given it to me just as he possessed it himself, free from hindrance, compulsion, and impediment. When then the coin which another uses is a different coin, if a man presents this coin, he receives that which is sold for it. Suppose that there comes into the province a thievish proconsul, what coin does he use? Silver coin. Show it to him, and carry off what you please. Suppose one comes who is an adulterer: what coin does he use? Little girls. Take, a man says, the coin, and sell me the small thing. Give, says the seller, and buy [what you want]. Another is eager to possess boys. Give him the coin, and receive what you wish. Another is fond of hunting: give him a fine nag or a dog. Though he groans and laments, he will sell for it that which you want. For another

[1] Comp. i. 19, 11.

compels him from within, he who has fixed (determined) this coin.[2]

Against (or with respect to) this kind of thing chiefly a man should exercise himself. As soon as you go out in the morning, examine every man whom you see, every man whom you hear; answer as to a question, What have you seen? A handsome man or woman? Apply the rule. Is this independent of the will, or dependent? Independent. Take it away. What have you seen? A man lamenting over the death of a child. Apply the rule. Death is a thing independent of the will. Take it away. Has the proconsul met you? Apply the rule. What kind of thing is a proconsul's office? Independent of the will, or dependent on it? Independent. Take this away also: it does not stand examination: cast it away: it is nothing to you.

If we practised this and exercised ourselves in it daily from morning to night, something indeed would be done. But now we are forthwith caught half asleep by every appearance, and it is only, if ever, that in the school we are roused a little. Then when we go out, if we see a man lamenting, we say, He is undone. If we see a consul, we say, He is happy. If we see an exiled man, we say, He is miserable. If we see a poor man, we say, He is wretched: he has nothing to eat.

We ought then to eradicate these bad opinions, and to this end we should direct all our efforts. For what is weeping and lamenting? Opinion. What is bad fortune? Opinion. What is civil sedition, what is divided opinion, what is blame, what is accusation, what is impiety, what is

[2] Mrs. Carter compares the Epistle to the Romans, vii. 21–23. Schweighaeuser says, the man either sees that the thing which he is doing is bad or unjust, or for any other reason he does not do the thing willingly; but he is compelled, and allows himself to be carried away by the passion which rules him. The 'another' who compels is God, Schweig. says, who has made the nature of man such, that he must postpone every thing else to that thing in which he places his Good: and he adds, that it is man's fault if he places his good in that thing, in which God has not placed it.

Some persons will not consider this to be satisfactory. The man is 'compelled and allows himself to be carried away,' etc. The notion of 'compulsion' is inconsistent with the exercise of the will. The man is unlucky. He is like him 'who sees,' as the Latin poet says, 'the better things and approves of them, but follows the worse.'

trifling? All these things are opinions, and nothing more, and opinions about things independent of the will, as if they were good and bad. Let a man transfer these opinions to things dependent on the will, and I engage for him that he will be firm and constant, whatever may be the state of things around him. Such as is a dish of water, such is the soul. Such as is the ray of light which falls on the water, such are the appearances. When the water is moved, the ray also seems to be moved, yet it is not moved. And when then a man is seized with giddiness, it is not the arts and the virtues which are confounded, but the spirit (the nervous power) on which they are impressed; but if the spirit be restored to its settled state, those things also are restored.[3]

CHAPTER IV.

AGAINST A PERSON WHO SHOWED HIS PARTIZANSHIP IN AN UNSEEMLY WAY IN A THEATRE.

THE governor of Epirus having shown his favour to an actor in an unseemly way and being publicly blamed on this account, and afterwards having reported to Epictetus that he was blamed and that he was vexed at those who blamed him, Epictetus said, What harm have they been doing? These men also were acting as partizans, as you were doing. The governor replied, Does then any person show his partizanship in this way? When they see you, said Epictetus, who are their governor, a friend of Caesar and his deputy, showing partizanship in this way, was it not to be expected that they also should show their partizanship in the same way? for if it is not right to show partizanship in this way, do not do so yourself; and if it is right, why are you angry if they followed your example? For whom have the many to imitate except you, who are their superiors? to whose example should they look when

[3] See Schweig.'s note on this obscure passage.

they go to the theatre except yours? See how the deputy of Caesar looks on: he has cried out, and I too then will cry out. He springs up from his seat, and I will spring up. His slaves sit in various parts of the theatre and call out. I have no slaves, but I will myself cry out as much as I can and as loud as all of them together. You ought then to know when you enter the theatre that you enter as a rule and example to the rest how they ought to look at the acting. Why then did they blame you? Because every man hates that which is a hindrance to him. They wished one person to be crowned; you wished another. They were a hindrance to you, and you were a hindrance to them. You were found to be the stronger; and they did what they could; they blamed that which hindered them. What then would you have? That you should do what you please, and they should not even say what they please? And what is the wonder? Do not the husbandmen abuse Zeus when they are hindered by him? do not the sailors abuse him? do they ever cease abusing Caesar? What then? does not Zeus know? is not what is said reported to Caesar? What then does he do? he knows that, if he punished all who abuse him, he would have nobody to rule over. What then? when you enter the theatre, you ought to say not, Let Sophron (some actor) be crowned, but you ought to say this, Come let me maintain my will in this matter so that it shall be conformable to nature: no man is dearer to me than myself. It would be ridiculous then for me to be hurt (injured) in order that another who is an actor may be crowned. Whom then do I wish to gain the prize? Why the actor who does gain the prize; and so he will always gain the prize whom I wish to gain it.—But I wish Sophron to be crowned.—Celebrate as many games as you choose in your own house, Nemean, Pythian, Isthmian, Olympian, and proclaim him victor. But in public do not claim more than your due, nor attempt to appropriate to yourself what belongs to all. If you do not consent to this, bear being abused: for when you do the same as the many, you put yourself on the same level with them.

CHAPTER V.

AGAINST THOSE WHO ON ACCOUNT OF SICKNESS GO AWAY HOME.

I AM sick here, said one of the pupils, and I wish to return home.—At home, I suppose, you were free from sickness. Do you not consider whether you are doing any thing here which may be useful to the exercise of your will, that it may be corrected? For if you are doing nothing towards this end, it was to no purpose that you came. Go away. Look after your affairs at home. For if your ruling power cannot be maintained in a state conformable to nature, it is possible that your land can, that you will be able to increase your money, you will take care of your father in his old age, frequent the public place, hold magisterial office: being bad you will do badly any thing else that you have to do. But if you understand yourself, and know that you are casting away certain bad opinions and adopting others in their place, and if you have changed your state of life from things which are not within your will to things which are within your will, and if you ever say, Alas! you are not saying what you say on account of your father, or your brother, but on account of yourself, do you still allege your sickness? Do you not know that both disease and death must surprise us while we are doing something? the husbandman while he is tilling the ground, the sailor while he is on his voyage? what would you be doing when death surprises you, for you must be surprised when you are doing something? If you can be doing anything better than this when you are surprised, do it. For I wish to be surprised by disease or death when I am looking after nothing else than my own will, that I may be free from perturbation, that I may be free from hindrance, free from compulsion, and in a state of liberty. I wish to be found practising these things that I may be able to say to God, Have I in any respect transgressed thy commands? have I in any respect wrongly used the powers which thou gavest me? have I misused my perceptions or my preconceptions (προλήψεσι)?[1] have I ever blamed thee? have I ever found fault with thy administration? I have been sick, because it was thy will, and so have others, but I was content to be sick. I have been poor because it was thy will, but I was content also. I have not filled a magisterial office, because it was not thy pleasure that I should: I have never desired it. Hast thou ever seen me for this reason discontented? have I not always approached thee with a cheerful countenance, ready to do thy commands and to obey thy signals? Is it now thy will that I should depart from the assemblage of men? I depart. I give thee all thanks that thou hast allowed me to join in this thy assemblage of men and to see thy works, and to comprehend this thy administration. May death surprise me while I am thinking of these things, while I am thus writing and reading.

But my mother will not hold my head when I am sick. Go to your mother then; for you are a fit person to have your head held when you are sick.—But at home I used to lie down on a delicious bed.—Go away to your bed: indeed you are fit to lie on such a bed even when you are in health: do not then lose what you can do there (at home).

But what does Socrates say?[2] As one man, he says, is pleased with improving his land, another with improving his horse, so I am daily pleased in observing that I am growing better. Better in what? in using nice little words? Man, do not say that. In little matters of speculation (θεωρήματα)? what are you saying?—And indeed I do not see what else there is on which philosophers employ their time.—Does it seem nothing to you to have never found fault with any person, neither with God nor man? to have blamed nobody? to carry the same face always in going out and coming in? This is what Socrates knew, and yet

[1] On 'preconceptions,' see i. 2.

[2] Xenophon (Memorab. i. 6, 14); but Epictetus does not quote the words, he only gives the meaning. Antoninus (viii. 43) says, 'Different things delight different people. But it is my delight to keep the ruling faculty sound without turning away either from any man or from any of the things which happen to men, but looking at and receiving all with welcome eyes, and using every thing according to its value.'

he never said that he knew any thing or taught any thing.[3] But if any man asked for nice little words or little speculations, he would carry him to Protagoras or to Hippias; and if any man came to ask for potherbs, he would carry him to the gardener. Who then among you has this purpose (motive to action)? for if indeed you had it, you would both be content in sickness, and in hunger, and in death. If any among you has been in love with a charming girl, he knows that I say what is true.[4]

CHAPTER VI.

MISCELLANEOUS.

WHEN some person asked him how it happened that since reason has been more cultivated by the men of the present age, the progress made in former times was greater. In what respect, he answered, has it been more cultivated now, and in what respect was the progress greater then? For in that in which it has now been more cultivated, in that also the progress will now be found. At present it has been cultivated for the purpose of resolving syllogisms, and progress is made. But in former times it was cultivated for the purpose of maintaining the governing faculty in a condition conformable to nature, and progress was made. Do not then mix things which are different, and do not expect, when you are labouring at one thing to make progress in another. But see if any man among us when he is intent upon this, the keeping himself in a state

[3] Socrates never professed to teach virtue, but by showing himself to be a virtuous man he expected to make his companions virtuous by imitating his example. (Xenophon, Memorab. i. 2, 3.)

[4] Upton explains this passage thus: 'He who loves knows what it is to endure all things for love.' If any man then being captivated with love for a girl would for her sake endure dangers and even death, what would he not endure if he possessed the love of God, the Universal, the chief of beautiful things?'

conformable to nature and living so always, does not make progress. For you will not find such a man.

The good man is invincible, for he does not enter the contest where he is not stronger. If you (his adversary) want to have his land and all that is on it, take the land; take his slaves, take his magisterial office, take his poor body. But you will not make his desire fail in that which it seeks, nor his aversion fall into that which he would avoid. The only contest into which he enters is that about things which are within the power of his will; how then will he not be invincible?

Some person having asked him what is Common sense, Epictetus replied, As that may be called a certain Common hearing which only distinguishes vocal sounds, and that which distinguishes musical sounds is not Common, but artificial; so there are certain things which men, who are not altogether perverted, see by the common notions which all possess. Such a constitution of the mind is named Common sense.[1]

It is not easy to exhort weak young men; for neither is it easy to hold (soft) cheese with a hook.[2] But those who have a good natural disposition, even if you try to turn them aside, cling still more to reason. Wherefore Rufus[3] generally attempted to discourage (his pupils), and he used this method as a test of those who had a good natural disposition and those who had not. For it was his habit to say, as a stone, if you cast it upwards, will be brought down to the earth by its own nature, so the man whose mind is naturally good, the more you repel him, the more he turns towards that to which he is naturally inclined.

[1] The Greek is *κοίνος νοῦς*, the Communis sensus of the Romans, and our Common sense. Horace (Sat. i. 3, 65) speaks of a man who 'communi sensu plane caret,' one who has not the sense or understanding which is the common property of men.

[2] This was a proverb used by Bion, as Diogenes Laertius says. The cheese was new and soft, as the antients used it.

[3] Rufus is mentioned i. 1, note 12.

CHAPTER VII.

TO THE ADMINISTRATOR OF THE FREE CITIES WHO WAS AN EPICUREAN.

WHEN the administrator[1] came to visit him, and the man was an Epicurean, Epictetus said, It is proper for us who are not philosophers to inquire of you who are philosophers,[2] as those who come to a strange city inquire of the citizens and those who are acquainted with it, what is the best thing in the world, in order that we also after inquiry may go in quest of that which is best and look at it, as strangers do with the things in cities. For that there are three things which relate to man, soul, body, and things external, scarcely any man denies. It remains for you philosophers to answer what is the best. What shall we say to men? Is the flesh the best? and was it for this that Maximus[3] sailed as far as Cassiope in winter (or bad weather) with his son, and accompanied him that he might be gratified in the flesh? When the man said that it was not, and added, Far be that from him.—Is it not fit then, Epictetus said, to be actively employed about the best? It is certainly of all things the most fit. What then do we possess which is better than the flesh? The soul, he replied. And the good things of the best, are they better, or the good things of the worse? The good things of the best. And are the good things of the best within the power of the will or not within the power of the will? They are within the power of the will. Is then the pleasure of the soul a thing within the power of the will? It is, he replied.

[1] The Greek is διορθωτής. The Latin word is Corrector, which occurs in inscriptions, and elsewhere.

[2] The Epicureans are ironically named Philosophers, for most of them were arrogant men. See what is said of them in Cicero's De Natura Deorum, i. 8. Schweig.

[3] Maximus was appointed by Trajan to conduct a campaign against the Parthians, in which he lost his life. Dion Cassius, ii. 1108, 1126, Reimarus.

Cassiope or Cassope is a city in Epirus, near the sea, and between Pandosia and Nicopolis, where Epictetus lived.

And on what shall this pleasure depend? On itself? But that can not be conceived: for there must first exist a certain substance or nature (οὐσία) of good, by obtaining which we shall have pleasure in the soul. He assented to this also. On what then shall we depend for this pleasure of the soul? for if it shall depend on things of the soul,[4] the substance (nature) of the good is discovered; for good can not be one thing, and that at which we are rationally delighted another thing; nor if that which precedes is not good, can that which comes after be good, for in order that the thing which comes after may be good, that which precedes must be good. But you would not affirm this, if you are in your right mind, for you would then say what is inconsistent both with Epicurus and the rest of your doctrines. It remains then that the pleasure of the soul is in the pleasure from things of the body: and again that those bodily things must be the things which precede and the substance (nature) of the good.

For this reason Maximus acted foolishly if he made the voyage for any other reason than for the sake of the flesh, that is, for the sake of the best. And also a man acts foolishly if he abstains from that which belongs to others, when he is a judge (δικαστής) and able to take it. But, if you please, let us consider this only, how this thing may be done secretly, and safely, and so that no man will know it. For not even does Epicurus himself declare stealing to be bad,[5] but he admits that detection is; and because it is impossible to have security against detection, for this reason he says, Do not steal. But I say to you that if stealing is done cleverly and cautiously, we shall not be detected: further also we have powerful friends in Rome both men and women, and the Hellenes (Greeks) are weak, and no man will venture to go up to Rome for the purpose (of complaining). Why do you refrain from your own good? This is senseless, foolish. But even if you tell me that you do refrain, I will not believe you. For as it is

[4] ψυχικοῖς is Lord Shaftesbury's emendation in place of ἀγαθοῖς, and it is accepted by Schweighaeuser.

[5] Diogenes Laertius (x. 151), quoted by Upton. 'Injustice,' says Epicurus, 'is not an evil in itself, but the evil is in the fear which there is on account of suspicion.'

impossible to assent to that which appears false, and to turn away from that which is true, so it is impossible to abstain from that which appears good. But wealth is a good thing, and certainly most efficient in producing pleasure. Why will you not acquire wealth? And why should we not corrupt our neighbor's wife, if we can do it without detection? and if the husband foolishly prates about the matter, why not pitch him out of the house? If you would be a philosopher such as you ought to be, if a perfect philosopher, if consistent with your own doctrines, [you must act thus]. If you would not, you will not differ at all from us who are called Stoics; for we also say one thing, but we do another: we talk of the things which are beautiful (good), but we do what is base. But you will be perverse in the contrary way, teaching what is bad, practising what is good.[6]

In the name of God,[7] are you thinking of a city of Epicureans? [One man says], 'I do not marry.'—'Nor I, for a man ought not to marry; nor ought we to beget children, nor engage in public matters.' What then will happen? whence will the citizens come? who will bring them up? who will be governor of the youth, who preside over gymnastic exercises? and in what also will the teacher instruct them? will he teach them what the Lacedaemonians were taught, or what the Athenians were taught? Come take a young man, bring him up according to your doctrines. The doctrines are bad, subversive of a state, pernicious to families, and not becoming to women. Dismiss them, man. You live in a chief city: it is your duty to be a magistrate, to judge justly, to abstain from that which belongs to others; no woman ought to seem beautiful to you except your own

[6] The MSS., with one exception, have δογματίζων τὰ καλὰ, ποιῶν τὰ αἰσχρα, but it was properly corrected by Wolf, as Upton remarks, who shows from Cicero, de Fin., ii. 25 and 31, that the MSS. are wrong. In the second passage Cicero says, 'nihil in hac praeclara epistola scriptum ab Epicuro congruens et conveniens decretis ejus reperietis. Ita redarguitur ipse a sese, vincunturque scripta ejus probitate ipsius ac moribus.' See Epictetus, ii. 18.

[7] Upton compares the passage (v. 333) in the Cyclops of Euripides, who speaks like an Epicurean. Not to marry and not to engage in public affairs were Epicurean doctrines. See Epictetus, i. 23, 3 and 6

wife, and no youth, no vessel of silver, no vessel of gold (except your own). Seek for doctrines which are consistent with what I say, and by making them your guide you will with pleasure abstain from things which have such persuasive power to lead us and overpower us. But if to the persuasive power of these things, we also devise such a philosophy as this which helps to push us on towards them and strengthens us to this end, what will be the consequence? In a piece of toreutic[8] art which is the best part? the silver or the workmanship? The substance of the hand is the flesh; but the work of the hand is the principal part (that which precedes and leads the rest). The duties then are also three:[9] those which are directed towards the existence of a thing; those which are directed towards its existence in a particular kind; and third, the chief or leading things themselves. So also in man we ought not to value the material, the poor flesh, but the principal (leading things, *τὰ προηγούμενα*). What are these? Engaging in public business, marrying, begetting children, venerating God, taking care of parents, and generally, having desires, aversions (*ἐκκλίνειν*), pursuits of things and avoidances, in the way in which we ought to do these things, and according to our nature. And how are we constituted by nature? Free, noble, modest: for what other animal blushes? what other is capable of receiving the appearance (the impression) of shame? and we are so constituted by nature as to subject pleasure to these things, as a minister, a servant, in order that it may call forth our activity, in order that it may keep us constant in acts which are conformable to nature.[10]

But I am rich and I want nothing.—Why then do you pretend to be a philosopher? Your golden and your silver vessels are enough for you. What need have you of principles (opinions)? But I am also a judge (*κριτής*) of the Greeks.—Do you know how to judge? Who taught you to

[8] The toreutic art is the art of working in metal, stone, or wood, and of making figures on them in relief or by cutting into the material.

[9] See Schweig.'s note.

[10] See Schweig.'s note.

know? Caesar wrote to me a codicil.[11] Let him write and give you a commission to judge of music; and what will be the use of it to you? Still how did you become a judge? whose hand did you kiss? the hand of Symphorus or Numenius? Before whose bed-chamber have you slept?[12] To whom have you sent gifts? Then do you not see that to be a judge is just of the same value as Numenius is? But I can throw into prison any man whom I please.—So you can do with a stone.—But I can beat with sticks whom I please.—So you may an ass. This is not a governing of men. Govern us as rational animals: show us what is profitable to us, and we will follow it: show us what is unprofitable, and we will turn away from it. Make us imitators of yourself, as Socrates made men imitators of himself. For he was like a governor of men, who made them subject to him their desires, their aversion, their movements towards an object and their turning away from it.—Do this: do not do this: if you do not obey, I will throw you into prison.—This is not governing men like rational animals. But I (say): As Zeus has ordained, so act: if you do not act so, you will feel the penalty, you will be punished.—What will be the punishment? Nothing else than not having done your duty: you will lose the character of fidelity, modesty, propriety. Do not look for greater penalties than these.

[11] A 'codicillus' is a small 'codex' and the original sense of 'codex' is a strong stem or stump. Lastly it was used for a book, and even for a will. 'Codicilli' were small writing-tablets, covered with wax, on which men wrote with a stylus or pointed metal. Lastly, codicillus is a book or writing generally; and a writing or letter by which the emperor conferred any office. Our word codicil has only one sense, which is a small writing added or subjoined to a will or testament; but this sense is also derived from the Roman use of the word. (Dig. 29, tit. 7, de jure codicillorum.)

[12] Upton supposes this to mean, whose bedchamber man are you? and he compares i. 19. But Schweig. says that this is not the meaning here, and that the meaning is this: He who before daybreak is waiting at the door of a rich man, whose favour he seeks, is said in a derisive way to be passing the night before a man's chamber.

CHAPTER VIII.

HOW WE MUST EXERCISE OURSELVES AGAINST APPEARANCES (φαντασίας).

As we exercise ourselves against sophistical questions, so we ought to exercise ourselves daily against appearances; for these appearances also propose questions to us. A certain person's son is dead. Answer; the thing is not within the power of the will: it is not an evil. A father has disinherited a certain son. What do you think of it? It is a thing beyond the power of the will, not an evil. Caesar has condemned a person. It is a thing beyond the power of the will, not an evil. The man is afflicted at this. Affliction is a thing which depends on the will: it is an evil. He has borne the condemnation bravely. That is a thing within the power of the will: it is a good. If we train ourselves in this manner, we shall make progress; for we shall never assent to any thing of which there is not an appearance capable of being comprehended. Your son is dead. What has happened? Your son is dead. Nothing more? Nothing. Your ship is lost. What has happened? Your ship is lost. A man has been led to prison. What has happened? He has been led to prison. But that herein he has fared badly, every man adds from his own opinion. But Zeus, you say, does not do right in these matters. Why? because he has made you capable of endurance? because he has made you magnanimous? because he has taken from that which befalls you the power of being evils? because it is in your power to be happy while you are suffering what you suffer; because he has opened the door to you,[1] when things do not please you?[2] Man, go out and do not complain.

Hear how the Romans feel towards philosophers, if you would like to know. Italicus, who was the most in repute of the philosophers, once when I was present being vexed with his own friends and as if he was suffering something intolerable said, "I cannot bear it, you are killing me: you will make me such as that man is;" pointing to me.[3]

[1] See i. 9. 20.

[2] See ii. 6. 22, ἄν σοι ποιῇ. Upton.

[3] Schweighaeuser says that he does not clearly see what Epictetus means; nor do I.

CHAPTER IX.

TO A CERTAIN RHETORICIAN WHO WAS GOING UP TO ROME ON A SUIT.

When a certain person came to him, who was going up to Rome on account of a suit which had regard to his rank, Epictetus enquired the reason of his going to Rome, and the man then asked what he thought about the matter. Epictetus replied, If you ask me what you will do in Rome, whether you will succeed or fail, I have no rule (*θεώρημα*) about this. But if you ask me how you will fare, I can tell you: if you have right opinions (*δόγματα*), you will fare well; if they are false, you will fare ill. For to every man the cause of his acting is opinion. For what is the reason why you desired to be elected governor of the Cnossians? Your opinion. What is the reason that you are now going up to Rome? Your opinion. And going in winter, and with danger and expense.—I must go.—What tells you this? Your opinion. Then if opinions are the causes of all actions, and a man has bad opinions, such as the cause may be, such also is the effect. Have we then all sound opinions, both you and your adversary? And how do you differ? But have you sounder opinions than your adversary? Why? You think so. And so does he think that his opinions are better; and so do madmen. This is a bad criterion. But show to me that you have made some inquiry into your opinions and have taken some pains about them. And as now you are sailing to Rome in order to become governor of the Cnossians, and you are not content to stay at home with the honours which you had, but you desire something greater and more conspicuous, so when did you ever make a voyage for the purpose of examining your own opinions, and casting them out, if you have any that are bad? Whom have you approached for this purpose? What time have you fixed for it? What age? Go over the times of your life by yourself, if you are ashamed of me (knowing the fact) when you were a boy, did you examine your own opinions? and did you not then, as you do all things now, do as you did do? and when you were become a youth and attended the rhetoricians, and yourself practised rhetoric, what did you imagine that you were deficient in? And when you were a young man and engaged in public matters, and pleaded causes yourself, and were gaining reputation, who then seemed your equal? And when would you have submitted to any man examining and showing that your opinions are bad? What then do you wish me to say to you?—Help me in this matter.—I have no theorem (rule) for this. Nor have you, if you came to me for this purpose, come to me as a philosopher, but as to a seller of vegetables or a shoemaker. For what purpose then have philosophers theorems? For this purpose, that whatever may happen, our ruling faculty may be and continue to be conformable to nature. Does this seem to you a small thing?—No; but the greatest. —What then? does it need only a short time? and is it possible to seize it as you pass by? If you can, seize it.

Then you will say, I met with Epictetus as I should meet with a stone or a statue: for you saw me, and nothing more. But he meets with a man as a man, who learns his opinions, and in his turn shows his own. Learn my opinions: show me yours; and then say that you have visited me. Let us examine one another: if I have any bad opinion, take it away: if you have any, show it. This is the meaning of meeting with a philosopher.—Not so, (you say): but this is only a passing visit, and while we are hiring the vessel, we can also see Epictetus. Let us see what he says. Then you go away and say: Epictetus was nothing; he used solecisms and spoke in a barbarous way. For of what else do you come as judges?—Well, but a man may say to me, if I attend to such matters[1] (as you do), I shall have no land, as you have none; I shall have no silver cups as you have none, nor fine beasts as you have none.—In answer to this it is perhaps sufficient to say: I have no need of such things: but if you possess many things, you have need of others: whether you choose or not, you are poorer than I am. What then have I need of? Of that which you have not: of firmness, of a

[1] See Schweig.'s note.

mind which is conformable to nature, of being free from perturbation. Whether I have a patron[2] or not, what is that to me? but it is something to you. I am richer than you: I am not anxious what Caesar will think of me: for this reason, I flatter no man. This is what I possess instead of vessels of silver and gold. You have utensils of gold; but your discourse, your opinions, your assents, your movements (pursuits), your desires are of earthen ware. But when I have these things conformable to nature, why should I not employ my studies also upon reason? for I have leisure: my mind is not distracted. What shall I do, since I have no distraction? What more suitable to a man have I than this? When you have nothing to do, you are disturbed, you go to the theatre or you wander about without a purpose. Why should not the philosopher labour to improve his reason? You employ yourself about crystal vessels: I employ myself about the syllogism named the lying:[3] you about myrrhine[4] vessels; I employ myself about the syllogism named the denying (τοῦ ἀποφάσκοντος). To you every thing appears small that you possess: to me all that I have appears great. Your desire is insatiable: mine is satisfied. To (children) who put their hand into a narrow-necked earthen vessel and bring out figs and nuts, this happens; if they fill the hand, they cannot take it out, and then they cry. Drop a few of them and you will draw things out. And do you part with your desires: do not desire many things and you will have what you want.

[2] The Roman word 'patronus,' which at that time had the sense of a protector.

[3] On the syllogism named 'lying' (ψευδόμενος) see Epict. ii. 17. 34.

[4] 'Murrhina vasa' were reckoned very precious by the Romans, and they gave great prices for them. It is not certain of what material they were made. Pliny (xxxvii. c. 2) has something about them.

CHAPTER X.

IN WHAT MANNER WE OUGHT TO BEAR SICKNESS.

When the need of each opinion comes, we ought to have it in readiness:[1] on the occasion of breakfast, such opinions as relate to breakfast; in the bath, those that concern the bath; in bed, those that concern bed.

> Let sleep not come upon thy languid eyes
> Before each daily action thou hast scann'd;
> What's done amiss, what done, what left undone;
> From first to last examine all, and then
> Blame what is wrong, in what is right rejoice.[2]

And we ought to retain these verses in such way that we may use them, not that we may utter them aloud, as when we exclaim 'Paean Apollo.'[3] Again in fever we should have ready such opinions as concern a fever; and we ought not, as soon as the fever begins, to lose and forget all. (A man who has a fever) may say: If I philosophize any longer, may I be hanged: wherever I go, I must take care of the poor body, that a fever may not come.[4] But what is philosophizing? Is it not a preparation against events which may happen? Do you not understand that you are saying something of this kind? "If I shall still prepare myself to bear with patience what happens, may I be hanged." But this is just as if a man after receiving

[1] M. Antoninus, iii. 13. 'As physicians have always their instruments and knives ready for cases which suddenly require their skill, so do thou have principles (δόγματα) ready for the understanding of things divine and human, and for doing every thing, even the smallest, with a recollection of the bond which unites the divine and human to one another. For neither wilt thou do anything well which pertains to man without at the same time having a reference to things divine; nor the contrary.'

[2] These verses are from the Golden verses attributed to Pythagoras. See iv. 6. 32.

[3] The beginning of a form of prayer, as in Macrobius, Sat. i. 17: 'namque Vestales Virgines ita indigitant: Apollo Maedice, Apollo Paean.'

[4] This passage is obscure. See Schweig.'s note here, and also his note on s. 6.

blows should give up the Pancratium. In the Pancratium it is in our power to desist and not to receive blows. But in the other matter if we give up philosophy, what shall we gain? What then should a man say on the occasion of each painful thing? It was for this that I exercised myself, for this I disciplined myself. God says to you, Give me a proof that you have duly practised athletics,[5] that you have eaten what you ought, that you have been exercised, that you have obeyed the aliptes (the oiler and rubber). Then do you show yourself weak when the time for action comes? Now is the time for the fever. Let it be borne well. Now is the time for thirst, bear it well; now is the time for hunger, bear it well. Is it not in your power? who shall hinder you? The physician will hinder you from drinking; but he cannot prevent you from bearing thirst well: and he will hinder you from eating; but he cannot prevent you from bearing hunger well.

But I cannot attend to my philosophical studies.[6] And for what purpose do you follow them? Slave, is it not that you may be happy, that you may be constant, is it not that you may be in a state conformable to nature and live so? What hinders you when you have a fever from having your ruling faculty conformable to nature? Here is the proof of the thing, here is the test of the philosopher. For this also is a part of life, like walking, like sailing, like journeying by land, so also is fever. Do you read when you are walking? No. Nor do you when you have a fever. But if you walk about well, you have all that belongs to a man who walks. If you bear a fever well, you have all that belongs to a man in a fever. What is it to bear a fever well? Not to blame God or man; not to be afflicted at that which happens, to expect death well and nobly, to do what must be done: when the physician comes in, not to be frightened at what he says; nor if he says, 'you are doing well,'[7] to be overjoyed. For what good has he told you? and when you were in health, what good was that to you? And even if he says, 'you

[5] εἰ νομίμως ἤθλησας. 'St. Paul hath made use of this very expression ἐὰν μὴ νομίμως ἀθλήσῃ, 2 Tim. ii. 3.' Mrs. Carter.

[6] The Greek is οὐ φιλολογῶ. See Schweighaeuser's note.

[7] See ii. 18, 14.

are in a bad way,' do not despond. For what is it to be ill? is it that you are near the severance of the soul and the body? what harm is there in this? If you are not near now, will you not afterwards be near? Is the world going to be turned upside down when you are dead? Why then do you flatter the physician?[8] Why do you say if you please, master, I shall be well?[9] Why do you give him an opportunity of raising his eyebrows (being proud; or showing his importance)?[10] Do you not value a physician, as you do a shoemaker when he is measuring your foot, or a carpenter when he is building your house, and so treat the physician as to the body which is not yours, but by nature dead? He who has a fever has an opportunity of doing this: if he does these things, he has what belongs to him. For it is not the business of a philosopher to look after these externals, neither his wine nor his oil nor his poor body, but his own ruling power. But as to externals how must he act? so far as not to be careless about them. Where then is there reason for fear? where is there then still reason for anger, and of fear about what belongs to others, about things which are of no value? For we ought to have these two principles in readiness, that except the will nothing is good nor bad; and that we ought not to lead events, but to follow them.[11]—My brother[12] ought not to have behaved thus to me.—No; but he will see to that: and, however he may behave, I will conduct myself towards him as I ought. For this is my own business: that belongs to another; no man can prevent this, the other thing can be hindered.

[8] Et quid opus Cratero magnos promittere montes? Persius, iii. 65. Craterus was a physician.

[9] Upton compares Matthew, viii. 2. 'Lord, if thou wilt, thou canst make me clean.'

[10] Compare M. Antoninus, iv. 48. τὰς ὀφρῦς . . . συσπάσαντες.

[11] To this Stoic precept Horace (Epict. i. 1. 19) opposes that of Aristippus.

Et mihi res, non me rebus, subjungere conor.

Both wisely said, if they are rightly taken. Schweig., who refers to i. 12. 17.

[12] Lord Shaftesbury proposed to read τὸν ἰατρόν for τὸν ἀδελφόν. But see Schweig.'s note.

CHAPTER XI.

CERTAIN MISCELLANEOUS MATTERS.

THERE are certain penalties fixed as by law for those who disobey the divine administration.[1] Whoever thinks any other thing to be good except those things which depend on the will, let him envy, let him desire, let him flatter, let him be perturbed: whoever considers any thing else to be evil, let him grieve, let him lament, let him weep, let him be unhappy. And yet, though so severely punished, we cannot desist.

Remember what the poet[2] says about the stranger:

Stranger, I must not, e'en if a worse man come.

This then may be applied even to a father: I must not, even if a worse man than you should come, treat a father unworthily; for all are from paternal Zeus. And (let the same be said) of a brother, for all are from the Zeus who presides over kindred. And so in the other relations of life we shall find Zeus to be an inspector.

CHAPTER XII.

ABOUT EXERCISE.

WE ought not to make our exercises consist in means contrary to nature and adapted to cause admiration, for if we do so, we who call ourselves philosophers, shall not differ at all from jugglers. For it is difficult even to

[1] 'As to the divine law, see iii. 24. 32, and Xenophon's Memorabilia, iv. 4. 21,' etc. Upton.

[2] The poet is Homer. The complete passage is in the Odyssey, xiv. v. 55, etc.

Stranger, I must not, e'en if a worse man come,
Ill treat a stranger, for all come from Zeus,
Strangers and poor.

walk on a rope; and not only difficult, but it is also dangerous. Ought we for this reason to practise walking on a rope, or setting up a palm tree,[1] or embracing statues? By no means. Every thing which is difficult and dangerous is not suitable for practice; but that is suitable which conduces to the working out of that which is proposed to us. And what is that which is proposed to us as a thing to be worked out? To live with desire and aversion (avoidance of certain things) free from restraint. And what is this? Neither to be disappointed in that which you desire, nor to fall into any thing which you would avoid. Towards this object then exercise (practice) ought to tend. For since it is not possible to have your desire not disappointed and your aversion free from falling into that which you would avoid, without great and constant practice, you must know that if you allow your desire and aversion to turn to things which are not within the power of the will, you will neither have your desire capable of attaining your object, nor your aversion free from the power of avoiding that which you would avoid. And since strong habit leads (prevails), and we are accustomed to employ desire and aversion only to things which are not within the power of our will, we ought to oppose to this habit a contrary habit, and where there is great slipperiness in the appearances, there to oppose the habit of exercise.

I am rather inclined to pleasure: I will incline to the contrary side[2] above measure for the sake of exercise. I

[1] "To set up a palm tree." He does not mean a real palm tree, but something high and upright. The climbers of palm trees are mentioned by Lucian, de Dea Syria (c. 29). Schweigh. has given the true interpretation when he says that on certain feast days in the country a high piece of wood is fixed in the earth and climbed by the most active youths by using only their hands and feet. In England we know what this is.

It is said that Diogenes used to embrace statues when they were covered with snow for the purpose of exercising himself. I suppose bronze statues, not marble which might be easily broken. The man would not remain long in the embrace of a metal statue in winter. But perhaps the story is not true. I have heard of a general, not an English general, setting a soldier on a cold cannon; but it was as a punishment.

[2] ἀνατοιχήσω. See the note of Schweighaeuser.

am averse to pain: I will rub and exercise against this the appearances which are presented to me for the purpose of withdrawing my aversion from every such thing. For who is a practitioner in exercise? He who practises not using his desire, and applies his aversion only to things which are within the power of his will, and practises most in the things which are difficult to conquer. For this reason one man must practise himself more against one thing and another against another thing. What then is it to the purpose to set up a palm tree, or to carry about a tent of skins, or a mortar and pestle?[3] Practise, man, if you are irritable, to endure if you are abused, not to be vexed if you are treated with dishonour. Then you will make so much progress that, even if a man strikes you you will say to yourself, Imagine that you have embraced a statue: then also exercise yourself to use wine properly so as not to drink much, for in this also there are men who foolishly practise themselves; but first of all you should abstain from it, and abstain from a young girl and dainty cakes. Then at last, if occasion presents itself, for the purpose of trying yourself at a proper time you will descend into the arena to know if appearances overpower you as they did formerly. But at first fly far from that which is stronger than yourself: the contest is unequal between a charming young girl and a beginner in philosophy. The earthen pitcher, as the saying is, and the rock do not agree.[4]

After the desire and the aversion comes the second topic (matter) of the movements towards action and the withdrawals from it; that you may be obedient to reason, that you do nothing out of season or place, or contrary to any propriety of the kind.[5] The third topic concerns the assents, which is related to the things which are persuasive and attractive. For as Socrates said, we ought not

[3] This was done for the sake of exercise says Upton; but I don't understand the passage.

[4] There is a like fable in Aesop of the earthen pitcher and the brazen. Upton.

[5] The text has ἀσυμμετρίαν. It would be easier to understand the passage, if we read συμμετριάν, as in iv. 1, 84 we have παρὰ τὰ μέτρα. See Schweig.'s note.

to live a life without examination,[6] so we ought not to accept an appearance without examination, but we should say, Wait, let me see what you are and whence you come; like the watch at night (who says) Show me the pass (the Roman tessera).[7] Have you the signal from nature which the appearance that may be accepted ought to have? And finally whatever means are applied to the body by those who exercise it, if they tend in any way towards desire and aversion, they also may be fit means of exercise; but if they are for display, they are the indications of one who has turned himself towards something external and who is hunting for something else and who looks for spectators who will say, Oh the great man. For this reason Apollonius said well, When you intend to exercise yourself for your own advantage, and you are thirsty from heat, take in a mouthful of cold water, and spit it out and tell nobody.[8]

CHAPTER XIII.

WHAT SOLITUDE IS, AND WHAT KIND OF PERSON A SOLITARY MAN IS.

SOLITUDE is a certain condition of a helpless man. For because a man is alone, he is not for that reason also solitary; just as though a man is among numbers, he is not therefore not solitary. When then we have lost either a brother, or a son or a friend on whom we were accustomed to repose, we say that we are left solitary, though we are often in Rome, though such a crowd meet us, though so many live in the same place, and sometimes we have a great number of slaves. For the man who is solitary, as

[6] See i. 26, 18, and iii. 2, 5.

[7] Polybius vi. 36.

[8] Schweighaeuser refers to Arrian's Expedition of Alexander (vi. 26) for such an instance of Alexander's abstinence. There was an Apollonius of Tyana, whose life was written by Philostratus: but it may be that this is not the man who is mentioned here.

it is conceived, is considered to be a helpless person and exposed to those who wish to harm him. For this reason when we travel, then especially do we say that we are lonely when we fall among robbers, for it is not the sight of a human creature which removes us from solitude, but the sight of one who is faithful and modest and helpful to us. For if being alone is enough to make solitude, you may say that even Zeus is solitary in the conflagration[1] and bewails himself saying, Unhappy that I am who have neither Hera, nor Athena, nor Apollo, nor brother, nor son, nor descendant nor kinsman. This is what some say that he does when he is alone at the conflagration.[2] For they do not understand how a man passes his life when he is alone, because they set out from a certain natural principle, from the natural desire of community and mutual love and from the pleasure of conversation among men. But none the less a man ought to be prepared in a manner for this also (being alone), to be able to be sufficient for himself and to be his own companion. For as Zeus dwells with himself, and is tranquil by himself, and thinks of his own administration and of its nature, and is employed in thoughts suitable to himself; so ought we also to be able to talk with ourselves, not to feel the want of others also, not to be unprovided with the means of passing our time; to observe the divine administration, and the relation of

[1] This was the doctrine of Heraclitus 'that all things were composed from (had their origin in) fire, and were resolved into it,' an opinion afterwards adopted by the Stoics. It is not so extravagant, as it may appear to some persons, to suppose that the earth had a beginning, is in a state of continual change, and will finally be destroyed in some way, and have a new beginning. See Seneca, Ep. 9 'cum resoluto mundo, diis in unum confusis, paulisper cessante natura, adquiescit sibi Jupiter, cogitationibus suis traditus.'

[2] The Latin translation is: 'hoc etiam nonnulli facturum eum in conflagratione mundi . . . . aiunt.' But the word is ποιεῖ; and this may mean that the conflagration has happened, and will happen again. The Greek philosophers in their speculations were not troubled with the consideration of time. Even Herodotus (ii. 11), in his speculations on the gulf, which he supposes that the Nile valley was once, speaks of the possibility of it being filled up in 20,000 years, or less. Modern speculators have only recently become bold enough to throw aside the notion of the earth and the other bodies in space being limited by time, as the ignorant have conceived it.

ourselves to every thing else; to consider how we formerly were affected towards things that happen and how at present; what are still the things which give us pain; how these also can be cured and how removed; if any things require improvement, to improve them according to reason.

For you see that Caesar appears to furnish us with great peace, that there are no longer enemies nor battles nor great associations of robbers nor of pirates, but we can travel at every hour and sail from east to west. But can Caesar give us security from fever also, can he from shipwreck, from fire, from earthquake or from lightning? well, I will say, can he give us security against love? He cannot. From sorrow? He cannot. From envy? He cannot. In a word then he cannot protect us from any of these things. But the doctrine of philosophers promises to give us security (peace) even against these things. And what does it say? Men, if you will attend to me, wherever you are, whatever you are doing, you will not feel sorrow, nor anger, nor compulsion, nor hindrance, but you will pass your time without perturbations and free from every thing. When a man has this peace, not proclaimed by Caesar, (for how should he be able to proclaim it?), but by God through reason, is he not content when he is alone? when he sees and reflects, Now no evil can happen to me; for me there is no robber, no earthquake, every thing is full of peace, full of tranquillity: every way, every city, every meeting, neighbour, companion is harmless. One person whose business it is, supplies me with food;[3] another with raiment; another with perceptions, and preconceptions (προλήψεις). And if he does not supply what is necessary, he (God) gives the signal for retreat, opens the door, and says to you, Go. Go whither? To nothing terrible, but to the place from which you came, to your friends and kinsmen, to the elements:[4] what there was in you of fire goes

[3] See iii. 1, 43.

[4] 'What a melancholy description of death and how gloomy the ideas in this *consolatory* chapter! All beings reduced to mere elements in successive conflagrations! A noble contrast to the Stoic notions on this subject may be produced from several passages in the Scripture—"Then shall the dust return to the earth, as it was; and

to fire; of earth, to earth; of air (spirit), to air; of water to water: no Hades, nor Acheron, nor Cocytus, nor Pyriphlegethon, but all is full of Gods and Daemons. When a man has such things to think on, and sees the sun, the moon and stars, and enjoys earth and sea, he is not solitary nor even helpless. Well then, if some man should

the spirit shall return to God who gave it," Eccles. xii. 7.' Mrs. Carter; who also refers to 1 Thess. iv. 14; John vi. 39, 40; xi. 25, 26; 1 Cor. vi. 14; xv. 53; 2 Cor. v. 14 etc.

Mrs. Carter quotes Ecclesiastes, but the author says nearly what Epicharmus said, quoted by Plutarch, *παραμυθ. πρὸς Ἀπολλώνιον*, vol. i. p. 435 ed. Wytt.

> συνεκρίθη καὶ διεκρίθη καὶ ἀπῆλθεν ὅθεν ἦλθε πάλιν,
> γᾶ μὲν ἐς γᾶν, πνεῦμα δ' ἄνω· τί τῶνδε χαλεπόν; οὐδὲ ἕν.

Euripides in a fragment of the Chrysippus, fr. 836, ed. Nauck, says

> τὰ μὲν ἐκ γαίας φύντ' εἰς γαῖαν,
> τὰ δ' ἀπ' αἰθερίου βλαστόντα γονῆς
> εἰς οὐράνιον πάλιν ἦλθε πόλον.

I have translated the words of Epictetus *ὅσον πνευματίου, εἰς πνευμάτιον* by 'of air (spirit), to air': but the *πνευμάτιον* of Epictetus may mean the same as the *πνεῦμα* of Epicharmus, and the same as the 'spirit' of Ecclesiastes.

An English commentator says that "the doctrine of a future retribution forms the great basis and the leading truth of this book (Ecclesiastes)," and that "the royal Preacher (Ecclesiastes) brings forward the prospect of a future life and retribution." I cannot discover any evidence of this assertion in the book. The conclusion is the best part of this ill-connected, obscure and confused book, as it appears in our translation. The conclusion is (xii. 13, 14): 'Fear God and keep his commandments: for this is the whole duty of man, for God shall bring every work into judgment with every secret thing, whether it be good or whether it be evil.' This is all that I can discover in the book which can support the commentator's statement; and even this may not mean what he affirms.

Schweighaeuser observes that here was the opportunity for Epictetus to say something of the immortality of the soul, if he had any thing to say. But he says nothing unless he means to say that the soul, the spirit, "returns to God who gave it" as the Preacher says. There is a passage (iii. 24, 94) which appears to mean that the soul of man after death will be changed into something else, which the universe will require for some use or purpose. It is strange, observes Schweig., that Epictetus, who studied the philosophy of Socrates, and speaks so eloquently of man's capacity and his duty to God, should say no more: but the explanation may be that he had no doctrine of man's immortality, in the sense in which that word is now used.

come upon me when I am alone and murder me? Fool, not murder You, but your poor body.

What kind of solitude then remains? what want? why do we make ourselves worse than children? and what do children do when they are left alone? They take up shells and ashes, and they build something, then pull it down, and build something else, and so they never want the means of passing the time. Shall I then, if you sail away, sit down and weep, because I have been left alone and solitary? Shall I then have no shells, no ashes? But children do what they do through want of thought (or deficiency in knowledge), and we through knowledge are unhappy.

Every great power (faculty) is dangerous to beginners.[5] You must then bear such things as you are able, but conformably to nature: but not . . . . Practise sometimes a way of living like a person out of health that you may at some time live like a man in health. Abstain from food, drink water, abstain sometimes altogether from desire, in order that you may some time desire consistently with reason; and if consistently with reason, when you have anything good in you, you will desire well.—Not so; but we wish to live like wise men immediately and to be useful to men—Useful how? what are you doing? have you been useful to yourself? But, I suppose, you wish to exhort them? You exhort them![6] You wish to be useful to them. Show to them in your own example what kind of men philosophy makes, and don't trifle. When you are eating, do good to those who eat with you; when you are drinking, to those who are drinking with you; by yielding to all, giving way, bearing with them, thus do them good, and do not spit on them your phlegm (bad humours).

[5] The text has ἀρχομένων, but it probably ought to be ἀρχομένῳ. Compare i. 1, 8, πᾶσα δύναμις ἐπισφαλής.

The text from φέρειν οὖν δεῖ to τῷ φθισικῷ is unintelligible. Lord Shaftesbury says that the passage is not corrupt, and he gives an explanation; but Schweig. says that the learned Englishman's exposition does not make the text plainer to him; nor does it to me. Schweig. observes that the passage which begins πᾶσα μεγάλη and what follows seem to belong to the next chapter xiv.

[6] See Schweig.'s note, and the Latin version

CHAPTER XIV.

CERTAIN MISCELLANEOUS MATTERS.

As bad[1] tragic actors cannot sing alone, but in company with many: so some persons cannot walk about alone. Man, if you are anything, both walk alone and talk to yourself, and do not hide yourself in the chorus. Examine a little at last, look around, stir yourself up, that you may know who you are.

When a man drinks water, or does anything for the sake of practice (discipline), whenever there is an opportunity he tells it to all: 'I drink water.' Is it for this that you drink water, for the purpose of drinking water? Man, if it is good for you to drink, drink; but if not, you are acting ridiculously. But if it is good for you and you do drink, say nothing about it to those who are displeased with water-drinkers. What then, do you wish to please these very men?

Of things that are done some are done with a final purpose (προηγουμένως), some according to occasion, others with a certain reference to circumstances, others for the purpose of complying with others, and some according to a fixed scheme of life.[2]

You must root out of men these two things, arrogance (pride) and distrust. Arrogance then is the opinion that you want nothing (are deficient in nothing): but distrust is the opinion that you cannot be happy when so many circumstances surround you. Arrogance is removed by confutation; and Socrates was the first who practised this. And (to know) that the thing is not impossible inquire and seek. This search will do you no harm; and in a manner this is philosophizing, to seek how it is possible to employ desire and aversion (ἐκκλίσει) without impediment.

I am superior to you, for my father is a man of consular rank. Another says, I have been a tribune, but you have

[1] All the MSS. have 'good' (καλοί), which the critics have properly corrected. As to σκόπει see Schweig.'s note.

[2] This section is not easy to translate.

not. If we were horses, would you say, My father was swifter? I have much barley and fodder, or elegant neck ornaments. If then while you were saying this, I said, Be it so: let us run then. Well, is there nothing in a man such as running in a horse, by which it will be known which is superior and inferior? Is there not modesty (αἰδὼς), fidelity, justice? Show yourself superior in these, that you may be superior as a man. If you tell me that you can kick violently, I also will say to you, that you are proud of that which is the act of an ass.

CHAPTER XV.

THAT WE OUGHT TO PROCEED WITH CIRCUMSPECTION TO EVERY THING.[1]

In every act consider what precedes and what follows, and then proceed to the act. If you do not consider, you will at first begin with spirit, since you have not thought at all of the things which follow; but afterwards when some consequences have shown themselves, you will basely desist (from that which you have begun).—I wish to conquer at the Olympic games.—[And I too, by the gods: for it is a fine thing]. But consider here what precedes and what follows; and then, if it is for your good, undertake the thing. You must act according to rules, follow strict diet, abstain from delicacies, exercise yourself by compulsion at fixed times, in heat, in cold; drink no cold

[1] Compare Encheiridion 29.

"This chapter has a great conformity to Luke xiv. 28 etc. But it is to be observed that Epictetus, both here and elsewhere, supposes some persons incapable of being philosophers; that is, virtuous and pious men: but Christianity requires and enables all to be such." Mrs. Carter.

The passage in Luke contains a practical lesson, and so far is the same as the teaching of Epictetus: but the conclusion in v. 33 does not appear to be helped by what immediately precedes v. 28–32. The remark that Christianity 'enables all to be such' is not true, unless Mrs. Carter gives to the word 'enables' a meaning which I do not see.

water, nor wine, when there is opportunity of drinking it.[2] In a word you must surrender yourself to the trainer, as you do to a physician. Next in the contest, you must be covered with sand,[3] sometimes dislocate a hand, sprain an ankle, swallow a quantity of dust, be scourged with the whip; and after undergoing all this, you must sometimes be conquered. After reckoning all these things, if you have still an inclination, go to the athletic practice. If you do not reckon them, observe you will behave like children who at one time play as wrestlers, then as gladiators, then blow a trumpet, then act a tragedy, when they have seen and admired such things. So you also do: you are at one time a wrestler (athlete), then a gladiator, then a philosopher, then a rhetorician; but with your whole soul you are nothing: like the ape you imitate all that you see; and always one thing after another pleases you, but that which becomes familiar displeases you. For you have never undertaken any thing after consideration, nor after having explored the whole matter and put it to a strict examination; but you have undertaken it at hazard and with a cold desire. Thus some persons having seen a philosopher and having heard one speak like Euphrates[4]—and yet who can speak like him?—wish to be philosophers themselves.

Man, consider first what the matter is (which you propose to do), then your own nature also, what it is able to bear. If you are a wrestler, look at your shoulders, your thighs, your loins: for different men are naturally formed for different things. Do you think that, if you do (what

[2] The commentators refer us to Paul, 1 Cor. c. 9, 25. Compare Horace, Ars Poetica, 39:

> Versate diu quid ferre recusent,
> Quid valeant humeri.

[3] Wolf thought that the word παρορύσσεσθαι might mean the loss of an eye; but other commentators give the word a different meaning. See Schweigh.'s note.

[4] In place of Euphrates the Encheiridion 29 had in the text 'Socrates,' which name the recent editors of the Encheiridion altered to 'Euphrates,' and correctly. The younger Pliny (i. Ep. 10) speaks in high terms of the merits and attractive eloquence of this Syrian philosopher Euphrates, who is mentioned by M. Antoninus (x. 31) and by others.

you are doing daily), you can be a philosopher? Do you think that you can eat as you do now, drink as you do now, and in the same way be angry and out of humour? You must watch, labour, conquer certain desires, you must depart from your kinsmen, be despised by your slave, laughed at by those who meet you, in every thing you must be in an inferior condition, as to magisterial office, in honours, in courts of justice. When you have considered all these things completely, then, if you think proper, approach to philosophy, if you would gain in exchange for these things freedom from perturbations, liberty, tranquillity. If you have not considered these things, do not approach philosophy: do not act like children, at one time a philosopher, then a tax collector, then a rhetorician, then a procurator (officer) of Caesar. These things are not consistent. You must be one man either good or bad: you must either labour at your own ruling faculty or at external things: you must either labour at things within or at external things: that is, you must either occupy the place of a philosopher or that of one of the vulgar.

A person said to Rufus [5] when Galba was murdered, Is the world now governed by Providence? But Rufus replied, Did I ever incidentally form an argument from Galba that the world is governed by Providence?

CHAPTER XVI.

THAT WE OUGHT WITH CAUTION TO ENTER INTO FAMILIAR INTERCOURSE WITH MEN.

If a man has frequent intercourse with others either for talk, or drinking together, or generally for social purposes, he must either become like them, or change them to his

[5] Rufus was a philosopher. See i. 1, i. 9. Galba is the emperor Galba, who was murdered. The meaning of the passage is rather obscure, and it is evident that it does not belong to this chapter. Lord Shaftesbury remarks that this passage perhaps belongs to chapter 11 or 14, or perhaps to the end of chapter 17.

own fashion. For if a man places a piece of quenched charcoal close to a piece that is burning, either the quenched charcoal will quench the other, or the burning charcoal will light that which is quenched. Since then the danger is so great, we must cautiously enter into such intimacies with those of the common sort, and remember that it is impossible that a man can keep company with one who is covered with soot without being partaker of the soot himself. For what will you do if a man speaks about gladiators, about horses, about athletes, or what is worse about men? Such a person is bad, such a person is good: this was well done, this was done badly. Further, if he scoff, or ridicule, or show an ill-natured disposition? Is any man among us prepared like a lute-player when he takes a lute, so that as soon as he has touched the strings, he discovers which are discordant, and tunes the instrument? such a power as Socrates had who in all his social intercourse could lead his companions to his own purpose? How should you have this power? It is therefore a necessary consequence that you are carried about by the common kind of people.

Why then are they more powerful than you? Because they utter these useless words from their real opinions: but you utter your elegant words only from your lips; for this reason they are without strength and dead, and it is nauseous[1] to listen to your exhortations and your miserable virtue, which is talked of every where (up and down). In this way the vulgar have the advantage over you: for every opinion (δόγμα) is strong and invincible. Until then the good (κομψαί) sentiments (ὑπολήψεις) are fixed in you, and you shall have acquired a certain power for your security, I advise you to be careful in your association with common persons: if you are not, every day like wax in the sun there will be melted away whatever you inscribe on your minds in the school. Withdraw then yourselves far from the sun so long as you have these waxen sentiments. For this reason also philosophers advise men to leave their native country, because antient habits distract them and do not allow a beginning to be

[1] The word is σικχᾶναι. See Antoninus v. 9.

made of a different habit; nor can we tolerate those who meet us and say: See such a one is now a philosopher, who was once so and so. Thus also physicians send those who have lingering diseases to a different country and a different air; and they do right. Do you also introduce other habits than those which you have: fix your opinions and exercise yourselves in them. But you do not so: you go hence to a spectacle, to a show of gladiators, to a place of exercise (ξυστόν), to a circus; then you come back hither, and again from this place you go to those places, and still the same persons. And there is no pleasing (good) habit, nor attention, nor care about self and observation of this kind, How shall I use the appearances presented to me? according to nature, or contrary to nature? how do I answer to them? as I ought, or as I ought not? Do I say to those things which are independent of the will, that they do not concern me? For if you are not yet in this state, fly from your former habits, fly from the common sort, if you intend ever to begin to be something.

CHAPTER XVII.

ON PROVIDENCE.

When you make any charge against Providence, consider, and you will learn that the thing has happened according to reason.—Yes, but the unjust man has the advantage.—In what?—In money.—Yes, for he is superior to you in this, that he flatters, is free from shame, and is watchful. What is the wonder? But see if he has the advantage over you in being faithful, in being modest: for you will not find it to be so; but wherein you are superior, there you will find that you have the advantage. And I once said to a man who was vexed because Philostorgus was fortunate: Would you choose to lie with Sura?[1]—

[1] Upton suggests that Sura may be Palfurius (Juvenal, iv. 53), or Palfurius Sura (Suetonius, Domitian, c. 13).

May it never happen, he replied, that this day should come? Why then are you vexed, if he receives something in return for that which he sells; or how can you consider him happy who acquires those things by such means as you abominate; or what wrong does Providence, if he gives the better things to the better men? Is it not better to be modest than to be rich?—He admitted this—Why are you vexed then, man, when you possess the better thing? Remember then always and have in readiness the truth, that this is a law of nature, that the superior has an advantage over the inferior in that in which he is superior; and you will never be vexed.

But my wife treats me badly.—Well, if any man asks you what this is, say, my wife treats me badly—Is there then nothing more? Nothing.—My father gives me nothing—[What is this? my father gives me nothing—Is there nothing else then?—Nothing] [2]: but to say that this is an evil is something which must be added to it externally, and falsely added. For this reason we must not get rid of poverty, but of the opinion about poverty, and then we shall be happy.

CHAPTER XVIII.

THAT WE OUGHT NOT TO BE DISTURBED BY ANY NEWS.

When any thing shall be reported to you which is of a nature to disturb, have this principle in readiness, that the news is about nothing which is within the power of your will. Can any man report to you that you have formed a bad opinion, or had a bad desire? By no means. But perhaps he will report that some person is dead. What then is that to you? He may report that some person speaks ill of you. What then is that to you? Or that your father is planning something or other. Against whom? Against your will (προαίρεσις)? How can he? But is it against your poor body, against your little pro-

[2] See Schweig.'s note.

perty? You are quite safe: it is not against you. But the judge declares that you have committed an act of impiety. And did not the judges (δίκασται) make the same declaration against Socrates? Does it concern you that the judge has made this declaration? No. Why then do you trouble yourself any longer about it? Your father has a certain duty, and if he shall not fulfil it, he loses the character of a father, of a man of natural affection, of gentleness. Do not wish him to lose any thing else on this account. For never does a man do wrong in one thing, and suffer in another. On the other side it is your duty to make your defence firmly, modestly, without anger: but if you do not, you also lose the character of a son, of a man of modest behavior, of generous character. Well then, is the judge free from danger? No; but he also is in equal danger. Why then are you still afraid of his decision? What have you to do with that which is another man's evil? It is your own evil to make a bad defence: be on your guard against this only. But to be condemned or not to be condemned, as that is the act of another person, so it is the evil of another person. A certain person threatens you. Me? No. He blames you. Let him see how he manages his own affairs. He is going to condemn you unjustly. He is a wretched man.

CHAPTER XIX.

WHAT IS THE CONDITION OF A COMMON KIND OF MAN AND OF A PHILOSOPHER.

THE first difference between a common person (ἰδιώτης) and a philosopher is this: the common person says, Woe to me for my little child, for my brother, for my father.[1] The philosopher, if he shall ever be compelled to say, Woe to me, stops and says, 'but for myself.' For nothing which is independent of the will can hinder or damage

[1] Compare iii. 5. 4.

the will, and the will can only hinder or damage itself. If then we ourselves incline in this direction, so as, when we are unlucky, to blame ourselves and to remember that nothing else is the cause of perturbation or loss of tranquillity except our own opinion, I swear to you by all the gods that we have made progress. But in the present state of affairs we have gone another way from the beginning. For example, while we were still children, the nurse, if we ever stumbled through want of care, did not chide us, but would beat the stone. But what did the stone do? Ought the stone to have moved on account of your child's folly? Again, if we find nothing to eat on coming out of the bath, the paedagogue never checks our appetite, but he flogs the cook. Man, did we make you the paedagogue of the cook and not of the child?[2] Correct the child, improve him. In this way even when we are grown up we are like children. For he who is unmusical is a child in music; he who is without letters is a child in learning: he who is untaught, is a child in life.

CHAPTER XX.

THAT WE CAN DERIVE ADVANTAGE FROM ALL EXTERNAL THINGS.

In the case of appearances which are objects of the vision,[1] nearly all have allowed the good and the evil to be in ourselves, and not in externals. No one gives the name of good to the fact that it is day, nor bad to the fact that it is night, nor the name of the greatest evil to the opinion that three are four. But what do men say? They

[2] I have not followed Schweighaeuser's text here. See his note.

[1] The original is θεωρητικῶν φαντασιῶν, which is translated in the Latin version 'visa theoretica,' but this does not help us. Perhaps the author means any appearances which are presented to us either by the eyes or by the understanding; but I am not sure what he means. It is said in the Index Graecitatis (Schweig.'s ed.): 'φαντασίαι θεωρητικαί, notiones theoreticae, iii. 20. 1, quibus opponuntur Practicae ad vitam regendam spectantes.'

say that knowledge is good, and that error is bad; so that even in respect to falsehood itself there is a good result, the knowledge that it is falsehood. So it ought to be in life also. Is health a good thing, and is sickness a bad thing? No, man. But what is it? To be healthy, and healthy in a right way, is good: to be healthy in a bad way is bad; so that it is possible to gain advantage even from sickness, I declare. For is it not possible to gain advantage even from death, and is it not possible to gain advantage from mutilation? Do you think that Menoeceus gained little by death?[2] Could a man who says so, gain so much as Menoeceus gained? Come, man, did he not maintain the character of being a lover of his country, a man of great mind, faithful, generous? And if he had continued to live, would he not have lost all these things? would he not have gained the opposite? would he not have gained the name of coward, ignoble, a hater of his country, a man who feared death?[3] Well, do you think that he gained little by dying? I suppose not. But did the father of Admetus[4] gain much by prolonging his life so ignobly and miserably? Did he not die afterwards? Cease, I adjure you by the gods, to admire material things. Cease to make yourselves slaves, first of things, then on account of things slaves of those who are able to give them or take them away.

Can advantage then be derived from these things? From all; and from him who abuses you. Wherein does the man who exercises before the combat profit the athlete? Very greatly. This man becomes my exerciser before the combat: he exercises me in endurance, in keeping my temper, in mildness. You say no: but he, who lays hold of my neck and disciplines my loins and shoulders,

[2] Menoeceus, the son of Creon, gave up his life by which he would save his country, as it was declared by an oracle. (Cicero, Tuscul. i. c. 48.) Juvenal (Sat. xiv. 238) says

> Quarum Amor in te
> Quantus erat patriae Deciorum in pectore; quantum
> Dilexit Thebas, si Graecia vera, Menoeceus.

Euripides, Phoenissae, v. 913.

[3] See Schweig.'s note.

[4] The father of Admetus was Phe es (Euripides, Alcestis).

does me good; and the exercise master (the aliptes, or oiler) does right when he says; 'Raise him up with both hands, and the heavier he (ἐκεῖνος) is, so much the more is my advantage.[5] But if a man exercises me in keeping my temper, does he not do me good?—This is not knowing how to gain an advantage from men. Is my neighbour bad? Bad to himself, but good to me: he exercises my good disposition, my moderation. Is my father bad? Bad to himself, but to me good. This is the rod of Hermes: touch with it what you please, as the saying is, and it will be of gold. I say not so: but bring what you please, and I will make it good.[6] Bring disease, bring death, bring poverty, bring abuse, bring trial on capital charges: all these things through the rod of Hermes shall be made profitable. What will you do with death? Why, what else than that it shall do you honour, or that it shall show you by act through it,[7] what a man is who follows the will of nature? What will you do with disease? I will show its nature, I will be conspicuous in it, I will be firm, I will be happy, I will not flatter the physician, I will not wish to die. What else do you seek? Whatever you shall give me, I will make it happy, fortunate, honoured, a thing which a man shall seek.

You say No: but take care that you do not fall sick: it is a bad thing. This is the same as if you should say, Take care that you never receive the impression (appearance) that three are four: that is bad. Man, how is it bad? If I think about it as I ought, how shall it then do me any damage? and shall it not even do me good? If then I think about poverty as I ought to do, about disease, about not having office,[8] is not that enough for me? will it not be an advan-

[5] The meaning is not clear, if we follow the original text. Schweig. cannot see the sense 'with both hands' in the Greek, nor can I. He also says that in the words ἆρον ὑπὲρ ἀμφοτέρας unless some masculine noun is understood which is not expressed, ἐκεῖνος must be referred to the aliptes; and he translates βαρύτερος by 'severior.'

[6] Mrs. Carter quotes the epistle to the Romans (viii. 28): 'and we know that all things work together for good to them that love God'; but she quotes only the first part of the verse and omits the conclusion, 'to them who are the called according to his purpose.'

[7] See Schweig.'s note.

[8] ἀναρχίας; see iv. 4, 2 and 23.

tage? How then ought I any longer to look to seek evil and good in externals? What happens? these doctrines are maintained here, but no man carries them away home; but immediately every one is at war with his slave, with his neighbours, with those who have sneered at him, with those who have ridiculed him. Good luck to Lesbius,[9] who daily proves that I know nothing.

CHAPTER XXI.

AGAINST THOSE WHO READILY COME TO THE PROFESSION OF SOPHISTS.

THEY who have taken up bare theorems (θεωρήματα) immediately wish to vomit them forth, as persons whose stomach is diseased do with food. First digest the thing, then do not vomit it up thus: if you do not digest it, the thing becomes truly an emetic, a crude food and unfit to eat. But after digestion show us some change in your ruling faculty, as athletes show in their shoulders by what they have been exercised and what they have eaten; as those who have taken up certain arts show by what they have learned. The carpenter does not come and say, Hear me talk about the carpenter's art; but having undertaken to build a house, he makes it, and proves that he knows the art. You also ought to do something of the kind; eat like a man, drink like a man, dress, marry, beget children, do the office of a citizen, endure abuse, bear with an unreasonable brother, bear with your father, bear with your son, neighbour, companion.[1] Show us these things that we may see that

[9] Some abusive fellow, known to some of the hearers of Epictetus. We ought perhaps to understand the words as if it were said, 'each of you ought to say to himself, Good luck to Lesbius etc.' Schweig.'s note.

[1] The practical teaching of the Stoics is contained in iii. c. 7, and it is good and wise. A modern writer says of modern practice: 'If we open our eyes and if we will honestly acknowledge to ourselves what we discover, we shall be compelled to confess that all the life and

you have in truth learned something from the philosophers. You say, No; but come and hear me read (philosophical) commentaries. Go away, and seek somebody to vomit them on. (He replies) And indeed I will expound to you the writings of Chrysippus as no other man can: I will explain his text most clearly: I will add also, if I can, the vehemence of Antipater and Archedemus.[2]

Is it then for this that young men shall leave their country and their parents, that they may come to this place, and hear you explain words? Ought they not to return with a capacity to endure, to be active in association with others, free from passions, free from perturbation, with such a provision for the journey of life with which they shall be able to bear well the things that happen and derive honour from them?[3] And how can you give them any of these things which you do not possess? Have you done from the beginning any thing else than employ yourself about the resolution of Syllo-

efforts of the civilized people of our times is founded on a view of the world, which is directly opposed to the view of the world which Jesus had' (Strauss, Der alte und der neue Glaube, p. 74).

[2] Cicero (Academ. Prior. ii. 47) names Antipater and Archidemus (Archedemus) the chief of dialecticians, and also 'opiniosissimi homines.'

[3] This passage is one of those which show the great good sense of Epictetus in the matter of education; and some other remarks to the same effect follow in this chapter. A man might justly say that we have no clear notion of the purpose of education. A modern writer, who seems to belong to the school of Epictetus says: "it cannot be denied that in all schools of all kinds it ought to be the first and the chief object to make children healthy, good, honest, and, if possible, sensible men and women; and if this is not done in a reasonable degree, I maintain that the education of these schools is good for nothing—I do not propose to make children good and honest and wise by precepts and dogmas and preaching, as you will see. They must be made good and wise by a cultivation of the understanding, by the practice of the discipline necessary for that purpose, and by the example of him who governs, directs and instructs." Further, "my men and women teachers have something which the others have not; they have a purpose, an end in their system of education; and what is education? What is human life without some purpose or end which may be attained by industry, order and the exercise of moderate abilities? Great abilities are rare, and they are often accompanied by qualities which make the abilities useless to him who has them, and even injurious to society."

gisms, of sophistical arguments (οἱ μεταπίπτοντες), and in those which work by questions? But such a man has a school; why should not I also have a school? These things are not done, man, in a careless way, nor just as it may happen; but there must be a (fit) age and life and God as a guide. You say, No. But no man sails from a port without having sacrificed to the Gods and invoked their help; nor do men sow without having called on Demeter; and shall a man who has undertaken so great a work undertake it safely without the Gods? and shall they who undertake this work come to it with success? What else are you doing, man, than divulging the mysteries? You say, there is a temple at Eleusis, and one here also. There is an Hierophant at Eleusis,[4] and I also will make an Hierophant: there is a herald, and I will establish a herald: there is a torchbearer at Eleusis, and I also will establish a torchbearer; there are torches at Eleusis, and I will have torches here. The words are the same: how do the things done here differ from those done there?—Most impious man, is there no difference? these things are done both in due place and in due time; and when accompanied with sacrifice and prayers, when a man is first purified, and when he is disposed in his mind to the thought that he is going to approach sacred rites and antient rites. In this way the mysteries are useful, in this way we come to the notion that all these things were established by the antients for the instruction and correction of life.[5] But you publish and divulge them out of time, out of place, without sacrifices, without purity; you have not the garments which the hierophant ought to have, nor the hair, nor the headdress, nor the voice, nor the age; nor have you purified yourself as he has: but you have committed to memory the words only, and you say, Sacred are the words by themselves.[6]

[4] There was a great temple of Demeter (Ceres) at Eleusis in Attica, and solemn mysteries, and an Hierophant or conductor of the ceremonies.

[5] See the note of T. Burnet, De Fide et Officiis Christianorum, Ed. Sec. p. 89.

[6] The reader, who has an inclination to compare religious forms antient and modern, may find something in modern practice to which the words of Epictetus are applicable.

You ought to approach these matters in another way: the thing is great, it is mystical, not a common thing, nor is it given to every man. But not even wisdom[7] perhaps is enough to enable a man to take care of youths: a man must have also a certain readiness and fitness for this purpose, and a certain quality of body, and above all things he must have God to advise him to occupy this office, as God advised Socrates to occupy the place of one who confutes error, Diogenes the office of royalty and reproof, and the office of teaching precepts. But you open a doctor's shop, though you have nothing except physic: but where and how they should be applied, you know not nor have you taken any trouble about it. See, that man says, I too have salves for the eyes. Have you also the

[7] This is a view of the fitness of a teacher which, as far as I know, is quite new; and it is also true. Perhaps there was some vague notion of this kind in modern Europe at the time when teachers of youths were only priests, and when it was supposed that their fitness for the office of teacher was secured by their fitness for the office of priest. In the present 'Ordering of Deacons' in the Church of England, the person, who is proposed as a fit person to be a deacon, is asked the following question by the bishop: 'Do you trust that you are inwardly moved by the Holy Ghost to take upon you this office and ministration to serve God for the promotion of his glory and the edifying of his people?' 'In the ordering of Priests' this question is omitted, and another question only is put, which is used also in the ordering of Deacons; 'Do you think in your heart that you be truly called, according to the will of our Lord Jesus Christ' etc. The teacher ought to have God to advise him to occupy the office of teacher, as Epictetus says. He does not say how God will advise: perhaps he supposed that this advice might be given in the way in which Socrates said that he received it.

'Wisdom perhaps is not enough' to enable a man to take care of youths. Whatever 'wisdom' may mean, it is true that a teacher should have a fitness and liking for the business. If he has not, he will find it disagreeable, and he will not do it well. He may and ought to gain a reasonable living by his labour: if he seeks only money and wealth, he is on the wrong track, and he is only like a common dealer in buying and selling, a butcher or a shoemaker, or a tailor, all useful members of society and all of them necessary in their several kinds. But the teacher has a priestly office, the making, as far as it is possible, children into good men and women. Should he be 'ordered' like a Deacon or a Priest, for his office is even more useful than that of Priest or Deacon? Some will say that this is ridiculous. Perhaps the wise will not think so.

power of using them? Do you know both when and how they will do good, and to whom they will do good? Why then do you act at hazard in things of the greatest importance? why are you careless? why do you undertake a thing that is in no way fit for you? Leave it to those who are able to do it, and to do it well. Do not yourself bring disgrace on philosophy through your own acts, and be not one of those who load it with a bad reputation. But if theorems please you, sit still, and turn them over by yourself; but never say that you are a philosopher, nor allow another to say it; but say: He is mistaken, for neither are my desires different from what they were before, nor is my activity directed to other objects, nor do I assent to other things, nor in the use of appearances have I altered at all from my former condition. This you must think and say about yourself, if you would think as you ought: if not act at hazard, and do what you are doing; for it becomes you.

CHAPTER XXII.

ABOUT CYNISM.

When one of his pupils inquired of Epictetus, and he was a person who appeared to be inclined to Cynism, what kind of person a Cynic ought to be and what was the notion (πρόληψις) of the thing, we will inquire, said Epictetus, at leisure: but I have so much to say to you that he who without God attempts so great a matter, is hateful to God, and has no other purpose than to act indecently in public. For in any well-managed house no man comes forward, and says to himself, I ought to be manager of the house. If he does so, the master turns round, and seeing him insolently giving orders, drags him forth and flogs him. So it is also in this great city (the world); for here also there is a master of the house who orders every thing. (He says) You are the sun; you can by going round make the year and seasons, and make the fruits grow and nourish them, and stir the winds and make them remit, and warm the bodies of men properly: go, travel round, and so administer things from the greatest to the least. You are a calf; when a lion shall appear, do your proper business (*i.e.* run away): if you do not, you will suffer. You are a bull: advance and fight, for this is your business, and becomes you, and you can do it. You can lead the army against Ilium; be Agamemnon. You can fight in single combat against Hector: be Achilles. But if Thersites[1] came forward and claimed the command, he would either not have obtained it; or if he did obtain it, he would have disgraced himself before many witnesses.

Do you also think about the matter carefully: it is not what it seems to you. (You say) I wear a cloak now and I shall wear it then: I sleep hard now, and I shall sleep hard then: I will take in addition a little bag now and a staff, and I will go about and begin to beg and to abuse those whom I meet; and if I see any man plucking the hair out of his body, I will rebuke him, or if he has dressed his hair, or if he walks about in purple—If you imagine the thing to be such as this, keep far away from it: do not approach it: it is not at all for you. But if you imagine it to be what it is, and do not think yourself to be unfit for it, consider what a great thing you undertake.

In the first place in the things which relate to yourself, you must not be in any respect like what you do now: you must not blame God or man: you must take away desire altogether, you must transfer avoidance (ἔκκλισις) only to the things which are within the power of the will: you must not feel anger nor resentment nor envy nor pity; a girl must not appear handsome to you, nor must you love a little reputation, nor be pleased with a boy or a cake. For you ought to know that the rest of men throw walls around them and houses and darkness when they do any such things, and they have many means of concealment. A man shuts the door, he sets somebody before

[1] See the description of Thersites in the Iliad, ii. 212.

the chamber: if a person comes, say that he is out, he is not at leisure. But the Cynic instead of all these things must use modesty as his protection: if he does not, he will be indecent in his nakedness and under the open sky. This is his house, his door: this is the slave before his bedchamber: this is his darkness. For he ought not to wish to hide any thing that he does: and if he does, he is gone, he has lost the character of a Cynic, of a man who lives under the open sky, of a free man: he has begun to fear some external thing, he has begun to have need of concealment, nor can he get concealment when he chooses. For where shall he hide himself and how? And if by chance this public instructor shall be detected, this paedagogue, what kind of things will he be compelled to suffer? when then a man fears these things, is it possible for him to be bold with his whole soul to superintend men? It cannot be: it is impossible.

In the first place then you must make your ruling faculty pure, and this mode of life also. Now (you should say), to me the matter to work on is my understanding, as wood is to the carpenter, as hides to the shoemaker; and my business is the right use of appearances. But the body is nothing to me: the parts of it are nothing to me. Death? Let it come when it chooses, either death of the whole or of a part. Fly, you say. And whither; can any man eject me out of the world? He cannot. But wherever I go, there is the sun, there is the moon, there are the stars, dreams, omens, and the conversation (ὁμιλία) with Gods.

Then, if he is thus prepared, the true Cynic cannot be satisfied with this; but he must know that he is sent a messenger from Zeus to men about good and bad things,[2] to show them that they have wandered and are seeking the substance of good and evil where it is not, but where it is, they never think; and that he is a spy, as Diogenes[3] was carried off to Philip after the battle of Chaeroneia as a spy. For in fact a Cynic is a spy of the things which

[2] The office which in our times corresponds to this description of the Cynic, is the office of a teacher of religion.

[3] See i. 24, note [3].

are good for men and which are evil, and it is his duty to examine carefully and to come and report truly, and not to be struck with terror so as to point out as enemies those who are not enemies, nor in any other way to be perturbed by appearances nor confounded.

It is his duty then to be able with a loud voice, if the occasion should arise, and appearing on the tragic stage to say like Socrates: Men, whither are you hurrying, what are you doing, wretches? like blind people you are wandering up and down: you are going by another road, and have left the true road: you seek for prosperity and happiness where they are not, and if another shows you where they are, you do not believe him. Why do you seek it without?[4] In the body? It is not there. If you doubt, look at Myro, look at Ophellius.[5] In possessions? It is not there. But if you do not believe me, look at Croesus: look at those who are now rich, with what lamentations their life is filled. In power? It is not there. If it is, those must be happy who have been twice and thrice consuls; but they are not. Whom shall we believe in these matters? You who from without see their affairs and are dazzled by an appearance, or the men themselves? What do they say? Hear them when they groan, when they grieve, when on account of these very consulships and glory and splendour they think that they are more wretched and in greater danger. Is it in royal power? It is not: if it were, Nero would have been happy, and Sardanapalus. But neither was Agamemnon

[4] Quod petis hic est,
Est Ulubris, animus si te non deficit aequus.
Horace, Ep. i. 11, 30.

Willst du immer weiter schweifen?
Sieh, das Gute liegt so nah.
Lerne nur das Glück ergreifen,
Denn das Glück ist immer da.
Goethe, Gedichte.

[5] These men are supposed to have been strong gladiators. Croesus is the rich king of Lydia, who was taken prisoner by Cyrus the Persian.

happy, though he was a better man than Sardanapalus and Nero; but while others are snoring, what is he doing?

> Much from his head he tore his rooted hair:
> Iliad, x. 15.

and what does he say himself?

> 'I am perplexed,' he says, 'and
> Disturb'd I am,' and 'my heart out of my bosom
> Is leaping.'
> Iliad x. 91.

Wretch, which of your affairs goes badly? Your possessions? No. Your body? No. But you are rich in gold and copper. What then is the matter with you? That part of you, whatever it is, has been neglected by you and is corrupted, the part with which we desire, with which we avoid, with which we move towards and move from things. How neglected? He knows not the nature of good for which he is made by nature and the nature of evil; and what is his own, and what belongs to another; and when any thing that belongs to others goes badly, he says, Wo to me, for the Hellenes are in danger. Wretched is his ruling faculty, and alone neglected and uncared for. The Hellenes are going to die destroyed by the Trojans. And if the Trojans do not kill them, will they not die? Yes; but not all at once. What difference then does it make? For if death is an evil, whether men die altogether, or if they die singly, it is equally an evil. Is any thing else then going to happen than the separation of the soul and the body?[6] Nothing. And if the Hellenes perish, is the door closed, and is it not in your power to die? It is. Why then do you lament (and say) Oh, you who are a king and have the sceptre of Zeus? An unhappy king does not exist more than an unhappy god. What then art thou? In truth a shepherd: for you weep as shepherds do, when a wolf has carried off one of their sheep: and these who

[6] Man then is supposed to consist of a soul and of a body. It may be useful to remember this when we are examining other passages in Epictetus.

are governed by you are sheep. And why did you come hither? Was your desire in any danger? was your aversion (ἔκκλισις)? was your movement (pursuits)? was your avoidance of things? He replies, No; but the wife of my brother was carried off. Was it not then a great gain to be deprived of an adulterous wife?—Shall we be despised then by the Trojans?—What kind of people are the Trojans, wise or foolish? If they are wise, why do you fight with them? If they are fools, why do you care about them?

In what then is the good, since it is not in these things? Tell us, you who are lord, messenger and spy. Where you do not think that it is, nor choose to seek it: for if you chose to seek it, you would have found it to be in yourselves; nor would you be wandering out of the way, nor seeking what belongs to others as if it were your own. Turn your thoughts into yourselves: observe the preconceptions which you have. What kind of a thing do you imagine the good to be? That which flows easily, that which is happy, that which is not impeded. Come, and do you not naturally imagine it to be great, do you not imagine it to be valuable? do you not imagine it to be free from harm? In what material then ought you to seek for that which flows easily, for that which is not impeded? in that which serves or in that which is free? In that which is free. Do you possess the body then free or is it in servile condition? We do not know. Do you not know that it is the slave of fever, of gout, ophthalmia, dysentery, of a tyrant, of fire, of iron, of every thing which is stronger? Yes, it is a slave. How then is it possible that any thing which belongs to the body can be free from hindrance? and how is a thing great or valuable which is naturally dead, or earth, or mud? Well then, do you possess nothing which is free? Perhaps nothing. And who is able to compel you to assent to that which appears false? No man. And who can compel you not to assent to that which appears true? No man. By this then you see that there is something in you naturally free. But to desire or to be averse from, or to move towards an object or to move from it, or to prepare yourself, or to propose to do any thing, which of you can do this, unless he has received an impression of the appearance of that which is profitable or a duty? No man. You have then in these things also something which is not hindered and is free. Wretched men, work out this, take care of this, seek for good here.

And how is it possible that a man who has nothing, who is naked, houseless, without a hearth, squalid, without a slave, without a city, can pass a life that flows easily? See, God has sent you a man to show you that it is possible.[7] Look at me, who am without a city, without a house, without possessions, without a slave; I sleep on the ground; I have no wife, no children, no praetorium, but only the earth and heavens, and one poor cloak. And what do I want? Am I not without sorrow? am I not without fear? Am I not free? When did any of you see me failing in the object of my desire? or ever falling into that which I would avoid? did I ever blame God or man?[8]

[7] "It is observable that Epictetus seems to think it a necessary qualification in a teacher sent from God for the instruction of mankind to be destitute of all external advantages and a suffering character. Thus doth this excellent man, who had carried human reason to so great a height, bear testimony to the propriety of that method which the divine wisdom hath thought fit to follow in the scheme of the Gospel; whose great author had not *where to lay his head;* and which some in later ages have inconsiderately urged as an argument against the Christian religion. The infinite disparity between the proposal of the example of Diogenes in Epictetus and of our Redeemer in the New Testament is too obvious to need any enlargement." Mrs. Carter.

[8] Some of the antients, who called themselves philosophers, did blame God and his administration of the world; and there are men who do the same now. If a man is dissatisfied with the condition of the world, he has the power of going out of it, as Epictetus often says; and if he knows, as he must know, that he cannot alter the nature of man and the conditions of human life, he may think it wise to withdraw from a state of things with which he is not satisfied. If he believes that there is no God, he is at liberty to do what he thinks best for himself; and if he does believe that there is a God, he may still think that his power of quitting the world is a power which he may exercise when he chooses. Many persons commit suicide, not because they are dissatisfied with the state of the world, but for other reasons. I have not yet heard of a modern philosopher who found fault with the condition of human things, and voluntarily retired from life. Our philosophers live as long as they can, and some of them take care of themselves and of all that they possess; they even provide well for the

did I ever accuse any man? did any of you ever see me with sorrowful countenance? And how do I meet with those whom you are afraid of and admire? Do not I treat them like slaves? Who, when he sees me, does not think that he sees his king and master?

This is the language of the Cynics, this their character, this is their purpose. You say No: but their characteristic is the little wallet, and staff, and great jaws: the devouring of all that you give them, or storing it up, or the abusing unseasonably all whom they meet, or displaying their shoulder as a fine thing.—Do you see how you are going to undertake so great a business? First take a mirror: look at your shoulders; observe your loins, your thighs. You are going, my man, to be enrolled as a combatant in the Olympic games, no frigid and miserable contest. In the Olympic games a man is not permitted to be conquered only and to take his departure; but first he must be disgraced in the sight of all the world, not in the sight of Athenians only, or of Lacedaemonians or of Nicopolitans; next he must be whipped also if he has entered[9] into the contests rashly: and before being whipped, he must suffer thirst and heat, and swallow much dust.

comfort of those whom they leave behind them. The conclusion seems to be that they prefer living in this world to leaving it, that their complaints are idle talk; and that being men of weak minds, and great vanity they assume the philosopher's name, and while they try to make others as dissatisfied as they profess themselves to be, they are really enjoying themselves after their fashion as much as they can. These men, though they may have the means of living with as much comfort as the conditions of human life permit, are dissatisfied, and they would, if they could, make as dissatisfied as themselves those who have less means of making life tolerable. These grumblers are not the men who give their money or their labour or their lives for increasing the happiness of mankind and diminishing the unavoidable sufferings of human life; but they find it easier to blame God, when they believe in him; or to find fault with things as they are, which is more absurd, when they do not believe in God, and when they ought to make the best that they can of the conditions under which we live.

[9] The text is *εἰκῆ ἐξελθόντα*. Meibomius suggested *εἰσελθόντα* in place of *ἐξελθόντα*: Schweig. appears to prefer *εἰσελθόντα*, and I have translated this word in the version. I think that there is no doubt about the emendation.

Reflect more carefully, know thyself,[10] consult the divinity, without God attempt nothing; for if he shall advise you (to do this or anything), be assured that he intends you to become great or to receive many blows. For this very amusing quality is conjoined to a Cynic: he must be flogged like an ass, and when he is flogged, he must love those who flog him, as if he were the father of all, and the brother of all.[11]—You say No; but if a man flogs you, stand in the public place and call out, 'Caesar, what do I suffer in this state of peace under thy protection?' Let us bring the offender before the proconsul.—But what is Caesar to a Cynic, or what is a proconsul or what is any other except him who sent the Cynic down hither, and whom he serves, namely Zeus? Does he call upon any other than Zeus? Is he not convinced that whatever he suffers, it is Zeus who is exercising him? Hercules when he was exercised by Eurystheus did not think that he was wretched, but without hesitation he attempted to execute all that he had in hand. And is he who is trained to the contest and exercised by Zeus going to call out and to be vexed, he who is worthy to bear the sceptre of Diogenes? Hear what Diogenes says to the passers by when he is in a fever, Miserable wretches, will you not stay? but are you going so long a journey to Olympia to see the destruction or the fight of athletes; and will you not choose to see the combat between a fever and a man?[12] Would such a man accuse God who sent him down as if God were treating him unworthily, a man who gloried in

[10] 'E caelo descendit γνῶθι σεαυτόν' Juvenal xi. 27. The expression 'Know thyself' is attributed to several persons, and to Socrates among them. Self-knowledge is one of the most difficult kinds of knowledge; and no man has it completely. Men either estimate their powers too highly, and this is named vanity, self conceit or arrogance; or they think too meanly of their powers and do not accomplish what they might accomplish, if they had reasonable self confidence.

[11] "Compare this with the Christian precepts of forbearance and love to enemies, Matthew v. 39-44. The reader will observe that Christ specifies higher injuries and provocations than Epictetus doth; and requires of *all* his followers, what Epictetus describes only as the duty of one or two *extraordinary* persons, as such." Mrs. Carter.

[12] Upton quotes Hieronymus lib. ii. adversus Jovianum, where the thing is told in a different way.

his circumstances, and claimed to be an example to those who were passing by? For what shall he accuse him of? because he maintains a decency of behaviour, because he displays his virtue more conspicuously?[13] Well, and what does he say of poverty, about death, about pain? How did he compare his own happiness with that of the great king (the king of Persia)? or rather he thought that there was no comparison between them. For where there are perturbations, and griefs, and fears, and desires not satisfied, and aversions of things which you cannot avoid, and envies and jealousies, how is there a road to happiness there? But where there are corrupt principles, there these things must of necessity be.

When the young man asked, if when a Cynic has fallen sick, and a friend asks him to come to his house and to be taken care of in his sickness, shall the Cynic accept the invitation, he replied, And where shall you find, I ask, a Cynic's friend?[14] For the man who invites ought to be such another as the Cynic that he may be worthy of being reckoned the Cynic's friend. He ought to be a partner in the Cynic's sceptre and his royalty, and a worthy minister, if he intends to be considered worthy of a Cynic's friendship, as Diogenes was a friend of Antisthenes, as Crates was a friend of Diogenes. Do you think that if a man comes to a Cynic and salutes him, that he is the Cynic's friend, and that the Cynic will think him worthy of receiving a Cynic into his house? So that if you please,[15] reflect on this also: rather look round for some convenient dunghill on which you shall bear your fever and which will shelter you from the north wind that you may not be chilled. But you seem to me to wish to go into some man's house and to be well fed there for a time. Why then do you think of attempting so great a thing (as the life of a Cynic)?

[13] I have not translated, because I do not understand, the words ὅτι κατηγορεῖ. See Schweig.'s note.

[14] This must be the meaning. Meibomius suggested that the true reading is Κυνικοῦ, and not Κυνικόν: and Schweig. seems to be of the same mind. I have repeated the word Cynic several times to remove all ambiguity in this section.

[15] See Schweig.'s note on ὥστε ἄν σοι δοκῇ.

But, said the young man, shall marriage and the procreation of children as a chief duty be undertaken by the Cynic?[16] If you grant me a community of wise men, Epictetus replies, perhaps no man will readily apply himself to the Cynic practice. For on whose account should he undertake this manner of life? However if we suppose that he does, nothing will prevent him from marrying and begetting children; for his wife will be another like himself, and his father in law another like himself, and his children will be brought up like himself. But in the present state of things which is like that of an army placed in battle order, is it not fit that the Cynic should without any distraction be employed only on the ministration of God,[17] able to go about among men,

[16] The Stoics recommended marriage, the procreation of children, the discharge of magisterial offices, and the duties of social life generally.

[17] "It is remarkable that Epictetus here uses the same word (ἀπερισπάστως) with St. Paul, 1 Cor. vii. 35, and urges the same consideration, of applying wholly to the service of God, to dissuade from marriage. His observation too that the state of things was then (ὡς ἐν παρατάξει) like *that of an army prepared for battle*, nearly resembles the Apostle's (ἐνεστῶσα ἀνάγκη) *present necessity*. St. Paul says 2 Tim. ii. 4 (οὐδεὶς στρατευόμενος ἐμπλέκεται etc.) no man that warreth entangleth himself with the affairs of life. So Epictetus says here that a Cynic must not be (ἐμπεπλεγμένον) in relations etc. From these and many other passages of Epictetus one would be inclined to think that he was not unacquainted with St. Paul's Epistles or that he had heard something of the Christian doctrine." Mrs. Carter.

I do not find any evidence of Epictetus being acquainted with the Epistles of Paul. It is possible that he had heard something of the Christian doctrine, but I have not observed any evidence of the fact. Epictetus and Paul have not the same opinion about marriage, for Paul says that 'if they cannot contain, let them marry: for it is better to marry than to burn.' Accordingly his doctrine is 'to avoid fornication let every man have his own wife, and let every woman have her own husband.' He does not directly say what a man should do when he is not able to maintain a wife; but the inference is plain what he will do (1 Cor. vii. 2). Paul's view of marriage differs from that of Epictetus, who recommends marriage. Paul does not: he writes, 'I say therefore to the unmarried and widows, It is good for them if they abide even as I.' He does not acknowledge marriage and the begetting of children as a duty; which Epictetus did.

In the present condition of the world Epictetus says that the 'minister of God' should not marry, because the cares of a family would distract him and make him unable to discharge his duties.

not tied down to the common duties of mankind, nor entangled in the ordinary relations of life, which if he neglects, he will not maintain the character of an honourable and good man? and if he observes them he will lose the character of the messenger, and spy and herald of God. For consider that it is his duty to do something towards his father in law, something to the other kinsfolks of his wife, something to his wife also (if he has one). He is also excluded by being a Cynic from looking after the sickness of his own family, and from providing for their support. And to say nothing of the rest, he must have a vessel for heating water for the child that he may wash it in the bath; wool for his wife when she is delivered of a child, oil, a bed, a cup: so the furniture of the house is increased. I say nothing of his other occupations, and of his distraction. Where then now is that king, he who devotes himself to the public interests,

> The people's guardian and so full of cares.
> Homer, Iliad ii. 25

whose duty it is to look after others, the married and those who have children; to see who uses his wife well, who uses her badly; who quarrels; what family is well administered, what is not; going about as a physician does and feels pulses? He says to one, you have a fever, to another you have a head-ache, or the gout: he says to one, abstain from food;[18] to another he says, eat; or do not use the bath; to another, you require the knife, or the cautery. How can he have time for this who is tied to the duties of common life? is it not his duty to supply clothing to his children, and to send them to the schoolmaster with writing tablets, and styles (for writing).[19] Besides must he not supply them with beds? for they

There is sound sense in this. A 'minister of God' should not be distracted by the cares of a family, especially if he is poor.

[18] The word is ἀνάτεινον. Compare ii. 17, 9.

[19] In the text it is γραφεῖα, τιλλάρια. It is probable that there should be only one word. See Schweig.'s note. Horace (Sat. i. 6. 73) speaks of boys going to school

> Laevo suspensi loculos tabulamque lacerto.

cannot be genuine Cynics as soon as they are born. If he does not do this, it would be better to expose the children as soon as they are born than to kill them in this way. Consider what we are bringing the Cynic down to, how we are taking his royalty from him.—Yes, but Crates took a wife.—You are speaking of a circumstance which arose from love and of a woman who was another Crates.[20] But we are inquiring about ordinary marriages and those which are free from distractions,[21] and making this inquiry we do not find the affair of marriage in this state of the world a thing which is especially suited to the Cynic.

How then shall a man maintain the existence of society? In the name of God, are those men greater benefactors to society who introduce into the world to occupy their own places two or three grunting children,[22] or those who superintend as far as they can all mankind, and see what they do, how they live, what they attend to, what they neglect contrary to their duty? Did they who left little children to the Thebans do them more good than Epaminondas who died childless? And did Priamus who begat fifty worthless sons or Danaus or Aeolus contribute more to the community than Homer? then shall the duty of a general or the business of a writer exclude a man from marriage or the begetting of children, and such a man shall not be judged to have accepted the condition of childlessness for nothing; and shall not the royalty of a Cynic be considered an equivalent for the want of children? Do we not perceive his grandeur and do we not justly contemplate the character of Diogenes; and do we instead of this turn our eyes to the present Cynics who are dogs that wait at tables, and in no respect imitate the Cynics of old except perchance in breaking wind, but in nothing else? For such matters would not have moved us at all nor should we have wondered if a Cynic should not marry or beget children.

[20] The wife of Crates was Hipparchia, who persisted against all advice in marrying Crates and lived with him exactly as he lived. Diogenes Laertius, vi. 96. Upton.

[21] There is some difficulty about ἀπερισπάστων here. Upton proposed to write ἀπεριστάτων, which he explains 'that which has nothing peculiar in it.'

[22] Schweig. translates κακόρυγχα 'male grunnientes': perhaps it means 'ugly-faced.'

Man, the Cynic is the father of all men; the men are his sons, the women are his daughters: he so carefully visits all, so well does he care for all. Do you think that it is from idle impertinence that he rebukes those whom he meets? He does it as a father, as a brother, and as the minister of the father of all, the minister of Zeus.

If you please, ask me also if a Cynic shall engage in the administration of the state. Fool, do you seek a greater form of administration than that in which he is engaged? Do you ask if he shall appear among the Athenians and say something about the revenues and the supplies, he who must talk with all men, alike with Athenians, alike with Corinthians, alike with Romans, not about supplies, nor yet about revenues, nor about peace or war, but about happiness and unhappiness, about good fortune and bad fortune, about slavery and freedom? When a man has undertaken the administration of such a state, do you ask me if he shall engage in the administration of a state? ask me also if he shall govern (hold a magisterial office): again I will say to you, Fool, what greater government shall he exercise than that which he exercises now?

It is necessary also for such a man (the Cynic) to have a certain habit of body: for if he appears to be consumptive, thin and pale, his testimony has not then the same weight. For he must not only by showing the qualities of the soul prove to the vulgar that it is in his power independent of the things which they admire to be a good man, but he must also show by his body that his simple and frugal way of living in the open air does not injure even the body. See, he says, I am a proof of this, and my own body also is. So Diogenes used to do, for he used to go about fresh looking, and he attracted the notice of the many by his personal appearance. But if a Cynic is an object of compassion, he seems to be a beggar: all persons turn away from him, all are offended with him; for neither ought he to appear dirty so that he shall not also in this respect drive away men; but his very roughness ought to be clean and attractive.

There ought also to belong to the Cynic much natural grace and sharpness; and if this is not so, he is a stupid fellow, and nothing else; and he must have these qualities that he may be able readily and fitly to be a match for all circumstances that may happen. So Diogenes replied to one who said, Are you the Diogenes who does not believe that there are gods?[23] And, how, replied Diogenes, can this be when I think that you are odious to the gods? On another occasion in reply to Alexander, who stood by him when he was sleeping, and quoted Homer's line (Iliad, ii. 24)

A man a councillor should not sleep all night,

he answered, when he was half asleep,

The people's guardian and so full of cares.

But before all the Cynic's ruling faculty must be purer than the sun; and if it is not, he must necessarily be a cunning knave and a fellow of no principle, since while he himself is entangled in some vice he will reprove others.[24] For see how the matter stands: to these kings and tyrants their guards and arms give the power of reproving some persons, and of being able even to punish those who do wrong though they are themselves bad; but to a Cynic instead of arms and guards it is conscience (τὸ συνειδός) which gives this power. When he knows that he has watched and laboured for mankind, and has slept pure, and sleep has left him still purer, and that he thought whatever he has thought as a friend of the gods, as a minister, as a participator of the power of Zeus, and that on all occasions he is ready to say

Lead me, O Zeus, and thou, O Destiny;[25]

and also, If so it pleases the gods, so let it be; why should he not have confidence to speak freely to his own brothers, to his children, in a word to his kinsmen? For this reason he is neither over curious nor a busybody when he is in

[23] Diogenes Laertius, vi. 42.

[24] The Cynic is in Epictetus the minister of religion. He must be pure, for otherwise how can he reprove vice? This is a useful lesson to those whose business it is to correct the vices of mankind.

[25] See ii. 23, 42, note [11].

this state of mind; for he is not a meddler with the affairs of others when he is superintending human affairs, but he is looking after his own affairs. If that is not so, you may also say that the general is a busybody, when he inspects his soldiers, and examines them and watches them and punishes the disorderly. But if while you have a cake under your arm, you rebuke others, I will say to you, Will you not rather go away into a corner and eat that which you have stolen; what have you to do with the affairs of others? For who are you? are you the bull of the herd, or the queen of the bees? Show me the tokens of your supremacy, such as they have from nature. But if you are a drone claiming the sovereignty over the bees, do you not suppose that your fellow citizens will put you down as the bees do the drones?

The Cynic also ought to have such power of endurance as to seem insensible to the common sort and a stone: no man reviles him, no man strikes him, no man insults him, but he gives his body that any man who chooses may do with it what he likes. For he bears in mind that the inferior must be overpowered by the superior in that in which it is inferior; and the body is inferior to the many, the weaker to the stronger. He never then descends into such a contest in which he can be overpowered; but he immediately withdraws from things which belong to others, he claims not the things which are servile. But where there is will and the use of appearances, there you will see how many eyes he has so that you may say, Argus was blind compared with him. Is his assent ever hasty, his movement (towards an object) rash, does his desire ever fail in its object, does that which he would avoid befal him, is his purpose unaccomplished, does he ever find fault, is he ever humiliated, is he ever envious? To these he directs all his attention and energy; but as to every thing else he snores supine. All is peace; there is no robber who takes away his will,[26] no tyrant. But what say you as to his body? I say there is. And his possessions? I say there is. And as to magistracies and honours?—What does he care for them?—When then any person would

[26] This is quoted by M. Antoninus, xi. 36.

frighten him through them, he says to him, Begone, look for children: masks are formidable to them; but I know that they are made of shell, and they have nothing inside.

About such a matter as this you are deliberating. Therefore, if you please, I urge you in God's name, defer the matter, and first consider your preparation for it. For see what Hector says to Andromache, Retire rather, he says, into the house and weave:

> War is the work of men
> Of all indeed, but specially 'tis mine.
> Il. vi. 490.

So he was conscious of his own qualification, and knew her weakness.

CHAPTER XXIII.

TO THOSE WHO READ AND DISCUSS FOR THE SAKE OF OSTENTATION.[1]

FIRST say to yourself Who you wish to be: then do accordingly what you are doing; for in nearly all other things we see this to be so. Those who follow athletic exercises first determine what they wish to be, then they do accordingly what follows. If a man is a runner in the long course, there is a certain kind of diet, of walking, rubbing, and exercise: if a man is a runner in the stadium, all these things are different; if he is a Pentathlete, they are still more different. So you will find it also in the arts. If you are a carpenter, you will have such and such things: if a worker in metal, such things. For every thing that we do, if we refer it to no end, we shall do it to no purpose; and if we refer it to

[1] Epictetus in an amusing manner touches on the practice of Sophists, Rhetoricians, and others, who made addresses only to get praise. This practice of reciting prose or verse compositions was common in the time of Epictetus, as we may learn from the letters of the younger Pliny, Juvenal, Martial, and the author of the treatise de Causis corruptae eloquentiae. Upton.

the wrong end, we shall miss the mark. Further, there is a general end or purpose, and a particular purpose. First of all, we must act as a man. What is comprehended in this? We must not be like a sheep, though gentle; nor mischievous, like a wild beast. But the particular end has reference to each person's mode of life and his will. The lute-player acts as a lute-player, the carpenter as a carpenter, the philosopher as a philosopher, the rhetorician as a rhetorician. When then you say, Come and hear me read to you: take care first of all that you are not doing this without a purpose; then if you have discovered that you are doing this with reference to a purpose, consider if it is the right purpose. Do you wish to do good or to be praised? Immediately you hear him saying, To me what is the value of praise from the many? and he says well, for it is of no value to a musician, so far as he is a musician, nor to a geometrician. Do you then wish to be useful? in what? tell us that we may run to your audience room. Now can a man do anything useful to others, who has not received something useful himself? No, for neither can a man do any thing useful in the carpenter's art, unless he is a carpenter; nor in the shoemaker's art, unless he is a shoemaker.

Do you wish to know then if you have received any advantage? Produce your opinions, philosopher. What is the thing which desire promises? Not to fail in the object. What does aversion promise? Not to fall into that which you would avoid. Well; do we fulfill their promise? Tell me the truth; but if you lie, I will tell you. Lately when your hearers came together rather coldly, and did not give you applause, you went away humbled. Lately again when you had been praised, you went about and said to all, What did you think of me? Wonderful, master, I swear by all that is dear to me. But how did I treat of that particular matter? Which? The passage in which I described Pan and the nymphs?[2] Excellently. Then do you tell me that in desire and in aversion you are acting according to nature? Be gone; try to persuade somebody else. Did you not praise a cer-

[2] Such were the subjects which the literary men of the day delighted in.

tain person contrary to your opinion? and did you not flatter a certain person who was the son of a senator? Would you wish your own children to be such persons?—I hope not—Why then did you praise and flatter him? He is an ingenuous youth and listens well to discourses—How is this?—He admires me. You have stated your proof. Then what do you think? do not these very people secretly despise you? When then a man who is conscious that he has neither done any good nor ever thinks of it, finds a philosopher who says, You have a great natural talent, and you have a candid and good disposition, what else do you think that he says except this, This man has some need of me? Or tell me what act that indicates a great mind has he shown? Observe; he has been in your company a long time; he has listened to your discourses, he has heard you reading; has he become more modest? has he been turned to reflect on himself? has he perceived in what a bad state he is? has he cast away self-conceit? does he look for a person to teach him? He does. A man who will teach him to live? No, fool, but how to talk; for it is for this that he admires you also. Listen and hear what he says: This man writes with perfect art, much better than Dion.[3] This is altogether another thing. Does he say, This man is modest, faithful, free from perturbations? and even if he did say it, I should say to him, Since this man is faithful, tell me what this faithful man is. And if he could not tell me, I should add this, First understand what you say, and then speak.

You then, who are in a wretched plight and gaping after applause and counting your auditors, do you intend to be useful to others?—To-day many more attended my discourse. Yes, many; we suppose five hundred. That is nothing; suppose that there were a thousand—Dion never had so many hearers—How could he?—And they understand what is said beautifully. What is fine, master, can move even a stone—See, these are the words of a

[3] Dion of Prusa in Bithynia was named Chrysostomus (golden-mouthed) because of his eloquence. He was a rhetorician and sophist, as the term was then understood, and was living at the same time as Epictetus. Eighty of his orations written in Greek are still extant, and some fragments of fifteen.

philosopher.. This is the disposition of a man who will do good to others; here is a man who has listened to discourses, who has read what is written about Socrates as Socratic, not as the compositions of Lysias and Isocrates. 'I have often wondered by what arguments.'[4] Not so, but 'by what argument': this is more exact than that— What, have you read the words at all in a different way from that in which you read little odes? For if you read them as you ought, you would not have been attending to such matters, but you would rather have been looking to these words: "Anytus and Melitus are able to kill me, but they cannot harm me:" "and I am always of such a disposition as to pay regard to nothing of my own except to the reason which on inquiry seems to me the best."[5] Hence who ever heard Socrates say, "I know something and I teach;" but he used to send different people to different teachers. Therefore they used to come to him and ask to be introduced to philosophers by him; and he would take them and recommend them.—Not so; but as he accompanied them he would say, Hear me to-day discoursing in the house of Quadratus.[6] Why should I hear you? Do you wish to show me that you put words together cleverly? You put them together, man; and what good will it do you?—But only praise me.—What do you mean by praising?—Say to me, admirable, wonderful.—Well, I say so. But if that is praise whatever it is which philosophers mean by the name (κατηγορία)[7] of

[4] These words are the beginning of Xenophon's Memorabilia, i. 1. The small critics disputed whether the text should be τίσι λόγοις, or τίνι λόγῳ.

[5] From the Crito of Plato, c. 6.

[6] The rich, says Upton, used to lend their houses for recitations, as we learn from Pliny, Ep. viii. 12 and Juvenal, vii. 40.

Si dulcedine famae
Succensus recites, maculosas commodat aedes.

Quadratus is a Roman name. There appears to be a confusion between Socrates and Quadratus. The man says, No. Socrates would not do so: but he would do, as a man might do now. He would say on the road; I hope you will come to hear me. I don't find anything in the notes on this passage; but it requires explanation.

[7] κατηγορία is one of Aristotle's common terms.

good, what have I to praise in you? If it is good to speak well, teach me, and I will praise you. — What then? ought a man to listen to such things without pleasure?— I hope not. For my part I do not listen even to a lute-player without pleasure. Must I then for this reason stand and play the lute? Hear what Socrates says, Nor would it be seemly for a man of my age, like a young man composing addresses, to appear before you.[8] Like a young man, he says. For in truth this small art is an elegant thing, to select words, and to put them together, and to come forward and gracefully to read them or to speak, and while he is reading to say, There are not many who can do these things, I swear by all that you value.

Does a philosopher invite people to hear him? As the sun himself draws men to him, or as food does, does not the philosopher also draw to him those who will receive benefit? What physician invites a man to be treated by him? Indeed I now hear that even the physicians in Rome do invite patients, but when I lived there, the physicians were invited. I invite you to come and hear that things are in a bad way for you, and that you are taking care of every thing except that of which you ought to take care, and that you are ignorant of the good and the bad and are unfortunate and unhappy. A fine kind of invitation: and yet if the words of the philosopher do not produce this effect on you, he is dead, and so is the speaker. Rufus was used to say: If you have leisure to praise me, I am speaking to no purpose.[9] Accordingly he used to speak in such a way that every one of us who were sitting there supposed that some one had accused him before Rufus: he so touched on what was doing, he so placed before the eyes every man's faults.

The philosopher's school, ye men, is a surgery: you ought not to go out of it with pleasure, but with pain. For you are not in sound health when you enter: one has dislocated his shoulder, another has an abscess, a third a fistula, and a fourth a head ache. Then do I sit and utter to

[8] From Plato's Apology of Socrates.
[9] Aulus Gellius v. 1. Seneca, Ep. 52. Upton.

you little thoughts and exclamations that you may praise me and go away, one with his shoulder in the same condition in which he entered, another with his head still aching, and a third with his fistula or his abscess just as they were? Is it for this then that young men shall quit home, and leave their parents and their friends and kinsmen and property, that they may say to you, Wonderful! when you are uttering your exclamations. Did Socrates do this, or Zeno, or Cleanthes?

What then? is there not the hortatory style? Who denies it? as there is the style of refutation, and the didactic style. Who then ever reckoned a fourth style with these, the style of display? What is the hortatory style? To be able to show both to one person and to many the struggle in which they are engaged, and that they think more about any thing than about what they really wish. For they wish the things which lead to happiness, but they look for them in the wrong place. In order that this may be done, a thousand seats must be placed and men must be invited to listen, and you must ascend the pulpit in a fine robe or cloak and describe the death of Achilles. Cease, I intreat you by the gods, to spoil good words and good acts as much as you can. Nothing can have more power in exhortation than when the speaker shows to the hearers that he has need of them. But tell me who when he hears you reading or discoursing is anxious about himself or turns to reflect on himself? or when he has gone out says, The philosopher hit me well: I must no longer do these things. But does he not, even if you have a great reputation, say to some person? He spoke finely about Xerxes;[10] and another says, No, but about the battle of Thermopylae. Is this listening to a philosopher?

[10] Cicero, de Officiis i. 18: 'Quae magno animo et fortiter excellenterque gesta sunt, ea nescio quomodo pleniore ore laudamus. Hinc Rhetorum campus de Marathone, Salamine, Plataeis, Thermopylis, Leuctris.'

CHAPTER XXIV.

THAT WE OUGHT NOT TO BE MOVED BY A DESIRE OF THOSE THINGS WHICH ARE NOT IN OUR POWER.

LET not that which in another is contrary to nature be an evil to you: for you are not formed by nature to be depressed with others nor to be unhappy with others, but to be happy with them. If a man is unhappy, remember that his unhappiness is his own fault: for God has made all men to be happy, to be free from perturbations. For this purpose he has given means to them, some things to each person as his own, and other things not as his own: some things subject to hindrance and compulsion and deprivation; and these things are not a man's own: but the things which are not subject to hindrances, are his own; and the nature of good and evil, as it was fit to be done by him who takes care of us and protects us like a father, he has made our own.—But you say, I have parted from a certain person, and he is grieved.—Why did he consider as his own that which belongs to another? why, when he looked on you and was rejoiced, did he not also reckon that you are mortal, that it is natural for you to part from him for a foreign country? Therefore he suffers the consequences of his own folly. But why do you [1] or for what purpose bewail yourself? Is it that you also have not thought of these things? but like poor women who are good for nothing, you have enjoyed all things in which you took pleasure, as if you would always enjoy them, both places and men and conversation; and now you sit and weep because you do not see the same persons and do not live in the same places.—Indeed you deserve this, to be more wretched than crows and ravens who have the power of flying where they please and changing their nests for others, and crossing the seas without lamenting or regretting their former condition.—Yes, but this happens to them because they are irrational creatures.—Was reason then given to us by the gods for

[1] See Schweig.'s note.

the purpose of unhappiness and misery, that we may pass our lives in wretchedness and lamentation? Must all persons be immortal and must no man go abroad, and must we ourselves not go abroad, but remain rooted like plants; and if any of our familiar friends goes abroad, must we sit and weep; and on the contrary, when he returns, must we dance and clap our hands like children?

Shall we not now wean ourselves and remember what we have heard from the philosophers? if we did not listen to them as if they were jugglers: they tell us that this world is one city,[2] and the substance out of which it has been formed is one, and that there must be a certain period, and that some things must give way to others, that some must be dissolved, and others come in their place; some to remain in the same place, and others to be moved; and that all things are full of friendship, first of the gods,[3] and then of men who by nature are made to be of one family; and some must be with one another, and others must be separated, rejoicing in those who are with them, and not grieving for those who are removed from them; and man in addition to being by nature of a noble temper and having a contempt of all things which are not in the power of his will, also possesses this property not to be rooted nor to be naturally fixed to the earth, but to go at different times to different places, sometimes from the urgency of certain occasions, and at others merely for the sake of seeing. So it was with Ulysses, who saw

> Of many men the states, and learned their ways.[4]

And still earlier it was the fortune of Hercules to visit all the inhabited world

> Seeing men's lawless deeds and their good rules of law:[5]

casting out and clearing away their lawlessness and introducing in their place good rules of law. And yet how many friends do you think that he had in Thebes, how many in Argos, how many in Athens? and how many do

[2] See ii. 5, 26.

[3] See iii. 13. 15.

[4] Homer, Odyssey i. 3.

[5] Odyssey, xvii. 487.

you think that he gained by going about? And he married also, when it seemed to him a proper occasion, and begot children, and left them without lamenting or regretting or leaving them as orphans; for he knew that no man is an orphan; but it is the father who takes care of all men always and continuously. For it was not as mere report that he had heard that Zeus is the father of men, for he thought that Zeus was his own father, and he called him so, and to him he looked when he was doing what he did. Therefore he was enabled to live happily in all places. And it is never possible for happiness and desire of what is not present to come together. For that which is happy must have all[6] that it desires, must resemble a person who is filled with food, and must have neither thirst nor hunger.—But Ulysses felt a desire for his wife and wept as he sat on a rock.—Do you attend to Homer and his stories in every thing? Or if Ulysses really wept, what was he else than an unhappy man? and what good man is unhappy? In truth the whole is badly administered, if Zeus does not take care of his own citizens that they may be happy like himself. But these things are not lawful nor right to think of: and if Ulysses did weep and lament, he was not a good man. For who is good if he knows not who he is? and who knows what he is, if he forgets that things which have been made are perishable, and that it is not possible for one human being to be with another always? To desire then things which are impossible is to have a slavish character, and is foolish: it is the part of a stranger, of a man who fights against God in the only way that he can, by his opinions.

But my mother laments when she does not see me.—Why has she not learned these principles? and I do not say this, that we should not take care that she may not lament, but I say that we ought not to desire in every way what is not our own. And the sorrow of another is another's sorrow: but my sorrow is my own. I then will stop my own sorrow by every means, for it is in my power: and the sorrow of another I will endeavour to stop as far as I can; but I will not attempt to do it by every means;

[6] ἀπέχειν. See iii. 2, 13. Paul to the Philippians, iv. 18.

for if I do, I shall be fighting against God, I shall be opposing Zeus and shall be placing myself against him in the administration of the universe; and the reward (the punishment) of this fighting against God and of this disobedience not only will the children of my children pay, but I also shall myself, both by day and by night, startled by dreams, perturbed, trembling at every piece of news, and having my tranquillity depending on the letters of others.—Some person has arrived from Rome. I only hope that there is no harm. But what harm can happen to you, where you are not?—From Hellas (Greece) some one is come: I hope that there is no harm.—In this way every place may be the cause of misfortune to you. Is it not enough for you to be unfortunate there where you are, and must you be so even beyond sea, and by the report of letters? Is this the way in which your affairs are in a state of security?—Well then suppose that my friends have died in the places which are far from me.—What else have they suffered than that which is the condition of mortals? Or how are you desirous at the same time to live to old age, and at the same time not to see the death of any person whom you love? Know you not that in the course of a long time many and various kinds of things must happen; that a fever shall overpower one, a robber another, and a third a tyrant? Such is the condition of things around us, such are those who live with us in the world: cold and heat, and unsuitable ways of living, and journeys by land, and voyages by sea, and winds, and various circumstances which surround us, destroy one man, and banish another, and throw one upon an embassy and another into an army. Sit down then in a flutter at all these things, lamenting, unhappy, unfortunate, dependent on another, and dependent not on one or two, but on ten thousands upon ten thousands.

Did you hear this when you were with the philosophers? did you learn this? do you not know that human life is a warfare? that one man must keep watch, another must go out as a spy, and a third must fight? and it is not possible that all should be in one place, nor is it better that it should be so. But you neglecting to do the commands of the general complain when any thing more hard than usual is imposed on you, and you do not observe what you make the army become as far as it is in your power; that if all imitate you, no man will dig a trench, no man will put a rampart round, nor keep watch, nor expose himself to danger, but will appear to be useless for the purposes of an army. Again, in a vessel if you go as a sailor, keep to one place and stick to it. And if you are ordered to climb the mast, refuse; if to run to the head of the ship, refuse; and what master of a ship will endure you? and will he not pitch you overboard as a useless thing, an impediment only and bad example to the other sailors? And so it is here also: every man's life is a kind of warfare, and it is long and diversified. You must observe the duty of a soldier and do every thing at the nod of the general; if it is possible, divining what his wishes are: for there is no resemblance between that general and this, neither in strength nor in superiority of character. You are placed in a great office of command and not in any mean place; but you are always a senator. Do you not know that such a man must give little time to the affairs of his household, but be often away from home, either as a governor or one who is governed, or discharging some office, or serving in war or acting as a judge? Then do you tell me that you wish, as a plant, to be fixed to the same places and to be rooted?—Yes, for it is pleasant.—Who says that it is not? but a soup is pleasant, and a handsome woman is pleasant. What else do those say who make pleasure their end? Do you not see of what men you have uttered the language? that it is the language of Epicureans and catamites? Next while you are doing what they do and holding their opinions, do you speak to us the words of Zeno and of Socrates? Will you not throw away as far as you can the things belonging to others with which you decorate yourself, though they do not fit you at all? For what else do they desire than to sleep without hindrance and free from compulsion, and when they have risen to yawn at their leisure, and to wash the face, then write and read what they choose, and then talk about some trifling matter being praised by their friends whatever they may say, then to go forth for a walk, and having walked about a little to bathe, and then eat and sleep, such sleep as is the fashion of such men? why need we say how? for one can easily conjecture. Come, do you also tell your own way of passing the time which you desire, you who are an admirer of truth and of Socrates and Diogenes. What do you wish to do in Athens? the same (that others do), or something else? Why then do you call yourself a Stoic? Well, but they who falsely call themselves Roman citizens,[7] are severely punished; and should those, who falsely claim so great and reverend a thing and name, get off unpunished? or is this not possible, but the law divine and strong and inevitable is this, which exacts the severest punishments from those who commit the greatest crimes? For what does this law say? Let him who pretends to things which do not belong to him be a boaster, a vain-glorious man:[8] let him who disobeys the divine administration be base, and a slave; let him suffer grief, let him be envious, let him pity;[9] and in a word let him be unhappy and lament.

Well then; do you wish me to pay court to a certain person? to go to his doors?[10]—If reason requires this to be done for the sake of country, for the sake of kinsmen, for the sake of mankind, why should you not go? You are not ashamed to go to the doors of a shoemaker, when you are in want of shoes, nor to the door of a gardener, when you want lettuces; and are you ashamed to go to the doors of the rich when you want any thing?—Yes, for I have no awe of a shoemaker—Don't feel any awe of the rich—Nor

[7] Suetonius (Claudius, 25) says: 'Peregrinae conditionis homines vetuit usurpare Romana nomina, duntaxat gentilia. Civitatem Romanam usurpantes in campo Esquilino securi percussit.' Upton.

[8] This is a denunciation of the hypocrite.

[9] 'Pity' perhaps means that he will suffer the perturbation of pity, when he ought not to feel it. I am not sure about the exact meaning.

[10] 'What follows hath no connection with what immediately preceded; but belongs to the general subject of the chapter.' Mrs Carter.

'The person with whom Epictetus chiefly held this discourse, seems to have been instructed by his friends to pay his respects to some great man at Nicopolis (perhaps the procurator, iii. 4. 1) and to visit his house.' Schweig.

will I flatter the gardener—And do not flatter the rich—How then shall I get what I want?—Do I say to you, go as if you were certain to get what you want? And do not I only tell you, that you may do what is becoming to yourself? Why then should I still go? That you may have gone, that you may have discharged the duty of a citizen, of a brother, of a friend. And further remember that you have gone to the shoemaker, to the seller of vegetables, who have no power in any thing great or noble, though he may sell dear. You go to buy lettuces: they cost an obolus (penny), but not a talent. So it is here also. The matter is worth going for to the rich man's door—Well, I will go—It is worth talking about—Let it be so; I will talk with him—But you must also kiss his hand and flatter him with praise—Away with that, it is a talent's worth: it is not profitable to me, nor to the state nor to my friends, to have done that which spoils a good citizen and a friend.—But you will seem not to have been eager about the matter, if you do not succeed. Have you again forgotten why you went? Know you not that a good man does nothing for the sake of appearance, but for the sake of doing right?—What advantage is it then to him to have done right?—And what advantage is it to a man who writes the name of Dion to write it as he ought?—The advantage is to have written it.—Is there no reward then [11]?—Do you seek a reward for a good man greater than doing what is good and just? At Olympia you wish for nothing more, but it seems to you enough to be crowned at the games. Does it seem to you so small and worthless a thing to be good and

[11] The reward of virtue is in the acts of virtue. The Stoics taught that virtue is its own reward. When I was a boy I have written this in copies, but I did not know what it meant. I know now that few people believe it; and like the man here, they inquire what reward they shall have for doing as they ought to do. A man of common sense would give no other answer than what Epictetus gives. But that will not satisfy all. The heathens must give the answer: 'For what more dost thou want when thou hast done a man a service? Art thou not content that thou hast done something conformable to thy nature, and dost thou seek to be paid for it? just as if the eye demanded a recompense for seeing or the feet for walking.' M. Antoninus, ix. 42. Compare Seneca, de Vita Beata, c. 9.

happy? For these purposes being introduced by the gods into this city (the world), and it being now your duty to undertake the work of a man, do you still want nurses also and a mamma, and do foolish women by their weeping move you and make you effeminate? Will you thus never cease to be a foolish child? know you not that he who does the acts of a child, the older he is, the more ridiculous he is?

In Athens did you see no one by going to his house?—I visited any man that I pleased—Here also be ready to see, and you will see whom you please: only let it be without meanness, neither with desire nor with aversion, and your affairs will be well managed. But this result does not depend on going nor on standing at the doors, but it depends on what is within, on your opinions. When you have learned not to value things which are external and not dependent on the will, and to consider that not one of them is your own, but that these things only are your own, to exercise the judgment well, to form opinions, to move towards an object, to desire, to turn from a thing, where is there any longer room for flattery, where for meanness? why do you still long for the quiet there (at Athens), and for the places to which you are accustomed? Wait a little and you will again find these places familiar: then, if you are of so ignoble a nature, again if you leave these also, weep and lament.

How then shall I become of an affectionate temper? By being of a noble disposition, and happy. For it is not reasonable to be mean-spirited nor to lament yourself, nor to depend on another, nor ever to blame God or man. I entreat you, become an affectionate person in this way, by observing these rules. But if through this affection, as you name it, you are going to be a slave and wretched, there is no profit in being affectionate. And what prevents you from loving another as a person subject to mortality, as one who may go away from you. Did not Socrates love his own children? He did; but it was as a free man, as one who remembered that he must first be a friend to the gods. For this reason he violated nothing which was becoming to a good man, neither in making his defence nor by fixing a penalty on himself,[12] nor even in the former part of his life when he was a senator or when he was a soldier. But we are fully supplied with every pretext for being of ignoble temper, some for the sake of a child, some for a mother, and others for brethren's sake. But it is not fit for us to be unhappy on account of any person, but to be happy on account of all, but chiefly on account of God who has made us for this end. Well, did Diogenes[13] love nobody, who was so kind and so much a lover of all that for mankind in general he willingly undertook so much labour and bodily sufferings? He did love mankind, but how? As became a minister of God, at the same time caring for men, and being also subject to God. For this reason all the earth was his country, and no particular place; and when he was taken prisoner he did not regret Athens nor his associates and friends there, but even he became familiar with the pirates and tried to improve them; and being sold afterwards he lived in Corinth as before at Athens; and he would have behaved the same, if he had gone to the country of the Perrhaebi.[14] Thus is freedom acquired. For this reason he used to say, Ever since Antisthenes made me free, I have not been a slave. How did Antisthenes make him free? Hear what he says: Antisthenes taught me what is my own, and what is not my own; possessions are not my own, nor kinsmen, domestics, friends, nor reputation, nor places familiar, nor mode of life; all these belong to others. What then is your own? The use of appearances. This he showed to me, that I possess it free from hindrance, and from com-

[12] It was the custom at Athens when the court (the dicasts) had determined to convict an accused person, in some cases at least, to ask him what penalty he proposed to be inflicted on himself; but Socrates refused to do this or to allow his friends to do it, for he said that to name the penalty was the same as admitting his guilt (Xenophon, Apologia, 23). Socrates said that if he did name a proper penalty for himself, it would be that he should daily be allowed to dine in the Prytaneium (Plato, Apology, c. 26; Cicero, De Oratore, i. 54).

[13] The character of Diogenes is described very differently by Epictetus from that which we read in common books.

[14] A people in Thessaly between the river Peneius and Mount Olympus. It is the same as if Epictetus had said to any remote country.

pulsion, no person can put an obstacle in my way, no person can force me to use appearances otherwise than I wish. Who then has any power over me? Philip or Alexander, or Perdiccas or the great king? How have they this power? For if a man is going to be overpowered by a man, he must long before be overpowered by things. If then pleasure is not able to subdue a man, nor pain, nor fame, nor wealth, but he is able, when he chooses, to spit out all his poor body in a man's face and depart from life, whose slave can he still be? But if he dwelt with pleasure in Athens, and was overpowered by this manner of life, his affairs would have been at every man's command; the stronger would have had the power of grieving him. How do you think that Diogenes would have flattered the pirates that they might sell him to some Athenian, that some time he might see that beautiful Piraeus, and the Long Walls and the Acropolis? In what condition would you see them? As a captive, a slave and mean: and what would be the use of it for you?—Not so: but I should see them as a free man—Show me, how you would be free. Observe, some person has caught you, who leads you away from your accustomed place of abode and says, You are my slave, for it is in my power to hinder you from living as you please, it is in my power to treat you gently, and to humble you: when I choose, on the contrary you are cheerful and go elated to Athens. What do you say to him who treats you as a slave? What means have you of finding one who will rescue you from slavery?[15] Or cannot you even look him in the face, but without saying more do you intreat to be set free? Man, you ought to go gladly to prison, hastening, going before those who lead you there. Then, I ask you, are you unwilling to live in Rome and desire to live in Hellas (Greece)? And when you must die, will you then also fill us with your lamentations, because you will not see Athens nor walk about in the Lyceion? Have you gone abroad for this? was it for this reason you have sought to find some person from whom you might receive benefit? What benefit? That you may

[15] On the word καρπιστήν see the notes in Schweig.'s edition. The word is supposed to be formed from καρπίς, καρφίς, festuca.

solve syllogisms more readily, or handle hypothetical arguments? and for this reason did you leave brother, country, friends, your family, that you might return when you had learned these things? So you did not go abroad to obtain constancy of mind, nor freedom from perturbation, nor in order that being secure from harm you may never complain of any person, accuse no person, and no man may wrong you, and thus you may maintain your relative position without impediment? This is a fine traffic that you have gone abroad for in syllogisms and sophistical arguments[16] and hypothetical: if you like, take your place in the agora (market or public place) and proclaim them for sale like dealers in physic.[17] Will you not deny even all that you have learned that you may not bring a bad name on your theorems as useless? What harm has philosophy done you? Wherein has Chrysippus injured you that you should prove by your acts that his labours are useless? Were the evils that you had there (at home) not enough, those which were the cause of your pain and lamentation, even if you had not gone abroad? Have you added more to the list? And if you again have other acquaintances and friends, you will have more causes for lamentation; and the same also if you take an affection for another country. Why then do you live to surround yourself with other sorrows upon sorrows through which you are unhappy? Then, I ask you, do you call this affection? What affection, man! If it is a good thing, it is the cause of no evil: if it is bad, I have nothing to do with it. I am formed by nature for my own good: I am not formed for my own evil.

What then is the discipline for this purpose? First of all the highest and the principal, and that which stands as it were at the entrance, is this; when you are delighted with anything, be delighted as with a thing which is not

[16] *Μεταπίπτοντας.* See i. 7.

[17] This is an old practice, to go about and sell physic to people. Cicero (Pro Cluentio, c. 14) speaks of such a quack (pharmacopola), who would do a poisoning job for a proper sum of money. I have seen a travelling doctor in France who went about in a cart, and rang a bell, at the sound of which people came round him. Some who were deaf had stuff poured into their ears, paid their money, and made way for others who had other complaints.

one of those which cannot be taken away, but as with something of such a kind, as an earthen pot is, or a glass cup, that when it has been broken, you may remember what it was, and may not be troubled. So in this matter also: if you kiss your own child, or your brother or friend, never give full license to the appearance (φαντασίαν), and allow not your pleasure to go as far as it chooses; but check it, and curb it as those who stand behind men in their triumphs and remind them that they are mortal.[18] Do you also remind yourself in like manner, that he whom you love is mortal, and that what you love is nothing of your own: it has been given to you for the present, not that it should not be taken from you, nor has it been given to you for all time, but as a fig is given to you or a bunch of grapes at the appointed season of the year. But if you wish for these things in winter, you are a fool. So if you wish for your son or friend when it is not allowed to you, you must know that you are wishing for a fig in winter.[19] For such as winter is to a fig, such is every event which happens from the universe to the things which are taken away according to its nature. And further, at the times when you are delighted with a thing, place before yourself the contrary appearances. What harm is it while you are kissing your child to say with a lisping voice, To-morrow you will die; and to a friend also, To-morrow you will go away or I shall, and never shall we see one another again?—But these are words of bad omen—And some incantations also are of bad omen; but because they are useful, I don't care for this; only let them be useful. But do you call things to be of bad omen except those which are significant of some evil? Cowardice is a word of bad omen, and meanness of spirit, and sorrow, and grief and shamelessness. These words are of bad omen: and yet we ought not to hesitate to utter them in order to protect ourselves against the things. Do you tell me that a name which is significant of any natural thing is of evil omen? say that even for the ears of corn to be

[18] It was the custom in Roman triumphs for a slave to stand behind the triumphant general in his chariot and to remind him that he was still mortal. Juvenal, x. 41.

[19] Compare Antoninus xi. 33 and 34.

reaped is of bad omen, for it signifies the destruction of the ears, but not of the world. Say that the falling of the leaves also is of bad omen, and for the dried fig to take the place of the green fig, and for raisins to be made from the grapes. For all these things are changes from a former state into other states; not a destruction, but a certain fixed economy and administration. Such is going away from home and a small change: such is death, a greater change, not from the state which now is to that which is not, but to that which is not now.[20]—Shall I then no longer exist?—You will not exist, but you will be something else, of which the world now has need:[21] for you also came into existence not when you chose, but when the world had need of you.[22]

[20] Marcus Antoninus, xi. 35. Compare Epict., iii. 13, 14, and iv. 7. 75.

[21] Upton altered the text *οὐκέτι οὖν ἔσομαι; Οὐκ ἔσῃ· ἀλλ' ἄλλο τι, οὗ νῦν ὁ κόσμος χρείαν ἔχει,* into *οὐκετι οὖν ἔσομαι; Ἔσῃ· ἀλλ' ἄλλο τι, οὗ νῦν ὁ κόσμος χρείαν οὐκ ἔχει.* He says that he made the alteration without MS. authority, but that the sense requires the change. Schweighaeuser does not accept the alteration, nor do I. Schweig. remarks that there may be some difficulty in the words *οὗ νῦν ὁ κόσμος χρείαν ἔχει.* He first supposes that the word 'now' (*νῦν*) means after a man's death; but next he suggests that *ἄλλο τι οὗ* means 'something different from that of which the world has now need.' A reader might not discover that there is any difficulty. He might also suggest that *νῦν* ought to be omitted, for if it were omitted, the sense would be still plainer. See iii. 13. 15, and iv. 7. 15.

[22] I am not sure if Epictetus ever uses *κόσμος* in the sense of 'Universe,' the 'universum' of philosophers. I think he sometimes uses it in the common sense of the world, the earth and all that is on it. Epictetus appears to teach that when a man dies, his existence is terminated. The body is resolved into the elements of which it is formed, and these elements are employed for other purposes. Consistently with this doctrine he may have supposed that the powers, which we call rational and intellectual, exist in man by virtue only of the organisation of his brain which is superior to that of all other animals; and that what we name the soul has no existence independent of the body. It was an old Greek hypothesis that at death the body returned to earth from which it came, and the soul (*πνεῦμα*) returned to the regions above, from which it came. I cannot discover any passage in Epictetus in which the doctrine is taught that the soul has an existence independent of the body. The opinions of Marcus Antoninus on this matter are contained in his book, iv. 14, 21, and perhaps elsewhere: but they are rather obscure. A recent writer has attempted to settle the question of the existence of departed souls by affirming that we can find

Wherefore the wise and good man, remembering who he is and whence he came, and by whom he was produced, is

no place for them either in heaven or in hell; for the modern scientific notion, as I suppose that it must be named, does not admit the conception of a place heaven or a place hell (Strauss, Der Alte und der Neue Glaube, p. 129).

We may name Paul a contemporary of Epictetus, for though Epictetus may have been the younger, he was living at Rome during Nero's reign (A.D. 54–68); and it is affirmed, whether correctly or not, I do not undertake to say, that Paul wrote from Ephesus his first epistle to the Corinthians (Cor. i. 16, 8) in the beginning of A.D. 56. Epictetus, it is said, lived in Rome till the time of the expulsion of the philosophers by Domitian, when he retired to Nicopolis an old man, and taught there. Paul's first epistle to the Corinthians (c. 15) contains his doctrine of the resurrection, which is accepted, I believe, by all, or nearly all, if there are any exceptions, who profess the Christian faith: but it is not understood by all in the same way.

Paul teaches that Christ died for our sins, that he was buried and rose again on the third day; and that after his resurrection he was seen by many persons. Then he asks, if Christ rose from the dead, how can some say that there is no resurrection of the dead? 'But if there be no resurrection of the dead, then is Christ not risen' (v. 13); and (v. 19), 'if in this life only we have hope in Christ, we are of all men most miserable.' But he affirms again (v. 20) that 'Christ is risen and become the first fruits of them that slept.' In v. 32, he asks what advantages he has from his struggles in Ephesus, 'if the dead rise not: let us eat and drink, for to-morrow we die.' He seems not to admit the value of life, if there is no resurrection of the dead; and he seems to say that we shall seek or ought to seek only the pleasures of sense, because life is short, if we do not believe in a resurrection of the dead. It may be added that there is not any direct assertion in this chapter that Christ ascended to heaven in a bodily form, or that he ascended to heaven in any way. He then says (v. 35), 'But some man will say, How are the dead raised up? and with what body do they come?' He answers this question (v. 36), 'Thou fool, that which thou sowest is not quickened except it die': and he adds that 'God giveth it (the seed) a body as it hath pleased him, and to every seed his own body.' We all know that the body, which is produced from the seed, is not the body 'that shall be:' and we also know that the seed which is sown does not die, and that if the seed died, no body would be produced from such seed. His conclusion is that the dead 'is sown a natural body; it is raised a spiritual body' (σῶμα πνευματικόν). I believe that the commentators do not agree about this 'spiritual body': but it seems plain that Paul did not teach that the body which will rise will be the same as the body which is buried. He says (v. 50) that 'flesh and blood cannot inherit the kingdom of God.' Yet in the Apostles' Creed we pronounce our belief in the 'resurrection of the body': but in the Nicene Creed it is said we look 'for the resurrection of the dead,' which is a different thing or may have a

attentive only to this, how he may fill his place with due regularity, and obediently to God. Dost thou still wish me to exist (live)? I will continue to exist as free, as noble in nature, as thou hast wished me to exist: for thou hast made me free from hindrance in that which is my own. But hast thou no further need of me? I thank thee; and so far I have remained for thy sake, and for the sake of no other person, and now in obedience to thee I depart. How dost thou depart? Again, I say, as thou hast pleased, as free, as thy servant, as one who has known thy commands and thy prohibitions. And so long as I shall stay in thy service, whom dost thou will me to be? A prince or a private man, a senator or a common person, a soldier or a general, a teacher or a master of a family? whatever place and position thou mayest assign to me, as Socrates says, I will die ten thousand times rather than desert them. And where dost thou will me to be? in Rome or Athens, or Thebes or Gyara. Only remember me there where I am. If thou sendest me to a place where there are no means for men living according to nature, I shall not depart (from life) in disobedience to thee, but as if thou wast giving me the signal to retreat: I do not leave thee, let this be far from my intention, but I perceive that thou hast no need of me. If means of living according to nature be allowed to me, I will seek no other place than that in which I am, or other men than those among whom I am.

Let these thoughts be ready to hand by night and by day: these you should write, these you should read: about these you should talk to yourself, and to others. Ask a man, Can you help me at all for this purpose? and further, go to another and to another. Then if any thing that is

different meaning from 'the resurrection of the body.' In the ministration of baptism to such as are of riper years, the person to be baptized is asked 'Dost thou believe in God the Father Almighty,' etc. in the terms of the Church Creeds, but in place of the resurrection of the body or of the dead, he is asked if he believes 'in the resurrection of the flesh.'

The various opinions of divines of the English church on the resurrection of the body are stated by A. Clissold in the 'Practical Nature of the Theological Writings of E. Swedenborg in a letter to Whately, Archbishop of Dublin, 1859, 2nd ed.'

said be contrary to your wish, this reflection first will immediately relieve you, that it is not unexpected. For it is a great thing in all cases to say, I knew that I begot a son who is mortal.[23] For so you also will say, I knew that I am mortal, I knew that I may leave my home, I knew that I may be ejected from it, I knew that I may be led to prison. Then if you turn round and look to yourself, and seek the place from which comes that which has happened, you will forthwith recollect that it comes from the place of things which are out of the power of the will, and of things which are not my own. What then is it to me? Then, you will ask, and this is the chief thing: And who is it that sent it? The leader, or the general, the state, the law of the state. Give it me then, for I must always obey the law in every thing. Then, when the appearance (of things) pains you, for it is not in your power to prevent this, contend against it by the aid of reason, conquer it: do not allow it to gain strength nor to lead you to the consequences by raising images such as it pleases and as it pleases. If you be in Gyara, do not imagine the mode of living at Rome, and how many pleasures there were for him who lived there and how many there would be for him who returned to Rome: but fix your mind on this matter, how a man who lives in Gyara ought to live in Gyara like a man of courage. And if you be in Rome, do not imagine what the life in Athens is, but think only of the life in Rome.

Then in the place of all other delights substitute this, that of being conscious that you are obeying God, that not in word, but in deed you are performing the acts of a wise and good man. For what a thing it is for a man to be able to say to himself, Now whatever the rest may say in solemn manner in the schools and may be judged to be saying in a way contrary to common opinion (or in a strange way), this I am doing; and they are sitting and are discoursing of my virtues and inquiring about me and praising me; and of this Zeus has willed that I shall receive from myself a demonstration, and shall myself know if he has a soldier such as he ought to have, a citizen such as

[23] Seneca de Consol. ad Pol. c. 30; Cicero, Tuscul. Disp. iii. 13.

he ought to have, and if he has chosen to produce me to the rest of mankind as a witness of the things which are independent of the will: See that you fear without reason, that you foolishly desire what you do desire: seek not the good in things external; seek it in yourselves: if you do not, you will not find it. For this purpose he leads me at one time hither, at another time sends me thither, shows me to men as poor, without authority, and sick; sends me to Gyara, leads me into prison, not because he hates me, far from him be such a meaning, for who hates the best of his servants? nor yet because he cares not for me, for he does not neglect any even of the smallest things;[24] but he does this for the purpose of exercising me and making use of me as a witness to others. Being appointed to such a service, do I still care about the place in which I am, or with whom I am, or what men say about me? and do I not entirely direct my thoughts to God and to his instructions and commands?

Having these things (or thoughts) always in hand, and exercising them by yourself, and keeping them in readiness, you will never be in want of one to comfort you and strengthen you. For it is not shameful to be without something to eat, but not to have reason sufficient for keeping away fear and sorrow. But if once you have gained exemption from sorrow and fear, will there any longer be a tyrant for you, or a tyrant's guard, or attendants on Caesar?[25] Or shall any appointment to offices at court cause you pain, or shall those who sacrifice in the Capitol on the occasion of being named to certain functions, cause pain to you who have received so great authority from Zeus?[26] Only do not make a proud display of it, nor boast of it; but shew it by your acts; and if no man perceives it, be satisfied that you are yourself in a healthy state and happy.

[24] Compare i. 12. 2, ii. 14. 11, iii. 26. 28. 'Compare this with the description of the universal care of Providence, Matthew, x. 29, 30, and the occasion on which it was produced.' Mrs. Carter.

[25] See i. 19. 19.

[26] On the strange words ὀρδινατίων and ὀπτικίοις, which occur in this sentence, see the notes in Schweighaeuser's edition.

CHAPTER XXV.

TO THOSE WHO FALL OFF (DESIST) FROM THEIR PURPOSE.

CONSIDER as to the things which you proposed to yourself at first, which you have secured, and which you have not; and how you are pleased when you recall to memory the one, and are pained about the other; and if it is possible, recover the things wherein you failed. For we must not shrink when we are engaged in the greatest combat, but we must even take blows.[1] For the combat before us is not in wrestling and the Pancration, in which both the successful and the unsuccessful may have the greatest merit, or may have little, and in truth may be very fortunate or very unfortunate; but the combat is for good fortune and happiness themselves. Well then, even if we have renounced the contest in this matter (for good fortune and happiness), no man hinders us from renewing the combat again, and we are not compelled to wait for another four years that the games at Olympia may come again[2]; but as soon as you have recovered and restored yourself, and employ the same zeal, you may renew the combat again; and if again you renounce it, you may again renew it; and if you once gain the victory, you are like him who has never renounced the combat. Only do not through a habit of doing the same thing (renouncing the combat) begin to do it with pleasure, and then like a bad athlete go about after being conquered in all the circuit of the games like quails who have run away.[3]

The sight of a beautiful young girl overpowers me. Well,

[1] Compare iii. 15, 4.

[2] These games were celebrated once in four years.

[3] 'All the circuit of the games' means the circuit of the Pythian, Isthmian, Nemean, and Olympic games. A man who had contended in these four games victoriously was named Periodonices, or Periodeutes. Upton.

The Greeks used to put quails in a cockpit, as those who are old enough may remember that we used to put game cocks to fight with one another. Schweighaeuser describes a way of trying the courage of these quails from Pollux (ix. 109); but I suppose that the birds fought also with one another.

have I not been overpowered before? An inclination arises in me to find fault with a person; for have I not found fault with him before? You speak to us as if you had come off (from these things) free from harm, just as if a man should say to his physician who forbids him to bathe, Have I not bathed before? If then the physician can say to him, Well, and what then happened to you after the bath? Had you not a fever, had you not a headache? And when you found fault with a person lately, did you not do the act of a malignant person, of a trifling babbler; did you not cherish this habit in you by adding to it the corresponding acts? And when you were overpowered by the young girl, did you come off unharmed? Why then do you talk of what you did before? You ought, I think, remembering what you did, as slaves remember the blows which they have received, to abstain from the same faults. But the one case is not like the other; for in the case of slaves the pain causes the remembrance: but in the case of your faults, what is the pain, what is the punishment; for when have you been accustomed to fly from evil acts?[4] Sufferings then of the trying character are useful to us, whether we choose or not.

[4] Upton supposed that the words 'Αλλ' οὐχ ὅμοιον . . . . to κακῶς ἐνεργῆσαι, in the translation, 'But the one case is not, . . . to 'fly from evil acts,' are said by the adversary of Epictetus, and Mrs. Carter has followed Upton in the translation. But then there is no sense in the last sentence Οἱ πόνοι ἄρα etc., in the translation, 'Sufferings then' etc. The reader may consult Schweighaeuser's note. I suppose that Epictetus is speaking the words 'But the one case' etc. to the end of the chapter. The adversary, who is not punished like a slave, and has no pains to remind him of his faults, is supposed so far not to have felt the consequences of his bad acts; but Epictetus concludes that sufferings of a painful character would be useful to him, as they are to all persons who do what they ought not to do. There is perhaps some difficulty in the word πειρατηρίων. But I think that Schweig. has correctly explained the passage.

ARE you not ashamed at being more cowardly and more mean than fugitive slaves? How do they when they run away leave their masters? on what estates do they depend, and what domestics do they rely on? Do they not after stealing a little which is enough for the first days, then afterwards move on through land or through sea, contriving one method after another for maintaining their lives? And what fugitive slave ever died of hunger?[2] But you are afraid lest necessary things should fail you, and are sleepless by night. Wretch, are you so blind, and don't you see the road to which the want of necessaries leads?—Well, where does it lead?—To the same place to which a fever leads, or a stone that falls on you, to death. Have you not often said this yourself to your companions? have you not read much of this kind, and written much? and how often have you boasted that you were easy as to death?

Yes: but my wife and children also suffer hunger.[3]—Well then, does their hunger lead to any other place? Is there not the same descent to some place for them also? Is not

[1] 'Compare this chapter with the beautiful and affecting discourses of our Saviour on the same subject, Matthew vi. 25-34; Luke xii 22-30.' Mrs. Carter. The first verse of Matthew begins, 'Take no thought for your life, what ye shall eat or what ye shall drink' etc No Christian literally follows the advice of this and the following verses, and he would be condemned by the judgment of all men if he did.

[2] It is very absurd to suppose that no fugitive slave ever died of hunger. How could Epictetus know that?

[3] He supposes that the man who is dying of hunger has also wife and children, who will suffer the same dreadful end. The consolation, if it is any, is that the rich and luxurious and kings will also die The fact is true. Death is the lot of all. But a painful death by hunger cannot be alleviated by a man knowing that all must die in some way. It seems as if the philosopher expected that even women and children should be philosophers, and that the husband in his philosophy should calmly contemplate the death of wife and children by starvation. This is an example of the absurdity to which even a wise man carried his philosophy; and it is unworthy of the teacher's general good sense.

there the same state below for them? Do you not choose then to look to that place full of boldness against every want and deficiency, to that place to which both the richest and those who have held the highest offices, and kings themselves and tyrants must descend? or to which you will descend hungry, if it should so happen, but they burst by indigestion and drunkenness. What beggar did you hardly ever see who was not an old man, and even of extreme old age? But chilled with cold day and night, and lying on the ground, and eating only what is absolutely necessary they approach near to the impossibility of dying.[4] Cannot you write? Cannot you teach (take care of) children? Cannot you be a watchman at another person's door?—But it is shameful to come to such a necessity.—Learn then first what are the things which are shameful, and then tell us that you are a philosopher: but at present do not, even if any other man call you so, allow it.

Is that shameful to you which is not your own act, that of which you are not the cause, that which has come to you by accident, as a headache, as a fever? If your parents were poor, and left their property to others, and if while they live, they do not help you at all, is this shameful to you? Is this what you learned with the philosophers? Did you never hear that the thing which is shameful ought to be blamed, and that which is blameable is worthy of blame? Whom do you blame for an act which is not his own, which he did not do himself? Did you then make your father such as he is, or is it in your power to improve him? Is this power given to you? Well then, ought you to wish the things which are not given to you, or to be ashamed if you do not obtain them? And have you also been accustomed while you were studying philosophy to look to others and to hope for nothing from yourself? Lament then and groan and eat with fear that you may not have food to-morrow.

[4] We see many old beggars who endure what others could not endure; but they all die at last, and would have died earlier if their beggar life had begun sooner. The living in the open air and wandering about help them to last longer; but the exposure to cold and wet and to the want of food hastens their end. The life of a poor old beggar is neither so long nor so comfortable as that of a man, who has a good home and sufficient food, and lives with moderation.

Tremble about your poor slaves lest they steal, lest they run away, lest they die. So live, and continue to live, you who in name only have approached philosophy, and have disgraced its theorems as far as you can by showing them to be useless and unprofitable to those who take them up; you who have never sought constancy, freedom from perturbation, and from passions: you who have not sought any person for the sake of this object, but many for the sake of syllogisms; you who have never thoroughly examined any of these appearances by yourself, Am I able to bear, or am I not able to bear? What remains for me to do? But as if all your affairs were well and secure, you have been resting on the third topic,[5] that of things being unchanged, in order that you may possess unchanged—what? cowardice, mean spirit, the admiration of the rich, desire without attaining any end, and avoidance (*ἔκκλισιν*) which fails in the attempt? About security in these things you have been anxious.

Ought you not to have gained something in addition from reason, and then to have protected this with security? And whom did you ever see building a battlement all round and not encircling it with a wall?[6] And what door-keeper is placed with no door to watch? But you practise in order to be able to prove—what? You practise that you may not be tossed as on the sea through sophisms,[7] and tossed about from what? Shew me first what you hold, what you measure, or what you weigh; and shew me the scales or the medimnus (the measure); or how long will you go on measuring the dust[8]? Ought you not to demonstrate those things which make men happy, which make things go on for them in the way as they wish, and why we ought to blame no man, accuse no man, and acquiesce in the administration of the universe? Shew me these. 'See, I

[5] See iii. c. 2.

[6] 'Plato using the same simile teaches that last of all disciplines dialectic ought to be learned.' Schweighaeuser.

[7] *ἀποσαλεύεσθαι.* Paul, Ep. to the Thessalonians (ii. 2. 2) has *εἰς τὸ μὴ ταχέως σαλευθῆναι ὑμᾶς ἀπὸ τοῦ νοός.* Upton.

[8] This is good advice. When you propose to measure, to estimate things, you should first tell us what the things are before you attempt to fix their value; and what is the measure or scales that you use.

shew them: I will resolve syllogisms for you.'—This is the measure, slave; but it is not the thing measured. Therefore you are now paying the penalty for what you neglected, philosophy: you tremble, you lie awake, you advise with all persons; and if your deliberations are not likely to please all, you think that you have deliberated ill. Then you fear hunger, as you suppose: but it is not hunger that you fear, but you are afraid that you will not have a cook, that you will not have another to purchase provisions for the table, a third to take off your shoes, a fourth to dress you, others to rub you, and to follow you, in order that in the bath, when you have taken off your clothes and stretched yourself out like those who are crucified you may be rubbed on this side and on that, and then the aliptes (rubber) may say (to the slave), Change his position, present the side, take hold of his head, shew the shoulder; and then when you have left the bath and gone home, you may call out, Does no one bring something to eat? And then, Take away the tables, sponge them: you are afraid of this, that you may not be able to lead the life of a sick man. But learn the life of those who are in health, how slaves live, how labourers, how those live who are genuine philosophers; how Socrates lived, who had a wife and children; how Diogenes lived, and how Cleanthes[9] who attended to the school and drew water. If you choose to have these things, you will have them every where, and you will live in full confidence. Confiding in what? In that alone in which a man can confide, in that which is secure, in that which is not subject to hindrance, in that which cannot be taken away, that is, in your own will. And why have you made yourself so useless and good for nothing that no man will choose to receive you into his house, no man to take care of you?: but if a utensil entire and useful were cast abroad, every man who found it, would take it up and think it a gain; but no man will take you up, and every man will consider you a loss. So cannot you discharge the office even of a dog,

[9] Cleanthes, the successor of Zeno in his school, was a great example of the pursuit of knowledge under difficulties: during the night he used to draw water from the wells for the use of the gardens: during the day he employed himself in his studies. He was the author of a noble hymn to Zeus, which is extant.

or of a cock? Why then do you choose to live any longer, when you are what you are?

Does any good man fear that he shall fail to have food? To the blind it does not fail, to the lame it does not: shall it fail to a good man? And to a good soldier there does not fail to be one who gives him pay, nor to a labourer, nor to a shoemaker: and to the good man shall there be wanting such a person?[10] Does God thus neglect the things that he has established, his ministers, his witnesses, whom alone he employs as examples to the uninstructed, both that he exists, and administers well the whole, and does not neglect human affairs, and that to a good man there is no evil either when he is living or when he is dead? What then when he does not supply him with food? What else does he do than[11] like a good general he has given me the signal to retreat? I obey, I follow, assenting to the words of the commander,[12] praising his acts: for I came when it pleased him, and I will also go away when it pleases him; and while I lived, it was my duty to praise God both by myself, and to each person severally and to many.[13] He does not supply me with many things, nor with abundance, he does not will me to live luxuriously; for neither did he supply Hercules who was his own son; but another (Eurystheus) was king of Argos and Mycenae, and Hercules obeyed orders, and laboured, and was exercised. And Eurystheus was what he was, neither king of Argos nor of Mycenae, for he was not even king of himself; but Hercules was ruler and leader of the whole earth and sea, who purged away lawlessness, and introduced justice and holiness;[14] and he did these things both naked and alone. And when Ulysses

[10] It seems strange that Epictetus should make such assertions when we know that they are not true. Shortly after he himself speaks even of the good man not being supplied with food by God.

[11] See i. 29. 29.

[12] The word is ἐπευφημῶν. Compare ἐπευφήμησαν, Homer, Iliad i. 22.

[13] See i. 16. 15.

[14] 'Compare Hebrews xi. and xii., in which the Apostle and Philosopher reason in nearly the same manner and even use the same terms; but how superior is the example urged by the Apostle to Hercules and Ulysses!' Mrs. Carter.

was cast out shipwrecked, did want humiliate him, did it break his spirit? but how did he go off to the virgins to ask for necessaries, to beg which is considered most shameful?[15]

> As a lion bred in the mountains trusting in his strength.—
> Od. vi. 130.

Relying on what? Not on reputation nor on wealth nor on the power of a magistrate, but on his own strength, that is, on his opinions about the things which are in our power and those which are not. For these are the only things which make men free, which make them escape from hindrance, which raise the head (neck) of those who are depressed, which make them look with steady eyes on the rich and on tyrants. And this was (is) the gift given to the philosopher. But you will not come forth bold, but trembling about your trifling garments and silver vessels. Unhappy man, have you thus wasted your time till now?

What then, if I shall be sick? You will be sick in such a way as you ought to be.—Who will take care of me?—God; your friends—I shall lie down on a hard bed—But you will lie down like a man—I shall not have a convenient chamber—You will be sick in an inconvenient chamber—Who will provide for me the necessary food?—Those who provide for others also. You will be sick like Manes.[16]—And what also will be the end of the sickness? Any other than death?—Do you then consider that this the chief of all evils to man and the chief mark of mean spirit and of cowardice is not death, but rather the fear of death? Against this fear then I advise you to exercise yourself: to this let all your reasoning tend, your exercises, and reading; and you will know that thus only are men made free.

[15] The story of Ulysses asking Nausicaa and her maids for help when he was cast naked on the land is in the Odyssey vi. 127.

[16] Manes is a slave's name. Diogenes had a slave named Manes, his only slave, who ran away, and though Diogenes was informed where the slave was, he did not think it worth while to have him brought back. He said, it would be a shame if Manes could live without Diogenes, and Diogenes could not live without Manes.

BOOK IV.

CHAPTER I.

ABOUT FREEDOM.

He is free who lives as he wishes to live;[1] who is neither subject to compulsion nor to hindrance, nor to force; whose movements to action (ὁρμαί) are not impeded, whose desires attain their purpose, and who does not fall into that which he would avoid (ἐκκλίσεις ἀπερίπτωτοι). Who then chooses to live in error? No man. Who chooses to live deceived, liable to mistake,[2] unjust, unrestrained, discontented, mean? No man. Not one then of the bad lives as he wishes; nor is he then free. And who chooses to live in sorrow, fear, envy, pity, desiring and failing in his desires, attempting to avoid something and falling into it? Not one. Do we then find any of the bad free from sorrow, free from fear, who does not fall into that which he would avoid, and does not obtain that which he wishes? Not one; nor then do we find any bad man free.[3]

If then a man who has been twice consul should hear this, if you add, But you are a wise man; this is nothing to you: he will pardon you. But if you tell him the truth, and say, You differ not at all from those who have been thrice sold as to being yourself not a slave, what else ought you to expect than blows? For he says, What, I a

[1] Cicero, Paradox. v. 'Quid est enim libertas? Potestas vivendi ut velis. Quis igitur vivit ut vult, nisi qui recta sequitur,' etc.

[2] προπίπτων. Comp. ii. 1. 10: ἐξαπατηθῆναι οὖν ἢ προπεσεῖν.

[3] 'Whoever committeth sin, is the servant of sin,' John viii. 34. Mrs. Carter.

slave, I whose father was free, whose mother was free, I whom no man can purchase: I am also of senatorial rank, and a friend of Caesar, and I have been a consul, and I own many slaves.—In the first place, most excellent senatorial man, perhaps your father also was a slave in the same kind of servitude, and your mother, and your grandfather and all your ancestors in an ascending series. But even if they were as free as it is possible, what is this to you? What if they were of a noble nature, and you of a mean nature; if they were fearless, and you a coward; if they had the power of self-restraint, and you are not able to exercise it.

And what, you may say, has this to do with being a slave? Does it seem to you to be nothing to do a thing unwillingly, with compulsion, with groans, has this nothing to do with being a slave? It is something, you say: but who is able to compel me, except the lord of all, Caesar? Then even you yourself have admitted that you have one master. But that he is the common master of all, as you say, let not this console you at all: but know that you are a slave in a great family. So also the people of Nicopolis are used to exclaim, By the fortune of Caesar,[4] we are free.

However, if you please, let us not speak of Caesar at present. But tell me this: did you never love any person, a young girl, or slave, or free? What then is this with respect to being a slave or free? Were you never commanded by the person beloved to do something which you did not wish to do? have you never flattered your little slave? have you never kissed her feet? And yet if any man compelled you to kiss Caesar's feet, you would think it an insult and excessive tyranny. What else then is slavery? Did you never go out by night to some place whither you did not wish to go, did you not expend what you did not wish to expend, did you not utter words with sighs and groans, did you not submit to abuse and to be

[4] A usual form of oath. See ii. 20. 29. Upton compares the Roman expression 'Per Genium,' as in Horace Epp. i. 7. 94—

> Quod te per Genium, dextramque, Deosque Penates
> Obsecro et obtestor.

excluded?[5] But if you are ashamed to confess your own acts, see what Thrasonides[6] says and does, who having seen so much military service as perhaps not even you have, first of all went out by night, when Geta (a slave) does not venture out, but if he were compelled by his master, would have cried out much and would have gone out lamenting his bitter slavery. Next, what does Thrasonides say? A worthless girl has enslaved me, me whom no enemy ever did. Unhappy man, who are the slave even of a girl, and a worthless girl. Why then do you still call yourself free? and why do you talk of your service in the army? Then he calls for a sword and is angry with him who out of kindness refuses it; and he sends presents to her who hates him, and intreats and weeps, and on the other hand having had a little success he is elated. But even then how? was he free enough neither to desire nor to fear?

Now consider in the case of animals, how we employ the notion of liberty. Men keep tame lions shut up, and feed them, and some take them about; and who will say that this lion is free?[7] Is it not the fact that the more he lives at his ease, so much the more he is in a slavish condition? and who if he had perception and reason would wish to be one of these lions? Well, these birds when they are caught and are kept shut up, how much do they suffer in their attempts to escape?[8] and some of them die of hunger rather than submit to such a kind of life. And as many of them as live, hardly live and with suffering pine away; and if they ever find any opening, they make their

[5] A lover's exclusion by his mistress was a common topic, and a serious cause of complaint (Lucretius, iv. 1172):

> At lacrimans exclusus amator limina saepe
> Floribus et sertis operit.

See also Horace, Odes, i. 25.

[6] Thrasonides was a character in one of Menander's plays, intitled Μισούμενος or the Hated.

[7] It must have been rather difficult to manage a tame lion; but we read of such things among the Romans. Seneca, Epp. 41.

[8] The keeping of birds in cages, parrots and others, was also common among the Romans. Ovid (Amor. ii. 6) has written a beautiful elegy on the death of a favourite parrot.

escape. So much do they desire their natural liberty, and to be independent and free from hindrance. And what harm is there to you in this? What do you say? I am formed by nature to fly where I choose, to live in the open air, to sing when I choose: you deprive me of all this, and say, what harm is it to you? For this reason we shall say that those animals only are free, which cannot endure capture, but as soon as they are caught, escape from captivity by death. So Diogenes also somewhere says that there is only one way to freedom, and that is to die content: and he writes to the Persian king, You cannot enslave the Athenian state any more than you can enslave fishes. How is that? cannot I catch them? If you catch them, says Diogenes, they will immediately leave you, as fishes do; for if you catch a fish, it dies; and if these men that are caught shall die, of what use to you is the preparation for war? These are the words of a free man who had carefully examined the thing, and, as was natural, had discovered it. But if you look for it in a different place from where it is, what wonder if you never find it?

The slave wishes to be set free immediately. Why? Do you think that he wishes to pay money to the collectors of twentieths?[9] No; but because he imagines that hitherto through not having obtained this, he is hindered and unfortunate. If I shall be set free, immediately it is all happiness, I care for no man, I speak to all as an equal and like to them, I go where I choose, I come from any place I choose, and go where I choose. Then he is set free; and forthwith having no place where he can eat, he looks for some man to flatter, some one with whom he shall sup: then he either works with his body and endures the most dreadful things;[10] and if he can obtain a manger, he falls into a slavery much worse than his former

[9] See ii. 1. 26. The εἰκοστῶναι were the Publicani, men who farmed this and other taxes. A tax of a twentieth of the value of a slave when manumitted was established at an early time (Livy vii. 16). It appears from this passage that the manumitted slave paid the tax out of his savings (peculium). See ii. 1. note 7.

[10] The reader may guess the meaning.

slavery; or even if he is become rich, being a man without any knowledge of what is good, he loves some little girl, and in his unhappiness laments and desires to be a slave again. He says, what evil did I suffer in my state of slavery? Another clothed me, another supplied me with shoes, another fed me, another looked after me in sickness; and I did only a few services for him. But now a wretched man, what things I suffer, being a slave to many instead of to one. But however, he says, if I shall acquire rings,[11] then I shall live most prosperously and happily. First, in order to acquire these rings, he submits to that which he is worthy of; then when he has acquired them, it is again all the same. Then he says, If I shall be engaged in military service, I am free from all evils. He obtains military service. He suffers as much as a flogged slave, and nevertheless he asks for a second service and a third. After this, when he has put the finishing stroke (the colophon) [12] to his career, and is become a senator, then he becomes a slave by entering into the assembly, then he serves the finer and most splendid slavery—not to be a fool, but to learn what Socrates taught, what is the nature of each thing that exists, and that a man should not rashly adapt preconceptions (προλήψεις) to the several things which are.[13] For this is the cause to men of all their evils, the not being able to adapt the general preconceptions to the several things. But we have different opinions (about the cause of our evils). One man thinks that he is sick: not so however, but the fact is that he does not adapt his preconceptions right. Another thinks that he is poor; another that he has a severe father or mother; and another again that Caesar is not favourable to him. But all this is one and only one thing, the not knowing how to adapt the preconceptions. For who has not a preconception of that which is bad,

[11] A gold ring was worn by the Equites; and accordingly to desire the gold ring is the same as to desire to be raised to the Equestrian class.

[12] The colophon. See ii. 14. note 5. After the words 'most splendid slavery' it is probable that some words have accidentally been omitted in the MSS.

[13] Compare i. 2. 6.

that it is hurtful, that it ought to be avoided, that it ought in every way to be guarded against? One preconception is not repugnant to another,[14] only where it comes to the matter of adaptation. What then is this evil, which is both hurtful, and a thing to be avoided? He answers not to be Caesar's friend.—He is gone far from the mark, he has missed the adaptation, he is embarrassed, he seeks the things which are not at all pertinent to the matter; for when he has succeeded in being Caesar's friend, never the less he has failed in finding what he sought. For what is that which every man seeks? To live secure, to be happy, to do every thing as he wishes, not to be hindered, nor compelled. When then he is become the friend of Caesar, is he free from hindrance? free from compulsion, is he tranquil, is he happy? Of whom shall we inquire? What more trustworthy witness have we than this very man who is become Caesar's friend? Come forward and tell us when did you sleep more quietly, now or before you became Caesar's friend? Immediately you hear the answer, Stop, I intreat you, and do not mock me: you know not what miseries I suffer, and sleep does not come to me; but one comes and says, Caesar is already awake, he is now going forth: then come troubles and cares—Well, when did you sup with more pleasure, now or before? Hear what he says about this also. He says that if he is not invited, he is pained: and if he is invited, he sups like a slave with his master, all the while being anxious that he does not say or do any thing foolish. And what do you suppose that he is afraid of; lest he should be lashed like a slave? How can he expect any thing so good? No, but as befits so great a man, Caesar's friend, he is afraid that he may lose his head. And when did you bathe more free from trouble, and take your gymnastic exercise more quietly? In fine, which kind of life did you prefer? your present or your former life? I can swear that no man is so stupid or so ignorant of truth as not to bewail his own misfortunes the nearer he is in friendship to Caesar.

[14] Compare i. 22.

Since then neither those who are called kings live as they choose, nor the friends of kings, who finally are those who are free? Seek, and you will find; for you have aids from nature for the discovery of truth. But if you are not able yourself by going along these ways only to discover that which follows, listen to those who have made the inquiry. What do they say? Does freedom seem to you a good thing? The greatest good. Is it possible then that he who obtains the greatest good can be unhappy or fare badly? No. Whomsoever then you shall see unhappy, unfortunate, lamenting, confidently declare that they are not free. I do declare it. We have now then got away from buying and selling and from such arrangements about matters of property: for if you have rightly assented to these matters, if the great king (the Persian king) is unhappy, he cannot be free, nor can a little king, nor a man of consular rank, nor one who has been twice consul.—Be it so.

Further then answer me this question also, does freedom seem to you to be something great and noble and valuable?—How should it not seem so? Is it possible then when a man obtains anything so great and valuable and noble to be mean?—It is not possible—When then you see any man subject to another or flattering him contrary to his own opinion, confidently affirm that this man also is not free; and not only if he do this for a bit of supper, but also if he does it for a government (province) or a consulship: and call these men little slaves who for the sake of little matters do these things, and those who do so for the sake of great things call great slaves, as they deserve to be.—This is admitted also—Do you think that freedom is a thing independent and self governing?—Certainly—Whomsoever then it is in the power of another to hinder and compel, declare that he is not free. And do not look, I intreat you, after his grandfathers and great grandfathers, or inquire about his being bought or sold; but if you hear him saying from his heart and with feeling, 'Master,' even if the twelve fasces precede him (as consul), call him a slave. And if you hear him say, 'Wretch that I am, how much I suffer,' call him a slave. If finally you see him lamenting, complaining, unhappy, call him a slave though he wears a praetexta.[15] If then he is doing nothing of this kind, do not yet say that he is free, but learn his opinions, whether they are subject to compulsion, or may produce hindrance, or to bad fortune; and if you find him such, call him a slave who has a holiday in the Saturnalia:[16] say that his master is from home: he will return soon, and you will know what he suffers. Who will return? Whoever has in himself the power over anything which is desired by the man, either to give it to him or to take it away? Thus then have we many masters? We have: for we have circumstances as masters prior to our present masters; and these circumstances are many. Therefore it must of necessity be that those who have the power over any of these circumstances must be our masters. For no man fears Caesar himself, but he fears death, banishment, deprivation of his property, prison, and disgrace. Nor does any man love Caesar, unless Caesar is a person of great merit, but he loves wealth, the office of tribune, praetor or consul. When we love, and hate and fear these things, it must be that those who have the power over them must be our masters. Therefore we adore them even as gods; for we think that what possesses the power of conferring the greatest advantage on us is divine. Then we wrongly assume (ὑποτάσσομεν) that a certain person has the power of conferring the greatest advantages; therefore he is something divine. For if we wrongly assume[17] that a certain person has the power of conferring the greatest advantages, it is a necessary consequence that the conclusion from these premises must be false.

What then is that which makes a man free from hindrance and makes him his own master? For wealth does not do it, nor consulship, nor provincial government,

[15] Sic praetextatos referunt Artaxata mores.—Juv. ii. 170.

See Epict. i. 2, note 4.

[16] Saturnalia. See i. 25, note 3.

At this season the slaves had liberty to enjoy themselves and to talk freely with their masters. Hence Horace says Sat. ii. 74—

Age, libertate Decembri,
Quando ita majores voluerunt, utere.

[17] "Insigne hoc exemplum est τοῦ εἰκῆ τὰς προλήψεις ἐφαρμόζειν ταῖς ἐπὶ μέρους οὐσίαις. De quo, vide i. 22, 9, ii. 11, 3, ii. 17, 7." Upton.

nor royal power; but something else must be discovered. What then is that which when we write makes us free from hindrance and unimpeded? The knowledge of the art of writing. What then is it in playing the lute? The science of playing the lute. Therefore in life also it is the science of life. You have then heard in a general way: but examine the thing also in the several parts. Is it possible that he who desires any of the things which depend on others can be free from hindrance? No—Is it possible for him to be unimpeded? No—Therefore he cannot be free. Consider then: whether we have nothing which is in our own power only, or whether we have all things, or whether some things are in our own power, and others in the power of others.—What do you mean?—When you wish the body to be entire (sound), is it in your power or not?—It is not in my power—When you wish it to be healthy?—Neither is this in my power.—When you wish it to be handsome?—Nor is this—Life or death?—Neither is this in my power.[18]—Your body then is another's, subject to every man who is stronger than yourself—It is—But your estate, is it in your power to have it when you please, and as long as you please, and such as you please?—No—And your slaves?—No—And your clothes?—No—And your house?—No—And your horses?—Not one of these things—And if you wish by all means your children to live, or your wife, or your brother, or your friends, is it in your power?—This also is not in my power.

Whether then have you nothing which is in your own power, which depends on yourself only and cannot be taken from you, or have you any thing of the kind?—I know not—Look at the thing then thus, and examine it. Is any man able to make you assent to that which is false[19]—No man—In the matter of assent then you are free

[18] Schweighaeuser observes that death is in our power, as the Stoics taught; and Epictetus often tells us that the door is open. He suggests that the true reading may be *καὶ οὐκ ἀποθανεῖν*. I think that the text is right. Epictetus asks is 'Life or death' in our power. He means no more than if he had said Life only.

[19] He means that which seems to you to be false. See iii. 22, 42. "In the matter of assent then": this is the third *τόπος* or 'locus' or division in philosophy (iii. 2, 1–5). As to the Will, compare i. 17, note

from hindrance and obstruction.—Granted—Well; and can a man force you to desire to move towards that to which you do not choose?—He can, for when he threatens me with death or bonds, he compels me to desire to move towards it. If then, you despise death and bonds, do you still pay any regard to him?—No—Is then the despising of death an act of your own or is it not yours?—It is my act—It is your own act then also to desire to move towards a thing: or is it not so?—It is my own act—But to desire to move away from a thing, whose act is that? This also is your act—What then if I have attempted to walk, sup-

10. Epictetus affirms that a man cannot be compelled to assent, that is to admit, to allow, or, to use another word, to believe in that which seems to him to be false, or, to use the same word again, to believe in that in which he does not believe. When the Christian uses the two creeds, which begin with the words, 'I believe etc.,' he knows or he ought to know, that he cannot compel an unbeliever to accept the same belief. He may by pains and penalties of various kinds compel some persons to profess or to express the same belief: but as no pains or penalties could compel some Christians to deny their belief, so I suppose that perhaps there are men who could not be compelled to express this belief when they have it not. The case of the believer and the unbeliever however are not the same. The believer may be strengthened in his belief by the belief that he will in some way be punished by God, if he denies that which he believes. The unbeliever will not have the same motive or reason for not expressing his assent to that which he does not believe. He believes that it is and will be all the same to him with respect to God, whether he gives his assent to that which he does not believe or refuses his assent. There remains nothing then to trouble him if he expresses his assent to that which he does not believe, except the opinion of those who know that he does not believe, or his own reflections on expressing his assent to that which he does not believe; or in other words his publication of a lie, which may probably do no harm to any man or in any way. I believe that some men are strong enough, under some circumstances at least, to refuse their assent to any thing which they do not believe; but I do not affirm that they would do this under all circumstances.

To return to the matter under consideration, a man cannot be compelled by any power to accept voluntarily a thing as true, when he believes that it is not true; and this act of his is quite independent of the matter whether his unbelief is well founded or not. He does not believe because he cannot believe. Yet it is said (Mark xvi. 16) in the received text, as it now stands, 'He that believeth and is baptized shall be saved; but he that believeth not, shall be damned' (condemned). The cause, as it is called, of this unbelief is explained by some theologians; but all men do not admit the explanation to be sufficient; and it does not concern the present subject.

pose another should hinder me—What part of you does he hinder? does he hinder the faculty of assent?—No: but my poor body—Yes, as he would do with a stone—Granted; but I no longer walk—And who told you that walking is your own act free from hindrance? for I said that this only was free from hindrance, to desire to move: but where there is need of body and its co-operation, you have heard long ago that nothing is your own.—Granted this also—And who can compel you to desire what you do not wish?—No man—And to propose or intend, or in short to make use of the appearances which present themselves, can any man compel you?—He cannot do this: but he will hinder me when I desire from obtaining what I desire.—If you desire any thing which is your own, and one of the things which cannot be hindered, how will he hinder you?—He cannot in any way—Who then tells you that he who desires the things that belong to another is free from hindrance?

Must I then not desire health? By no means, nor any thing else that belongs to another: for what is not in your power to acquire or to keep when you please, this belongs to another. Keep then far from it not only your hands, but more than that, even your desires. If you do not, you have surrendered yourself as a slave; you have subjected your neck, if you admire[20] any thing not your own, to every thing that is dependent on the power of others and perishable, to which you have conceived a liking.—Is not my hand my own?—It is a part of your own body;[21] but it is by nature earth, subject to hindrance, compulsion, and the slave of every thing which is stronger. And why do I say your hand? You ought to possess your whole body as a poor ass loaded, as long as it is possible, as long as you are allowed. But if there be a press,[22] and

[20] The word 'admire' is *θαυμάσῃς* in the original. The word is often used by Epictetus, and Horace uses 'admirari' in this Stoical sense. See i. 29. 2, note.

[21] See Schweig.'s note on *μέρος*.

[22] The word is *ἀγγαρεία*, a word of Persian origin (Herodotus, viii. 98). It means here the seizure of animals for military purposes when it is necessary. Upton refers to Matthew 5, v. 41, Mark 15, c. 21 for similar uses of the verb *ἀγγαρεύω*

a soldier should lay hold of it, let it go, do not resist, nor murmur; if you do, you will receive blows, and never the less you will also lose the ass. But when you ought to feel thus with respect to the body, consider what remains to be done about all the rest, which is provided for the sake of the body. When the body is an ass, all the other things are bits belonging to the ass, pack-saddles, shoes,[23] barley, fodder. Let these also go: get rid of them quicker and more readily than of the ass.

When you have made this preparation, and have practised this discipline, to distinguish that which belongs to another from that which is your own, the things which are subject to hindrance from those which are not, to consider the things free from hindrance to concern yourself, and those which are not free not to concern yourself, to keep your desire steadily fixed to the things which do concern yourself, and turned from the things which do not concern yourself; do you still fear any man? No one. For about what will you be afraid? about the things which are your own, in which consists the nature of good and evil? and who has power over these things? who can take them away? who can impede them? No man can, no more than he can impede God. But will you be afraid about your body and your possessions, about things which are not yours, about things which in no way concern you? and what else have you been studying from the beginning than to distinguish between your own and not your own, the things which are in your power and not in your power, the things subject to hindrance and not subject? and why have you come to the philosophers? was it that you may never the less be unfortunate and unhappy? You will then in this way, as I have supposed you to have done, be without fear and disturbance. And what is grief to you? for fear comes from what you expect, but grief from that which is present.[24] But what further will you desire? For of the things which are within the power of the will, as being good and present, you have a proper and regulated desire:

[23] Here he speaks of asses being shod. The Latin translation of the word (ὑποδηματια) in Epictetus is 'ferreas calces.' I suppose they could use nothing but iron.

[24] See Schweig.'s note.

but of the things which are not in the power of the will you do not desire any one, and so you do not allow any place to that which is irrational, and impatient, and above measure hasty.[25]

When then you are thus affected towards things, what man can any longer be formidable to you? For what has a man which is formidable to another, either when you see him or speak to him or finally are conversant with him? Not more than one horse has with respect to another, or one dog to another, or one bee to another bee. Things indeed are formidable to every man; and when any man is able to confer these things on another or to take them away, then he too becomes formidable. How then is an acropolis (a stronghold or fortress, the seat of tyranny) demolished? Not by the sword, not by fire, but by opinion. For if we abolish the acropolis which is in the city, can we abolish also that of fever, and that of beautiful women? Can we in a word abolish the acropolis which is in us and cast out the tyrants within us,[26] whom we have daily over us, sometimes the same tyrants, at other times different tyrants? But with this we must begin, and with this we must demolish the acropolis and eject the tyrants, by giving up the body, the parts of it, the faculties of it, the possessions, the reputation, magisterial offices, honours, children, brothers, friends, by considering all these things as belonging to others. And if tyrants have been ejected from us, why do I still shut in the acropolis by a wall of circumvallation,[27] at least on my account; for if it still stands, what does it do to me? why do I still eject (the tyrant's) guards? For where do I perceive them? against others they have their fasces, and their spears and their swords. But I have never been hindered in my will, nor compelled when I did not will. And how is this possible? I have placed

[25] See Schweig.'s note.

[26] Schweig. suggests καταβεβλήκαμεν instead of ἀποβεβλήκαμεν, though all his MSS. have the word in the text. I do not think that his proposed alteration is an improvement.

[27] The word is ἀποτειχίζω, which means what I have translated. The purpose of circumvallation was to take and sometimes also to destroy a fortress. Schweig. translates the word by 'destruam,' and that is perhaps not contrary to the meaning of the text; but it is not the exact meaning of the word.

my movements towards action (ὁρμήν) in obedience to God.[28] Is it his will that I shall have fever? It is my will also. Is it his will that I should move towards any thing? It is my will also. Is it his will that I should obtain any thing? It is my wish also.[29] Does he not will? I do not wish. Is it his will that I die, is it his will that I be put to the rack? It is my will then to die: it is my will then to be put to the rack. Who then is still able to hinder me contrary to my own judgment, or to compel me? No more than he can hinder or compel Zeus.

Thus the more cautious of travellers also act. A traveller has heard that the road is infested by robbers; he does not venture to enter on it alone, but he waits for the companionship on the road either of an ambassador, or of a quaestor, or of a proconsul, and when he has attached himself to such persons he goes along the road safely. So in the world[30] the wise man acts. There are many companies of robbers, tyrants, storms, difficulties, losses of that which is dearest. Where is there any place of refuge? how shall he pass along without being attacked by robbers? what company shall he wait for that he may pass along in safety? to whom shall he attach himself? To what person generally? to the rich man, to the man of consular rank? and what is the use of that to me? Such a man is stripped himself, groans and laments. But what if the fellow companion himself turns against me and becomes my robber, what shall I do? I will be a friend of Caesar: when I am Caesar's companion no man will wrong me. In the first place, that I may become illustrious, what things must I endure and

[28] In this passage and in what follows we find the emphatic affirmation of the duty of conformity and of the subjection of man's will to the will of God. The words are conclusive evidence of the doctrine of Epictetus that a man ought to subject himself in all things to the will of God or to that which he believes to be the will of God. No Christian martyr ever proclaimed a more solemn obedience to God's will. The Christian martyr indeed has given perfect proof of his sincerity by enduring torments and death: the heathen philosopher was not put to the same test, and we cannot therefore say that he would have been able to bear it.

[29] In this passage the distinction must be observed between θέλω and βούλομαι, which the Latin translators have not observed, nor Mrs. Carter. See Schweig.'s note on s. 90.

[30] ἐν τῷ κόσμῳ: he means 'on earth.'

suffer? how often and by how many must I be robbed? Then, if I become Caesar's friend, he also is mortal. And if Caesar from any circumstance becomes my enemy, where is it best for me to retire? Into a desert? Well, does fever not come there? What shall be done then? Is it not possible to find a safe fellow traveller, a faithful one, strong, secure against all surprises? Thus he considers and perceives that if he attaches himself to God, he will make his journey in safety.

How do you understand 'attaching yourself to God?' In this sense, that whatever God wills, a man also shall will; and what God does not will, a man also shall not will. How then shall this be done? In what other way than by examining the movements (ὁρμάς, the acts) of God[31] and his administration? What has he given to me as my own and in my own power? what has he reserved to himself? He has given to me the things which are in the power of the will (τὰ προαιρετικὰ): he has put them in my power free from impediment and hindrance. How was he able to make the earthy body free from hindrance? [He could not], and accordingly he has subjected to the revolution of the whole (τῇ τῶν ὅλων περιόδῳ)[32] possessions, household things, house, children, wife. Why then do I fight against God? why do I will what does not depend on the will? why do I will to have absolutely what is not granted to me? But how ought I to will to have things? In the way in which they are given and as long as they are given. But he who has given takes away.[33] Why then do I resist? I do not say that I shall be a fool if I use force to one who is stronger, but I shall first be unjust. For whence had I things when I came into the world?—

[31] Schweig. expresses his surprise that Epictetus has applied this word (ὁρμάς) to God. He says that Wolf has translated it 'Dei appetitionem,' and Upton 'impetum.' He says that he has translated it 'consilium.'

It is not unusual for men to speak of God in the same words in which they speak of man.

[32] See ii. 1. 18. Schweig. expected that Epictetus would have said 'body and possessions etc.' I assume that Epictetus did say 'body and possessions etc.,' and that his pupil or some copyist of MSS. has omitted the word 'body.'

[33] 'The Lord gave and the Lord hath taken away. Job i. 21.' Mrs. Carter.

My father gave them to me—And who gave them to him? and who made the sun? and who made the fruits of the earth? and who the seasons? and who made the connection of men with one another and their fellowship?

Then after receiving everything from another and even yourself, are you angry and do you blame the giver if he takes any thing from you? Who are you, and for what purpose did you come into the world? Did not he (God) introduce you here, did he not show you the light, did he not give you fellow workers, and perceptions and reason? and as whom did he introduce you here? did he not introduce you as subject to death, and as one to live on the earth with a little flesh, and to observe his administration, and to join with him in the spectacle and the festival for a short time? Will you not then, as long as you have been permitted, after seeing the spectacle and the solemnity, when he leads you out, go with adoration of him and thanks for what you have heard and seen?—No; but I would still enjoy the feast.—The initiated too would wish to be longer in the initiation:[34] and perhaps also those at Olympia to see other athletes; but the solemnity is ended: go away like a grateful and modest man; make room for others: others also must be born, as you were, and being born they must have a place, and houses and necessary things. And if the first do not retire, what remains? Why are you insatiable? Why are you not content? why do you contract the world?—Yes, but I would have my little children with me and my wife—What, are they yours? do they not belong to the giver, and to him who made you? then will you not give up what belongs to others? will you not give way to him who is superior?—Why then did he introduce me into the world on these conditions?—And if the conditions do not suit you, depart.[35] He has no need of a spectator who

[34] The initiated (*μύσται*) are those who were introduced with solemn ceremonies into some great religious body. These ceremonies are described by Dion Prus. Orat. xii., quoted by Upton.

[35] "And is this all the comfort, every serious reader will be apt to say, which one of the best philosophers, in one of his noblest discourses, can give to the good man under severe distress? 'Either tell yourself that present suffering void of future hope, is no evil, or give up your existence and mingle with the elements of the Universe'! Unspeakably more rational and more worthy of infinite goodness is our blessed

is not satisfied. He wants those who join in the festival, those who take part in the chorus, that they may rather applaud, admire, and celebrate with hymns the solemnity. But those who can bear no trouble, and the cowardly he will not unwillingly see absent from the great assembly (πανήγυρις); for they did not when they were present behave as they ought to do at a festival nor fill up their place properly, but they lamented, found fault with the deity, fortune, their companions; not seeing both what they had, and their own powers, which they received for contrary purposes, the powers of magnanimity, of a generous mind, manly spirit, and what we are now inquiring about, freedom.—For what purpose then have I received these things? —To use them—How long?—So long as he who has lent them chooses.—What if they are necessary to me?—Do not attach yourself to them and they will not be necessary: do not say to yourself that they are necessary, and then they are not necessary.

This study you ought to practise from morning to evening, beginning with the smallest things and those most liable to damage, with an earthen pot, with a cup. Then proceed in this way to a tunic, to a little dog, to a horse, to a small estate in land: then to yourself, to your body, to the parts of your body, to your children, to your wife, to your brothers. Look all round and throw these things from you (which are not yours). Purge your opinions, so that nothing cleave to you of the things which are not your own, that nothing grow to you, that nothing give you pain when it is torn from you;[36] and say, while you

Master's exhortation to the persecuted Christian: 'Rejoice and be exceedingly glad, for great is your reward in heaven.'" Mrs. Carter.

I do not think that Mrs. Carter has represented correctly the teaching of Epictetus. He is addressing men who were not Christians, but were, as he assumes, believers in God or in the Gods, and his argument is that a man ought to be contented with things as they are, because they are from God. If he cannot be contented with things as they are, and make the best of them, the philosopher can say no more to the man. He tells him to depart. What else could he say to a grumbler, who is also a believer in God? If he is not a believer, Epictetus might say the same to him also. The case is past help or advice.

The Christian doctrine, of which probably Epictetus knew nothing, is very different. It promises future happiness on certain conditions to Christians, but to Christians only, if I understand it right.

[36] See the note of Schweig. on this passage.

are daily exercising yourself as you do there (in the school), not that you are philosophizing, for this is an arrogant (offensive) expression, but that you are presenting an asserter of freedom:[37] for this is really freedom. To this freedom Diogenes was called by Antisthenes, and he said that he could no longer be enslaved by any man. For this reason when he was taken prisoner,[38] how did he behave to the pirates? Did he call any of them master? and I do not speak of the name, for I am not afraid of the word, but of the state of mind, by which the word is produced. How did he reprove them for feeding badly their captives? How was he sold? Did he seek a master? no; but a slave. And when he was sold how did he behave to his master?[39] Immediately he disputed with him and said to his master that he ought not to be dressed as he was, nor shaved in such a manner; and about the children he told them how he ought to bring them up. And what was strange in this? for if his master had bought an exercise master, would he have employed him in the exercises of the palaestra as a servant or as a master? and so if he had bought a physician or an architect. And so in every matter, it is absolutely necessary that he who has skill must be the superior of him who has not. Whoever then generally possesses the science of life, what else must he be than master? For who is master in a ship? The man who governs the helm? Why? Because he who will not obey him suffers for it. But a master can give me stripes. Can he do it then without suffering for it? So I also used to think. But because he cannot do it without suffering for it, for this reason it is not in his power: and no man can do what is unjust without suffering for it. And what is the penalty for him who puts his own slave in chains?[40] what do you think that is? The fact of putting the slave in chains:—and you also will admit this,

[37] The word is *καρπίστην δίδως*. See iii. 24. 76 and the note 15: also Upton's note on this passage. Schweig. says that he does not quite understand why Epictetus here says *διδόναι καρπίστην*, 'dare vindicem' or 'adsertorem,' instead of saying 'vindicare sese in libertatem.'

[38] See iii. 24. 66, ii. 13. 24.

[39] See the same story in Aulus Gellius (ii. c. 18), who says that Xeniades, a Corinthian, bought Diogenes, manumitted him and made him the master of his children.

[40] See Schweig.'s note 15.

if you choose to maintain the truth, that man is not a wild beast, but a tame animal. For when is a vine doing badly? When it is in a condition contrary to its nature. When is a cock? Just the same. Therefore a man also is so. What then is a man's nature? To bite, to kick, and to throw into prison and to behead? No; but to do good, to co-operate with others, to wish them well. At that time then he is in a bad condition, whether you chose to admit it or not, when he is acting foolishly.

Socrates then did not fare badly?—No; but his judges and his accusers did.—Nor did Helvidius[41] at Rome fare badly?—No; but his murderer did. How do you mean?—The same as you do when you say that a cock has not fared badly when he has gained the victory and been severely wounded; but that the cock has fared badly when he has been defeated and is unhurt: nor do you call a dog fortunate, who neither pursues game nor labours, but when you see him sweating,[42] when you see him in pain and panting violently after running. What paradox (unusual thing) do we utter if we say that the evil in every thing is that which is contrary to the nature of the thing? Is this a paradox? for do you not say this in the case of all other things? Why then in the case of man only do you think differently? But because we say that the nature of man is tame (gentle) and social and faithful, you will not say that this is a paradox?[43] It is not—What then is it a paradox to say that a man is not hurt when he is whipped, or put in chains, or beheaded? does he not, if he suffers nobly, come off even with increased advantage and profit? But is he not hurt, who suffers in a most pitiful and disgraceful way, who in place of a man becomes a wolf, or viper or wasp?

Well then let us recapitulate the things which have been agreed on. The man who is not under restraint is free, to whom things are exactly in that state in which he wishes them to be; but he who can be restrained or compelled or hindered, or thrown into any circumstances

[41] See i. 2, note 5.

[42] I do not know if dogs sweat; at least in a state of health I have never seen it. But this is a question for the learned in dog science.

[43] See Schweig.'s note.

against his will, is a slave. But who is free from restraint? He who desires nothing that belongs to (is in the power of) others. And what are the things which belong to others? Those which are not in our power either to have or not to have, or to have of a certain kind or in a certain manner.[44] Therefore the body belongs to another, the parts of the body belong to another, possession (property) belongs to another. If then you are attached to any of these things as your own, you will pay the penalty which it is proper for him to pay who desires what belongs to another. This road leads to freedom, this is the only way of escaping from slavery, to be able to say at last with all your soul

> Lead me, O Zeus, and thou O destiny,
> The way that I am bid by you to go.[45]

But what do you say, philosopher? The tyrant summons you to say something which does not become you. Do you say it or do you not? Answer me—Let me consider—Will you consider now? But when you were in the school, what was it which you used to consider? Did you not study what are the things that are good and what are bad, and what things are neither one nor the other?—I did.—What then was our opinion?—That just and honourable acts were good; and that unjust and disgraceful (foul) acts were bad.—Is life a good thing?—No.—Is death a bad thing?—No.—Is prison?—No.—But what did we think about mean and faithless words and betrayal of a friend and flattery of a tyrant?—That they are bad.—Well then, you are not considering, nor have you considered nor deliberated. For what is the matter for consideration, is it whether it is becoming for me, when I have it in my power, to secure for myself the greatest of good things, and not to secure for myself (that is, not to avoid) the greatest evils? A fine inquiry indeed, and necessary, and one that demands much deliberation. Man, why do you mock us? Such an inquiry is never made. If you really

[44] As Upton remarks, Epictetus is referring to the four categories of the Stoics.

[45] Epictetus, Encheiridion c. 52. M. Antoninus, Gatak. 2d. ed. 1697, Annot. p. 96.

imagined that base things were bad and honourable things were good, and that all other things were neither good nor bad, you would not even have approached this enquiry, nor have come near it; but immediately you would have been able to distinguish them by the understanding as you would do (in other cases) by the vision. For when do you inquire if black things are white, if heavy things are light, and do not comprehend the manifest evidence of the senses? How then do you now say that you are considering whether things which are neither good nor bad ought to be avoided more than things which are bad? But you do not possess these opinions; and neither do these things seem to you to be neither good nor bad, but you think that they are the greatest evils; nor do you think those other things (mean and faithless words, etc.) to be evils, but matters which do not concern us at all. For thus from the beginning you have accustomed yourself. Where am I? In the schools: and are any listening to me? I am discoursing among philosophers. But I have gone out of the school. Away with this talk of scholars and fools. Thus a friend is overpowered by the testimony of a philosopher:[46] thus a philosopher becomes a parasite; thus he lets himself for hire for money: thus in the senate a man does not say what he thinks; in private (in the school) he proclaims his opinions.[47] You are a cold and miserable little opinion, suspended from idle words as from a hair. But keep yourself strong and fit for the uses of life and initiated by being exercised in action. How do you hear (the report)?—I do not say, that your child is dead—for how could you bear that?—but that your oil is spilled, your wine drunk up. Do you act in such a way that one standing by you while you are making a great noise, may say this only, Philo-

[46] Stoicus occidit Barcam, delator amicum,
Discipulumque senex.
Juvenal, iii. 116.

Epictetus is supposed to allude to the crime of Egnatius Celer who accused Barea Soranus at Rome in the reign of Nero (Tacit. Ann. xvi. 32).

[47] Mrs. Carter says that 'there is much obscurity and some variety of reading in several lines of the original.' But see Schweig.'s notes. Epictetus is showing that talk about philosophy is useless: philosophy should be practical.

sopher, you say something different in the school. Why do you deceive us? Why, when you are only a worm, do you say that you are a man? I should like to be present when some of the philosophers is lying with a woman, that I might see how he is exerting himself, and what words he is uttering, and whether he remembers his title of philosopher, and the words which he hears or says or reads.

And what is this to liberty? Nothing else than this, whether you who are rich choose or not.—And who is your evidence for this?—who else than yourselves? who have a powerful master (Caesar), and who live in obedience to his nod and motion, and who faint if he only looks at you with a scowling countenance; you who court old women[48] and old men, and say, I cannot do this: it is not in my power. Why is it not in your power? Did you not lately contend with me and say that you are free? But Aprulla[49] has hindered me? Tell the truth then, slave, and do not run away from your masters, nor deny, nor venture to produce any one to assert your freedom (καρπιστήν), when you have so many evidences of your slavery. And indeed when a man is compelled by love to do something contrary to his opinion (judgment), and at the same time sees the better, but has not the strength to follow it, one might consider him still more worthy of excuse as being held by a certain violent and in a manner a divine power.[50] But who could endure you who are in

[48] Horace Sat. ii. 5.

[49] Aprulla is a Roman woman's name. It means some old woman who is courted for her money.

[50] Compare Plato (Symposium, p. 206): 'All men conceive both as to the body and as to the soul, and when they have arrived at a certain age, our nature desires to procreate. But it cannot procreate in that which is ugly, but in that which is beautiful. For the conjunction of man and woman is generation; but this act is divine, and this in the animal which is mortal is divine, conceiving and begetting.' See what is said in ii. 23, note 10 on marrying. In a certain sense the procreation of children is a duty, and consequently the providing for them is also a duty. It is the fulfilling of the will and purpose of the Deity to people the earth; and therefore the act of procreation is divine. So a man's duty is to labour in some way, and if necessary, to earn his living and sustain the life which he has received; and this is also a divine act. Paul's opinion of marriage is contained in 1 Cor. i. 7. Some of his teaching on this matter has been justly condemned. He has no conception of the true nature of marriage; at least he does not show that he has in

love with old women and old men, and wipe the old women's noses, and wash them and give them presents, and also wait on them like a slave when they are sick, and at the same time wish them dead, and question the physicians whether they are sick unto death? And again, when in order to obtain these great and much admired magistracies and honours, you kiss the hands of these slaves of others, and so you are not the slave even of free men. Then you walk about before me in stately fashion a praetor or a consul. Do I not know how you became a praetor, by what means you got your consulship, who gave it to you? I would not even choose to live, if I must live by help of Felicion[51] and endure his arrogance and servile insolence: for I know what a slave is, who is fortunate, as he thinks, and puffed up by pride.

You then, a man may say, are you free? I wish, by the Gods, and pray to be free; but I am not yet able to face my masters, I still value my poor body, I value greatly the preservation of it entire, though I do not possess it entire.[52] But I can point out to you a free man, that you may no longer seek an example. Diogenes was free. How was he free?—not because he was born of free parents,[53] but because he was himself free, because he had cast off all the handles of slavery, and it was not possible for any man to approach him, nor had any man the means of laying hold of him to enslave him. He had everything easily loosed, everything only hanging to him. If you laid hold of his property, he would have rather let it go and be yours, than he would have followed you for it: if you had laid hold of his leg, he would have let go his leg; if of all his body, all his poor body; his intimates, friends, country, just the same. For he knew

this chapter. His teaching is impracticable, contrary to that of Epictetus, and to the nature and constitution of man; and it is rejected by the good sense of Christians who affect to receive his teaching; except, I suppose, by the superstitious body of Christians, who recommend and commend the so-called religious, and unmarried life.

[51] Felicion. See i. 19, p. 62.

[52] Epictetus alludes to his lameness: compare i. 8. 14, i. 16. 20, and other passages. Upton.

[53] Schweig. doubts if the words οὐ γὰρ ἦν, which I have omitted, are genuine, and gives his reasons for the doubt.

from whence he had them, and from whom, and on what conditions. His true parents indeed, the Gods, and his real country he would never have deserted, nor would he have yielded to any man in obedience to them and to their orders, nor would any man have died for his country more readily. For he was not used to inquire when he should be considered to have done anything on behalf of the whole of things (the universe, or all the world), but he remembered that every thing which is done comes from thence and is done on behalf of that country and is commanded by him who administers it.[54] Therefore see what Diogenes himself says and writes:—"For this reason, he says, Diogenes, it is in your power to speak both with the King of the Persians and with Archidamus the king of the Lacedaemonians, as you please." Was it because he was born of free parents? I suppose all the Athenians and all the Lacedaemonians because they were born of slaves, could not talk with them (these kings) as they wished, but feared and paid court to them. Why then does he say that it is in his power? Because I do not consider the poor body to be my own, because I want nothing, because law [55] is every thing to me, and nothing else is. These were the things which permitted him to be free.

And that you may not think that I show you the example of a man who is a solitary person,[56] who has neither wife nor children, nor country, nor friends nor kinsmen, by whom he could be bent and drawn in various directions, take Socrates and observe that he had a wife and children, but he did not consider them as his own; that he had a country, so long as it was fit to have one, and in such a manner as was fit; friends and kinsmen also, but he held all in subjection to law and to the obedience due to it. For this reason he was the first to go out as a soldier, when it was necessary, and in war he exposed himself to danger

[54] Schweig. has a note on this difficult passage, which is rather obscure.

[55] The sense of 'law' (ὁ νόμος) can be collected from what follows. Compare the discourse of Socrates on obedience to the law. (Criton, c. 11, &c.)

[56] See Schweig.'s note on ἀπεριστάτου.

most unsparingly;[57] and when he was sent by the tyrants to seize Leon, he did not even deliberate about the matter, because he thought that it was a base action, and he knew that he must die (for his refusal), if it so happened.[58] And what difference did that make to him? for he intended to preserve something else, not his poor flesh, but his fidelity, his honourable character. These are things which could not be assailed nor brought into subjection. Then when he was obliged to speak in defence of his life, did he behave like a man who had children, who had a wife? No, but he behaved like a man who has neither. And what did he do when he was (ordered) to drink the poison,[59] and when he had the power of escaping from prison, and when Crito said to him, Escape for the sake of your children, what did Socrates say?[60] did he consider the power of escape as an unexpected gain? By no means: he considered what was fit and proper; but the rest he did not even look at or take into the reckoning. For he did not choose, he said, to save his poor body, but to save that which is increased and saved by doing what is just, and is impaired and destroyed by doing what is unjust. Socrates will not save his life by a base act; he who would not put the Athenians to the vote when they clamoured that he should do so,[61] he who refused to obey

[57] Socrates fought at Potidaea, Amphipolis and Delium. He is said to have gained the prize for courage at Delium. He was a brave soldier as well as a philosopher, a union of qualities not common (Plato's Apology.)

[58] Socrates with others was ordered by the Thirty tyrants, who at that time governed Athens, to arrest Leon in the island of Salamis and to bring him to be put to death. But Socrates refused to obey the order. Few men would have done what he did under the circumstances. (Plato's Apology; M. Antoninus, vii. 66.)

[59] Cicero, Tuscul. Disp. i. 29.

[60] The Dialogue of Plato, named Criton, contains the arguments which were used by his friends to persuade Socrates to escape from prison, and the reply of Socrates.

[61] This alludes to the behaviour of Socrates when he refused to put to the vote the matter of the Athenian generals and their behaviour after the naval battle of Arginusae. The violence of the weather prevented the commanders from collecting and honorably burying those who fell in the battle; and the Athenians after their hasty fashion, wished all the commanders to be put to death. But Socrates, who was in office at this time, resisted the unjust clamour of the people. Xenophon, Hellenica, i. c. 7, 15; Plato, Apologia; Xenophon, Memorab. i. 1, 18.

the tyrants, he who discoursed in such a manner about virtue and right behaviour. It is not possible to save such a man's life by base acts, but he is saved by dying, not by running away. For the good actor also preserves his character by stopping when he ought to stop, better than when he goes on acting beyond the proper time. What then shall the children of Socrates do? "If," said Socrates, "I had gone off to Thessaly, would you have taken care of them; and if I depart to the world below, will there be no man to take care of them?" See how he gives to death a gentle name and mocks it. But if you and I had been in his place, we should have immediately answered as philosophers that those who act unjustly must be repaid in the same way, and we should have added, "I shall be useful to many, if my life is saved, and if I die, I shall be useful to no man." For, if it had been necessary, we should have made our escape by slipping through a small hole. And how in that case should we have been useful to any man? for where would they have been then staying?[62] or if we were useful to men while we were alive, should we not have been much more useful to them by dying when we ought to die, and as we ought? And now Socrates being dead, no less useful to men, and even more useful, is the remembrance of that which he did or said when he was alive.[63]

[62] The original is ποῦ γὰρ ἂν ἔτι ἔμενον ἐκεῖνοι; this seems to mean, if we had escaped and left the country, where would those have been to whom we might have been useful? They would have been left behind, and we could have done nothing for them.

[63] This is the conclusion about Socrates, whom Epictetus highly valued: the remembrance of what Socrates did and said is even more useful than his life. "The life of the dead," says Cicero of Servius Sulpicius, the great Roman jurist and Cicero's friend, "rests in the remembrance of the living." Epictetus has told us of some of the acts of Socrates, which prove him to have been a brave and honest man He does not tell us here what Socrates said, which means what he taught; but he knew what it was. Modern writers have expounded the matter at length, and in a form which Epictetus would not or could not have used.—Socrates left to others the questions which relate to the material world, and he first taught, as we are told, the things which concern man's daily life and his intercourse with other men: in other words he taught Ethic (the principles of morality). Fields and trees, he said, will teach me nothing, but man in his social state will; and man then is the proper subject of the philosophy of Socrates. The beginning of this knowledge was, as he said, to know himself according

Think of these things, these opinions, these words: look to these examples, if you would be free, if you desire the thing according to its worth. And what is the wonder if you buy so great a thing at the price of things so many and so great? For the sake of this which is called liberty, some hang themselves, others throw themselves down precipices, and sometimes even whole cities have perished: and will you not for the sake of the true and unassailable and secure liberty give back to God when he demands them the things which he has given? Will you not, as Plato says, study not to die only, but also to endure torture, and exile, and scourging and in a word to give up all which is not your own? If you will not, you will be

to the precept of the Delphic oracle, Know thyself (γνῶθι σεαυτόν): and the object of his philosophy was to comprehend the nature of man as a moral being in all relations; and among these the relation of man to God as the father of all, creator and ruler of all, as Plato expresses it. Socrates taught that what we call death is not the end of man; death is only the road to another life. The death of Socrates was conformable to his life and teaching. "Socrates died not only with the noblest courage and tranquillity, but he also refused, as we are told, to escape from death, which the laws of the state permitted, by going into exile or paying a fine, because as he said, if he had himself consented to a fine or allowed others to propose it, (Xenophon, Apol. § 22), such an act would have been an admission of his guilt. Both (Socrates and Jesus) offered themselves with the firmest resolution for a holy cause, which was so far from being lost through their death that it only served rather to make it the general cause of mankind." (Das Christliche des Platonismus oder Socrates und Christus, by F. C. Baur.)

This essay by Baur is very ingenious. Perhaps there are some readers who will disagree with him on many points in the comparison of Socrates and Christus. However the essay is well worth the trouble of reading.

The opinion of Rousseau in his comparison of Jesus and Socrates is in some respects more just than that of Baur, though the learning of the Frenchman is very small when compared with that of the German. "What prejudices, what blindness must a man have," says Rousseau, "when he dares to compare the son of Sophroniscus with the son of Mary!—The death of Socrates philosophising tranquilly with his friends is the most gentle that a man could desire; that of Jesus expiring in torments, insulted, jeered, cursed by a whole people, is the most horrible that a man could dread. Socrates taking the poisoned cup blesses him who presents it and weeps; Jesus in his horrible punishment prays for his savage executioners. Yes, if the life and the death of Socrates are those of a sage, the life and the death of Jesus are those of a God." (Rousseau, Emile, vol. iii. p. 166. Amsterdam, 1765.)

a slave among slaves, even if you be ten thousand times a consul; and if you make your way up to the Palace (Caesar's residence), you will no less be a slave; and you will feel, that perhaps philosophers utter words which are contrary to common opinion (paradoxes). as Cleanthes also said, but not words contrary to reason. For you will know by experience that the words are true, and that there is no profit from the things which are valued and eagerly sought to those who have obtained them; and to those who have not yet obtained them there is an imagination (φαντασία), that when these things are come, all that is good will come with them; then, when they are come, the feverish feeling is the same, the tossing to and fro is the same, the satiety, the desire of things which are not present; for freedom is acquired not by the full possession of the things which are desired, but by removing the desire. And that you may know that this is true, as you have laboured for those things, so transfer your labour to these; be vigilant for the purpose of acquiring an opinion which will make you free; pay court to a philosopher instead of to a rich old man: be seen about a philosopher's doors: you will not disgrace yourself by being seen; you will not go away empty nor without profit, if you go to the philosopher as you ought, and if not (if you do not succeed), try at least: the trial (attempt) is not disgraceful.

CHAPTER II.

ON FAMILIAR INTIMACY.

To this matter before all you must attend, that you be never so closely connected with any of your former intimates or friends as to come down to the same acts as he does.[1] If you do not observe this rule, you will ruin yourself. But if the thought arises in your mind, "I shall seem disobliging to him and he will not have the same feeling towards me," remember that nothing is done with-

[1] He means that you must not do as he does, because he does this or that act. The advice is in substance, Do not do as your friend does simply because he is your friend.

out cost, nor is it possible for a man if he does not do the same things to be the same man that he was. Choose then which of the two you will have, to be equally loved by those by whom you were formerly loved, being the same with your former self; or being superior, not to obtain from your friends the same that you did before. For if this is better, immediately turn away to it, and let not other considerations draw you in a different direction. For no man is able to make progress (improvement), when he is wavering between opposite things; but if you have preferred this (one thing) to all things, if you choose to attend to this only, to work out this only, give up every thing else. But if you will not do this, your wavering will produce both these results: you will neither improve as you ought, nor will you obtain what you formerly obtained. For before by plainly desiring the things which were worth nothing, you pleased your associates. But you cannot excel in both kinds, and it is necessary that so far as you share in the one, you must fall short in the other. You cannot, when you do not drink with those with whom you used to drink, be agreeable to them as you were before. Choose then whether you will be a hard drinker and pleasant to your former associates or a sober man and disagreeable to them. You cannot, when you do not sing with those with whom you used to sing, be equally loved by them. Choose then in this matter also which of the two you will have. For if it is better to be modest and orderly than for a man to say, He is a jolly fellow, give up the rest, renounce it, turn away from it, have nothing to do with such men. But if this behaviour shall not please you, turn altogether to the opposite: become a catamite, an adulterer, and act accordingly, and you will get what you wish. And jump up in the theatre and bawl out in praise of the dancer. But characters so different cannot be mingled: you cannot act both Thersites and Agamemnon. If you intend to be Thersites,[2] you must be humpbacked and bald: if Agamemnon, you must be tall and handsome, and love those who are placed in obedience to you.

[2] See Iliad, ii. 216; and for the description of Agamemnon, Iliad, iii. 167.

CHAPTER III.

WHAT THINGS WE SHOULD EXCHANGE FOR OTHER THINGS.

KEEP this thought in readiness, when you lose any thing external, what you acquire in place of it; and if it be worth more, never say, I have had a loss; neither[1] if you have got a horse in place of an ass, or an ox in place of a sheep, nor a good action in place of a bit of money, nor in place of idle talk such tranquillity as befits a man, nor in place of lewd talk if you have acquired modesty. If you remember this, you will always maintain your character such as it ought to be. But if you do not, consider that the times of opportunity are perishing, and that whatever pains you take about yourself, you are going to waste them all and overturn them. And it needs only a few things for the loss and overturning of all, namely a small deviation from reason. For the steerer of a ship to upset it, he has no need of the same means as he has need of for saving it: but if he turns it a little to the wind, it is lost; and if he does not do this purposely, but has been neglecting his duty a little, the ship is lost. Something of the kind happens in this case also: if you only fall a nodding a little, all that you have up to this time collected is gone. Attend therefore to the appearances of things, and watch over them; for that which you have to preserve is no small matter, but it is modesty and fidelity and constancy, freedom from the affects, a state of mind undisturbed, freedom from fear, tranquillity, in a word liberty. For what will you sell these things? See what is the value of the things which you will obtain in exchange for these.—But shall I not obtain any such thing for it?—See, and if you do in return get that, see what you receive in place of it.[2] I possess decency, he possesses a tribuneship: he possesses a praetorship, I possess modesty. But I do not make acclamations where it is not becoming: I will not stand up where I ought not;[3]

[1] See Schweig.'s note.

[2] The text is obscure, and perhaps there is something wrong. Schweighaeuser has a long note on the passage.

[3] He alludes to the factions in the theatres, iii. 4, 4; iv. 2–9. Upton.

for I am free, and a friend of God, and so I obey him willingly. But I must not claim (seek) any thing else, neither body nor possession, nor magistracy, nor good report, nor in fact any thing. For he (God) does not allow me to claim (seek) them: for if he had chosen, he would have made them good for me; but he has not done so, and for this reason I cannot transgress his commands.[4] Preserve that which is your own good in every thing; and as to every other thing, as it is permitted, and so far as to behave consistently with reason in respect to them, content with this only. If you do not, you will be unfortunate, you will fail in all things, you will be hindered, you will be impeded. These are the laws which have been sent from thence (from God); these are the orders. Of these laws a man ought to be an expositor, to these he ought to submit, not to those of Masurius and Cassius.[5]

CHAPTER IV.

TO THOSE WHO ARE DESIROUS OF PASSING LIFE IN TRANQUILLITY.

REMEMBER that not only the desire of power and of riches makes us mean and subject to others, but even the desire of tranquillity, and of leisure, and of travelling abroad, and of learning. For to speak plainly, whatever the external thing may be, the value which we set upon it places us in subjection to others. What then is the difference between desiring to be a senator or not desiring to be one; what is the difference between desiring power or being content with a private station; what is the difference between saying, I am unhappy, I have nothing to do, but I am bound to my books as a corpse; or saying, I am unhappy, I have no leisure for reading? For as salutations[1] and power are things external and independent of

[4] See i. 25. note 1; iv. 7. 17.

[5] Masurius Sabinus was a great Roman jurisconsult in the times of Augustus and Tiberius. He is sometimes named Masurius only (Persius, v. 90). C. Cassius Longinus was also a jurist, and, it is said, a descendant of the Cassius, who was one of the murderers of the dictator C. Caesar. He lived from the time of Tiberius to that of Vespasian.

[1] ἀσπασμοί. See this chapter further on.

the will, so is a book. For what purpose do you choose to read? Tell me. For if you only direct your purpose to being amused or learning something, you are a silly fellow and incapable of enduring labour.[2] But if you refer reading to the proper end, what else is this than a tranquil and happy life (εὔροια)? But if reading does not secure for you a happy and tranquil life, what is the use of it? But it does secure this, the man replies, and for this reason I am vexed that I am deprived of it.—And what is this tranquil and happy life, which any man can impede, I do not say Caesar or Caesar's friend, but a crow, a piper, a fever, and thirty thousand other things? But a tranquil and happy life contains nothing so sure as continuity and freedom from obstacle. Now I am called to do something: I will go then with the purpose of observing the measures (rules) which I must keep,[3] of acting with modesty, steadiness, without desire and aversion to things external;[4] and then that I may attend to men, what they say, how they are moved;[5] and this not with any bad disposition, or that I may have something to blame or to ridicule; but I turn to myself, and ask if I also commit the same faults. How then shall I

[2] See Bishop Butler's remarks in the Preface to his Sermons vol. ii. He speaks of the 'idle way of reading and considering things: by this means, time even in solitude is happily got rid of without the pain of attention: neither is any part of it more put to the account of idleness, one can scarce forbear saying, is spent with less thought than great part of that which is spent in reading.'

[3] Sed verae numerosque modosque ediscere vitae. Hor. Epp. ii. 2. 144. M. Antoninus, iii. 1.

[4] 'The readers perhaps may grow tired with being so often told what they will find it very difficult to believe, That because externals are not in our power, they are nothing to us. But in excuse for this frequent repetition, it must be considered that the Stoics had reduced themselves to a necessity of dwelling on this consequence, extravagant as it is, by rejecting stronger aids. One cannot indeed avoid highly admiring the very few, who attempted to amend and exalt themselves on this foundation. No one perhaps ever carried the attempt so far in practice, and no one ever spoke so well in support of the argument as Epictetus. Yet, notwithstanding his great abilities and the force of his example, one finds him strongly complaining of the want of success; and one sees from this circumstance as well as from others in the Stoic writings, That virtue can not be maintained in the world without the hope of a future reward.' Mrs. Carter.

[5] Compare Horace, Sat. i. 4. 133: Neque enim cum lectulus etc.

cease to commit them? Formerly I also acted wrong, but now I do not: thanks to God.

Come, when you have done these things and have attended to them, have you done a worse act than when you have read a thousand verses or written as many? For when you eat, are you grieved because you are not reading? are you not satisfied with eating according to what you have learned by reading, and so with bathing and with exercise? Why then do you not act consistently in all things, both when you approach Caesar, and when you approach any person? If you maintain yourself free from perturbation, free from alarm, and steady; if you look rather at the things which are done and happen than are looked at yourself; if you do not envy those who are preferred before you; if surrounding circumstances (ὕλαι) do not strike you with fear or admiration, what do you want? Books? How or for what purpose? for is not this (the reading of books) a preparation for life? and is not life itself (living) made up of certain other things than this? This is just as if an athlete should weep when he enters the stadium, because he is not being exercised outside of it. It was for this purpose that you used to practise exercise; for this purpose were used the haltéres (weights),[6] the dust, the young men as antagonists; and do you seek for those things now when it is the time of action? This is just as if in the topic (matter) of assent when appearances present themselves, some of which can be comprehended, and some cannot be comprehended, we should not choose to distinguish them but should choose to read what has been written about comprehension (κατάληψις).

What then is the reason of this? The reason is that we have never read for this purpose, we have never written for this purpose, so that we may in our actions use in a way conformable to nature the appearances presented to us; but we terminate in this, in learning what is said, and in being able to expound it to another, in resolving a syllogism,[7] and in handling the hypothetical syllogism. For

[6] See i. 4. note 5, iii. 15. 4; and i. 24. 1, i. 29. 34. The athletes were oiled, but they used to rub themselves with dust to be enabled to lay hold of one another.

[7] M. Antoninus, i. 17, thanks the Gods that he did not waste his time in the resolution of syllogisms.

this reason where our study (purpose) is, there alone is the impediment. Would you have by all means the things which are not in your power? Be prevented then, be hindered, fail in your purpose. But if we read what is written about action (efforts, ὁρμή),[8] not that we may see what is said about action, but that we may act well: if we read what is said about desire and aversion (avoiding things), in order that we may neither fail in our desires, nor fall into that which we try to avoid; if we read what is said about duty (officium), in order that remembering the relations (of things to one another) we may do nothing irrationally nor contrary to these relations; we should not be vexed in being hindered as to our readings, but we should be satisfied with doing the acts which are conformable (to the relations), and we should be reckoning not what so far we have been accustomed to reckon: To-day I have read so many verses, I have written so many; but (we should say), To-day I have employed my action as it is taught by the philosophers; I have not employed my desire; I have used avoidance (ἐκκλίσει) only with respect to things which are within the power of my will; I have not been afraid of such a person, I have not been prevailed upon by the entreaties of another; I have exercised my patience,[9] my abstinence, my co-operation with others; and so we should thank God for what we ought to thank him.

But now we do not know that we also in another way are like the many. Another man is afraid that he shall not have power: you are afraid that you will. Do not do so, my man; but as you ridicule him who is afraid that he shall not have power, so ridicule yourself also. For it makes no difference whether you are thirsty like a man who has a fever, or have a dread of water like a man who is mad. Or how will you still be able to say as Socrates did, If so it pleases God, so let it be? Do you think that Socrates if he had been eager to pass his leisure in the Lyceum or in the Academy and to discourse daily with the young men, would have readily served in military

[8] See iii. c. 2.

[9] See Aulus Gellius xvii. 19, where he quotes Epictetus on what Gellius expresses by 'intolerantia' and 'incontinentia.' Compare M. Antoninus (v. 33) on the precept 'Ανέχου and 'Απέχου.

expeditions so often as he did; and would he not have lamented and groaned, Wretch that I am; I must now be miserable here, when I might be sunning myself in the Lyceum? Why, was this your business, to sun yourself? And is it not your business to be happy, to be free from hindrance, free from impediment? And could he still have been Socrates, if he had lamented in this way: how would he still have been able to write Paeans in his prison?[10]

In short remember this, that what you shall prize which is beyond your will, so far you have destroyed your will. But these things are out of the power of the will, not only power (authority), but also a private condition: not only occupation (business), but also leisure.—Now then must I live in this tumult?—Why do you say tumult?—I mean among many men.—Well what is the hardship? Suppose that you are at Olympia: imagine it to be a panegyris (public assembly), where one is calling out one thing, another is doing another thing, and a third is pushing another person: in the baths there is a crowd: and who of us is not pleased with this assembly, and leaves it unwillingly? Be not difficult to please nor fastidious about what happens.—Vinegar is disagreeable, for it is sharp; honey is disagreeable, for it disturbs my habit of body. I do not like vegetables. So also I do not like leisure; it is a desert: I do not like a crowd; it is confusion.—But if circumstances make it necessary for you to live alone or with a few, call it quiet, and use the thing as you ought: talk with yourself, exercise the appearances (presented to you), work up your preconceptions.[11] If you fall into a crowd, call it a celebration of games, a panegyris, a festival: try to enjoy the festival with other men. For what is a more pleasant sight to him who loves mankind than a number of men? We see with pleasure herds of horses or oxen: we are delighted when we see many ships: who is pained when he sees many men?—But they deafen me with their cries.—Then your hearing is impeded. What then is this to you? Is then the power of making use of appearances hindered? And who prevents you

[10] Plato in the Phaedon (c. 4) says that Socrates in his prison wrote a hymn to Apollo.

[11] i. 22.

from using according to nature inclination to a thing and aversion from it; and movement towards a thing and movement from it? What tumult (confusion) is able to do this?

Do you only bear in mind the general rules: what is mine, what is not mine; what is given (permitted) to me; what does God will that I should do now? what does he not will? A little before he willed you to be at leisure, to talk with yourself, to write about these things, to read, to hear, to prepare yourself. You had sufficient time for this. Now he says to you: Come now to the contest, show us what you have learned, how you have practised the athletic art. How long will you be exercised alone? Now is the opportunity for you to learn whether you are an athlete worthy of victory, or one of those who go about the world and are defeated. Why then are you vexed? No contest is without confusion. There must be many who exercise themselves for the contest, many who call out to those who exercise themselves, many masters, many spectators.—But my wish is to live quietly.—Lament then and groan as you deserve to do. For what other is a greater punishment than this to the untaught man and to him who disobeys the divine commands, to be grieved, to lament, to envy, in a word to be disappointed and to be unhappy? Would you not release yourself from these things?—And how shall I release myself?—Have you not often heard, that you ought to remove entirely desire, apply aversion (turning away) to those things only which are within your power, that you ought to give up every thing, body, property, fame, books, tumult, power, private station? for whatever way you turn, you are a slave, you are subjected, you are hindered, you are compelled, you are entirely in the power of others. But keep the words of Cleanthes in readiness.

Lead me, O Zeus, and thou necessity.[12]

Is it your will that I should go to Rome? I will go to Rome. To Gyara? I will go to Gyara. To Athens? I

[12] Compare Encheiridion, 52. Cleanthes was a Stoic philosopher, who also wrote some poetry. See p. 292, note.

will go to Athens. To prison? I will go to prison. If you should once say, When shall a man go to Athens? you are undone. It is a necessary consequence that this desire, if it is not accomplished, must make you unhappy; and if it is accomplished, it must make you vain, since you are elated at things at which you ought not to be elated; and on the other hand, if you are impeded, it must make you wretched because you fall into that which you would not fall into. Give up then all these things.—Athens is a good place.—But happiness is much better; and to be free from passions, free from disturbance, for your affairs not to depend on any man. There is tumult at Rome and visits of salutation.[13] But happiness is an equivalent for all troublesome things. If then the time comes for these things, why do you not take away the wish to avoid them? what necessity is there to carry a burden like an ass, and to be beaten with a stick? But if you do not so, consider that you must always be a slave to him who has it in his power to effect your release, and also to impede you, and you must serve him as an evil genius.[14]

There is only one way to happiness, and let this rule be ready both in the morning and during the day and by night: the rule is not to look towards things which are out of the power of our will, to think that nothing is our own, to give up all things to the Divinity, to Fortune; to make them the superintendents of these things, whom Zeus also has made so; for a man to observe that only which is his own, that which cannot be hindered; and when we read, to refer our reading to this only, and our writing and our listening. For this reason I cannot call the man industrious, if I hear this only, that he reads and writes; and even if a man adds that he reads all night, I cannot say so, if he knows not to what he should refer his reading. For neither do you say that a man is industrious if he keeps awake for a girl;[15] nor do I. But if he does it (reads and writes) for reputation, I say that he is a

[13] He alludes to the practice of dependents paying formal visits in the morning at the houses of the great and powerful at Rome. Upton refers to Virgil, Georgics, ii. 461.

[14] Compare i. 19. 6.

[15] Compare Horace Sat. i. 5. 83.

lover of reputation. And if he does it for money, I say that he is a lover of money, not a lover of labour; and if he does it through love of learning, I say that he is a lover of learning, But if he refers his labour to his own ruling power (ἡγεμονικόν), that he may keep it in a state conformable to nature and pass his life in that state, then only do I say that he is industrious. For never commend a man on account of these things which are common to all, but on account of his opinions (principles); for these are the things which belong to each man, which make his actions bad or good. Remembering these rules, rejoice in that which is present, and be content with the things which come in season.[16] If you see any thing which you have learned and inquired about occurring to you in your course of life (or opportunely applied by you to the acts of life), be delighted at it. If you have laid aside or have lessened bad disposition and a habit of reviling; if you have done so with rash temper, obscene words, hastiness, sluggishness; if you are not moved by what you formerly were, and not in the same way as you once were, you can celebrate a festival daily, to-day because you have behaved well in one act, and to-morrow because you have behaved well in another. How much greater is this a reason for making sacrifices than a consulship or the government of a province? These things come to you from yourself and from the gods. Remember this, who gives these things and to whom, and for what purpose. If you cherish yourself in these thoughts, do you still think that it makes any difference where you shall be happy, where you shall please God? Are not the gods equally distant from all places?[17] Do they not see from all places alike that which is going on?

[16] See Antoninus, vi. 2; and ix. 6 'Thy present opinion founded on understanding, and thy present conduct directed to social good, and thy present disposition of contentment with everything which happens —that is enough.'

[17] Compare Upton's note on ἀπέχουσι, and Schweig.'s version, and the Index Graecitatis. These commentators do not appear to be quite certain about the meaning of the text.

CHAPTER V.

AGAINST THE QUARRELSOME AND FEROCIOUS.

The wise and good man neither himself fights with any person, nor does he allow another, so far as he can prevent it. And an example of this as well as of all other things is proposed to us in the life of Socrates, who not only himself on all occasions avoided fights (quarrels), but would not allow even others to quarrel. See in Xenophon's Symposium [1] how many quarrels he settled, how further he endured Thrasymachus and Polus and Callicles; how he tolerated his wife, and how he tolerated his son [2] who attempted to confute him and to cavil with him. For he remembered well that no man has in his power another man's ruling principle. He wished therefore for nothing else than that which was his own. And what is this? Not that this or that man may act according to nature; for that is a thing which belongs to another; but that while others are doing their own acts, as they choose, he may never the less be in a condition conformable to nature and live in it, only doing what is his own to the end that others also may be in a state conformable to nature. For this is the object always set before him by the wise and good man. Is it to be commander (a praetor) [3] of an army? No: but if it is permitted him, his object is in this matter to maintain his own ruling principle. Is it to marry? No; but if marriage is allowed to him, in this matter his object is to maintain himself in a condition conformable to nature. But if he would have his son not to do wrong or his wife, he would have what belongs to another not to belong to another: and to be instructed is this, to learn what things are a man's own and what belongs to another.

How then is there left any place for fighting (quarrelling) to a man who has this opinion (which he ought to have)? Is he surprised at any thing which happens,

[1] See ii. 12. 15.
[2] See Xenophon, Memorabilia, ii. 2.
[3] The word στρατηγῆσαι may be translated either way.

and does it appear new to him?[4] Does he not expect that which comes from the bad to be worse and more grievous than what actually befals him? And does he not reckon as pure gain whatever they (the bad) may do which falls short of extreme wickedness? Such a person has reviled you. Great thanks to him for not having struck you. But he has struck me also. Great thanks that he did not wound you. But he wounded me also. Great thanks that he did not kill you. For when did he learn or in what school that man is a tame[5] animal, that men love one another, that an act of injustice is a great harm to him who does it. Since then he has not learned this and is not convinced of it, why shall he not follow that which seems to be for his own interest? Your neighbour has thrown stones. Have you then done any thing wrong? But the things in the house have been broken. Are you then a utensil? No; but a free power of will.[6] What then is given to you (to do) in answer to this? If you are like a wolf, you must bite in return, and throw more stones. But if you consider what is proper for a man, examine your storehouse, see with what faculties you came into the world. Have you the disposition of a wild beast, have you the disposition of revenge for an injury? When is a horse wretched? When he is deprived of his natural faculties, not when he cannot crow like a cock, but when he cannot run. When is a dog wretched? Not when he cannot fly, but when he cannot track his game. Is then a man also unhappy in this way, not because he cannot strangle lions or embrace statues,[7] for he did not come into the world in the possession of certain powers from nature for this purpose, but because he has lost his probity and his fidelity? People ought to meet and lament such a man for the misfortunes into which he

[4] See iv. 1. 77, and the use of θαυμάζειν.

[5] See ii. 10. 14, iv. 1. 120. So Plato says (Legg. vi.), that a man who has had right education is wont to be the most divine and the tamest of animals. Upton.

On the doing wrong to another, see Plato's Critc, and Epictetus iv. 1. 167.

[6] See iii. 1. 40.

[7] Like Hercules and Diogenes See iii. 12. 2.

has fallen; not indeed to lament because a man has been born or has died,[8] but because it has happened to him in his life time to have lost the things which are his own, not that which he received from his father, not his land and house, and his inn,[9] and his slaves; for not one of these things is a man's own, but all belong to others, are servile, and subject to account (ὑπεύθυνα), at different times given to different persons by those who have them in their power: but I mean the things which belong to him as a man, the marks (stamps) in his mind with which he came into the world, such as we seek also on coins, and if we find them, we approve of the coins, and if we do not find the marks, we reject them. What is the stamp on this Sestertius?[10] The stamp of Trajan. Present it. It is the stamp of Nero. Throw it away: it cannot be accepted, it is counterfeit.[11] So also in this case: What is

[8] The allusion is to a passage (a fragment) in the Cresphontes of Euripides translated by Cicero into Latin Iambics (Tusc. Disp. i. 48)—

ἔδει γὰρ ἡμᾶς σύλλογον ποιουμένους
τὸν φύντα θρηνεῖν εἰς ὅσ' ἔρχεται κάκα.
τὸν δ'αὖ θανόντα καὶ πόνων πεπαυμένον
χαίροντας, εὐφημοῦντας ἐκπέμπειν δόμων.

Herodotus (v. 4) says of the Trausi, a Thracian tribe: 'when a child is born, the relatives sit round it and lament over all the evils which it must suffer on coming into the world and enumerate all the calamities of mankind: but when one dies, they hide him in the earth with rejoicing and pleasure, reckoning all the evils from which he is now released and in possession of all happiness.'

[9] The word is πανδοκεῖον, which Schweig. says that he does not understand. He supposes the word to be corrupt; unless we take it to mean the inn in which a man lives who has no home. I do not understand the word here.

[10] See the note of Schweig. on the word τετράσσαρον in the text.

[11] This does not mean, it is said, that Nero issued counterfeit coins, for there are extant many coins of Nero which both in form and in the purity of the metal are complete. A learned numismatist, Francis Wise, fellow of Trinity College Oxford, in a letter to Upton, says that he can discover no reason for Nero's coins being rejected in commercial dealings after his death except the fact of the tyrant having been declared by the Senate to be an enemy to the Commonwealth. (Suetonius, Nero, c. 49.) When Domitian was murdered, the Senate ordered his busts to be taken down, as the French now do after a revolution and all memorials of him to be destroyed (Suetonius, Domitian, c. 23). Dion also reports (LX.) that when Caligula was

the stamp of his opinions? It is gentleness, a sociable disposition, a tolerant temper, a disposition to mutual affection. Produce these qualities. I accept them: I consider this man a citizen, I accept him as a neighbour, a companion in my voyages. Only see that he has not Nero's stamp. Is he passionate, is he full of resentment, is he fault-finding? If the whim seizes him, does he break the heads of those who come in his way? (If so), why then did you say that he is a man? Is every thing judged (determined) by the bare form? If that is so, say that the form in wax [12] is an apple and has the smell and the taste of an apple. But the external figure is not enough: neither then is the nose enough and the eyes to make the man, but he must have the opinions of a man. Here is a man who does not listen to reason, who does not know when he is refuted: he is an ass: in another man the sense of shame is become dead: he is good for nothing, he is any thing rather than a man. This man seeks whom he may meet and kick or bite, so that he is not even a sheep or an ass, but a kind of wild beast.

What then? would you have me to be despised?—By whom? by those who know you? and how shall those who know you despise a man who is gentle and modest? Perhaps you mean by those who do not know you? What is that to you? For no other artisan cares for the opinion of those who know not his art.—But they will be more hostile to me [13] for this reason.—Why do you say 'me'? Can any man injure your will, or prevent you from using in a natural way the appearances which are presented to

murdered, it was ordered that all the brass coin which bore his image should be melted, and, I suppose, coined again. There is more on this subject in Wise's letter.

I do not believe that genuine coins would be refused in commercial dealings for the reasons which Wise gives, at least not refused in parts distant from Rome. Perhaps Epictetus means that some people would not touch the coins of the detestable Nero.

[12] He says *τὸ κήρινον*, which Mrs. Carter translates 'a piece of wax.' Perhaps it means 'a piece of wax in the form of an apple.'

[13] The word is *ἐπιφύησονται*, the form of which is not Greek. Schweig. has no remark on it, and he translates the word by 'adorientur.' The form ought to be *ἐπιφύσονται*. See Stephens' Lexicon on the word *ἐπιφύομαι*. Probably the word is corrupted.

you? In no way can he. Why then are you still disturbed and why do you choose to show yourself afraid?[14] And why do you not come forth and proclaim that you are at peace with all men whatever they may do, and laugh at those chiefly who think that they can harm you? These slaves, you can say, know not either who I am, nor where lies my good or my evil, because they have no access to the things which are mine.

In this way also those who occupy a strong city mock the besiegers, (and say): What trouble these men are now taking for nothing: our wall is secure, we have food for a very long time, and all other resources. These are the things which make a city strong and impregnable: but nothing else than his opinions makes a man's soul impregnable. For what wall is so strong, or what body is so hard, or what possession is so safe, or what honour (rank, character) so free from assault (as a man's opinions)? All (other) things every where are perishable, easily taken by assault, and if any man in any way is attached to them, he must be disturbed, expect what is bad, he must fear, lament, find his desires disappointed, and fall into things which he would avoid. Then do we not choose to make secure the only means of safety which are offered to us, and do we not choose to withdraw ourselves from that which is perishable and servile and to labour at the things which are imperishable and by nature free; and do we not remember that no man either hurts another or does good to another, but that a man's opinion about each thing, is that which hurts him, is that which overturns him; this is fighting, this is civil discord, this is war? That which made Eteocles and Polynices[15] enemies was nothing else than this opinion which they had about royal power, their opinion about exile, that the one is the extreme of evils, the other the greatest good. Now this is the nature of

[14] Mrs. Carter renders φοβερόν by 'formidable,' and in the Latin translation it is rendered 'formidabilem,' but that cannot be the meaning of the word here.

[15] Eteocles and Polynices were the sons of the unfortunate Oedipus, who quarrelled about the kingship of Thebes and killed one another. This quarrel is the subject of the Seven against Thebes of Aeschylus and the Phoenissae of Euripides. See ii. 22. note 3.

every man to seek the good, to avoid the bad;[16] to consider him who deprives us of the one and involves us in the other an enemy and treacherous, even if he be a brother, or a son or a father. For nothing is more akin to us than the good: therefore if these things (externals) are good and evil, neither is a father a friend to sons, nor a brother to a brother, but all the world is every where full of enemies, treacherous men, and sycophants. But if the will (προαίρεσις, the purpose, the intention) being what it ought to be, is the only good; and if the will being such as it ought not to be, is the only evil, where is there any strife, where is there reviling? about what? about the things which do not concern us? and strife with whom? with the ignorant, the unhappy, with those who are deceived about the chief things?

Remembering this Socrates managed his own house and endured a very ill tempered wife and a foolish (ungrateful?) son.[17] For in what did she show her bad temper? In pouring water on his head as much as she liked, and in trampling on the cake (sent to Socrates). And what is this to me, if I think that these things are nothing to me? But this is my business; and neither tyrant shall check my will nor a master; nor shall the many check me who am only one, nor shall the stronger check me who am the weaker; for this power of being free from check (hindrance) is given by God to every man. For these opinions make love in a house (family),

[16] 'Every man in everything he does naturally acts upon the forethought and apprehension of avoiding evil or obtaining good.' Bp. Butler, Analogy, Chap. 2. The bishop's 'naturally' is the φύσις of Epictetus.

[17] Socrates' wife Xanthippe is charged by her eldest son Lamprocles with being so ill-tempered as to be past all endurance (Xenophon, Memorab. ii. 2, 7). Xenophon in this chapter has reported the conversation of Socrates with his son on this matter.

Diogenes Laertius (ii.) tells the story of Xanthippe pouring water on the head of Socrates, and dirty water, as Seneca says (De Constantia, c. 18). Aelian (xi. 12) reports that Alcibiades sent Socrates a large and good cake, which Xanthippe trampled under her feet. Socrates only laughed and said, Well then, you will not have your share of it. The philosopher showed that his philosophy was practical by enduring the torment of a very ill-tempered wife, one of the greatest calamities that can happen to a man, and the trouble of an undutiful son.

concord in a state, among nations peace, and gratitude to God; they make a man in all things cheerful (confident) in externals as about things which belong to others, as about things which are of no value.[18] We indeed are able to write and to read these things, and to praise them when they are read, but we do not even come near to being convinced of them. Therefore what is said of the Lacedaemonians, "Lions at home, but in Ephesus foxes," will fit in our case also, "Lions in the school, but out of it foxes."[19]

CHAPTER VI.

AGAINST THOSE WHO LAMENT OVER BEING PITIED.

I AM grieved, a man says, at being pitied. Whether then is the fact of your being pitied a thing which concerns you or those who pity you? Well, is it in your power to stop this pity?—It is in my power, if I show them that I do not require pity.—And whether then are you in the condition of not deserving (requiring) pity, or are you not in that condition?—I think that I am not: but these persons do not pity me, for the things for which, if they ought to pity me, it would be proper, I mean, for my faults; but they pity me for my poverty, for not possessing honourable offices, for diseases and deaths and other such things—Whether then are you prepared to convince the many, that not one of these things is an evil, but that it is possible for a man who is poor and has no office (ἀνάρχοντι) and enjoys no honour to be happy; or to shew yourself to them as rich and in power? For the second of these things belong to a man who is boastful, silly and good for nothing. And consider by what means the pre-

[18] This is one of the wisest and noblest expressions of Epictetus.

[19] See Aristophanes, the Peace, v. 1188:

> πολλὰ γὰρ δή μ' ἠδίκησαν,
> ὄντες οἴκοι μὲν λέοντες,
> ἐν μάχῃ δ' ἀλώπεκες. Upton.

tence must be supported. It will be necessary for you to hire slaves and to possess a few silver vessels, and to exhibit them in public, if it is possible, though they are often the same, and to attempt to conceal the fact that they are the same, and to have splendid garments, and all other things for display, and to show that you are a man honoured by the great, and to try to sup at their houses, or to be supposed to sup there, and as to your person to employ some mean arts, that you may appear to be more handsome and nobler than you are. These things you must contrive, if you choose to go by the second path in order not to be pitied. But the first way is both impracticable and long, to attempt the very thing which Zeus has not been able to do, to convince all men what things are good and bad.[1] Is this power given to you? This only is given to you, to convince yourself; and you have not convinced yourself. Then I ask you, do you attempt to persuade other men? and who has lived so long with you as you with yourself? and who has so much power of convincing you as you have of convincing yourself; and who is better disposed and nearer to you than you are to yourself? How then have you not yet convinced yourself in order to learn? At present are not things upside down? Is this what you have been earnest about doing,[2] to learn to be free from grief and free from disturbance, and not to be humbled (abject), and to be free? Have you not heard then that there is only one way which leads to this end, to give up (dismiss) the things which do not depend on the will, to withdraw from them, and to admit that they belong to others? For another man then to have an opinion about you, of what kind is it?—It is a thing independent

[1] Here it is implied that there are things which God cannot do. Perhaps he means that as God has given man certain powers of will and therefore of action, he cannot at the same time exercise the contradictory powers of forcing man's will and action; for this would be at the same time to give power and to take it away. Butler remarks (Analogy, chap. 5) "the present is so far from proving in event a discipline of virtue to the generality of men that on the contrary they seem to make it a discipline of vice." In fact all men are not convinced and cannot be convinced in the present constitution of things 'what things are good and bad.'

[2] Something is perhaps wrong in the text here. See Schweig.'s note.

of the will.—Then is it nothing to you?—It is nothing—When then you are still vexed at this and disturbed, do you think that you are convinced about good and evil?

Will you not then letting others alone be to yourself both scholar and teacher?—The rest of mankind will look after this, whether it is to their interest to be and to pass their lives in a state contrary to nature: but to me no man is nearer than myself. What then is the meaning of this, that I have listened to the words of the philosophers and I assent to them, but in fact I am no way made easier (more content)? Am I so stupid? And yet in all other things such as I have chosen, I have not been found very stupid; but I learned letters quickly, and to wrestle, and geometry, and to resolve syllogisms. Has not then reason convinced me? and indeed no other things have I from the beginning so approved and chosen (as the things which are rational): and now I read about these things, hear about them, write about them; I have so far discovered no reason stronger than this (living according to nature). In what then am I deficient? Have the contrary opinions not been eradicated from me? Have the notions (opinions) themselves not been exercised nor used to be applied to action, but as armour are laid aside and rusted and cannot fit me? And yet neither in the exercises of the palaestra, nor in writing or reading am I satisfied with learning, but I turn up and down the syllogisms which are proposed, and I make others, and sophistical syllogisms also.[3] But the necessary theorems by proceeding from which a man can become free from grief, fear, passions (affects), hindrance, and a free man, these I do not exercise myself in nor do I practise in these the proper practice (study). Then I care about what others will say of me, whether I shall appear to them worth notice, whether I shall appear happy.—

Wretched man, will you not see what you are saying about yourself? What do you appear to yourself to be? in your opinions, in your desires, in your aversions from things (*ἐν τῷ ἐκκλίνειν*), in your movements (purposes, *ἐν ὁρμῇ*) in your preparation (for anything), in your de-

[3] In place of *μεταπίπτοντας* Schweig. suggests that Arrian wrote *καὶ τἄλλα ὡσαύτως* or something of the kind. On *μεταπίπτοντας* see Epictetus, i. 7.

signs (plans), and in other acts suitable to a man? But do you trouble yourself about this, whether others pity you? —Yes, but I am pitied not as I ought to be.—Are you then pained at this? and is he who is pained, an object of pity? —Yes—How then are you pitied not as you ought to be? For by the very act that you feel (suffer) about being pitied, you make yourself deserving of pity. What then says Antisthenes? Have you not heard? 'It is a royal thing, O Cyrus, to do right (well) and to be ill spoken of.'[4] My head is sound, and all think that I have the head ache. What do I care for that? I am free from fever, and people sympathize with me as if I had a fever, (and say), Poor man, for so long a time you have not ceased to have fever. I also say with a sorrowful countenance, In truth it is now a long time that I have been ill. What will happen then? As God may please: and at the same time I secretly laugh at those who are pitying me. What then hinders the same being done in this case also? I am poor, but I have a right opinion about poverty. Why then do I care if they pity me for my poverty? I am not in power (not a magistrate); but others are: and I have the opinion which I ought to have about having and not having power. Let them look to it who pity me:[5] but I am neither hungry nor thirsty nor do I suffer cold; but because they are hungry or thirsty they think that I too am. What then shall I do for them? Shall I go about and proclaim and say, Be not mistaken, men, I am very well, I do not trouble myself about poverty, nor want of power, nor in a word about anything else than right opinions. These I have free from restraint, I care for nothing at all.—What foolish talk is this? How do I possess right opinions when I am not content with being what I am, but am uneasy about what I am supposed to be?

But you say, others will get more and be preferred to me—What then is more reasonable than for those who have laboured about any thing to have more in that thing in which they have laboured? They have laboured for power, you have laboured about opinions; and they have laboured for wealth, you for the proper use of appearances.

[4] M. Antoninus, vii. 36.

[5] ὄψονται. See i. 4, note 4.

See if they have more than you in this about which you have laboured, and which they neglect; if they assent better than you with respect to the natural rules (measures) of things; if they are less disappointed than you in their desires; if they fall less into things which they would avoid than you do; if in their intentions, if in the things which they propose to themselves, if in their purposes, if in their motions towards an object they take a better aim; if they better observe a proper behaviour, as men, as sons, as parents, and so on as to the other names by which we express the relations of life. But if they exercise power, and you do not, will you not choose to tell yourself the truth, that you do nothing for the sake of this (power), and they do all? But it is most unreasonable that he who looks after anything should obtain less than he who does not look after it.

Not so: but since I care about right opinions, it is more reasonable for me to have power.—Yes in the matter about which you do care, in opinions. But in a matter in which they have cared more than you, give way to them. The case is just the same as if because you have right opinions, you thought that in using the bow you should hit the mark better than an archer, and in working in metal you should succeed better than a smith. Give up then your earnestness about opinions and employ yourself about the things which you wish to acquire; and then lament, if you do not succeed; for you deserve to lament. But now you say that you are occupied with other things, that you are looking after other things; but the many say this truly, that one act has no community with another.[6] He who has risen in the morning seeks whom (of the house of Caesar) he shall salute, to whom he shall say something agreeable, to whom he shall send a present, how he shall please the dancing man, how by bad behaviour to one he may please another. When he prays, he prays about

[6] Schweig. says that he has not observed that this proverb is mentioned by any other writer, and that he does not quite see the meaning of it, unless it be what he expresses in the Latin version (iv. 10. 24), 'alterum opus cum altero nihil commune habet.' I think that the context explains it: if you wish to obtain a particular end, employ the proper means, and not the means which do not make for that end.

these things; when he sacrifices, he sacrifices for these things: the saying of Pythagoras

Let sleep not come upon thy languid eyes [7]

he transfers to these things. Where have I failed in the matters pertaining to flattery? What have I done? Any thing like a free man, any thing like a noble minded man? And if he finds any thing of the kind, he blames and accuses himself: "Why did you say this? Was it not in your power to lie? Even the philosophers say that nothing hinders us from telling a lie." But do you, if indeed you have cared about nothing else except the proper use of appearances, as soon as you have risen in the morning reflect, "What do I want in order to be free from passion (affects), and free from perturbation? What am I? Am I a poor body, a piece of property, a thing of which something is said? I am none of these. But what am I? I am a rational animal. What then is required of me?" Reflect on your acts. Where have I omitted the things which conduce to happiness (εὔροιαν)? What have I done which is either unfriendly or unsocial? what have I not done as to these things which I ought to have done?

So great then being the difference in desires, actions, wishes, would you still have the same share with others in those things about which you have not laboured, and they have laboured? Then are you surprised if they pity you, and are you vexed? But they are not vexed if you pity them. Why? Because they are convinced that they have that which is good, and you are not convinced. For this reason you are not satisfied with your own, but you desire that which they have: but they are satisfied with their own, and do not desire what you have: since if you were really convinced, that with respect to what is good, it is you who are the possessor of it and that they have missed it, you would not even have thought of what they say about you.

[7] See iii. i. note 2. Epictetus is making a parody of the verses of Pythagoras. See Schweig.'s remarks on the words 'He who has risen etc.' I have of necessity translated κακοηθισάμενος in an active sense; but if this is right, I do not understand how the word is used so.

CHAPTER VII.

ON FREEDOM FROM FEAR.

WHAT makes the tyrant formidable? The guards, you say, and their swords, and the men of the bedchamber and those who exclude them who would enter. Why then if you bring a boy (child) to the tyrant when he is with his guards, is he not afraid; or is it because the child does not understand these things? If then any man does understand what guards are and that they have swords, and comes to the tyrant for this very purpose because he wishes to die on account of some circumstance and seeks to die easily by the hand of another, is he afraid of the guards? No, for he wishes for the thing which makes the guards formidable. If then any man neither wishing to die nor to live by all means, but only as it may be permitted, approaches the tyrant, what hinders him from approaching the tyrant without fear? Nothing. If then a man has the same opinion about his property as the man whom I have instanced has about his body; and also about his children and his wife, and in a word is so affected by some madness or despair that he cares not whether he possesses them or not, but like children who are playing with shells care (quarrel) about the play, but do not trouble themselves about the shells, so he too has set no value on the materials (things), but values the pleasure that he has with them and the occupation, what tyrant is then formidable to him or what guards or what swords?

Then through madness is it possible for a man to be so disposed towards these things, and the Galilaeans through habit,[1] and is it possible that no man can learn from reason

[1] See Schweig.'s note on the text. By the Galilaeans it is probable that Epictetus means the Christians, whose obstinacy Antoninus also mentions (xi. 3). Epictetus, a contemporary of St. Paul, knew little about the Christians, and only knew some examples of their obstinate adherence to the new faith and the fanatical behaviour of some of the converts. That there were wild fanatics among the early Christians is proved on undoubted authority; and also that there always have been such, and now are such. The abuse of any doctrines or religious opinions is indeed no argument against such doctrines or religious opinions; and it is a fact quite consistent with experience that the best things are liable to be perverted, misunderstood, and misused.

and from demonstration that God has made all the things in the universe and the universe itself completely free from hindrance and perfect, and the parts of it for the use of the whole? All other animals indeed are incapable of comprehending the administration of it; but the rational animal man has faculties for the consideration of all these things, and for understanding that it is a part, and what kind of a part it is, and that it is right for the parts to be subordinate to the whole. And besides this being naturally noble, magnanimous and free, man sees that of the things which surround him some are free from hindrance and in his power, and the other things are subject to hindrance and in the power of others; that the things which are free from hindrance are in the power of the will; and those which are subject to hindrance are the things which are not in the power of the will. And for this reason if he thinks that his good and his interest be in these things only which are free from hindrance and in his own power, he will be free, prosperous, happy, free from harm, magnanimous, pious, thankful to God[2] for all things; in no matter finding fault with any of the things which have not been put in his power, nor blaming any of them.[3] But if he thinks that his good and his interest are in externals and in things which are not in the power of his will, he must of necessity be hindered, be impeded, be a slave to those who have the power over the things which he admires (desires) and fears; and he must of necessity be impious because he thinks that he is harmed by God, and he must be unjust because he always claims more than belongs to him; and he must of necessity be abject and mean.

What hinders a man, who has clearly separated (comprehended) these things, from living with a light heart and bearing easily the reins, quietly expecting every thing which can happen, and enduring that which has already happened? Would you have me to bear poverty? Come and you will know what poverty is when it has found one who can act well the part of a poor man. Would you

[2] 'This agrees with Eph. v. 20: "Giving thanks always for all things to God."' Mrs. Carter. The words are the same in both except that the Apostle has εὐχαριστοῦντες, and Epictetus has χάριν ἔχον.

[3] See Schweig.'s note.

have me to possess power? Let me have power, and also the trouble of it. Well, banishment? Wherever I shall go, there it will be well with me; for here also where I am, it was not because of the place that it was well with me, but because of my opinions which I shall carry off with me:  for neither can any man deprive me of them; but my opinions alone are mine and they cannot be taken from me, and I am satisfied while I have them, wherever I may be and whatever I am doing. But now it is time to die. Why do you say to die? Make no tragedy show of the thing, but speak of it as it is: it is now time for the matter (of the body) to be resolved into the things out of which it was composed. And what is the formidable thing here? what is going to perish of the things which are in the universe?[4] what new thing or wondrous is going to happen? Is it for this reason that a tyrant is formidable? Is it for this reason that the guards appear to have swords which are large and sharp? Say this to others; but I have considered about all these things; no man has power over me. I have been made free; I know his commands, no man can now lead me as a slave. I have a proper person to assert my freedom;[5] I have proper judges. (I say) are you not the master of my body? What then is that to me? Are you not the master of my property? What then is that to me? Are you not the master of my exile or of my chains? Well, from all these things and all the poor body itself I depart at your bidding, when you please. Make trial of your power, and you will know how far it reaches.

Whom then can I still fear? Those who are over the bedchamber?[6] Lest they should do, what? Shut me out? If they find that I wish to enter, let them shut me out. Why then do you go to the doors? Because I think it befits me, while the play (sport) lasts, to join in it. How then are you not shut out? Because unless some

[4] He says that the body will be resolved into the things of which it is composed: none of them will perish. The soul, as he has said elsewhere, will go to him who gave it (iii. 13. note 4). But I do not suppose that he means that the soul will exist as having a separate consciousness.

[5] καρπιστήν, see iv. 1. 113.

[6] See i. 19. note 6.

one allows me to go in, I do not choose to go in, but am always content with that which happens; for I think that what God chooses is better than what I choose.[7] I will attach myself as a minister and follower to him; I have the same movements (pursuits) as he has, I have the same desires; in a word, I have the same will (συνθέλω). There is no shutting out for me, but for those who would force their way in. Why then do not I force my way in? Because I know that nothing good is distributed within to those who enter. But when I hear any man called fortunate because he is honoured by Caesar, I say, what does he happen to get? A province (the government of a province). Does he also obtain an opinion such as he ought? The office of a Prefect. Does he also obtain the power of using his office well? Why do I still strive to enter (Caesar's chamber)? A man scatters dried figs and nuts: the children seize them, and fight with one another; men do not, for they think them to be a small matter. But if a man should throw about shells, even the children do not seize them. Provinces are distributed: let children look to that. Money is distributed: let children look to that. Praetorships, consulships are distributed: let children scramble for them, let them be shut out, beaten, kiss the hands of the giver, of the slaves: but to me these are only dried figs and nuts. What then? If you fail to get them, while Caesar is scattering them about, do not be troubled: if a dried fig come into your lap, take it and eat it; for so far you may value even a fig. But if I shall stoop down and turn another over, or be turned over by another, and shall flatter those who have got into (Caesar's) chamber, neither is a dried fig worth the trouble, nor any thing else of the things which are not good, which the philosophers have persuaded me not to think good.

Show me the swords of the guards. See how big they are, and how sharp. What then do these big and sharp

[7] 'Nevertheless not as I will, but as thou wilt,' Matthew xxvi. 39. Mrs. Carter. 'Our resignation to the will of God may be said to be perfect, when our will is lost and resolved up into his; when we rest in his will as our end, as being itself most just and right and good.' Bp. Butler, Sermon on the Love of God.

swords do? They kill. And what does a fever do? Nothing else. And what else a (falling) tile? Nothing else. Would you then have me to wonder at these things and worship them, and go about as the slave of all of them? I hope that this will not happen: but when I have once learned that every thing which has come into existence must also go out of it, that the universe may not stand still nor be impeded, I no longer consider it any difference whether a fever shall do it or a tile, or a soldier. Bnt if a man must make a comparison between these things, I know that the soldier will do it with less trouble (to me), and quicker. When then I neither fear any thing which a tyrant can do to me, nor desire any thing which he can give, why do I still look on with wonder (admiration)? Why am I still confounded? Why do I fear the guards? Why am I pleased if he speaks to me in a friendly way, and receives me, and why do I tell others how he spoke to me? Is he a Socrates, is he a Diogenes that his praise should be a proof of what I am? Have I been eager to imitate his morals? But I keep up the play and go to him, and serve him so long as he does not bid me to do any thing foolish or unreasonable. But if he says to me, Go and bring Leon [8] of Salamis, I say to him, Seek another, for I am no longer playing. (The tyrant says): Lead him away (to prison). I follow; that is part of the play. But your head will be taken off—Does the tyrant's head always remain where it is, and the heads of you who obey him?—But you will be cast out unburied?—If the corpse is I, I shall be cast out; but if I am different from the corpse, speak more properly according as the fact is, and do not think of frightening me. These things are formidable to children and fools. But if any man has once entered a philosopher's school and knows not what he is, he deserves to be full of fear and to flatter those whom afterwards [9] he used to flatter; (and) if he has not yet learned that he is not flesh nor bones nor sinews (νεῦρα), but he is that which makes

[8] See iv. 1. note 59.

[9] I do not see the meaning of ὕστερον: it may perhaps mean 'after leaving the school.' See Schweig.'s note.

use of these parts of the body and governs them and follows (understands) the appearances of things.[10]

Yes, but this talk makes us despise the laws—And what kind of talk makes men more obedient to the laws who employ such talk? And the things which are in the power of a fool are not law.[11] And yet see how this talk makes us disposed as we ought to be even to these men (fools); since it teaches us to claim in opposition to them none of the things in which they are able to surpass us. This talk teaches us as to the body to give it up, as to property to give that up also, as to children, parents, brothers, to retire from these, to give up all; it only makes an exception of the opinions, which even Zeus has willed to be the select property of every man. What transgression of the laws is there here, what folly? Where you are superior and stronger, there I gave way to you: on the other hand, where I am superior, do you yield to me; for I have studied (cared for) this, and you have not. It is your study to live in houses with floors formed of various stones,[12] how your slaves and dependents shall serve you, how you shall wear fine clothing, have many hunting men, lute players, and tragic actors. Do I claim any of these? have you made any study of opinions, and of your own rational faculty? Do you know of what parts it is composed, how they are brought together, how

[10] Here Epictetus admits that there is some power in man which uses the body, directs and governs it. He does not say what the power is nor what he supposes it to be. "Upon the whole then our organs of sense and our limbs are certainly instruments, which the living persons, ourselves, make use of to perceive and move with." Butler's Analogy, chap. i.

[11] The will of a fool does not make law, he says. Unfortunately it does, if we use the word law in the strict sense of law: for law is a general command from a person, an absolute king, for example, who has power to enforce it on those to whom the command is addressed or if not to enforce it, to punish for disobedience to it. This strict use of the word 'law' is independent of the quality of the command, which may be wise or foolish, good or bad. But Epictetus does not use the word 'law' in the strict sense.

[12] The word is λιθοστρώτοις, which means what we name Mosaic floors or pavements. The word λιθόστρωτον is used by John xix. 13, and rendered in our version by 'pavement.'

they are connected, what powers it has, and of what kind? Why then are you vexed, if another who has made it his study, has the advantage over you in these things? But these things are the greatest. And who hinders you from being employed about these things and looking after them? And who has a better stock of books, of leisure, of persons to aid you? Only turn your mind at last to these things, attend, if it be only a short time, to your own ruling faculty[13] (ἡγεμονικόν): consider what this is that you possess, and whence it came, this which uses all other (faculties), and tries them, and selects and rejects. But so long as you employ yourself about externals you will possess them (externals) as no man else does; but you will have this (the ruling faculty) such as you choose to have it, sordid and neglected.

CHAPTER VIII.

AGAINST THOSE WHO HASTILY RUSH INTO THE USE OF THE PHILOSOPHIC DRESS.

NEVER praise nor blame a man because of the things which are common (to all, or to most),[1] and do not ascribe to him any skill or want of skill; and thus you will be free from rashness and from malevolence. "This man bathes very quickly. Does he then do wrong? Certainly not. But what does he do? He bathes very

[13] This term (τὸ ἡγεμονικόν) has been often used by Epictetus (i. 26 15. etc), and by M. Antoninus. Here Epictetus gives a definition or description of it: it is the faculty by which we reflect and judge and determine, a faculty which no other animal has, a faculty which in many men is neglected, and weak because it is neglected; but still it ought to be what its constitution forms it to be, a faculty which "plainly bears upon it marks of authority over all the rest, and claims the absolute direction of them all, to allow or forbid their gratification" (Bp. Butler, Preface to his Sermons). The words in the text (ἐκλεγόμενον, ἀπεκλεγόμενον, selection and rejection) are expressed by Cicero (De Fin. ix. ii. 11) by 'eligere' and 'rejicere.'

[1] See iv. 4. 44.

quickly. Are all things then done well? By no means: but the acts which proceed from right opinions are done well; and those which proceed from bad opinions are done ill. But do you, until you know the opinion from which a man does each thing, neither praise nor blame the act. But the opinion is not easily discovered from the external things (acts). This man is a carpenter. Why? Because he uses an axe. What then is this to the matter? This man is a musician because he sings. And what does that signify? This man is a philosopher. Because he wears a cloak and long hair. And what does a juggler wear? For this reason if a man sees any philosopher acting indecently, immediately he says, See what the philosopher is doing; but he ought because of the man's indecent behaviour rather to say that he is not a philosopher. For if this is the preconceived notion (πρόληψις) of a philosopher and what he professes, to wear a cloak and long hair, men would say well; but if what he professes is this rather, to keep himself free from faults, why do we not rather, because he does not make good his professions, take from him the name of philosopher? For so we do in the case of all other arts. When a man sees another handling an axe badly, he does not say, what is the use of the carpenter's art? See how badly carpenters do their work; but he says just the contrary, This man is not a carpenter, for he uses an axe badly. In the same way if a man hears another singing badly, he does not say, See how musicians sing; but rather, This man is not a musician. But it is in the matter of philosophy only that people do this. When they see a man acting contrary to the profession of a philosopher, they do not take away his title, but they assume him to be a philosopher, and from his acts deriving the fact that he is behaving indecently they conclude that there is no use in philosophy.

What then is the reason of this? Because we attach value to the notion (πρόληψιν) of a carpenter, and to that of a musician, and to the notion of other artisans in like manner, but not to that of a philosopher, and we judge from externals only that it is a thing confused and ill defined. And what other kind of art has a name from the dress and the hair; and has not both theorems and a material and an end? What then is the material (matter) of the philosopher? Is it a cloak? No, but reason. What is his end? is it to wear a cloak? No, but to possess the reason in a right state. Of what kind are his theorems? Are they those about the way in which the beard becomes great or the hair long? No, but rather what Zeno says, to know the elements of reason, what kind of a thing each of them is, and how they are fitted to one another, and what things are consequent upon them. Will you not then see first if he does what he professes when he acts in an unbecoming manner, and then blame his study (pursuit)? But now when you yourself are acting in a sober way, you say in consequence of what he seems to you to be doing wrong, Look at the philosopher, as if it were proper to call by the name of philosopher one who does these things; and further, This is the conduct of a philosopher. But you do not say, Look at the carpenter, when you know that a carpenter is an adulterer or you see him to be a glutton; nor do you say, See the musician. Thus to a certain degree even you perceive (understand) the profession of a philosopher, but you fall away from the notion, and you are confused through want of care.

But even the philosophers themselves as they are called pursue the thing (philosophy) by beginning with things which are common to them and others: as soon as they have assumed a cloak and grown a beard, they say, I am a philosopher.[2] But no man will say, I am a musician, if he has bought a plectrum (fiddlestick) and a lute: nor will he say, I am a smith, if he has put on a cap and apron. But the dress is fitted to the art; and they take their name from the art, and not from the dress. For this reason Euphrates[3] used to say well, A long time I strove to be a philosopher without people knowing it; and this, he said, was useful to me: for first I knew that when I did any thing well, I did not do it

[2] Compare Horace, Ep. i. 19, 12 etc.

> Quid, si quis vultu torvo ferus et pede nudo
> Exiguaeque togae simulet textore Catonem,
> Virtutemne repraesentet moresque Catonis?

[3] See iii. 15. 8.

for the sake of the spectators, but for the sake of myself: I ate well for the sake of myself; I had my countenance well composed and my walk: all for myself and for God. Then, as I struggled alone, so I alone also was in danger: in no respect through me, if I did anything base or unbecoming, was philosophy endangered; nor did I injure the many by doing any thing wrong as a philosopher. For this reason those who did not know my purpose used to wonder how it was that while I conversed and lived altogether with all philosophers, I was not a philosopher myself. And what was the harm for me to be known to be a philosopher by my acts and not by outward marks?[4] See how I eat, how I drink, how I sleep, how I bear and forbear, how I co-operate, how I employ desire, how I employ aversion (turning from things), how I maintain the relations (to things) those which are natural or those which are acquired, how free from confusion, how free from hindrance. Judge of me from this, if you can. But if you are so deaf and blind that you cannot conceive even Hephaestus[5] to be a good smith, unless you see the cap on his head, what is the harm in not being recognized by so foolish a judge?

So Socrates was not known to be a philosopher by most persons; and they used to come to him and ask to be introduced to philosophers. Was he vexed then as we are, and did he say, And do you not think that I am a philosopher? No, but he would take them and introduce them, being satisfied with one thing, with being a philosopher; and being pleased also with not being thought to be a philosopher, he was not annoyed: for he thought of his own occupation. What is the work of an honourable and good man? To have many pupils? By no means. They will look to this matter who are earnest about it. But was it his business to examine carefully difficult theorems? Others will look after these matters also. In what then

[4] "Yea a man may say, Thou hast faith, and I have works: shew me thy faith without thy works, and I will shew thee my faith by my works," Epistle of James, ii. 18. So a moral philosopher may say, I show my principles, not by what I profess, but by that which I do.

[5] See the statues of Hephaestus, Montfaucon, Antiq. vol. i. lib. iii. c. 1. Upton.

was he,[6] and who was he and whom did he wish to be? He was in that (employed in that) wherein there was hurt (damage) and advantage. If any man can damage me, he says, I am doing nothing: if I am waiting for another man to do me good, I am nothing. If I wish for any thing, and it does not happen, I am unfortunate. To such a contest he invited every man, and I do not think that he would have declined the contest with any one.[7] What do you suppose? was it by proclaiming and saying, I am such a man? Far from it, but by being such a man. For further, this is the character of a fool and a boaster to say, I am free from passions and disturbance: do not be ignorant, my friends, that while you are uneasy and disturbed about things of no value, I alone am free from all perturbation. So is it not enough for you to feel no pain, unless you make this proclamation: Come together all who are suffering gout, pains in the head, fever, ye who are lame, blind, and observe that I am sound (free) from every ailment—This is empty and disagreeable to hear, unless like Aesculapius you are able to show immediately by what kind of treatment they also shall be immediately free from disease, and unless you show your own health as an example.

For such is the Cynic who is honoured with the sceptre and the diadem by Zeus, and says, That you may see, O men, that you seek happiness and tranquillity not where it is, but where it is not, behold I am sent to you by God as an example,[8] I who have neither property nor house, nor wife nor children, not even a bed, nor coat nor household utensil; and see how healthy I am: try me, and if you see that I am free from perturbations, hear the remedies and how I have been cured (treated). This is both philanthropic and noble. But see whose work it is, the work of Zeus, or of him whom he may judge worthy of this service, that he may never exhibit any thing to the many, by which he shall make of no effect his own tes-

[6] 'In what then was he' seems to mean 'in what did he employ himself'?

[7] The text of Schweighaeuser is *οὐκ ἂν μοι δοκῇ ἐκστῆναι οὐδενί*: he says 'temere *οὐκ ἂν μοι δοκεῖ* ed. Bas. et seqq.' But *δοκεῖ* is right.

[8] Compare iii. c. 22.

timony, whereby he gives testimony to virtue, and bears evidence against external things:

> His beauteous face pales not, nor from his cheeks
> He wipes a tear.—Odyssey, xi. 528.

And not this only, but he neither desires nor seeks any thing, nor man nor place nor amusement, as children seek the vintage or holidays; always fortified by modesty as others are fortified by walls and doors and doorkeepers.

But now (these men) being only moved to philosophy, as those who have a bad stomach are moved to some kinds of food which they soon loathe, straightway (rush) towards the sceptre and to the royal power. They let the hair grow, they assume the cloak, they show the shoulder bare, they quarrel with those whom they meet; and if they see a man in a thick winter coat,[9] they quarrel with him. Man, first exercise yourself in winter weather: see your movements (inclinations) that they are not those of a man with a bad stomach or those of a longing woman. First strive that it be not known what you are: be a philosopher to yourself (or, philosophize to yourself) a short time. Fruit grows thus: the seed must be buried for some time, hid, grow slowly in order that it may come to perfection. But if it produces the ear before the jointed stem, it is imperfect, a produce of the garden of Adonis.[10] Such a poor plant are you also: you have blossomed too soon; the cold weather will scorch you up. See what the husbandmen say about seeds when there is warm weather too early. They are afraid lest the seeds should be too luxuriant, and then a single frost should lay hold of them and show that they are too forward. Do you also consider, my man: you have shot out too soon, you have hurried towards a little fame before the proper

[9] The word is φαινόλη, which seems to be the Latin 'paenula.'

[10] 'The gardens of Adonis' are things growing in earthen vessels, carried about for show only, not for use. 'The gardens of Adonis' is a proverbial expression applied to things of no value, to plants, for instance, which last only a short time, have no roots, and soon wither. Such things, we may suppose, were exhibited at the festivals of Adonis. Schweig.'s note.

season: you think that you are something, a fool among fools: you will be caught by the frost, and rather you have been frost-bitten in the root below, but your upper parts still blossom a little, and for this reason you think that you are still alive and flourishing. Allow us to ripen in the natural way: why do you bare (expose) us? why do you force us? we are not yet able to bear the air. Let the root grow, then acquire the first joint, then the second, and then the third: in this way then the fruit will naturally force itself out,[11] even if I do not choose. For who that is pregnant and filled with such great principles does not also perceive his own powers and move towards the corresponding acts? A bull is not ignorant of his own nature and his powers, when a wild beast shows itself, nor does he wait for one to urge him on; nor a dog when he sees a wild animal. But if I have the powers of a good man, shall I wait for you to prepare me for my own (proper) acts? At present I have them not, believe me. Why then do you wish me to be withered up before the time, as you have been withered up?

CHAPTER IX.

TO A PERSON WHO HAD BEEN CHANGED TO A CHARACTER OF SHAMELESSNESS.[1]

When you see another man in the possession of power (magistracy), set against this the fact that you have not the want (desire) of power; when you see another rich, see what you possess in place of riches: for if you possess nothing in place of them, you are miserable; but if you have not the want of riches, know that you possess more than this man possesses and what is worth much more. Another man possesses a handsome woman (wife): you

[11] See Schweig.'s note.

[1] 'They, who are desirous of taking refuge in Heathenism from the strictness of the Christian morality, will find no great consolation in reading this chapter of Epictetus.' Mrs. Carter.

have the satisfaction of not desiring a handsome wife. Do these things appear to you to be small? And how much would these persons give, these very men who are rich, and in possession of power, and live with handsome women, to be able to despise riches, and power and these very women whom they love and enjoy? Do you not know then what is the thirst of a man who has a fever? He possesses that which is in no degree like the thirst of a man who is in health: for the man who is in health ceases to be thirsty after he has drunk; but the sick man being pleased for a short time has a nausea, he converts the drink into bile, vomits, is griped, and more thirsty. It is such a thing to have desire of riches and to possess riches, desire of power and to possess power, desire of a beautiful woman and to sleep with her: to this is added jealousy, fear of being deprived of the thing which you love, indecent words, indecent thoughts, unseemly acts.

And what do I lose? you will say. My man, you were modest, and you are so no longer. Have you lost nothing? In place of Chrysippus and Zeno you read Aristides and Evenus;[2] have you lost nothing? In place of Socrates and Diogenes, you admire him who is able to corrupt and seduce most women. You wish to appear handsome and try to make yourself so, though you are not. You like to display splendid clothes that you may attract women; and if you find any fine oil (for the hair),[3] you imagine that you are happy. But formerly you did not think of any such thing, but only where there should be decent talk, a worthy man, and a generous conception. Therefore you slept like a man, walked forth like a man, wore a manly dress, and used to talk in a way becoming a good

[2] Aristides was a Greek, but his period is not known. He was the author of a work named Milesiaca or Milesian stories. All that we know of the work is that it was of a loose description, amatory and licentious. It was translated into Latin by L. Cornelius Sisenna, a contemporary of the Dictator Sulla; and it is mentioned by Plutarch (Life of Crassus, c. 32), and several times by Ovid (Tristia ii. 413 etc.). Evenus was perhaps a poet. We know nothing of this Evenus, but we may conjecture from being here associated with Aristides what his character was.

[3] See Schweig.'s note on the word μυραλειφίον, which he has in his text. It should be μυραλοιφίον, if the word exists.

man; then do you say to me, I have lost nothing? So do men lose nothing more than coin? Is not modesty lost? Is not decent behaviour lost? is it that he who has lost these things has sustained no loss? Perhaps you think that not one of these things is a loss. But there was a time when you reckoned this the only loss and damage, and you were anxious that no man should disturb you from these (good) words and actions.

Observe, you are disturbed from these good words and actions by nobody, but by yourself. Fight with yourself, restore yourself to decency, to modesty, to liberty. If any man ever told you this about me, that a person forces me to be an adulterer, to wear such a dress as yours, to perfume myself with oils, would you not have gone and with your own hand have killed the man who thus calumniated me? Now will you not help yourself? and how much easier is this help? There is no need to kill any man, nor to put him in chains; nor to treat him with contumely, nor to enter the Forum (go to the courts of law), but it is only necessary for you to speak to yourself who will be most easily persuaded, with whom no man has more power of persuasion than yourself. First of all, condemn what you are doing, and then when you have condemned it, do not despair of yourself, and be not in the condition of those men of mean spirit, who, when they have once given in, surrender themselves completely and are carried away as if by a torrent. But see what the trainers of boys do. Has the boy fallen? Rise, they say, wrestle again till you are made strong. Do you also do something of the same kind: for be well assured that nothing is more tractable than the human soul. You must exercise the Will,[4] and the thing is done, it is set right: as on the other hand, only fall a nodding (be careless), and the thing is lost: for from within comes ruin and from within comes help. Then (you say) what good do I gain? And

[4] The orginal is θελῆσαι δεῖ. Seneca (Ep. 80): 'Quid tibi opus est ut sis bonus? Velle.' Upton.

The power of the Will is a fundamental principle with Epictetus. The will is strong in some, but very feeble in others; and sometimes, as experience seems to show, it is incapable of resisting the power of old habits.

what greater good do you seek than this?[5] From a shameless man you will become a modest man, from a disorderly you will become an orderly man, from a faithless you will become a faithful man, from a man of unbridled habits a sober man. If you seek any thing more than this, go on doing what you are doing: not even a God can now help you.

CHAPTER X.

WHAT THINGS WE OUGHT TO DESPISE, AND WHAT THINGS WE OUGHT TO VALUE.

THE difficulties of all men are about external things, their helplessness is about externals. What shall I do, how will it be, how will it turn out, will this happen, will that? All these are the words of those who are turning themselves to things which are not within the power of the will. For who says, How shall I not assent to that which is false? how shall I not turn away from the truth? If a man be of such a good disposition as to be anxious about these things, I will remind him of this, Why are you anxious? The thing is in your own power: be assured: do not be precipitate in assenting before you apply the natural rule. On the other side, if a man is anxious (uneasy) about desire, lest it fail in its purpose and miss its end, and with respect to the avoidance of things, lest he should fall into that which he would avoid, I will first kiss (love) him, because he throws away the things about which others are in a flutter (others

[5] Virtue is its own reward, said the Stoics. This is the meaning of Epictetus, and it is consistent with his principles that a man should live conformably to his nature, and so he will have all the happiness of which human nature is capable. Mrs. Carter has a note here, which I do not copy, and I hardly understand. It seems to refer to the Christian doctrine of a man being rewarded in a future life according to his works: but we have no evidence that Epictetus believed in a future life, and he therefore could not go further than to maintain that virtuous behaviour is the best thing in this short life, and will give a man the happiness which he can obtain in no other way.

desire) and their fears, and employs his thoughts about his own affairs and his own condition. Then I shall say to him, if you do not choose to desire that which you will fail to obtain nor to attempt to avoid that into which you will fall, desire nothing which belongs to (which is in the power of) others, nor try to avoid any of the things which are not in your power. If you do not observe this rule, you must of necessity fail in your desires and fall into that which you would avoid. What is the difficulty here? where is there room for the words, How will it be? and How will it turn out? and will this happen or that?

Now is not that which will happen independent of the will? Yes. And the nature of good and of evil is it not in the things which are within the power of the will? Yes. Is it in your power then to treat according to nature every thing which happens? Can any person hinder you? No man. No longer then say to me, How will it be? For however it may be, you will dispose of it well,[1] and the result to you will be a fortunate one. What would Hercules have been if he said, How shall a great lion not appear to me, or a great boar, or savage men? And what do you care for that? If a great boar appear, you will fight a greater fight: if bad men appear, you will relieve the earth of the bad. Suppose then that I lose my life in this way. You will die a good man, doing a noble act. For since we must certainly die, of necessity a man must be found doing something, either following the employment of a husbandman, or digging, or trading, or serving in a consulship or suffering from indigestion or from diarrhœa. What then do you wish to be doing when you are found by death? I for my part would wish to be found doing something which belongs to a man, beneficent, suitable to the general interest, noble. But if I cannot be found doing things so great, I would be found doing at least that which I

[1] See a passage in Plutarch on Tranquillity from Euripides, the great storehouse of noble thoughts, from which antient writers drew much good matter; and perhaps it was one of the reasons why so many of his plays and fragments have been preserved.

> We must not quarrel with the things that are,
> For they care not for us; but he who feels them
> If he disposes well of things, fares well.

cannot be hindered from doing, that which is permitted me to do, correcting myself, cultivating the faculty which makes use of appearances, labouring at freedom from the affects (labouring at tranquillity of mind), rendering to the relations of life their due; if I succeed so far, also (I would be found) touching on (advancing to) the third topic (or head) safety in the forming judgments about things.[2] If death surprises me when I am busy about these things, it is enough for me if I can stretch out my hands to God and say: The means which I have received from thee for seeing thy administration (of the world) and following it, I have not neglected: I have not dishonoured thee by my acts: see how I have used my perceptions, see how I have used my preconceptions: have I ever blamed thee? have I been discontented with any thing that happens, or wished it to be otherwise? have I wished to transgress the (established) relations (of things)? That thou hast given me life, I thank thee for what thou hast given: so long as I have used the things which are thine I am content; take them back and place them wherever thou mayest choose; for thine were all things, thou gavest them to me [3]—Is it not enough to depart in this state of mind, and what life is better and more becoming than that of a man who is in this state of mind? and what end is more happy?[4]

[2] See iii. c. 2.

[3] "Thine they were, and thou gavest them to me." John xvii. 6. Mrs. Carter.

[4] 'I wish it were possible to palliate the ostentation of this passage, by applying it to the ideal perfect character: but it is in a general way that Epictetus hath proposed such a dying speech, as cannot without shocking arrogance be uttered by any one born to die. Unmixed as it is with any acknowledgment of faults or imperfections, at present, or with any sense of guilt on account of the past, it must give every sober reader a very disadvantageous opinion of some principles of the philosophy, on which it is founded, as contradictory to the voice of conscience, and formed on absolute ignorance or neglect of the condition and circumstances of such a creature as man.' Mrs. Carter.

I am inclined to think that Epictetus does refer to the 'ideal perfect character'; but others may not understand him in this way. When Mrs. Carter says 'but it is in a general . . . dying speech,' she can hardly suppose, as her words seem to mean, that Epictetus proposed such a dying speech for every man or even for many men, for he knew and has told us how bad many men are, and how few are good according to his measure and rule: in fact his meaning is plainly expressed. The

But that this may be done (that such a declaration may be made), a man must receive (bear) no small things, nor are the things small which he must lose (go without). You cannot both wish to be a consul and to have these things (the power of making such a dying speech), and to be eager to have lands, and these things also; and to be solicitous about slaves and about yourself. But if you wish for any thing which belongs to another, that which is your own is lost. This is the nature of the thing: nothing is given or had for nothing.[5] And where is the wonder? If you wish to be a consul, you must keep awake, run about, kiss hands, waste yourself with exhaustion at other men's doors, say and do many things unworthy of a free man, send gifts to many, daily presents to some. And what is the thing that is got? Twelve bundles of rods (the consular fasces), to sit three or four times on the tribunal, to exhibit the games in the Circus and to give suppers in small baskets.[6] Or, if you

dying speech may even be stronger in the sense in which Mrs. Carter understands it, in my translation, where I have rendered one passage in the text by the words 'I have not dishonoured thee by my acts,' which she translates, 'as far as in me lay, I have not dishonoured thee;' which apparently means, 'as far as I could, I have not dishonoured thee.' The Latin translation 'quantum in me fuit,' seems rather ambiguous to me.

There is a general confession of sins in the prayer book of the Church of England, part of which Epictetus would not have rejected, I think. Of course the words which form the peculiar Christian character of the confession would have been unintelligible to him. It is a confession which all persons of all conditions are supposed to make. If all persons made the confession with sincerity, it ought to produce a corresponding behaviour and make men more ready to be kind to one another, for all who use it confess that they fail in their duty, and it ought to lower pride and banish arrogance from the behaviour of those who in wealth and condition are elevated above the multitude. But I have seen it somewhere said, I cannot remember where, but said in no friendly spirit to Christian prayer, that some men both priests and laymen prostrate themselves in humility before God and indemnify themselves by arrogance to man.

[5] See iv. 2. 2.

[6] These were what the Romans named 'sportulæ,' in which the rich used to give some eatables to poor dependents who called to pay their respects to the great at an early hour.

Nunc sportula primo
Limine parva sedet turbae rapienda togatae.
Juvenal, Sat. i. 95.

do not agree about this, let some one show me what there is besides these things. In order then to secure freedom from passions (ἀπαθείας), tranquillity, to sleep well when you do sleep, to be really awake when you are awake, to fear nothing, to be anxious about nothing, will you spend nothing and give no labour? But if any thing belonging to you be lost while you are thus busied, or be wasted badly, or another obtains what you ought to have obtained, will you immediately be vexed at what has happened? Will you not take into the account on the other side what you receive and for what, how much for how much? Do you expect to have for nothing things so great? And how can you? One work (thing) has no community with another. You cannot have both external things after bestowing care on them and your own ruling faculty:[7] but if you would have those, give up this. If you do not, you will have neither this nor that, while you are drawn in different ways to both.[8] The oil will be spilled, the household vessels will perish: (that may be), but I shall be free from passions (tranquil).—There will be a fire when I am not present, and the books will be destroyed: but I shall treat appearances according to nature—Well; but I shall have nothing to eat. If I am so unlucky, death is a harbour; and death is the harbour for all; this is the place of refuge; and for this reason not one of the things in life is difficult: as soon as you choose, you are out of the house, and are smoked no more.[9] Why then are you anxious, why do you lose your sleep, why do you not straightway, after considering wherein your good is and your evil, say, Both of them are in my power? Neither can any man deprive me of the good, nor involve me in the bad against my will. Why do I not throw myself down and snore? for all that I have is safe. As to the things which belong to others, he will look to them who gets them, as they may be given by him who has the power.[10] Who am I who wish to have

[7] "You cannot serve God and Mammon." Matthew vi. 24. Mrs. Carter.

[8] See iv. 2, 5.

[9] Compare i. 25, 18, and i. 9, 20.

[10] See the note in Schweig.'s ed.

them in this way or in that? is a power of selecting them given to me? has any person made me the dispenser of them? Those things are enough for me over which I have power: I ought to manage them as well as I can: and all the rest, as the master of them (God) may choose.

When a man has these things before his eyes, does he keep awake and turn hither and thither? What would he have, or what does he regret, Patroclus or Antilochus or Menelaus?[11] For when did he suppose that any of his friends was immortal, and when had he not before his eyes that on the morrow or the day after he or his friend must die? Yes, he says, but I thought that he would survive me and bring up my son.—You were a fool for that reason, and you were thinking of what was uncertain. Why then do you not blame yourself, and sit crying like girls?—But he used to set my food before me.—Because he was alive, you fool, but now he cannot: but Automedon[12] will set it before you, and if Automedon also dies, you will find another. But if the pot, in which your meat was cooked, should be broken, must you die of

[11] Epictetus refers to the passage in the Iliad xxiv. 5, where Achilles is lamenting the death of Patroclus and cannot sleep.

[12] "This is a wretched idea of friendship; but a necessary consequence of the Stoic system. What a fine contrast to this gloomy consolation are the noble sentiments of an Apostle? Value your deceased friend, says Epictetus, as a broken pipkin; forget him, as a thing worthless, lost and destroyed. St. Paul, on the contrary, comforts the mourning survivors; bidding them not sorrow, as those who have no hope: but remember that the death of good persons is only a sleep; from which they will soon arise to a happy immortality." Mrs. Carter.

Epictetus does not say, 'value your deceased friend as a broken pipkin.' Achilles laments that he has lost the services of his friend at table, a vulgar kind of complaint: he is thinking of his own loss, instead of his friend. The answer is such a loss as he laments is easily repaired: the loss of such a friend is as easily repaired as the loss of a cooking vessel. Mrs. Carter in her zeal to contrast the teaching of the Apostle with that of Epictetus seems to forget for the time that Epictetus, so far as we know, did not accept or did not teach the doctrine of a future life. As to what he thought of friendship, if it was a real friendship, such as we can conceive, I am sure that he did not think of it, as Mrs. Carter says that he did; for true friendship implies many of the virtues which Epictetus taught and practised. He has a chapter on Friendship, ii. 22, which I suppose that Mrs. Carter did not think of, when she wrote this note.

hunger, because you have not the pot which you are accustomed to? Do you not send and buy a new pot? He says:

No greater ill than this could fall on me. (Iliad xix. 321.)

Why is this your ill? Do you then instead of removing it blame your mother (Thetis) for not foretelling it to you that you might continue grieving from that time? What do you think? do you not suppose that Homer wrote this that we may learn that those of noblest birth, the strongest and the richest, the most handsome, when they have not the opinions which they ought to have, are not prevented from being most wretched and unfortunate?

CHAPTER XI.

ABOUT PURITY (CLEANLINESS).

Some persons raise a question whether the social feeling[1] is contained in the nature of man; and yet I think that these same persons would have no doubt that love of purity is certainly contained in it, and that if man is distinguished from other animals by any thing, he is distinguished by this. When then we see any other animal cleaning itself, we are accustomed to speak of the act with surprise, and to add that the animal is acting like a man: and on the other hand, if a man blames an animal for being dirty, straightway as if we were making an excuse for it, we say that of course the animal is not a human creature. So we suppose that there is something superior in man, and that we first receive it from the Gods. For since the Gods by their nature are pure and free from corruption, so far as men approach them by reason, so far do they cling to purity and to a love (habit)

[1] The word is τὸ κοινωνικόν. Compare i. 23, 1, ii. 10, 14, ii. 20, 6.

of purity. But since it is impossible that man's nature (*οὐσία*) can be altogether pure being mixed (composed) of such materials, reason is applied, as far as it is possible, and reason endeavours to make human nature love purity.[2]

The first then and highest purity is that which is in the soul; and we say the same of impurity. Now you could not discover the impurity of the soul as you could discover that of the body: but as to the soul, what else could you find in it than that which makes it filthy in respect to the acts which are her own? Now the acts of the soul are movement towards an object or movement from it, desire, aversion, preparation, design (purpose), assent. What then is it which in these acts makes the soul filthy and impure? Nothing else than her own bad judgments (*κρίματα*). Consequently the impurity of the soul is the soul's bad opinions; and the purification of the soul is the planting in it of proper opinions; and the soul is pure which has proper opinions, for the soul alone in her own acts is free from perturbation and pollution.

Now we ought to work at something like this in the body also, as far as we can. It was impossible for the defluxions of the nose not to run when man has such a mixture in his body. For this reason nature has made hands and the nostrils themselves as channels for carrying off the humours. If then a man sucks up the defluxions, I say that he is not doing the act of a man. It was impossible for a man's feet not to be made muddy and not be soiled at all when he passes through dirty places. For this reason nature (God) has made water and hands. It was impossible that some impurity should not remain in the teeth from eating: for this reason, she says, wash the teeth. Why? In order that you may be a man and not a wild beast or a hog. It was impossible that from the sweat and the pressing of the clothes there should not remain some impurity about the body which requires to be cleaned away. For this reason water, oil, hands,

[2] In the text there are two words, *καθαρός* which means 'pure,' and *καθάριος* which means 'of a pure nature,' 'loving purity.'

towels, scrapers (strigils),[3] nitre, sometimes all other kinds of means are necessary for cleaning the body. You do not act so: but the smith will take off the rust from the iron (instruments), and he will have tools prepared for this purpose, and you yourself wash the platter when you are going to eat, if you are not completely impure and dirty: but will you not wash the body nor make it clean? Why? he replies. I will tell you again; in the first place, that you may do the acts of a man; then, that you may not be disagreeable to those with whom you associate. You do something of this kind even[4] in this matter, and you do not perceive it: you think that you deserve to stink. Let it be so: deserve to stink. Do you think that also those who sit by you, those who recline at table with you, that those who kiss you deserve the same?[5] Either go into a desert, where you deserve to go, or live by yourself, and smell yourself. For it is just that you alone should enjoy your own impurity. But when you are in a city, to behave so inconsiderately and foolishly, to what character do you think that it belongs? If nature had entrusted to you a horse, would you have overlooked and neglected him? And now think that you have been entrusted with your own body as with a horse; wash it, wipe it, take care that no man turns away from it, that no one gets out of the way for it. But who does not get out of the way of a dirty man, of a stinking man, of a man whose skin is foul, more than he does out of the way of a man who is daubed with muck? That smell is from without, it is put upon him; but the other smell is

[3] The ξύστρα, as Epictetus names it, was the Roman 'strigilis,' which was used for the scraping and cleaning of the body in bathing. Persius (v. 126) writes—

'I, puer, et strigiles Crispini ad balnea defer.'

The strigiles "were of bronze or iron of various forms. They were applied to the body much in the same way as we see a piece of hoop applied to a sweating horse." Pompeii, edited by Dr. Dyer.

[4] See Schweig.'s note.

[5] See Schweig.'s note. If the text is right, the form of expression is inexact and does not clearly express the meaning; but the meaning may be easily discovered.

from want of care, from within, and in a manner from a body in putrefaction.

But Socrates washed himself seldom—Yes, but his body was clean and fair: and it was so agreeable and sweet that the most beautiful and the most noble loved him, and desired to sit by him rather than by the side of those who had the handsomest forms. It was in his power neither to use the bath nor to wash himself, if he chose; and yet the rare use of water had an effect. [If you do not choose to wash with warm water, wash with cold.[6]] But Aristophanes says

> Those who are pale, unshod, 'tis those I mean.
> (Nubes v. 102.)

For Aristophanes says of Socrates that he also walked the air and stole clothes from the palaestra.[7] But all who have written about Socrates bear exactly the contrary evidence in his favour; they say that he was pleasant not only to hear, but also to see.[8] On the other hand they write the same about Diogenes.[9] For we ought not even by the appearance of the body to deter the multitude from philosophy; but as in other things, a philosopher should show himself cheerful and tranquil, so also he should in the things that relate to the body: See, ye men, that I have nothing, that I want nothing: see how I am without a house, and without a city, and an exile, if it happens to be so,[10] and without a hearth I live more free from trouble and more happily than all of noble birth and than the rich. But look at my poor body also and observe that it is not injured by my hard way of living—But if a man says this to me, who has the appearance (dress) and face of a condemned man, what God shall persuade me to approach philosophy, if[11] it makes men such persons? Far from it; I would not choose to do so, even if I

[6] See what is said of this passage in the latter part of this chapter.

[7] Aristophanes, Nubes, v. 225, and v. 179.

[8] Xenophon, Memorab. iii. 12.

[9] See iii. 22, 88.

[10] Diogenes, it is said, was driven from his native town Sinope in Asia on a charge of having debased or counterfeited the coinage. Upton. It is probable that this is false.

[11] On the word ὥστε see Schweig.'s note.

were going to become a wise man. I indeed would rather that a young man, who is making his first movements towards philosophy, should come to me with his hair carefully trimmed than with it dirty and rough, for there is seen in him a certain notion (appearance) of beauty and a desire of (attempt at) that which is becoming; and where he supposes it to be, there also he strives that it shall be. It is only necessary to show him (what it is), and to say: Young man, you seek beauty, and you do well: you must know then that it (is produced) grows in that part of you where you have the rational faculty: seek it there where you have the movements towards and the movements from things, where you have the desires towards, and the aversion from things: for this is what you have in yourself of a superior kind; but the poor body is naturally only earth: why do you labour about it to no purpose? if you shall learn nothing else, you will learn from time that the body is nothing. But if a man comes to me daubed with filth, dirty, with a moustache down to his knees, what can I say to him, by what kind of resemblance can I lead him on? For about what has he busied himself which resembles beauty, that I may be able to change him and say, Beauty is not in this, but in that? Would you have me to tell him, that beauty consists not in being daubed with muck, but that it lies in the rational part? Has he any desire of beauty? has he any form of it in his mind? Go and talk to a hog, and tell him not to roll in the mud.

For this reason the words of Xenocrates touched Polemon also, since he was a lover of beauty, for he entered (the room) having in him certain incitements (ἐναύσματα) to love of beauty, but he looked for it in the wrong place.[12] For nature has not made even the animals dirty which live with man. Does a horse ever wallow in the mud, or a well bred dog? But the hog, and the dirty geese, and worms and spiders do, which are banished furthest from human intercourse. Do you then being a man choose to be not as one of the animals which live with man, but rather a worm, or a spider? Will

[12] As to Polemon see iii. c. 1, 14.

you not wash yourself somewhere some time in such manner as you choose?[13] Will you not wash off the dirt from your body? Will you not come clean that those with whom you keep company may have pleasure in being with you? But do you go with us even into the temples in such a state, where it is not permitted to spit or blow the nose, being a heap of spittle and of snot?

What then? does any man (that is, do I) require you to ornament yourself? Far from it; except to ornament that which we really are by nature, the rational faculty, the opinions, the actions; but as to the body only so far as purity, only so far as not to give offence. But if you are told that you ought not to wear garments dyed with purple, go and daub your cloak with muck or tear it.[14] But how shall I have a neat cloak? Man, you have water; wash it. Here is a youth worthy of being loved,[15] here is an old man worthy of loving and being loved in return, a fit person for a man to intrust to him a son's instruction, to whom daughters and young men shall come, if opportunity shall so happen, that the teacher shall deliver his lessons to them on a dunghill.[16] Let this not be so: every deviation comes from something which is in man's nature; but this (deviation) is near being something not in man's nature.

[13] It has been suggested that the words s. 19, [if you do not choose to wash with warm water, wash with cold, p. 369] belong to this place.

[14] This is the literal translation: but it means, 'will you go, etc., tear it?'

[15] 'The youth, probably, means the scholar, who neglects neatness; and the old man, the tutor, that gives him no precept or example of it.' Mrs. Carter.

[16] The Greek is λέγῃ τὰς σχόλας. Cicero uses the Latin 'scholas habere,' 'to hold philosophical disputations:' Tusc. Disp. i 4. Upton.

CHAPTER XII.

ON ATTENTION

WHEN you have remitted your attention for a short time, do not imagine this, that you will recover it when you choose; but let this thought be present to you, that in consequence of the fault committed to-day your affairs must be in a worse condition for all that follows. For first, and what causes most trouble, a habit of not attending is formed in you; then a habit of deferring your attention. And continually from time to time you drive away by deferring it the happiness of life, proper behaviour, the being and living conformably to nature.[1] If then the procrastination of attention is profitable, the complete omission of attention is more profitable; but if it is not profitable, why do you not maintain your attention constant?—To-day I choose to play—Well then, ought you not to play with attention?—I choose to sing—What then hinders you from doing so with attention? Is there any part of life excepted, to which attention does not extend? For will you do it (any thing in life) worse by using attention, and better by not attending at all? And what else of the things in life is done better by those who do not use attention? Does he who works in wood work better by not attending to it? Does the captain of a ship manage it better by not attending? and is any of the smaller acts done better by inattention? Do you not see that when you have let your mind loose, it is no longer in your power to recall it, either to propriety, or to modesty, or to moderation: but you do every thing that comes into your mind in obedience to your inclinations.

To what things then ought I to attend? First to those general (principles) and to have them in readiness, and without them not to sleep, not to rise, not to drink, not to

[1] See Schweig.'s note on the words εἰώθει ὑπερτιθέμενον, in place of which he proposes ἐξωθῇ ὑπερτιθέμενος. Compare Persius, Sat. v. 66.

"Cras hoc fiet." Idem cras fiet, etc.,

and Martial, v. 58.

eat, not to converse (associate) with men; that no man is master of another man's will, but that in the will alone is the good and the bad. No man then has the power either to procure for me any good or to involve me in any evil, but I alone myself over myself have power in these things. When then these things are secured to me, why need I be disturbed about external things? What tyrant is formidable, what disease, what poverty, what offence (from any man)? Well, I have not pleased a certain person. Is he then (the pleasing of him) my work, my judgment? No. Why then should I trouble myself about him?—But he is supposed to be some one (of importance)—He will look to that himself; and those who think so will also. But I have one whom I ought to please, to whom I ought to subject myself, whom I ought to obey, God and those who are next to him.[2] He has placed me with myself, and has put my will in obedience to myself alone, and has given me rules for the right use of it; and when I follow these rules in syllogisms, I do not care for any man who says any thing else (different): in sophistical argument, I care for no man. Why then in greater matters do those annoy me who blame me? What is the cause of this perturbation? Nothing else than because in this matter (topic) I am not disciplined. For all knowledge (science) despises ignorance and the ignorant; and not only the sciences, but even the arts. Produce any shoemaker that you please, and he ridicules the many in respect to his own work[3] (business). Produce any carpenter.

First then we ought to have these (rules) in readiness, and to do nothing without them, and we ought to keep the soul directed to this mark, to pursue nothing external, and nothing which belongs to others (or is in the power of others), but to do as he has appointed who has the

[2] Compare iv. 4, 39, i. 14, 12; and Encheirid. c. 32, and the remark of Simplicius. Schweig. explains the words τοῖς μετ' ἐκεῖνον thus: 'qui post Illum (Deum) et sub Illo rebus humanis praesunt; qui proximum ab Illo locum tenent.'

[3] Compare ii. 13, 15 and 20; and Antoninus, vi. 35: 'Is it not strange if the architect and the physician shall have more respect to the reason (the principles) of their own arts than man to his own reason, which is common to him and the gods?'

power; we ought to pursue altogether the things which are in the power of the will, and all other things as it is permitted. Next to this we ought to remember who we are,[4] and what is our name, and to endeavour to direct our duties towards the character (nature) of our several relations (in life) in this manner: what is the season for singing, what is the season for play, and in whose presence; what will be the consequence of the act;[5] whether our associates will despise us, whether we shall despise them;[6] when to jeer (σκῶψαι), and whom to ridicule; and on what occasion to comply and with whom; and finally, in complying how to maintain our own character.[7] But wherever you have deviated from any of these rules, there is damage immediately, not from any thing external, but from the action itself.

What then? is it possible to be free from faults, (if you do all this)? It is not possible; but this is possible, to direct your efforts incessantly to being faultless. For we must be content if by never remitting this attention we shall escape at least a few errors. But now when you have said, To-morrow I will begin to attend, you must be told that you are saying this, To-day I will be shameless, disregardful of time and place, mean; it will be in the power of others to give me pain; to-day I will be passionate, and envious. See how many evil things you are permitting yourself to do. If it is good to use attention to-morrow, how much better is it to do so to-day? if to-morrow it is in your interest to attend, much more is it to-day, that you may be able to do so to-morrow also, and may not defer it again to the third day.[8]

[4] 'Quid sumus, aut quidnam victuri gignimur.' Persius, Sat. iii. 67.

[5] Schweig. thinks that the text will be better translated according to Upton's notion and H. Stephen's (hors de propos) by 'Quid sit abs re futurum,' 'what will be out of season.' Perhaps he is right.

[6] Schweig. says that the sense of the passage, as I have rendered it, requires the reading to be καταφρονήσουσι; and it is so, at least in the better Greek writers.

[7] See iii. 14, 7, i. 29, 64.

[8] Compare Antoninus, viii. 22: "Attend to the matter which is before thee, whether it is an opinion, or an act, or a word.

Thou sufferest this justly, for thou choosest rather to become good to-morrow than to be good to-day."

CHAPTER XIII.

AGAINST OR TO THOSE WHO READILY TELL THEIR OWN AFFAIRS.

When a man has seemed to us to have talked with simplicity (candour) about his own affairs, how is it that at last we are ourselves also induced to discover to him[1] our own secrets and we think this to be candid behaviour? In the first place because it seems unfair for a man to have listened to the affairs of his neighbour, and not to communicate to him also in turn our own affairs: next, because we think that we shall not present to them the appearance of candid men when we are silent about our own affairs. Indeed men are often accustomed to say, I have told you all my affairs, will you tell me nothing of your own? where is this done?—Besides, we have also this opinion that we can safely trust him who has already told us his own affairs; for the notion rises in our mind that this man could never divulge our affairs because he would be cautious that we also should not divulge his. In this way also the incautious are caught by the soldiers at Rome. A soldier sits by you in a common dress and begins to speak ill of Caesar; then you, as if you had received a pledge of his fidelity by his having begun the abuse, utter yourself also what you think, and then you are carried off in chains.[2]

Something of this kind happens to us also generally. Now as this man has confidently intrusted his affairs to me, shall I also do so to any man whom I meet? (No),

[1] Schweig. writes πῶς ποτε, etc., and translates 'excitamur quodammodo et ipsi,' etc. He gives the meaning, but the πῶς ποτε is properly a question.

[2] The man, whether a soldier or not, was an informer, one of those vile men who carried on this shameful business under the empire. He was what Juvenal names a 'delator.' Upton, who refers to the life of Hadrian by Aelius Spartianus, speaks even of this emperor employing soldiers named Frumentarii for the purpose of discovering what was said and done in private houses. John the Baptist (Luke iii. 14) in answer to the question of the soldiers, 'And what shall we do?' said unto them 'Do violence to no man, neither accuse any falsely; and be content with your wages.' Upton.

for when I have heard, I keep silence, if I am of such a disposition; but he goes forth and tells all men what he has heard. Then if I hear what has been done, if I be a man like him, I resolve to be revenged, I divulge what he has told me; I both disturb others and am disturbed myself. But if I remember that one man does not injure another, and that every man's acts injure and profit him, I secure this, that I do not any thing like him, but still I suffer what I do suffer through my own silly talk.

True: but it is unfair when you have heard the secrets of your neighbour for you in your turn to communicate nothing to him.—Did I ask you for your secrets, my man? did you communicate your affairs on certain terms, that you should in return hear mine also? If you are a babbler and think that all who meet you are friends, do you wish me also to be like you? But why, if you did well in intrusting your affairs to me, and it is not well for me to intrust mine to you, do you wish me to be so rash? It is just the same as if I had a cask which is water-tight, and you one with a hole in it, and you should come and deposit with me your wine that I might put it into my cask, and then should complain that I also did not intrust my wine to you, for you have a cask with a hole in it. How then is there any equality here? You intrusted your affairs to a man who is faithful, and modest, to a man who thinks that his own actions alone are injurious and (or) useful, and that nothing external is. Would you have me intrust mine to you, a man who has dishonoured his own faculty of will, and who wishes to gain some small bit of money or some office or promotion in the court (emperor's palace), even if you should be going to murder your own children, like Medea? Where (in what) is this equality (fairness)? But show yourself to me to be faithful, modest, and steady: show me that you have friendly opinions; show that your cask has no hole in it; and you will see how I shall not wait for you to trust me with your affairs, but I myself shall come to you and ask you to hear mine. For who does not choose to make use of a good vessel? Who does not value a benevolent and faithful adviser? who will not willingly receive a man who is ready to bear a share, as we may say, of the difficulty of his circumstances, and by this very act to ease the burden, by taking a part of it.'

True: but I trust you; you do not trust me.—In the first place, not even do you trust me, but you are a babbler, and for this reason you cannot hold any thing; for indeed, if it is true that you trust me, trust your affairs to me only; but now whenever you see a man at leisure, you seat yourself by him and say: Brother, I have no friend more benevolent than you nor dearer; I request you to listen to my affairs. And you do this even to those who are not known to you at all. But if you really trust me, it is plain that you trust me because I am faithful and modest, not because I have told my affairs to you. Allow me then to have the same opinion about you. Show me that if one man tells his affairs to another, he who tells them is faithful and modest. For if this were so, I would go about and tell my affairs to every man, if that would make me faithful and modest. But the thing is not so, and it requires no common opinions (principles). If then you see a man who is busy about things not dependent on his will and subjecting his will to them, you must know that this man has ten thousand persons to compel and hinder him. He has no need of pitch or the wheel to compel him to declare what he knows:[3] but a little girl's nod, if it should so happen, will move him, the blandishment of one who belongs to Caesar's court, desire of a magistracy or of an inheritance, and things without end of that sort. You must remember then among general principles that secret discourses (discourses about secret matters) require fidelity and corresponding opinions. But where can we now find these easily? Or if you cannot answer that question, let some one point out to me a man who can say: I care only about the things which are my own, the things which are not subject to hindrance, the things which are by nature free. This I hold to be the nature of the good: but let all other things be as they are allowed; I do not concern myself.

[3] The wheel and pitch were instruments of torture to extract confessions. See ii. 6, 18, and Schweig.'s note there.

THE ENCHEIRIDION, OR MANUAL.[1]

I.

Of things some are in our power, and others are not. In our power are opinion (ὑπόληψις), movement towards a thing (ὁρμή), desire, aversion (ἔκκλισις, turning from a thing); and in a word, whatever are our own acts: not in our power are the body, property, reputation, offices (magisterial power), and in a word, whatever are not our own acts. And the things in our power are by nature free, not subject to restraint nor hindrance: but the things not in our power are weak, slavish, subject to restraint, in the power of others. Remember then that if you think the things which are by nature slavish to be free, and the things which are in the power of others to be your own, you will be hindered, you will lament, you will be disturbed, you will blame both gods and men: but if you think that only which is your own to be your own, and if you think that what is another's, as it really is, belongs to another, no man will ever compel you, no man will hinder you, you will never blame any man, you will accuse no man, you will do nothing involuntarily (against your will), no man will harm you, you will have no enemy, for you will not suffer any harm.

If then you desire (aim at) such great things, remember that you must not (attempt to) lay hold of them with a small effort; but you must leave alone some things entirely, and postpone others for the present. But if you wish for these things also (such great things), and power

[1] In Schweighaeuser's edition the title is ''Επικτήτου ἐγχειρίδιον. Epicteti Manuale ex recensione et interpretatione Joannis Uptoni. Notabiliorem Lectionis varietatem adjecit Joh. Schweighaeuser.' There are also notes by Upton, and some by Schweighaeuser.

(office) and wealth, perhap
very things (power and w
those former things (such
will fail in those things t
and freedom are secured.
ing to every harsh appear
and in no manner what you
it by the rules which you
chiefly, whether it relates t
power or to things which a
relates to any thing which i
say, that it does not concern

Remember that desire contains in it the profession (hope) of obtaining that which you desire, and the profession (hope) in aversion (turning from a thing) is that you will not fall into that which you attempt to avoid: and he who fails in his desire is unfortunate; and he who falls into that which he would avoid, is unhappy. If then you attempt to avoid only the things contrary to nature which are within your power, you will not be involved in any of the things which you would avoid. But if you attempt to avoid disease or death or poverty, you will be unhappy. Take away then aversion from all things which are not in our power, and transfer it to the things contrary to nature which are in our power. But destroy desire completely for the present. For if you desire anything which is not in our power, you must be unfortunate: but of the things in our power, and which it would be good to desire, nothing yet is before you. But employ only the power of moving towards an object and retiring from it; and these powers indeed only slightly and with exceptions and with remission.[3]

[1] This passage will be obscure in the original, unless it is examined well. I have followed the explanation of Simplicius, iv. (i. 4.)

[2] Appearances are named 'harsh' or 'rough' when they are 'contrary to reason and overexciting and in fact make life rough (uneven) by the want of symmetry and by inequality in the movements' Simplicius, v. (i. 5.)

[3] See the notes in Schweig.'s edition.

III.

In every thing which pleases the soul, or supplies a want, or is loved, remember to add this to the (description, notion); what is the nature of each thing, beginning from the smallest? If you love an earthen vessel, say it is an earthen vessel which you love; for when it has been broken, you will not be disturbed. If you are kissing your child or wife, say that it is a human being whom you are kissing, for when the wife or child dies, you will not be disturbed.

IV.

When you are going to take in hand any act, remind yourself what kind of an act it is. If you are going to bathe, place before yourself what happens in the bath: some splashing the water, others pushing against one another, others abusing one another, and some stealing: and thus with more safety you will undertake the matter, if you say to yourself, I now intend to bathe, and to maintain my will in a manner conformable to nature. And so you will do in every act: for thus if any hindrance to bathing shall happen, let this thought be ready: it was not this only that I intended, but I intended also to maintain my will in a way conformable to nature; but I shall not maintain it so, if I am vexed at what happens.

V.

Men are disturbed not by the things which happen, but by the opinions about the things: for example, death is nothing terrible, for if it were, it would have seemed so to Socrates; for the opinion about death, that it is terrible, is the terrible thing. When then we are impeded or disturbed or grieved, let us never blame others, but ourselves, that is, our opinions. It is the act of an ill-instructed man to blame others for his own bad condition; it is the act of one who has begun to be instructed, to lay the blame on himself; and of one whose instruction is completed, neither to blame another, nor himself.

VI.

Be not elated at any advantage (excellence), which belongs to another. If a horse when he is elated should

I am beautiful, one might endure it. But when you are elated, and say, I have a beautiful horse, you must know that you are elated at having a good horse.[1] What then is your own? The use of appearances. Consequently when in the use of appearances you are conformable to nature, then you will be elated, for then you will be elated at something good which is your own.

VII.

As on a voyage when the vessel has reached a port, if you go out to get water, it is an amusement by the way to pick up a shell fish or some bulb, but your thoughts ought to be directed to the ship, and you ought to be constantly watching if the captain should call, and then you must throw away all those things, that you may not be bound and pitched into the ship like sheep: so in life also, if there be given to you instead of a little bulb and a shell a wife and child, there will be nothing to prevent (you from taking them). But if the captain should call, run to the ship, and leave all those things without regard to them. But if you are old, do not even go far from the ship, lest when you are called you make default.

VIII.

Seek not that the things which happen[2] should happen as you wish; but wish the things which happen to be as they are, and you will have a tranquil flow of life.

IX.

Disease is an impediment to the body, but not to the will, unless the will itself chooses. Lameness is an impediment to the leg, but not to the will. And add this reflection on the occasion of every thing that happens; for you will find it an impediment to something else, but not to yourself.

[1] Upton proposes to read ἐφ' ἵππου ἀγαθῷ instead of ἐπὶ ἵππῳ ἀγαθῷ. The meaning then will be 'elated at something good which is in the horse.' I think that be is right.

[2] The text has τὰ γενόμενα: but it should be τὰ γινόμενα. See Upton's note.

X.

On the occasion of every accident (event) that befals you, remember to turn to yourself and inquire what power you have for turning it to use. If you see a fair man or a fair woman, you will find that the power to resist is temperance (continence). If labour (pain) be presented to you, you will find that it is endurance. If it be abusive words, you will find it to be patience. And if you have been thus formed to the (proper) habit, the appearances will not carry you along with them.

XI.

Never say about any thing, I have lost it, but say I have restored it. Is your child dead? It has been restored. Is your wife dead? She has been restored. Has your estate been taken from you? Has not then this also been restored? But he who has taken it from me is a bad man. But what is it to you, by whose hands the giver demanded it back? So long as he may allow you, take care of it as a thing which belongs to another, as travellers do with their inn.

XII.

If you intend to improve, throw away such thoughts as these: if I neglect my affairs, I shall not have the means of living: unless I chastise my slave, he will be bad. For it is better to die of hunger and so to be released from grief and fear than to live in abundance with perturbation; and it is better for your slave to be bad than for you to be unhappy.[1] Begin then from little things. Is the oil spilled? Is a little wine stolen? Say on the occasion, at such price is sold freedom from perturbation; at such price is sold tranquillity, but nothing is got for nothing. And when you call your slave, consider that it is possible that he does not hear; and if he does hear, that

[1] He means, Do not chastise your slave while you are in a passion, lest, while you are trying to correct him, and it is very doubtful whether you will succeed, you fall into a vice which is a man's great and only calamity. Schweig.

he will do nothing which you wish. But matters are not so well with him, but altogether well with you, that it should be in his power for you to be not disturbed.[1]

XIII.

If you would improve, submit to be considered without sense and foolish with respect to externals. Wish to be considered to know nothing: and if you shall seem to some to be a person of importance, distrust yourself. For you should know that it is not easy both to keep your will in a condition conformable to nature and (to secure) external things: but if a man is careful about the one, it is an absolute necessity that he will neglect the other.

XIV.

If you would have your children and your wife and your friends to live for ever, you are silly; for you would have the things which are not in your power to be in your power, and the things which belong to others to be yours. So if you would have your slave to be free from faults, you are a fool; for you would have badness not to be badness, but something else.[2] But if you wish not to fail in your desires, you are able to do that. Practise then this which you are able to do. He is the master of every man who has the power over the things, which another person wishes or does not wish, the power to confer them on him or to take them away. Whoever then wishes to be free, let him neither wish for any thing nor avoid anything which depends on others: if he does not observe this rule, he must be a slave.

[1] The passage seems to mean, that your slave has not the power of disturbing you, because you have the power of not being disturbed. See Upton's note on the text.

[2] Θέλειν is used here, as it often is among the Stoics, to 'wish absolutely,' 'to will.' When Epictetus says 'you would have badness not to be badness,' he means that 'badness' is in the will of him who has the badness, and as you wish to subject it to your will, you are a fool. It is your business, as far as you can, to improve the slave: you may wish this. It is his business to obey your instruction: this is what he ought to wish to do; but for him to will to do this, that lies in himself, not in you. Schweig.

XV.

Remember that in life you ought to behave as at a banquet. Suppose that something is carried round and is opposite to you. Stretch out your hand and take a portion with decency. Suppose that it passes by you. Do not detain it. Suppose that it is not yet come to you. Do not send your desire forward to it, but wait till it is opposite to you. Do so with respect to children, so with respect to a wife, so with respect to magisterial offices, so with respect to wealth, and you will be some time a worthy partner of the banquets of the gods. But if you take none of the things which are set before you, and even despise them, then you will be not only a fellow banqueter with the gods, but also a partner with them in power. For by acting thus Diogenes and Heracleitus and those like them were deservedly divine, and were so called.

XVI.

When you see a person weeping in sorrow either when a child goes abroad or when he is dead, or when the man has lost his property, take care that the appearance do not hurry you away with it, as if he were suffering in external things.[1] But straightway make a distinction in your own mind, and be in readiness to say, it is not that which has happened that afflicts this man, for it does not afflict another, but it is the opinion about this thing which afflicts the man. So far as words then do not be unwilling to show him sympathy,[2] and even if it happens so, to lament with him. But take care that you do not lament internally also.

[1] This is obscure. 'It is true that the man is wretched, not because of the things external which have happened to him, but through the fact that he allows himself to be affected so much by external things which are placed out of his power.' Schweig.

[2] It has been objected to Epictetus that he expresses no sympathy with those who suffer sorrow. But here he tells you to show sympathy, a thing which comforts most people. But it would be contrary to his teaching, if he told you to suffer mentally with another.

XVII.

Remember that thou art an actor in a play,[1] of such a kind as the teacher (author)[2] may choose; if short, of a short one; if long, of a long one: if he wishes you to act the part of a poor man, see that you act the part naturally; if the part of a lame man, of a magistrate, of a private person, (do the same). For this is your duty, to act well the part that is given to you; but to select the part, belongs to another.

XVIII.

When a raven has croaked inauspiciously, let not the appearance hurry you away with it; but straightway make a distinction in your mind and say, None of these things is signified to me, but either to my poor body, or to my small property, or to my reputation, or to my children or to my wife: but to me all significations are auspicious if I choose. For whatever of these things results, it is in my power to derive benefit from it.

XIX.

You can be invincible, if you enter into no contest in which it is not in your power to conquer. Take care then when you observe a man honoured before others or possessed of great power or highly esteemed for any reason, not to suppose him happy, and be not carried away by the appearance. For if the nature of the good is in our power, neither envy nor jealousy will have a place in us. But you yourself will not wish to be a general or senator (πρύτανις) or consul, but a free man: and there is only one way to this, to despise (care not for) the things which are not in our power.

XX.

Remember that it is not he who reviles you or strikes you, who insults you, but it is your opinion about these things as being insulting. When then a man irritates you, you must know that it is your own opinion which

[1] Compare Antoninus, xi. 6, xii. 36.
[2] Note, ed. Schweig.

has irritated you. Therefore especially try not to be carried away by the appearance. For if you once gain time and delay, you will more easily master yourself.

XXI.

Let death and exile and every other thing which appears dreadful be daily before your eyes; but most of all death: and you will never think of any thing mean nor will you desire any thing extravagantly.

XXII.

If you desire philosophy, prepare yourself from the beginning to be ridiculed, to expect that many will sneer at you, and say, He has all at once returned to us as a philosopher; and whence does he get this supercilious look for us? Do you not show a supercilious look; but hold on to the things which seem to you best as one appointed by God to this station. And remember that if you abide in the same principles, these men who first ridiculed will afterwards admire you: but if you shall have been overpowered by them, you will bring on yourself double ridicule.

XXIII.

If it should ever happen to you to be turned to externals in order to please some person, you must know that you have lost your purpose in life.[1] Be satisfied then in every thing with being a philosopher; and if you wish to seem also to any person to be a philosopher, appear so to yourself, and you will be able to do this.

XXIV.

Let not these thoughts afflict you, I shall live unhonoured and be nobody nowhere. For if want of honour (*ἀτιμία*) is an evil, you cannot be in evil through the means (fault) of another any more than you can be involved in any thing base. Is it then your business to obtain the rank of a magistrate, or to be received at a banquet? By no means. How then can this be want of

[1] 'If I yet pleased men, I should not be the servant of Christ.' Gal. i. 10. Mrs. Carter.

honor (dishonor)? And how will you be nobody nowhere, when you ought to be somebody in those things only which are in your power, in which indeed it is permitted to you to be a man of the greatest worth? But your friends will be without assistance! What do you mean by being without assistance? They will not receive money from you, nor will you make them Roman-citizens. Who then told you that these are among the things which are in our power, and not in the power of others? And who can give to another what he has not himself? Acquire money then, your friends say, that we also may have something. If I can acquire money and also keep myself modest, and faithful and magnanimous, point out the way, and I will acquire it. But if you ask me to lose the things which are good and my own, in order that you may gain the things which are not good, see how unfair and silly you are. Besides, which would you rather have, money or a faithful and modest friend? For this end then rather help me to be such a man, and do not ask me to do this by which I shall lose that character. But my country, you say, as far as it depends on me, will be without my help. I ask again, what help do you mean? It will not have porticoes or baths through you.[1] And what does this mean? For it is not furnished with shoes by means of a smith, nor with arms by means of a shoemaker. But it is enough if every man fully discharges the work that is his own: and if you provided it with another citizen faithful and modest, would you not be useful to it? Yes. Then you also cannot be useless to it. What place then, you say, shall I hold in the city? Whatever you can, if you maintain at the same time your fidelity and modesty. But if when you wish to be useful to the state, you shall lose these qualities, what profit could you be to it, if you were made shameless and faithless?

XXV.

Has any man been preferred before you at a banquet, or in being saluted, or in being invited to a consultation? If these things are good, you ought to rejoice that he has obtained them: but if bad, be not grieved because you

[1] See the text.

have not obtained them; and remember that you cannot, if you do not the same things in order to obtain what is not in our own power, be considered worthy of the same (equal) things. For how can a man obtain an equal share with another when he does not visit a man's doors as that other man does, when he does not attend him when he goes abroad, as the other man does; when he does not praise (flatter) him as another does? You will be unjust then and insatiable, if you do not part with the price, in return for which those things are sold, and if you wish to obtain them for nothing. Well, what is the price of lettuces? An obolus [1] perhaps. If then a man gives up the obolus, and receives the lettuces, and if you do not give up the obolus and do not obtain the lettuces, do not suppose that you receive less than he who has got the lettuces; for as he has the lettuces, so you have the obolus which you did not give. In the same way then in the other matter also you have not been invited to a man's feast, for you did not give to the host the price at which the supper is sold; but he sells it for praise (flattery), he sells it for personal attention. Give then the price,[2] if it is for your interest, for which it is sold. But if you wish both not to give the price and to obtain the things, you are insatiable and silly. Have you nothing then in place of the supper? You have indeed, you have the not flattering of him, whom you did not choose to flatter; you have the not enduring [3] of the man when he enters the room.

XXVI.

We may learn the wish (will) of nature from the things in which we do not differ from one another: for instance, when your neighbour's slave has broken his cup, or any thing else, we are ready to say forthwith, that it is one of the things which happen. You must know then that when your cup also is broken, you ought to think as you did when your neighbour's cup was broken. Transfer this reflection to greater things also. Is another man's child or wife dead? There is no one who would not say, this

[1] The sixth part of a drachma. [2] 'Price' is here τὸ διαφέρον.
[3] See Schweig.'s note.

is an event incident to man. But when a man's own child or wife is dead, forthwith he calls out, Wo to me, how wretched I am. But we ought to remember how we feel when we hear that it has happened to others.

XXVII.

As a mark is not set up for the purpose of missing the aim, so neither does the nature of evil exist in the world.[1]

XXVIII.

If any person was intending to put your body in the power of any man whom you fell in with on the way, you would be vexed: but that you put your understanding in the power of any man whom you meet, so that if he should revile you, it is disturbed and troubled, are you not ashamed at this?

XXIX.[2]

In every act observe the things which come first, and those which follow it; and so proceed to the act. If you do not, at first you will approach it with alacrity, without having thought of the things which will follow; but afterwards, when certain base (ugly) things have shewn themselves, you will be ashamed. A man wishes to conquer at the Olympic games. I also wish indeed, for it

[1] This passage is explained in the commentary of Simplicius, (xxxiv., in Schweig.'s ed. xxvii. p. 264), and Schweighaeuser agrees with the explanation, which is this: Nothing in the world (universe) can exist or be done (happen) which in its proper sense, in itself and in its nature is bad; for every thing is and is done by the wisdom and will of God and for the purpose which he intended: but to miss a mark is to fail in an intention; and as a man does not set up a mark, or does not form a purpose for the purpose of missing the mark or the purpose, so it is absurd (inconsistent) to say that God has a purpose or design, and that he purposed or designed anything which in itself and in its nature is bad. The commentary of Simplicius is worth reading. But how many will read it? Perhaps one in a million.

[2] 'Compare iii. 15, from which all this passage has been transferred to the Encheiridion by the copyists.' Upton. On which Schweighaeuser remarks, 'Why should we not say by Arrian, who composed the Encheiridion from the Discourses of Epictetus?' See the notes of Upton and Schweig. on some differences in the readings of the passage in iii. 15, and in this passage.

is a fine thing. But observe both the things which come first, and the things which follow; and then begin the act. You must do every thing according to rule, eat according to strict orders, abstain from delicacies, exercise yourself as you are bid at appointed times, in heat, in cold, you must not drink cold water, nor wine as you choose; in a word, you must deliver yourself up to the exercise master as you do to the physician, and then proceed to the contest. And sometimes you will strain the hand, put the ankle out of joint, swallow much dust, sometimes be flogged, and after all this be defeated. When you have considered all this, if you still choose, go to the contest: if you do not, you will behave like children, who at one time play at wrestlers, another time as flute players, again as gladiators, then as trumpeters, then as tragic actors: so you also will be at one time an athlete, at another a gladiator, then a rhetorician, then a philosopher, but with your whole soul you will be nothing at all; but like an ape you imitate every thing that you see, and one thing after another pleases you. For you have not undertaken any thing with consideration, nor have you surveyed it well; but carelessly and with cold desire. Thus some who have seen a philosopher and having heard one speak, as Euphrates speaks,—and who can speak as he does?—they wish to be philosophers themselves also. My man, first of all consider what kind of thing it is: and then examine your own nature, if you are able to sustain the character. Do you wish to be a pentathlete or a wrestler? Look at your arms, your thighs, examine your loins. For different men are formed by nature for different things. Do you think that if you do these things, you can eat in the same manner, drink in the same manner, and in the same manner loathe certain things? You must pass sleepless nights, endure toil, go away from your kinsmen, be despised by a slave, in every thing have the inferior part, in honour, in office, in the courts of justice, in every little matter. Consider these things, if you would exchange for them, freedom from passions, liberty, tranquillity. If not, take care that, like little children, you be not now a philosopher, then a servant of the publicani, then a rhetorician, then a procurator (manager) for Caesar. These things are not consistent. You must be one man, either good or bad. You must either cultivate your own ruling faculty, or external things; you must either exercise your skill on internal things or on external things; that is you must either maintain the position of a philosopher or that of a common person.

XXX.

Duties are universally measured by relations (ταῖς σχέσεσι). Is a man a father? The precept is to take care of him, to yield to him in all things, to submit when he is reproachful, when he inflicts blows. But suppose that he is a bad father. Were you then by nature made akin to a good father? No; but to a father. Does a brother wrong you? Maintain then your own position towards him, and do not examine what he is doing, but what you must do that your will shall be conformable to nature. For another will not damage you, unless you choose: but you will be damaged then when you shall think that you are damaged. In this way then you will discover your duty from the relation of a neighbour, from that of a citizen, from that of a general, if you are accustomed to contemplate the relations.

XXXI.

As to piety towards the Gods you must know that this is the chief thing, to have right opinions about them, to think that they exist, and that they administer the All well and justly; and you must fix yourself in this principle (duty), to obey them, and to yield to them in every thing which happens, and voluntarily to follow it as being accomplished by the wisest intelligence. For if you do so, you will never either blame the Gods, nor will you accuse them of neglecting you. And it is not possible for this to be done in any other way than by withdrawing from the things which are not in our power, and by placing the good and the evil only in those things which are in our power. For if you think that any of the things which are not in our power is good or bad, it is absolutely necessary that, when you do not obtain what you wish, and when you fall into those things which you do not wish, you will find fault and hate those who are the cause of them; for every animal is formed by nature to this, to fly from and to turn from the things which appear harmful and the things which are the cause of the harm, but to follow and admire the things which are useful and the causes of the useful. It is impossible then for a person who thinks that he is harmed to be delighted with that which he thinks to be the cause of the harm, as it is also impossible to be pleased with the harm itself. For this reason also a father is reviled by his son, when he gives no part to his son of the things which are considered to be good: and it was this which made Polynices and Eteocles[1] enemies, the opinion that royal power was a good. It is for this reason that the cultivator of the earth reviles the Gods, for this reason the sailor does, and the merchant, and for this reason those who lose their wives and their children. For where the useful (your interest) is, there also piety is.[2] Consequently he who takes care to desire as he ought and to avoid (ἐκκλίνειν) as he ought, at the same time also cares after piety. But to make libations and to sacrifice and to offer first fruits according to the custom of our fathers, purely and not meanly nor carelessly nor scantily nor above our ability, is a thing which belongs to all to do.

XXXII.

When you have recourse to divination, remember that you do not know how it will turn out, but that you are come to inquire from the diviner. But of what kind it is, you know when you come, if indeed you are a philo-

[1] See ii. 22, 13, iv. 5, 9.

[2] 'It is plain enough that the philosopher does not say this, that the reckoning of our private advantage ought to be the sole origin and foundation of piety towards God.' Schweig., and he proceeds to explain the sentence, which at first appears rather obscure. Perhaps Arrian intends to say that the feeling of piety coincides with the opinion of the useful, the profitable; and that the man who takes care to desire as he ought to do and to avoid as he ought to do, thus also cares after piety, and so he will secure his interest (the profitable) and he will not be discontented.

In i. 27, 14 (p. 81) it is said ἐὰν μὴ ἐν τῷ αὐτῷ ᾖ τὸ εὐσεβὲς καὶ συμφέρον, οὐ δύναται σωθῆναι τὸ εὐσεβὲς ἔν τινι. This is what is said here (s. 31).

sopher. For if it is any of the things which are not in our power, it is absolutely necessary that it must be neither good nor bad. Do not then bring to the diviner desire or aversion (ἔκκλισιν): if you do, you will approach him with fear. But having determined in your mind that every thing which shall turn out (result) is indifferent, and does not concern you, and whatever it may be, for it will be in your power to use it well, and no man will hinder this, come then with confidence to the Gods as your advisers. And then when any advice shall have been given, remember whom you have taken as advisers, and whom you will have neglected, if you do not obey them. And go to divination, as Socrates said that you ought, about those matters in which all the inquiry has reference to the result, and in which means are not given either by reason nor by any other art for knowing the thing which is the subject of the inquiry. Wherefore when we ought to share a friend's danger or that of our country, you must not consult the diviner whether you ought to share it. For even if the diviner shall tell you that the signs of the victims are unlucky, it is plain that this is a token of death or mutilation of part of the body or of exile. But reason prevails that even with these risks we should share the dangers of our friend and of our country. Therefore attend to the greater diviner, the Pythian God, who ejected from the temple him who did not assist his friend when he was being murdered.[1]

XXXIII.

Immediately prescribe some character and some form to yourself, which you shall observe both when you are alone and when you meet with men.

And let silence be the general rule, or let only what is necessary be said, and in few words. And rarely and when the occasion calls we shall say something; but about none of the common subjects, not about gladiators, nor horse races, nor about athletes, nor about eating or drinking, which are the usual subjects; and

[1] The story is told by Aelian (iii. c. 44), and by Simplicius in his commentary on the Encheiridion (p. 411, ed. Schweig.). Upton.

especially not about men, as blaming them or praising them, or comparing them. If then you are able, bring over by your conversation the conversation of your associates to that which is proper; but if you should happen to be confined to the company of strangers, be silent.

Let not your laughter be much, nor on many occasions, nor excessive.

Refuse altogether to take an oath, if it is possible: if it is not, refuse as far as you are able.

Avoid banquets which are given by strangers[1] and by ignorant persons. But if ever there is occasion to join in them, let your attention be carefully fixed, that you slip not into the manners of the vulgar (the uninstructed). For you must know, that if your companion be impure, he also who keeps company with him must become impure, though he should happen to be pure.

Take (apply) the things which relate to the body as far as the bare use, as food, drink, clothing, house, and slaves: but exclude every thing which is for show or luxury.

As to pleasure with women, abstain as far as you can before marriage: but if you do indulge in it, do it in the way which is conformable to custom.[2] Do not however be disagreeable to those who indulge in these pleasures, or reprove them; and do not often boast that you do not indulge in them yourself.

If a man has reported to you, that a certain person speaks ill of you, do not make any defence (answer) to what has been told you: but reply, The man did not know the rest of my faults, for he would not have mentioned these only.

It is not necessary to go to the theatres often: but if there is ever a proper occasion for going, do not show yourself as being a partisan of any man except yourself, that is, desire only that to be done which is done, and for him only to gain the prize who gains the prize; for in this way you will meet with no hindrance. But abstain entirely from shouts and laughter at any (thing

[1] 'Convivia cum hominibus extraneis et rudibus, disciplina non imbutis' is the Latin version.

[2] The text is ὡς νόμιμον: and the Latin explanation is 'qua fas est uti; qua uti absque flagitio licet.'

or person), or violent emotions. And when you are come away, do not talk much about what has passed on the stage, except about that which may lead to your own improvement. For it is plain, if you do talk much that you admired the spectacle (more than you ought).[1]

Do not go to the hearing of certain persons' recitations nor visit them readily.[2] But if you do attend, observe gravity and sedateness, and also avoid making yourself disagreeable.

When you are going to meet with any person, and particularly one of those who are considered to be in a superior condition, place before yourself what Socrates or Zeno would have done in such circumstances, and you will have no difficulty in making a proper use of the occasion.

When you are going to any of those who are in great power, place before yourself that you will not find the man at home, that you will be excluded, that the door will not be opened to you, that the man will not care about you. And if with all this it is your duty to visit him, bear what happens, and never say to yourself that it was not worth the trouble. For this is silly, and marks the character of a man who is offended by externals.

In company take care not to speak much and excessively about your own acts or dangers: for as it is pleasant to you to make mention of your own dangers, it is not so pleasant to others to hear what has happened to you. Take care also not to provoke laughter; for this is a slippery way towards vulgar habits, and is also adapted to diminish the respect of your neighbours. It is a dangerous habit also to approach obscene talk. When then any thing of this kind happens, if there is a good opportunity, rebuke the man who has proceeded to this talk: but if there is not an opportunity, by your silence at least, and blushing and expression of dissatisfaction by your countenance, show plainly that you are displeased at such talk.

[1] To admire (θαυμάζειν) is contrary to the precept of Epictetus; i. 29, ii. 6, iii. 20. Upton.

[2] Such recitations were common at Rome, when authors read their works and invited persons to attend. These recitations are often mentioned in the letters of the younger Pliny. See Epictetus, iii. 23.

XXXIV.

If you have received the impression (φαντασίαν) of any pleasure, guard yourself against being carried away by it; but let the thing wait for you, and allow yourself a certain delay on your own part. Then think of both times, of the time when you will enjoy the pleasure, and of the time after the enjoyment of the pleasure when you will repent and will reproach yourself. And set against these things how you will rejoice if you have abstained from the pleasure, and how you will commend yourself. But if it seem to you seasonable to undertake (do) the thing, take care that the charm of it, and the pleasure, and the attraction of it shall not conquer you: but set on the other side the consideration how much better it is to be conscious that you have gained this victory.

XXXV.

When you have decided that a thing ought to be done and are doing it, never avoid being seen doing it, though the many shall form an unfavourable opinion about it. For if it is not right to do it, avoid doing the thing; but if it is right, why are you afraid of those who shall find fault wrongly?

XXXVI.

As the proposition it is either day or it is night is of great importance for the disjunctive argument, but for the conjunctive is of no value,[1] so in a symposium (entertainment) to select the larger share is of great value for the body, but for the maintenance of the social feeling is worth nothing. When then you are eating with another, remember to look not only to the value for the body of the things set before you, but also to the value of the behaviour towards the host which ought to be observed.[2]

[1] Compare i. 25, 11, etc.
[2] See the note of Schweig. on xxxvi.

XXXVII.

If you have assumed a character above your strength, you have both acted in this matter in an unbecoming way, and you have neglected that which you might have fulfilled.

XXXVIII.

In walking about as you take care not to step on a nail or to sprain your foot, so take care not to damage your own ruling faculty: and if we observe this rule in every act, we shall undertake the act with more security.

XXXIX.

The measure of possession (property) is to every man the body, as the foot is of the shoe.[1] If then you stand on this rule (the demands of the body), you will maintain the measure: but if you pass beyond it, you must then of necessity be hurried as it were down a precipice. As also in the matter of the shoe, if you go beyond the (necessities of the) foot, the shoe is gilded, then of a purple colour, then embroidered:[2] for there is no limit to that which has once passed the true measure.

XL.

Women forthwith from the age of fourteen[3] are called by the men mistresses (κυρίαι, dominae). Therefore since they see that there is nothing else that they can obtain, but only the power of lying with men, they begin to decorate themselves, and to place all their hopes in this.

[1] Cui non conveniet sua res, ut calceus olim,
Si pede major erit, subvertet; si minor, uret.
Horat. Epp. i. 10, 42, and Epp. i. 7, 98.

[2] The word is κεντητόν 'acu pictum,' ornamented with needlework.

[3] Fourteen was considered the age of puberty in Roman males, but in females the age of twelve (Justin. Inst. I. tit. 22). Compare Gaius, i. 196.

It is worth our while then to take care that they may know that they are valued (by men) for nothing else than appearing (being) decent and modest and discreet.

XLI.

It is a mark of a mean capacity to spend much time on the things which concern the body, such as much exercise, much eating, much drinking, much easing of the body, much copulation. But these things should be done as subordinate things: and let all your care be directed to the mind.

XLII.[1]

When any person treats you ill or speaks ill of you, remember that he does this or says this because he thinks that it is his duty. It is not possible then for him to follow that which seems right to you, but that which seems right to himself. Accordingly if he is wrong in his opinion, he is the person who is hurt, for he is the person who has been deceived; for if a man shall suppose the true conjunction[2] to be false, it is not the conjunction which is hindered, but the man who has been deceived about it. If you proceed then from these opinions, you will be mild in temper to him who reviles you: for say on each occasion, It seemed so to him.

XLIII.

Every thing has two handles, the one by which it may be borne, the other by which it may not. If your brother acts unjustly, do not lay hold of the act by that handle wherein he acts unjustly, for this is the handle which cannot be borne: but lay hold of the other, that he is your brother, that he was nurtured with you, and you will lay hold of the thing by that handle by which it can be borne.

[1] See Mrs. C.'s note, in which she says 'Epictetus seems to be in part mistaken here,' etc.; and I think that he is.

[2] τὸ ἀληθὲς συμπεπλεγμένον is rendered in the Latin by 'verum conjunctum.' Mrs. Carter renders it by 'a true proposition,' which I suppose to be the meaning.

XLIV.

These reasonings do not cohere: I am richer than you, therefore I am better than you; I am more eloquent than you, therefore I am better than you. On the contrary these rather cohere, I am richer than you, therefore my possessions are greater than yours: I am more eloquent than you, therefore my speech is superior to yours. But you are neither possession nor speech.

XLV.

Does a man bathe quickly (early)? do not say that he bathes badly, but that he bathes quickly. Does a man drink much wine? do not say that he does this badly, but say that he drinks much. For before you shall have determined the opinion,[1] how do you know whether he is acting wrong? Thus it will not happen to you to comprehend some appearances which are capable of being comprehended, but to assent to others.

XLVI.

On no occasion call yourself a philosopher, and do not speak much among the uninstructed about theorems (philosophical rules, precepts): but do that which follows from them. For example at a banquet do not say how a man ought to eat, but eat as you ought to eat. For remember that in this way Socrates[2] also altogether avoided ostentation: persons used to come to him and ask to be recommended by him to philosophers, and he used to take them to philosophers: so easily did he submit to being overlooked. Accordingly if any conversation should arise among uninstructed persons about any theorem, generally be silent; for there is great danger that you will immediately vomit up what you have not digested. And when a man shall say to you, that you know nothing, and you are not vexed, then be sure that you have begun the work (of philosophy). For even sheep do not vomit up

[1] Mrs. Carter translates this, "Unless you perfectly understand the principle [from which anyone acts]."

[2] See iii. 23, 22; iv. 8, 2.

their grass and show to the shepherds how much they have eaten; but when they have internally digested the pasture, they produce externally wool and milk. Do you also show not your theorems to the uninstructed, but show the acts which come from their digestion.

XLVII.

When at a small cost you are supplied with every thing for the body, do not be proud of this; nor, if you drink water, say on every occasion, I drink water. But consider first how much more frugal the poor are than we, and how much more enduring of labour. And if you ever wish to exercise yourself in labour and endurance, do it for yourself, and not for others: do not embrace statues.[1] But if you are ever very thirsty, take a draught of cold water, and spit it out, and tell no man.

XLVIII.

The condition and characteristic of an uninstructed person is this: he never expects from himself profit (advantage) nor harm, but from externals. The condition and characteristic of a philosopher is this: he expects all advantage and all harm from himself. The signs (marks) of one who is making progress are these: he censures no man, he praises no man, he blames no man, he accuses no man, he says nothing about himself as if he were somebody or knew something; when he is impeded at all or hindered, he blames himself: if a man praises him, he ridicules the praiser to himself: if a man censures him, he makes no defence: he goes about like weak persons, being careful not to move any of the things which are placed, before they are firmly fixed: he removes all desire from himself, and he transfers aversion (ἔκκλισιν) to those things only of the things within our power which are contrary to nature: he employs a moderate movement towards every thing: whether he is considered foolish or ignorant, he cares not: and in a word he watches himself as if he were an enemy and lying in ambush.

[1] See iii. 12.

XLIX.

When a man is proud because he can understand and explain the writings of Chrysippus, say to yourself, If Chrysippus had not written obscurely, this man would have had nothing to be proud of. But what is it that I wish? To understand Nature and to follow it. I inquire therefore who is the interpreter: and when I have heard that it is Chrysippus, I come to him (the interpreter). But I do not understand what is written, and therefore I seek the interpreter. And so far there is yet nothing to be proud of. But when I shall have found the interpreter, the thing that remains is to use the precepts (the lessons). This itself is the only thing to be proud of. But if I shall admire the exposition, what else have I been made unless a grammarian instead of a philosopher? except in one thing, that I am explaining Chrysippus instead of Homer. When then any man says to me, Read Chrysippus to me, I rather blush, when I cannot show my acts like to and consistent with his words.

L.

Whatever things (rules) are proposed[1] to you [for the conduct of life] abide by them, as if they were laws, as if you would be guilty of impiety if you transgressed any of them. And whatever any man shall say about you, do not attend to it: for this is no affair of yours. How long will you then still defer thinking yourself worthy of the best things, and in no matter transgressing the distinctive reason?[2] Have you accepted the theorems (rules), which it was your duty to agree to, and have you agreed to them? what teacher then do you still expect that you defer to him the correction of yourself? You are no longer a youth, but already a full-grown man. If then you are

[1] This may mean, 'what is proposed to you by philosophers,' and especially in this little book. Schweighaeuser thinks that it may mean 'what you have proposed to yourself:' but he is inclined to understand it simply, 'what is proposed above, or taught above.'

[2] τὸν διαιροῦντα λόγον. 'Eam partitionem rationis intelligo, qua initio dixit, Quaedam in potestate nostra esse, quaedam non esse.' Wolf.

negligent and slothful, and are continually making procrastination after procrastination, and proposal (intention) after proposal, and fixing day after day, after which you will attend to yourself, you will not know that you are not making improvement, but you will continue ignorant (uninstructed) both while you live and till you die. Immediately then think it right to live as a full-grown man, and one who is making proficiency, and let every thing which appears to you to be the best be to you a law which must not be transgressed. And if any thing laborious, or pleasant or glorious or inglorious be presented to you, remember that now is the contest, now are the Olympic games, and they cannot be deferred; and that it depends on one defeat and one giving way that progress is either lost or maintained. Socrates in this way became perfect, in all things improving himself, attending to nothing except to reason. But you, though you are not yet a Socrates, ought to live as one who wishes to be a Socrates.

LI.

The first and most necessary place (part, *τόπος*) in philosophy is the use of theorems (precepts, *θεωρήματα*), for instance, that we must not lie: the second part is that of demonstrations, for instance, How is it proved that we ought not to lie: the third is that which is confirmatory of these two and explanatory, for example, How is this a demonstration? For what is demonstration, what is consequence, what is contradiction, what is truth, what is falsehood? The third part (topic) is necessary on account of the second, and the second on account of the first; but the most necessary and that on which we ought to rest is the first. But we do the contrary. For we spend our time on the third topic, and all our earnestness is about it: but we entirely neglect the first. Therefore we lie; but the demonstration that we ought not to lie we have ready to hand.

LII.

In every thing (circumstance) we should hold these maxims ready to hand:

Lead me, O Zeus, and thou O Destiny,
The way that I am bid by you to go:
To follow I am ready. If I choose not,
I make myself a wretch, and still must follow.[1]

But whoso nobly yields unto necessity,
We hold him wise, and skill'd in things divine.[2]

And the third also: O Crito, if so it pleases the Gods, so let it be; Anytus and Melitus are able indeed to kill me, but they cannot harm me.[3]

[1] The first four verses are by the Stoic Cleanthes, the pupil of Zeno, and the teacher of Chrysippus. He was a native of Assus in Mysia; and Simplicius, who wrote his commentary on the Encheiridion in the sixth century, A.D., saw even at this late period in Assus a beautiful statue of Cleanthes erected by a decree of the Roman senate in honour of this excellent man. (Simplicius, ed. Schweig. p. 522.)

[2] The two second verses are from a play of Euripides, a writer who has supplied more verses for quotation than any antient tragedian.

[3] The third quotation is from the Criton of Plato. Socrates is the speaker. The last part is from the Apology of Plato, and Socrates is also the speaker. The words 'and the third also,' Schweighaeuser says, have been introduced from the commentary of Simplicius.

Simplicius concludes his commentary thus: Epictetus connects the end with the beginning, which reminds us of what was said in the beginning, that the man who places the good and the evil among the things which are in our power, and not in externals, will neither be compelled by any man nor ever injured.

FRAGMENTS OF EPICTETUS.

THESE Fragments are entitled "Epicteti Fragmenta maxime ex Ioanne Stobaeo, Antonio, et Maximo collecta" (ed. Schweig.). There are some notes and emendations on the Fragments; and a short dissertation on them by Schweighaeuser.

Nothing is known of Stobaeus nor of his time, except the fact that he has preserved some extracts of an ethical kind from the New Platonist Hierocles, who lived about the middle of the fifth century A.D.; and it is therefore concluded that Stobaeus lived after Hierocles. The fragments attributed to Epictetus are preserved by Stobaeus in his work entitled Ἀνθολόγιον, or Florilegium or Sermones.

Antonius Monachus, a Greek monk, also made a Florilegium, entitled Melissa (the bee). His date is uncertain, but it was certainly much later than the time of Stobaeus.

Maximus, also named the monk, and reverenced as a saint, is said to have been a native of Constantinople, and born about A.D. 580.

Some of the Fragments contained in the edition of Schweighaeuser are certainly not from Epictetus. Many of the fragments are obscure; but they are translated as accurately as I can translate them, and the reader must give to them such meaning as he can.

I.

The life which is implicated with fortune (depends on fortune) is like a winter torrent: for it is turbulent, and full of mud, and difficult to cross, and tyrannical, and noisy, and of short duration.

II.

A soul which is conversant with virtue is like an ever flowing source, for it is pure and tranquil and potable and sweet[1] and communicative (social), and rich and harmless and free from mischief.

III.

If you wish to be good, first believe that you are bad.

IV.

It is better to do wrong seldom and to own it, and to act right for the most part, than seldom to admit that you have done wrong and to do wrong often.

V.

Check (punish) your passions (πάθη), that you may not be punished by them.

VI.

Do not so much be ashamed of that (disgrace) which proceeds from men's opinion as fly from that which comes from the truth.

VII.

If you wish to be well spoken of, learn to speak well (of others): and when you have learned to speak well of them, try to act well, and so you will reap the fruit of being well spoken of.

VIII.

Freedom and slavery, the one is the name of virtue, and the other of vice: and both are acts of the will. But where there is no will, neither of them touches (affects)

[1] Consult the Lexicons for this sense of νόστιμος.

these things. But the soul is accustomed to be master of the body, and the things which belong to the body have no share in the will. For no man is a slave who is free in his will.[1]

IX.

It is an evil chain, fortune (a chain) of the body, and vice of the soul. For he who is loose (free) in the body, but bound in the soul is a slave: but on the contrary he who is bound in the body, but free (unbound) in the soul, is free.

X.

The bond of the body is loosened by nature through death, and by vice through money:[2] but the bond of the soul is loosened by learning, and by experience and by discipline.

XI.

If you wish to live without perturbation and with pleasure, try to have all who dwell with you good. And you will have them good, if you instruct the willing, and dismiss those who are unwilling (to be taught): for there will fly away together with those who have fled away both wickedness and slavery; and there will be left with those who remain with you goodness and liberty.

XII.

It is a shame for those who sweeten drink with the gifts of the bees, by badness to embitter reason which is the gift of the gods.

XIII.

No man who loves money, and loves pleasure, and loves fame, also loves mankind, but only he who loves virtue.

[1] See Schweig.'s note.

[2] "He does not say this 'that it is bad if a man by money should redeem himself from bonds,' but he means that 'even a bad man, if he has money, can redeem himself from the bonds of the body and so secure his liberty.'" Schweig.

XIV.

As you would not choose to sail in a large and decorated and gold-laden ship (or ship ornamented with gold), and to be drowned; so do not choose to dwell in a large and costly house and to be disturbed (by cares).

XV.

When we have been invited to a banquet, we take what is set before us: but if a guest should ask the host to set before him fish or sweet cakes, he would be considered to be an unreasonable fellow. But in the world we ask the Gods for what they do not give; and we do this though the things are many which they have given.

XVI.

They are amusing fellows, said he (Epictetus), who are proud of the things which are not in our power. A man says, I am better than you, for I possess much land, and you are wasting with hunger. Another says, I am of consular rank. Another says, I am a Procurator (ἐπίτροπος). Another, I have curly hair. But a horse does not say to a horse, I am superior to you, for I possess much fodder, and much barley, and my bits are of gold and my harness is embroidered: but he says, I am swifter than you. And every animal is better or worse from his own merit (virtue) or his own badness. Is there then no virtue in man only? and must we look to the hair, and our clothes and to our ancestors?

XVII.

The sick are vexed with the physician who gives them no advice, and think that he has despaired of them. But why should they not have the same feeling towards the philosopher, and think that he has despaired of their coming to a sound state of mind, if he says nothing at all that is useful to a man?

XVIII.

Those who are well constituted in the body endure both heat and cold: and so those who are well constituted in the soul endure both anger and grief and excessive joy and the other affects.

XIX.

Examine yourself whether you wish to be rich or to be happy. If you wish to be rich, you should know that it is neither a good thing nor at all in your power: but if you wish to be happy, you should know that it is both a good thing and in your power, for the one is a temporary loan of fortune, and happiness comes from the will.

XX.

As when you see a viper or an asp or a scorpion in an ivory or golden box, you do not on account of the costliness of the material love it or think it happy, but because the nature of it is pernicious, you turn away from it and loathe it; so when you shall see vice dwelling in wealth and in the swollen fulness of fortune, be not struck by the splendour of the material, but despise the false character of the morals.

XXI.

Wealth is not one of the good things; great expenditure is one of the bad; moderation (σωφροσύνη) is one of the good things. And moderation invites to frugality and the acquisition of good things: but wealth invites to great expenditure and draws us away from moderation. It is difficult then for a rich man to be moderate, or for a moderate man to be rich.[1]

[1] 'How hardly shall they that have riches enter the kingdom of God.' Mark x. 23 (Mrs. Carter). This expression in Mark sets forth the danger of riches, a fact which all men know who use their observation. In the next verse the truth is expressed in this form, 'How hard it is for them that trust in riches to enter into the kingdom of God.' The Stoics viewed wealth as among the things which are indifferent, neither good nor bad.

XXII.

As if you were begotten or born in a ship, you would not be eager to be the master of it (κυβερνήτης), so—.[1] For neither there (in the ship) will the ship naturally be connected with you, nor wealth in the other case; but reason is every where naturally connected with you. As then reason is a thing which naturally belongs to you and is born in you, consider this also as specially your own and take care of it.

XXIII.

If you had been born among the Persians, you would not have wished to live in Hellas (Greece), but to have lived in Persia happy: so if you are born in poverty, why do you seek to grow rich, and why do you not remain in poverty and be happy?[2]

[1] The other member of the comparison has been omitted by some accident in the MSS. Wolf in his Latin version supplied by conjecture the omission in this manner: 'ita neque in terris divitiae tibi expetendae sunt.' Schweig.

[2] To some persons the comparison will not seem apt. Also the notion that every man should be taught to rise above the condition in which he is born is, in the opinion of some persons, a better teaching. I think that it is not. Few persons have the talents and the character which enable them to rise from a low condition; and the proper lesson for them is to stay in the condition in which they are born and to be content with it. Those who have the power of rising from a low condition will rise whether they are advised to attempt it or not: and generally they will not be able to rise without doing something useful to society. Those who have ability sufficient to raise themselves from a low estate, and at the same time to do it to the damage of society, are perhaps only few, but certainly there are such persons. They rise by ability, by the use of fraud, by bad means almost innumerable. They gain wealth, they fill high places, they disturb society, they are plagues and pests, and the world looks on sometimes with stupid admiration until death removes the dazzling and deceitful image, and honest men breathe freely again

In the Church of England Catechism there are two answers to two questions, one on our duty to God, the other on our duty to our neighbour. Both the answers would be accepted by Epictetus, except such few words as were not applicable to the circumstances of his age. The second answer ends with the words 'to learn and labour to get mine own living and to do my duty in that state of life unto which it shall please God to call me.'

XXIV.

As it is better to lie compressed in a narrow bed and be healthy than to be tossed with disease on a broad couch, so also it is better to contract yourself within a small competence and to be happy than to have a great fortune and to be wretched.

XXV.

It is not poverty which produces sorrow, but desire; nor does wealth release from fear, but reason (the power of reasoning, λογισμός). If then you acquire this power of reasoning, you will neither desire wealth nor complain of poverty.

XXVI.

Neither is a horse elated nor proud of his manger and trappings and coverings, nor a bird of his little shreds of cloth and of his nest: but both of them are proud of their swiftness, one proud of the swiftness of the feet, and the other of the wings. Do you also then not be greatly proud of your food and dress and, in short, of any external things, but be proud of your integrity and good deeds (εὐποιΐα).

XXVII.

To live well differs from living extravagantly: for the first comes from moderation and a sufficiency (αὐταρκείας) and good order and propriety and frugality; but the other comes from intemperance and luxury and want of order and want of propriety. And the end (the consequence) of the one is true praise, but of the other blame. If then you wish to live well, do not seek to be commended for profuse expenditure.

XXVIII.

Let the measure to you of all food and drink be the first satisfying of the desire; and let the food and the pleasure be the desire (appetite) itself: and you will neither take more than is necessary, nor will you want cooks, and you will be satisfied with the drink that comes in the way.

XXIX.

Make your manner of eating neither luxurious nor gloomy, but lively and frugal, that the soul may not be perturbed through being deceived by the pleasures of the body, and that it may despise them; and that the soul may not be injured by the enjoyment of present luxury, and the body may not afterwards suffer from disease.[1]

XXX.

Take care that the food which you put into the stomach does not fatten (nourish) you, but the cheerfulness of the mind: for the food is changed into excrement, and ejected, and the urine also flows out at the same time; but the cheerfulness, even if the soul be separated, remains always uncorrupted.[2]

XXXI.

In banquets remember that you entertain two guests, body and soul: and whatever you shall have given to the body you soon eject: but what you shall have given to the soul, you keep always.

XXXII.

Do not mix anger with profuse expenditure and serve them up to your guests. Profusion which fills the body is quickly gone; but anger sinks into the soul and remains for a long time. Consider then that you be not transported with anger and insult your guests at a great expense; but rather please them with frugality and by gentle behaviour.[3]

[1] Mrs. Carter says, 'I have not translated this fragment, because I do not understand it.' Schweighaeuser says also that he does not understand it. I have given what may be the meaning; but it is not an exact translation, which in the present state of the text is not possible.

[2] This fragment is perhaps more corrupt than XXIX. See Schweig.'s note. I see no sense in *ἔπαινος*, and I have used the word *οὖρος*, which is a possible reading. The conclusion appears quite unintelligible.

[3] See Schweig.'s note.

XXXIII.

In your banquets (meals) take care that those who serve (your slaves) are not more than those who are served; for it is foolish for many souls (persons) to wait on a few couches (seats).

XXXIV.

It is best if even in the preparations for a feast you take a part of the labour, and at the enjoyment of the food, while you are feasting, you share with those who serve the things which are before you. But if such behaviour be unsuitable to the occasion, remember that you are served when you are not labouring by those who are labouring, when you are eating by those who are not eating, when you are drinking by those who are not drinking, while you are talking by those who are silent, while you are at ease by those who are under constraint; and if you remember this, you will neither being heated with anger be guilty of any absurdity yourself, nor by irritating another will you cause any mischief.[1]

XXXV.

Quarrelling and contention are every where foolish, and particularly in talk over wine they are unbecoming: for a man who is drunk could not teach a man who is sober, nor on the other hand could a drunken man be convinced by a sober man. But where there is not sobriety, it will appear that to no purpose have you laboured for the result of persuasion.[2]

XXXVI.

Grasshoppers (cicadae) are musical: snails have no voice. Snails have pleasure in being moist, but grasshoppers in being dry. Next the dew invites forth the snails and for this they crawl out: but on the contrary the sun when he is hot, rouses the grasshoppers and they sing in the sun. Therefore if you wish to be a musical

[1] I am not sure about the exact meaning of the conclusion. See Schweig.'s note.

[2] This is not a translation of the conclusion. Perhaps it is something like the meaning. See Schweig.'s note.

man and to harmonize well with others, when over the cups the soul is bedewed with wine, at that time do not permit the soul to go forth and to be polluted; but when in company (parties) it is fired by reason, then bid her to utter oracular words and to sing the oracles of justice.

XXXVII.

Examine in three ways him who is talking with you, as superior, or as inferior, or as equal: and if he is superior, you should listen to him and be convinced by him: but if he is inferior, you should convince him; if he is equal, you should agree with him; and thus you will never be guilty of being quarrelsome.

XXXVIII.

It is better by assenting to truth to conquer opinion, than by assenting to opinion to be conquered by truth.

XXXIX.

If you seek truth, you will not seek by every means to gain a victory; and if you have found truth, you will have the gain of not being defeated.

XL.

Truth conquers with itself; but opinion conquers among those who are external.[1]

XLI.

It is better to live with one free man and to be without fear and free, than to be a slave with many.

XLII.

What you avoid suffering, do not attempt to make others suffer. You avoid slavery: take care that others are not your slaves. For if you endure to have a slave, you appear to be a slave yourself first. For vice has no community with virtue, nor freedom with slavery.

[1] This is not clear.

XLIII.

As he who is in health would not choose to be served (ministered to) by the sick, nor for those who dwell with him to be sick, so neither would a free man endure to be served by slaves, or for those who live with him to be slaves.

XLIV.

Whoever you are who wish to be not among the number of slaves, release yourself from slavery: and you will be free, if you are released from desire. For neither Aristides nor Epaminondas nor Lycurgus through being rich and served by slaves were named the one just, the other a god, and the third a saviour, but because they were poor and delivered Hellas (Greece) from slavery.[1]

XLV.

If you wish your house to be well managed, imitate the Spartan Lycurgus. For as he did not fence his city with walls, but fortified the inhabitants by virtue and preserved the city always free;[2] so do you not cast around (your house) a large court and raise high towers, but strengthen the dwellers by good will and fidelity and friendship, and then nothing harmful will enter it, not even if the whole band of wickedness shall array itself against it.

XLVI.

Do not hang your house round with tablets and pictures, but decorate it with moderation (σωφροσύνη): for the one is of a foreign (unsuitable) kind, and a temporary deception of the eyes; but the other is a natural and indelible, and perpetual ornament of the house.

[1] It is observed that the term 'just' applies to Aristides; the term 'god' was given to Lycurgus by the Pythia or Delphic oracle; the name 'saviour' by his own citizens to Epaminondas.

[2] Schweig. quotes Polybius ix. 10, 1, 'a city is not adorned by external things, but by the virtue of those who dwell in it.' Alcaeus says, 22, Bergk, Poetae Lyrici Graeci, 1843,—

οὐ λίθοι
τειχέων εὖ δεδομάμενοι,
ἀλλ' ἄνδρες πόλιος πύργος ἀρήϊοι

XLVII.

Instead of an herd of oxen, endeavour to assemble herds of friends in your house.

XLVIII.

As a wolf resembles a dog, so both a flatterer, and an adulterer and a parasite, resemble a friend. Take care then that instead of watch dogs you do not without knowing it let in mischievous wolves.

XLIX.

To be eager that your house should be admired by being whitened with gypsum, is the mark of a man who has no taste: but to set off (decorate) our morals by the goodness of our communication (social habits) is the mark of a man who is a lover of beauty and a lover of man.

L.

If you begin by admiring little things,[1] you will not be thought worthy of great things: but if you despise the little, you will be greatly admired.

LI.

Nothing is smaller (meaner) than love of pleasure, and love of gain and pride. Nothing is superior to magnanimity, and gentleness, and love of mankind, and beneficence.

LII.

They bring forward (they name, they mention) the peevish philosophers (the Stoics), whose opinion it is that pleasure is not a thing conformable to nature, but is a thing which is consequent on the things which are conformable to nature, as justice, temperance, freedom. What

[1] Schweig. says that in the reading ἐὰν θαυμάζῃς τὰ μικρὰ πρῶτον the word πρῶτον is wanting in four MSS., and that Schow omitted πρῶτον, and that he has followed Schow. But πρῶτον is in Schweig.'s text.

then? is the soul pleased and made tranquil by the pleasures of the body which are smaller, as Epicurus says; and is it not pleased with its own good things, which are the greatest? And indeed nature has given to me modesty, and I blush much when I think of saying any thing base (indecent). This motion (feeling) does not permit me to make (consider) pleasure the good and the end (purpose) of life.[1]

LIII.

In Rome the women have in their hands Plato's Polity (the Republic), because it allows (advises) the women to be common, for they attend only to the words of Plato, not to his meaning. Now he does not recommend marriage and one man to cohabit with one woman, and then that the women should be common: but he takes away such a marriage, and introduces another kind of marriage. And in fine, men are pleased with finding excuses for their faults. Yet philosophy says that we ought not to stretch out even a finger without a reason.[2]

LIV.

Of pleasures those which occur most rarely give the greatest delight.

LV.

If a man should transgress moderation, the things which give the greatest delight would become the things which give the least.

LVI.

It is just to commend Agrippinus for this reason, that though he was a man of the highest worth, he never praised himself; but even if another person praised him, he would blush. And he was such a man (Epictetus said) that he would write in praise of any thing disagreeable that befel him; if it was a fever, he would write of a fever; if he was disgraced, he would write of disgrace; if he were banished, of banishment. And on one occasion (he mentioned) when he was going to dine, a messenger

[1] See Schweig.'s note.

[2] See Schweig.'s note.

brought him news that Nero commanded him to go into banishment; on which Agrippinus said, Well then we will dine at Aricia.[1]

LVII.

Diogenes said that no labour was good, unless the end (purpose) of it was courage and strength (τόνος) of the soul, but not of the body.

LVIII.

As a true balance is neither corrected by a true balance nor judged by a false balance, so also a just judge is neither corrected by just judges nor is he judged (condemned) by unjust judges.

LIX.

As that which is straight does not need that which is straight, so neither does the just need that which is just.[2]

LX.

Do not give judgment in one court (of justice) before you have been tried yourself before justice.[3]

LXI.

If you wish to make your judgments just, listen not to (regard not) any of those who are parties (to the suit), nor to those who plead in it, but listen to justice itself.

LXII.

You will fail (stumble) least in your judgments, if you yourself fail (stumble) least in your life.

LXIII.

It is better when you judge justly to be blamed undeservedly by him who has been condemned than when you judge unjustly to be justly blamed by (before) nature.[4]

[1] See i. 1, note 13 and 14.
[2] Rather obscure, says Schweig. Compare Frag. lviii. and lxvi.
[3] Compare lviii. Schweig.
[4] See Schweig.'s note.

LXIV.

As the stone which tests the gold is not at all tested itself by the gold, so it is with him who has the faculty of judging.[1]

LXV.

It is shameful for the judge to be judged by others.

LXVI.

As nothing is straighter than that which is straight, so nothing is juster than that which is just.

LXVII.

Who among us does not admire the act of Lycurgus the Lacedaemonian? For after he was maimed in one of his eyes by one of the citizens, and the young man was delivered up to him by the people that he might punish him as he chose, Lycurgus spared him: and after instructing him and making him a good man he brought him into the theatre. When the Lacedaemonians expressed their surprise, Lycurgus said, I received from you this youth when he was insolent and violent: I restore him to you gentle and a good citizen.[2]

LXVIII.

Pittacus after being wronged by a certain person and having the power of punishing him let him go, saying, Forgiveness is better than revenge: for forgiveness is the sign of a gentle nature, but revenge the sign of a savage nature.[3]

[1] Schweig. suggests that ὁ λόγος has been omitted before the words ὁ τὸ κριτήριον ἔχων.
See the fragment of Chilo on the stone which tries gold. Bergk, Poetae Lyrici Graeci, ed. 1, p. 568.
[2] See Schweig.'s note.
[3] Pittacus was one of the seven wise men, as they are named. Some authorities state that he lived in the seventh century B.C. By this maxim he anticipated one of the Christian doctrines by six centuries.

LXIX.

But before every thing this is the act of nature to bind together and to fit together the movement towards the appearance of that which is becoming (fit) and useful.

LXX.

To suppose that we shall be easily despised by others, if we do not in every way do some damage to those who first show us their hostility, is the mark of very ignoble and foolish men: for (thus) we affirm that the man is considered to be contemptible because of his inability to do damage; but much rather is a man considered to be contemptible because of his inability to do what is good (useful).[1]

LXXI.

When you are attacking (or going to attack) any person violently and with threats, remember to say to yourself first, that you are (by nature) mild (gentle); and if you do nothing savage, you will continue to live without repentance and without blame.

LXXII.

A man ought to know that it is not easy for him to have an opinion (or fixed principle), if he does not daily say the same things, and hear the same things, and at the same time apply them to life.

LXXIII.

[Nicias was so fond of labour (assiduous) that he often asked his slaves, if he had bathed and if he had dined.][2]

[1] See Mrs. Carter's note, who could only translate part of this fragment: and Schweig.'s emendation and note.

[2] LXXIII.-LXXV.—Schweig. has inclosed these three fragments in [ ]. They are not from Epictetus, but from Plutarch's treatise εἰ πρεσβυτέρῳ πολιτευτέον.

LXXIV.

[The slaves of Archimedes used to drag him by force from his table of diagrams and anoint him; and Archimedes would then draw his figures on his own body when it had been anointed.]

LXXV.

[Lampis the shipowner being asked how he acquired his wealth, answered, With no difficulty, my great wealth; but my small wealth (my first gains), with much labour.]

LXXVI.

Solon having been asked by Periander over their cups (*παρὰ πότον*), since he happened to say nothing, Whether he was silent for want of words or because he was a fool, replied: No fool is able to be silent over his cups.[1]

LXXVII.

Attempt on every occasion to provide for nothing so much as that which is safe: for silence is safer than speaking. And omit speaking whatever is without sense and reason.

LXXVIII.

As the fire-lights in harbours by a few pieces of dry-wood raise a great flame and give sufficient help to ships which are wandering on the sea; so also an illustrious man in a state which is tempest-tossed, while he is himself satisfied with a few things does great services to his citizens.

LXXIX.

As if you attempted to manage a ship, you would certainly learn completely the steersman's art, [so if you would administer a state, learn the art of managing a state]. For it will be in your power, as in the first case to manage the whole ship, so in the second case also to manage the whole state.[2]

[1] See Schweig.'s note.

[2] See Schweig.'s note. There is evidently something omitted in the text, which omission is supplied by the words inclosed thus [ ]. Schweig. proposes to change *κυβερνᾷν* into *κυβιστᾶν*. See his remark on *πᾶσαν . . πόλιν*. Perhaps he is right.

LXXX.

If you propose to adorn your city by the dedication of offerings (monuments), first dedicate to yourself (decorate yourself with) the noblest offering of gentleness, and justice and beneficence.

LXXXI.

You will do the greatest services to the state, if you shall raise not the roofs of the houses, but the souls of the citizens: for it is better that great souls should dwell in small houses than for mean slaves to lurk in great houses.

LXXXII.

Do not decorate the walls of your house with the valuable stones from Euboea and Sparta; but adorn the minds (breasts) of the citizens and of those who administer the state with the instruction which comes from Hellas (Greece). For states are well governed by the wisdom (judgement) of men, but not by stone and wood.[1]

LXXXIII.

As, if you wished to breed lions, you would not care about the costliness of their dens, but about the habits of the animals; so, if you attempt to preside over your citizens, be not so anxious about the costliness of the buildings as careful about the manly character of those who dwell in them.

LXXXIV.[2]

As a skilful horse-trainer does not feed (only) the good colts and allow to starve those who are disobedient to the rein, but he feeds both alike, and chastises the one more

[1] The marbles of Carystus in Euboea and the marbles of Taenarum near Sparta were used by the Romans, and perhaps by the Greeks also, for architectural decoration. (Strabo, x. 446, and viii. 367, ed. Cas.) Compare Horace, Carm. ii. 18.

Non ebur neque aureum
Mea renidet in domo lacunar, etc.

[2] This fragment contains a lesson for the administration of a state. The good must be protected, and the bad must be improved by discipline and punishment.

and forces him to be equal to the other:[1] so also a careful man and one who is skilled in political power, attempts to treat well those citizens who have a good character, but does not will that those who are of a contrary character should be ruined at once; and he in no manner grudges both of them their food, but he teaches and urges on with more vehemence him who resists reason and law.

LXXXV.

As a goose is not frightened by cackling nor a sheep by bleating, so let not the clamour of a senseless multitude alarm you.

LXXXVI.[2]

As a multitude, when they without reason demand of you any thing of your own, do not disconcert you, so do not be moved from your purpose even by a rabble when they unjustly attempt to move you.

LXXXVII.

What is due to the state pay as quickly as you can, and you will never be asked for that which is not due.

LXXXVIII.

As the sun does not wait for prayers and incantations to be induced to rise, but immediately shines and is saluted by all: so do you also not wait for clappings of hands, and shouts and praise to be induced to do good, but be a doer of good voluntarily, and you will be beloved as much as the sun.

LXXXIX.

Neither should a ship rely on one small anchor, nor should life rest on a single hope.

XC.

We ought to stretch our legs and stretch our hopes only to that which is possible.

[1] I am not sure what *μέρει* means.

[2] See in the Index Graecitatis the word *δυσωπεῖν*.

XCI.

When Thales was asked what is most universal, he answered, Hope, for hope stays with those who have nothing else.

XCII.

It is more necessary to heal the soul than the body, for to die is better than to live a bad life.

XCIII.

Pyrrho used to say that there is no difference between dying and living: and a man said to him, Why then do you not die? Pyrrho replied, Because there is no difference.

XCIV.[1]

Admirable is nature, and, as Xenophon says, a lover of animated beings. The body then, which is of all things the most unpleasant and the most foul (dirty), we love and take care of; for if we were obliged for five days only to take care of our neighbour's body, we should not be able to endure it. Consider then what a thing it would be to rise in the morning and rub the teeth of another, and after doing some of the necessary offices to wash those parts. In truth it is wonderful that we love a thing to which we perform such services every day. I fill this bag, and then I empty it;[2] what is more troublesome? But I must act as the servant of God. For this reason I remain

[1] Compare Xenophon, Memorab. i. 4, 17.

The body is here, and elsewhere in Epictetus, considered as an instrument, which another uses who is not the body; and that which so uses the body must be something which is capable of using the body and a power which possesses what we name intelligence and consciousness. Our bodies, as Bishop Butler says, are what we name matter, and differ from other matter only in being more closely connected with us than other matter. It would be easy to pass from these notions to the notion that this intelligence and power, or to use a common word, the soul, is something which exists independent of the body, though we only know the soul while it acts within and on the body, and by the body.

[2] This bag is the body, or that part of it which holds the food which is taken into the mouth.

(here), and I endure to wash this miserable body, to feed it and to clothe it. But when I was younger, God imposed on me also another thing, and I submitted to it. Why then do you not submit, when Nature who has given us this body takes it away? I love the body, you may say. Well, as I said just now, Nature gave you also this love of the body: but Nature says, Leave it now, and have no more trouble (with it).

XCV.

When a man dies young, he blames the gods. When he is old and does not die, he blames the gods because he suffers when he ought to have already ceased from suffering. And nevertheless, when death approaches, he wishes to live, and sends to the physician and intreats him to omit no care or trouble. Wonderful, he said, are men, who are neither willing to live nor to die.[1]

XCVI.

To the longer life and the worse, the shorter life, if it is better, ought by all means to be preferred.

XCVII.

When we are children our parents deliver us to a paedagogue to take care on all occasions that we suffer no harm. But when we are become men, God delivers us to our innate conscience (*συνειδήσει*) to take care of us. This guardianship then we must in no way despise, for we shall both displease God and be enemies to our own conscience.[2]

XCVIII.

[We ought to use wealth as the material for some act, not for every act alike.]

[1] See Schweig.'s excellent note on this fragment. There is manifestly a defect in the text, which Schweig.'s note supplies.

[2] Mrs. Carter suggests that *ἀπάρεστον* in the text should be *ἀπάρεστοι*: and so Schweig. has it.

XCIX.

[Virtue then should be desired by all men more than wealth which is dangerous to the foolish; for the wickedness of men is increased by wealth. And the more a man is without sense, the more violent is he in excess, for he has the means of satisfying his mad desire for pleasures.]

C.

What we ought not to do, we should not even think of doing.

CI.

Deliberate much before saying or doing anything, for you will not have the power of recalling what has been said or done.

CII.

Every place is safe to him who lives with justice.

CIII.

Crows devour the eyes of the dead, when the dead have no longer need of them. But flatterers destroy the souls of the living and blind their eyes.

CIV.

The anger of an ape and the threats of a flatterer should be considered as the same.

CV.

Listen to those who wish to advise what is useful, but not to those who are eager to flatter on all occasions; for the first really see what is useful, but the second look to that which agrees with the opinion of those who possess power, and imitating the shadows of bodies they assent to what is said by the powerful.

CVI.

The man who gives advice ought first to have regard to the modesty and character (reputation) of those whom he advises; for those who have lost the capacity of blushing are incorrigible.

CVII.

To admonish is better than to reproach: for admonition is mild and friendly, but reproach is harsh and insulting; and admonition corrects those who are doing wrong, but reproach only convicts them.

CVIII.

Give of what you have to strangers (ξένοις) and to those who have need: for he who gives not to him who wants, will not receive himself when he wants.

CIX.

A pirate had been cast on the land and was perishing through the tempest. A man took clothing and gave it to him, and brought the pirate into his house, and supplied him with every thing else that was necessary. When the man was reproached by a person for doing kindness to the bad, he replied, I have shown this regard not to the man, but to mankind.[1]

CX.

A man should choose (pursue) not every pleasure, but the pleasure which leads to the good.[2]

CXI.

It is the part of a wise man to resist pleasures, but of a foolish man to be a slave to them.

[1] Mrs. Carter in her notes often refers to the Christian precepts, but she says nothing here. The fragment is not from Epictetus; but, whether the story is true or not, it is an example of the behaviour of a wise and good man.

[2] See Schweig.'s interpretation and emendation. I doubt if he is right.

CXII.

Pleasure, like a kind of bait, is thrown before (in front of) every thing which is really bad, and easily allures greedy souls to the hook of perdition.

CXIII.

Choose rather to punish your appetites than to be punished through them.

CXIV.

No man is free who is not master of himself.

CXV.

The vine bears three bunches of grapes: the first is that of pleasure, the second of drunkenness, the third of violence.

CXVI.

Over your wine do not talk much to display your learning; for you will utter bilious stuff.[1]

CXVII.

He is intoxicated who drinks more than three cups: and if he is not intoxicated, he has exceeded moderation.

CXVIII.

Let your talk of God be renewed every day, rather than your food.

CXIX.

Think of God more frequently than you breathe.

CXX.

If you always remember that whatever you are doing in the soul or in the body, God stands by as an inspector, you will never err (do wrong) in all your prayers and in all your acts, but you will have God dwelling with you.[2]

[1] χολερὰ γὰρ ἀποφθέγξῃ. See Schweig.'s note.

[2] This is the doctrine of God being in man. See the Index.

CXXI.

As it is pleasant to see the sea from the land, so it is pleasant for him who has escaped from troubles to think of them.[1]

CXXII.

Law intends indeed to do service to human life, but it is not able when men do not choose to accept her services; for it is only in those who are obedient to her that she displays her special virtue.

CXXIII.

As to the sick physicians are as saviours, so to those also who are wronged are the laws.

CXXIV.

The justest laws are those which are the truest.

CXXV.

To yield to law and to a magistrate and to him who is wiser than yourself, is becoming.

CXXVI.

The things which are done contrary to law are the same as things which are not done.

CXXVII.

In prosperity it is very easy to find a friend; but in adversity it is most difficult of all things.

CXXVIII.

Time relieves the foolish from sorrow, but reason relieves the wise.

CXXIX.

He is a wise man who does not grieve for the things which he has not, but rejoices for those which he has.

[1] Compare Lucretius ii. the beginning.

CXXX.

Epictetus being asked how a man should give pain to his enemy answered, By preparing himself to live the best life that he can.[1]

CXXXI.

Let no wise man be averse to undertaking the office of a magistrate (τοῦ ἄρχειν): for it is both impious for a man to withdraw himself from being useful to those who have need of our services, and it is ignoble to give way to the worthless; for it is foolish to prefer being ill-governed to governing well.

CXXXII.

Nothing is more becoming to him who governs than to despise no man and not show arrogance, but to preside over all with equal care.[2]

CXXXIII.

[In poverty any man lives (can live) happily, but very seldom in wealth and power (ἀρχαῖς). The value of poverty excels so much that no just man (νόμιμος) would exchange poverty for disreputable wealth, unless indeed the richest of the Athenians Themistocles, the son of Neocles, was better than Aristides and Socrates, though he was poor in virtue. But the wealth of Themistocles and Themistocles himself have perished and have left no name. For all things die with death in a bad man, but the good is eternal.][3]

CXXXIV.

Remember that such was, and is, and will be the nature of the universe, and that it is not possible that the things which come into being can come into being otherwise than they do now; and that not only men have participated in this change and transmutation, and all other living things which are on the earth, but also the things

[1] Compare M. Antoninus, vi. 6.

[2] For οὐδὲν Mrs. Carter prefers οὐδὲν μᾶλλον: and also Schweig. does, or οὐδὲν ἄλλο μᾶλλον.

[3] This fragment is not from Epictetus. See Schweig.'s note.

which are divine. And indeed the very four elements are changed and transmuted up and down, and earth becomes water and water becomes air, and the air again is transmuted into other things, and the same manner of transmutation takes place from above to below. If a man attempts to turn his mind towards these thoughts, and to persuade himself to accept with willingness that which is necessary, he will pass through life with complete moderation and harmony.

CXXXV.

He who is dissatisfied with things present and what is given by fortune is an ignorant man (ἰδιώτης) in life: but he who bears them nobly and rationally and the things which proceed from them is worthy of being considered a good man.

CXXXVI.

All things obey and serve the world (the universe), earth and sea and sun and the rest of the stars, and the plants of earth and animals. And our body obeys it also both in disease and in health when it (the universe) chooses, both in youth and in age, and when it is passing through the other changes. What is reasonable then and in our power is this, for our judgment not to be the only thing which resists it (the universe): for it is strong and superior, and it has determined better about us by administering (governing) us also together with the whole. And besides, this opposition also is unreasonable and does nothing more than cause us to be tormented uselessly and to fall into pain and sorrow.

The fragments which follow are in part assigned to Epictetus, in part to others.

CXXXVII.

Contentment, as it is a short road and pleasant, has great delight and little trouble.

CXXXVIII.

Fortify yourself with contentment, for this is an impregnable fortress.

CXXXIX.

Let nothing be valued more than truth: not even selection of a friendship which lies without the influence of the affects, by which (affects) justice is both confounded (disturbed) and darkened.[1]

CXL.

Truth is a thing immortal and perpetual, and it gives to us a beauty which fades not away in time nor does it take away[2] the freedom of speech which proceeds from justice; but it gives to us the knowledge of what is just and lawful, separating from them the unjust and refuting them.

CXLI.

We should not have either a blunt knife or a freedom of speech which is ill managed.

CXLII.

Nature has given to men one tongue, but two ears, that we may hear from others twice as much as we speak.

CXLIII.

Nothing really pleasant or unpleasant subsists by nature, but all things become so through habit (custom).[3]

CXLIV.

Choose the best life, for custom (habit) will make it pleasant.

CXLV.

Be careful to leave your sons well instructed rather than rich, for the hopes of the instructed are better than the wealth of the ignorant.

[1] The meaning of the second part is confused and uncertain. See Schweig.'s note.

[2] In place of ἀφαιρεῖ τὴν Mrs. Carter proposes to read ἀφαιρετήν.

[3] See Schweig.'s note.

CXLVI.

A daughter is a possession to her father which is not his own.

CXLVII.

The same person advised to leave modesty to children rather than gold.

CXLVIII.

The reproach of a father is agreeable medicine, for it contains more that is useful than it contains of that which gives pain.

CXLIX.

He who has been lucky in a son in law has found a son: but he who has been unlucky, has lost also a daughter.

CL.

The value of education (knowledge) like that of gold is valued in every place.

CLI.

He who exercises wisdom exercises the knowledge which is about God.

CLII.

Nothing among animals is so beautiful as a man adorned by learning (knowledge).[1]

CLIII.

We ought to avoid the friendship of the bad and the enmity of the good.

CLIV.

The necessity of circumstances proves friends and detects enemies.

CLV.

When our friends are present, we ought to treat them well; and when they are absent, to speak of them well.

[1] See Schweig.'s note.

CLVI.

Let no man think that he is loved by any man when he loves no man.

CLVII.

You ought to choose both physician and friend not the most agreeable, but the most useful.

CLVIII.

If you wish to live a life free from sorrow, think of what is going to happen as if it had already happened.

CLIX.

Be free from grief not through insensibility like the irrational animals, nor through want of thought like the foolish, but like a man of virtue by having reason as the consolation of grief.

CLX.

Whoever are least disturbed in mind by calamities, and in act struggle most against them, these are the best men in states and in private life.

CLXI.

Those who have been instructed, like those who have been trained in the palaestra, though they may have fallen, rise again from their misfortune quickly and skilfully.

CLXII.

We ought to call in reason like a good physician as a help in misfortune.

CLXIII.

A fool having enjoyed good fortune like intoxication to a great amount becomes more foolish.

CLXIV.

Envy is the antagonist of the fortunate.

CLXV.

He who bears in mind what man is will never be troubled at any thing which happens.

CLXVI.

For making a good voyage a pilot (master) and wind are necessary: and for happiness reason and art.

CLXVII.

We should enjoy good fortune while we have it, like the fruits of autumn.

CLXVIII.

He is unreasonable who is grieved (troubled) at the things which happen from the necessity of nature.

Some Fragments of Epictetus omitted by Upton and by Meibomius.

CLXIX.

Of the things which are, God has put some of them in our power, and some he has not. In our own power he has placed that which is the best and the most important, that indeed through which he himself is happy, the use of appearances (*φαντασιῶν*). For when this use is rightly employed, there is freedom, happiness, tranquillity, constancy: and this is also justice and law, and temperance, and every virtue. But all other things he has not placed in our power. Wherefore we also ought to be of one mind with God, and making this division of things, to look after those which are in our power; and of the things not in our power, to intrust them to the Universe (*τῷ κόσμῳ*), and whether it should require our children, or our country, or our body, or any thing else, willingly to give them up.[1]

[1] This is a valuable fragment, and I think, a genuine fragment of Epictetus.
There is plainly a defect in the text, which Schweighaeuser has judiciously supplied.

CLXX.

When a young man was boasting in the theatre and saying, I am wise, for I have conversed with many wise men; Epictetus said, I also have conversed with many rich men, but I am not rich.

CLXXI.

The same person said, It is not good for him who has been well taught to talk among the untaught, as it is not right for him who is sober to talk among those who are drunk.

CLXXII.

Epictetus being asked, What man is rich, answered, He who is content (who has enough).

CLXXIII.

Xanthippe was blaming Socrates, because he was making small preparation for receiving his friends: but Socrates said, If they are our friends, they will not care about it; and if they are not, we shall care nothing about them.

CLXXIV.

When Archelaus was sending for Socrates to make him rich, Socrates told the messengers to return this answer: At Athens four measures (choenices) of meal are sold for one obolus (the sixth of a drachme), and the fountains run with water: if what I have is not enough (sufficient) for me, yet I am sufficient for what I have, and so it becomes sufficient for me. Do you not see that it was with no nobler voice that Polus acted the part of Oedipus as king than of Oedipus as a wanderer and beggar at Colonus? Then shall the good man appear to be inferior to Polus, and unable to act well every character (personage) imposed on him by the Deity? and shall he not imitate Ulysses, who even in rags made no worse figure than in the soft purple robe?[1]

[1] See Schweig.'s note on this fragment; and his remark on the words οὐκ εὐφωνότερον οὐδὲν, and his proposed emendation.

CLXXV.

What do I care, he (Epictetus) says, whether all things are composed of atoms (ἀτόμων), or of similar parts (ὁμοιομερῶν) or of fire and earth? for is it not enough to know the nature of the good and the evil, and the measures (μέτρα) of the desires and the aversions (ἐκκλίσεων), and also the movements towards things and from them; and using these as rules to administer the affairs of life, but not to trouble ourselves about the things above us? For these things are perhaps incomprehensible to the human mind: and if any man should even suppose them to be in the highest degree comprehensible, what then is the profit of them, if they are comprehended? And must we not say that those men have needless trouble who assign these things as necessary to the philosopher's discourse? Is then also the precept written at Delphi superfluous, which is Know thyself? It is not so, he says. What then is the meaning of it? If a man gave to a choreutes (member of chorus) the precept to know himself, would he not have observed in the precept that he must direct his attention to himself? [1]

CLXXVI.

You are a little soul carrying a dead body, as Epictetus said.[2]

CLXXVII.

He (Epictetus) said that he had discovered an art in giving assent; and in the topic (matter) of the movements he had discovered that we must observe attention, that the movements be subject to exception, (μεθ' ὑπεξαιρέσεως), that they be social, that they be according to the worth of each thing; and that we ought to abstain entirely from desire, and to employ aversion (ἐκκλίσει) to none of the things which are not in our power.[3]

[1] See Schweig.'s note, and his remark on the last line of the text.

[2] See M. Antoninus, iv. 41.

[3] See the translation of M. Antoninus, xi. 37; where I have translated this passage a little differently from the present translation. The meaning is the same. I do not know which is the better translation.

CLXXVIII.

About no common thing, he said, the contest (dispute) is, but about being mad or not.[1]

CLXXIX.

AUL. GELLIUS, XVII. 19.

Favorinum ego audivi dicere Epictetum philosophum dixisse, 'plerosque istos qui philosophari videntur, philosophos esse hujuscemodi, ἄνευ τοῦ πράττειν, μέχρι τοῦ λέγειν.'[2] Id significat, factis procul, verbis tenus. Jam illud est vehementius, quod Arrianus solitum eum dictitare in libris, quos de Dissertationibus ejus composuit, scriptum reliquit. Nam, 'quum,' inquit, 'animadverterat hominem pudore amisso, importuna industria, corruptis moribus, audacem, confidentem lingua, caeteraque omnia praeter animum procurantem; istiusmodi,' inquit, 'hominem quum viderat studia quoque et disciplinas philosophiae contrectare, et physica adire et meditari dialectica, multaque id genus theoremata suspicari sciscitarique, inclamabat deum atque hominum fidem, ac plerumque, inter clamandum his eum verbis increpabat: Ἄνθρωπε, ποῦ βάλλεις; σκέψαι εἰ κεκάθαρται τὸ ἀγγεῖον. ἂν γὰρ εἰς τὴν οἴησιν βάλλῃς, ἀπώλετο. ἢν σαπῇ, ἢ οὖρον ἢ ὄξος γένοιτ' ἄν, ἢ τι τούτων χεῖρον.' Nihil profecto his verbis gravius, nihil verius; quibus declarabat maximus philosophorum, 'literas atque doctrinas Philosophiae, quum in hominem falsum atque degenerem, tamquam in vas spurcum atque pollutum influxissent, verti, mutari, corrumpi, et (quod ipse κυνικώτερον ait) urinam fieri, aut si quid est urina spurcius.' Praeterea idem ille Epictetus, quod ex eodem Favorino audivimus, solitus dicere est: 'duo esse vitia multo omnium gravissima et taeterrima, intolerantiam et incontinentiam, quum aut injurias quae sunt ferendae non toleramus neque ferimus, aut a quibus rebus voluptatibusque nos tenere debemus non tenemus. Itaque,' inquit, 'si quis haec duo verba cordi habeat, eaque sibi

[1] See M. Antoninus, xi. 38.

[2] Arrian, Dissert. ii. 19.

imperando atque observando curet, is erit pleraque impeccabilis vitamque vivet tranquillissimam. Verba duo haec dicebat, 'Ἀνέχου καὶ Ἀπέχου.'

CLXXX.

AUL. GELLIUS, XIX. 1.

Philosophus in disciplina Stoica celebratus . . . . ex sarcinula sua librum protulit Epicteti philosophi quintum Διαλεξέων: quas ab Arriano digestas congruere scriptis Zenonis et Chrysippi non dubium est. In eo libro Graeca scilicet oratione scriptum ad hanc sententiam legimus: 'Visa animi,' quas φαντασίας philosophi appellant, 'quibus mens hominis prima statim specie accidentis ad animum rei pellitur, non voluntatis sunt, neque arbitraria, sed vi quadam sua inferunt sese hominibus noscitanda. Probationes autem quas συγκαταθέσεις vocant, quibus eadem visa noscuntur ac dijudicantur, voluntariae sunt fiuntque hominum arbitratu. Propterea quum sonus aliquis aut caelo aut ex ruina aut repentinus [nescius] periculi nuntius vel quid aliud ejusmodi factum, sapientis quoque animum paulisper moveri et contrahi et pallescere necessum est, non opinione alicujus mali praecepta, sed quibusdam motibus rapidis et inconsultis officium mentis atque rationis praevertentibus. Mox tamen ille sapiens ibidem [idem?] τὰς τοιαύτας φαντασίας, id est, visa istaec animi sui terrifica non approbat: hoc est οὐ συγκατατίθεται οὐδὲ προσεπιδοξάζει, sed abjicit respuitque, nec ei metuendum esse in his quidquam videtur. Atque hoc inter insipientis sapientisque animum differre dicunt, quod insipiens, qualia esse primo animi sui pulsu visa sunt saeva et aspera, talia esse vero putat, et eadem incepta tamquam jure metuenda sint, sua quoque assensione approbat καὶ προσεπιδοξάζει (hoc enim verbo Stoici quum super ista re disserunt utuntur). Sapiens autem quum breviter et strictim colore atque vultu motus est, οὐ συγκατατίθεται, sed statum vigoremque sententiae suae retinet, quam de hujuscemodi visis semper habuit, ut de minime metuendis, sed fronte falsa et formidine inani territantibus.'

CLXXXI.

ARNOBIUS ADVERS. GENTES, IN FINE LIBRI SECUNDI.

Quum de animarum agitur salute ac de respectu nostri; 'aliquid et sine ratione faciendum est,'[1] ut Epictetum dixisse approbat Arrianus.

[1] 'Nempe ubi ratio deficit, ibi sola fiducia in Deum reposita et obsequio voluntati ejus ab ipso declaratae unice subjecto agendum est.' Schweig. See Encheirid. xxxii.

INDEX.

Academics, the, 17
——, the folly of the, 171, 172
——, the, cannot blind their own senses though they have tried, 176
Achilles, 40
Act, every, consider what it is, 381
Acts which bear testimony to a man's words, 94
——, indolence and indifference as to, Epictetus blames, 130
Actor in a play, man an, 386
Admetus, father of, 242
Administrator of all things, the proof that there is an, 144
Adonis, gardens of, 356
Adultery, 107
Affect, an, how it is produced, 202
Affection, natural, 37
Affectionate, how to become, 277
Agamemnon and Achilles, quarrel of, 191
'Αγγαρεία, a press, 305
Agrippinus, Paconius, 7, 9, 417
Alcibiades, 200
Alexander and Menelaus, 179
—— and Hephaestion, 178
Aliptic art, the, 136
Anaxagoras, 114
'Ανέχου καὶ 'Απέχου, 439
Animals, what they are made for, 50
Annonae, Praefectus, 35
Antipater, 136
Antisthenes, Xenophon, and Plato, 157, 158
——, noble saying of, 342
—— made Diogenes free, 278
Anxiety, on, 136
Anytus and Melitus, 88
'Αφορμαί, 22
'Αποτειχίζειν, 307
Appearances, φαντασίαι, right use of, 4, 20, 45, 64
——, and the aids to be provided against them, 80
——, we act according to, 86
——, the nature of Good and also of Evil is in the use of, 97
——, the faculty of understanding the use of, 118
—— drive away reason, 161
—— lead on; and must be resisted, 161
——, right use of, free from restraint, 167
—— often disturb and perplex, 176
——, how we must exercise ourselves against, 218
—— should be examined, 380
Aqueduct, Marcian, at Rome, 150
Archedemus, 108
Archelaus and Socrates, 436
Archimedes, 421
Arguments, sophistical, 23, 25
Argument, he who is strong in, 193
Aristides, 415
—— and Evenus, 358
Aristophanes and Socrates, 369, 430
Arnobius, 440
Arrian, 1
Arrogance, self-conceit, οἴησις, 28
—— and distrust, 233
——, boasting, and pride, advice

against, 286, 384, 387, 394, 395, 399
Assent, cause of, 83
—— to that which appears false cannot be compelled, 253
Asses, shod, 306
Attention, on, 372
Aversion, ἔκκλισις, 54

Babbler, a, 376, 377
Bath, the, 68
Beauty, 195, 196
——, where it is, 370
Beggars, remarks on, 290
Belief cannot be compelled, 304
Best men, the, 434
Body, the, could not be made free from hindrance, 309
—— and spirit must be separated, 99
——, the, an instrument used by another power, 424
Books, what used for, 327
——, a few better than many, 79
Brotherhood of men, 46
Butler, Bp., 3, 134, 198, 326, 338, 348, 350

Caesar's friend is not happy, 300
Cages, birds kept in, by the Romans, 297
Carystus and Taenarum, marbles of, 422
Cassiope or Cassope, 213
Catechism of the Church of England, 410
Caution about familiar intercourse with men, 236
Character, on assuming a, above your strength, 398
Characters, different, cannot be mingled, 323
Christianity, Mrs. Carter's opinion of the power of, 234
Christians, promise of future happiness to, on certain conditions, 311
Chrysippus, 14, 17, 36, 43, 53, 54, 113, 402
——, the Pseudomenos of, 157
—— on Possibilities, 163
Chrysippus on the resolution of syllogisms, 188
—— and Antipater, 203
—— and Zeno, 358
Circumspection, on, 234
Circumstances, difficult, a lesson for, 96
—— show what men are, 70
Cleanliness, 368
Cleanthes, 31, 163, 404
——, an example of the pursuit of knowledge under difficulties, 292
Codicillus, a, 217
Colophon, the, 143
Common sense, 212
Company, behaviour in, 394, 396, 400
Conceit of thinking that we know something, 158
Confess, some things which a man will not, 173
Confession, general, of sins in the Prayer Book of the Church of England, 363
Conflagration, the great, 229
Conjunctive or complex axiom, 124
Conscience, τὸ συνειδός, power of, 262
Consciousness that he knows nothing, a man who knows nothing ought to have the, 174
Contest unequal between a charming young girl and a beginner in philosophy, 227
Contradictions, effect of demonstrating, 193
Convince himself, a power given to man to, 340
Courage and caution, 97, 98
—— and caution, when they are applicable, 101
Cowardice leads men to frequent divination, 117
Crates, a Cynic, and his wife, 260
Criton, Plato's Dialogue, named, 319
Cynic, the true; his office corresponds to the modern teacher of religion, 250

Cynic, a, does not wish to hide anything, 250
——, the true, a messenger from Zeus, 250
——, the father of all men and women, 261
Cynic's ruling faculty must be pure, 262
—— power of endurance, 263
Cynic, the, sent by God as an example, 355
Cynism, a man must not attempt it without God, 248
——, on, 248

Daemon, every man's, 48
Darkness, men seek, to conceal their acts, 249
Death, 81
——, fear of, 54
—— or pain, and the fear of pain or death, 98
——, what a man should be doing when death surprises him, 209
——, what it is, 230, 282
——, exhortation to receive it thankfully, 310
—— and birth, how viewed by a savage tribe, 335
——, the resolution of the matter of the body into the things of which it was composed, 347
——, a man must be found doing something when it comes; and what it should be, 361
——, when it comes, what Epictetus wishes to be able to say to God, 362
—— is the harbour for all, 364
—— should be daily before a man's eyes, 387
Demetrius, a Cynic, 75
Demonstration, what it is; and contradiction, 189, 190
De Morgan's Formal Logic, 28
Design, 19
Desire of things impossible is foolish, 272
Desires, consequences of, 358
Desire and aversion, what they are, 380
Determinations, right, only should be maintained, 145
Deviation, every, comes from something which is in man's nature, 371
Dialectic, to be learned last, 291
Difficulties, our, are about external things, 360
Diodorus Cronus, 162
Diogenes, 71, 139, 203, 226, 369, 418
——, when he was asked for letters of recommendation, 106
—— and Philip, 250
—— in a fever, 256
—— a friend of Antisthenes, 257
—— and the Cynics of Epictetus' time, 260
——, his personal appearance, 261
——, how he loved mankind, 278
Diogenes' opinion on freedom, 298
Diogenes and Antisthenes, 312
——, free, 317, 318
—— and Heraclitus, 385
Dion of Prusa, 266
Dirty persons, not capable of being improved, 370
Disputation or discussion, 133
Divination, 116, 393
Diviner, internal, 116
Doctors, travelling, 280
Domitian banishes philosophers from Rome, 71
Door, the open, 72, 99
Duty, what is a man's, 112
—— to God and to our neighbour, 410
Duties of life discovered from names, 127
—— of marriage, begetting children and other, 216
—— are measured by relations (σχέσεσι), 392

Education, Epictetus knew what it ought to be, 53, 58
——, what it is, 67
——, what ought to be the purpose of, 245

Ἡγεμονικόν, τὸ, the governing faculty, 49, 332
——, the ruling faculty, described, 351
Encheiridion, 1
End, man's true, 20
End, every thing that we do ought to be referred to an, 264
Enthymema, 28
Envy, the notion of; Socrates and Bp. Butler, 134
Epaminondas, 415
Epaphroditus, 6, 62, 78
Epictetus, 1, 2, 220
——, and the style of the Gospels, 13
——, mistake of, 31
—— misunderstood, 56, 311
—— and the New Testament writers, resemblances between, 93
——, extravagant assertion of, 114
—— perhaps confounds Jews and Christians, 126
——, how he could know what God is, 141
——, what was the effect of his teaching, 149
—— disclaims knowledge of certain things, 82, 163
——, his purpose in teaching, 166
——, great good sense of, in education, 245
——, some unwise remarks of, 289, 293
—— affirms that a man cannot be compelled to assent to that which seems to him to be false, 303
—— advises not to do as your friend does simply because he is your friend, 322
——, what reflections he recommends, 344
—— misunderstood by Mrs. Carter, 365
Epictetus' advice as to giving pain to an enemy, 430
Epictetus, wise sayings of, 436
Epicurus, 69, 417
——, doctrines of, 65, 66
——, the opinions of, 125
Epicurus, his opinions disproved, 168, 169
——, his opinion of honesty, 179
——, on the end of our being, and other works of, 185
Epicurus' opinion of injustice, 214
Epicureans and Academics, 167
Epicureans and catamites, 274
Epicurean, an, 213
Epirus, governor of, 207
Eriphyle and Amphiaraus, 181
Error, the property of, 192
Errors of others, we should not be angry with the, 56
Eteocles and Polynices, 177, 337
Eucharist in the Church of England service, 120
Euphrates, the philosopher, 235
—— did not act well for the sake of the spectators, 353
Euripides, 113, 178, 404
Euripides' Medea, 83
Euripides, fragment of, on death, 336
——, the great storehouse of noble thoughts, 361
Events, all, how to use, 383
Evidence, the assertion that all things are incapable of sure, 167
Evil, the origin of, is the abuse of rationality and liberty, 123
——, the, in everything, is that which is contrary to the nature of the thing, 313
——, the nature of, does not exist in the world, 390
—— to men, the cause of all their, is the being unable to adapt the preconceptions (προλήψεις) to the several things, 299
Exercise, on, 225
Exercising himself, method of a man, 206
Externals to the will, 92
——, some according to nature, and others contrary, 111
——, men admire and are busy about, 148
——, judgment from, fallacious, 352
—— things, that advantage can be derived from, 241

Face, the, does not express the hidden character, 106
Faculty, rational, 3
——, ruling, 236
——, the ruling, how restored to the original authority, 159
——, the ruling, the material for the wise and good man, 204
Faith and works, 354
False, impossibility of assenting to that which appears, 215
Familiar intimacy, on, 322
Faults, not possible for a man to be free from all, 374
Favorinus, 438
Fever, a goddess at Rome, 60, 68
Firmness in danger, 109
Fool, a, cannot be persuaded, 146
Forgiveness better than revenge, 419
Fragments of Epictetus, 405
Free persons only allowed to be educated, 100
Free, what is, 253, 254
——, no bad man is, 295
——, who are, the question answered, 301, 302
Freedom is obtained not by desires satisfied, but by removing desire, 322
—— and slavery, 406
Friendship, 176
——, the test of, 177
——, advice about, 181
——, what it depends on, 180
——, Epictetus' opinions of, 365

Galilaeans, 126, 345
Games, Greek, 287
Gellius, A., 438, 439
Gladiators, 91
Glorious objects in nature, the, 151
God, what is, 65
——, nature of; how far described by Epictetus, 118
——, the works of, 122
——, a guide, 117, 246
God's gifts, 23
God knows all things, 141
—— in man, 48
—— in man, an old doctrine, 119
God, the spirit of, in man, the doctrine of Paul and of Epictetus, 120, 121
—— dwelling with a man, 428
Gods everywhere, 250
God's law about the Good, 87
—— law that the stronger is always superior to the weaker, 88, 89
God and man, kinship of, 30
—— and man, and man's opinions of God, 141, 142
——, address to, 152
——, the wise and good man's address to; and his submission to God's will, 284
—— beyond man's understanding, 21, 65
—— ought to be obeyed, 373
——, obedience to, the pleasure of, 285, 286
God's will, 330
—— will should be the measure of our desires, 156
—— will, absolute conformity to, taught by Epictetus, 308, 309
—— will, when resignation to it is perfect, Bp. Butler, 348
God, blaming, 166
God's power over all things, 46, 47
God, supposed limitation of his power, 340
——, what a man should be able to say to, 209
——, the father of all, 12, 23, 61
——, a friend of, 157
——, without, nothing should be attempted, 256
——, what he chooses is better than what man chooses, 348
—— and his administration of the world, those who blame, 254
God's existence, to deny, and eat his bread, 172
God only, looking to, and fixing your affections on him only, 153
—— has sent a man to show how a life under difficulties is possible, 254
—— has made all things perfect,

and the parts of the universe for the use of the whole, 346
God and the gods, 12
Gods, various opinions on the, 41, 42
——, actions acceptable to the, 45
——, man must learn the nature of the, and try to be like them, 141
——, we ask for what they do not give, 408
Goethe, 19, 251
Gold tested by a certain stone, 419
Good and bad, each a certain kind of will, 87
——, bad, and things indifferent, 164
—— and evil consist in the will, intention, 130
—— could not exist without evil, 43
—— and evil; Chrysippus and Simplicius, 43
——, the, where it is, 253
——, the nature (οὐσία) of, 118
—— man, a, not unhappy, 272
Gospel precepts which Christians do not observe, 289
Gyarus, Gyara, 75
Gyara, 284, 285, 330

Habit, how to oppose, 80
—— and faculty, how maintained and increased, 158, 159
——, how weakened and destroyed, 160
Habits must be opposed by contrary habits, 226, 227
Habit cherished by corresponding acts, 288
Halteres, 15, 327
Hand-kissing, 62
Handles, two, every thing has, 399
Happiness and desire of what is not present never come together, 272
——, only one way to, 331
Harpaston, a ball, 110
Hearing, he who is fit for, moves the speaker, 192
Hector's address to Andromache, 264
Hellenes, quarrels among the, 178
Helvidius, Priscus, 10
Heraclitus, 229
—— and Zeno, 99
Hercules, 152, 161, 256, 361
Hippocrates, 154
Homer, what he meant when he wrote certain things, 366
Hope, Thales' opinion of, 424
Human intelligence is a part of the divine, 44
—— race, the, continuance of, how secured, 187
—— being, a, definition of 198
Hypocrite, the, 356
Hypothesis (ὑπόθεσις), 91

Ideas innate, of good and evil, 131
Idiotes, ἰδιώτης, the meaning of, 95
——, ἰδιώτης, a common person, 240
Ignorance the cause of doing wrong, 78
Ignorant man, description of an, 190
Iliad, the, is only appearances and the use of appearances, 84
Immortality of the soul; Socrates and Epictetus, 231
Impressions, φαντασίαι, guard against, 397
Indifferent, things which are, 64
Indifference of things; of the things which are neither good nor bad, 112
Informers at Rome, 375
Initiated, the, μύσται, 310
Injustice, an act of, a great harm to the doer, 334
Inn, an, πανδοκεῖον, 187
Interest, self; and common interest or utility, 61
——, every animal attached to its own, 178
Invincible, how a man should be, 59
——, how a man can be, 386

Jesus, prayer of, 31
—— and Socrates compared by Baur, 321
——, and of Socrates, the death of, contrasted by Rousseau, 321

Καλὸς καὶ ἀγαθός, 201
Know thyself, the maxim, 58, 197
—— thyself, the beginning of knowledge, 320
Know thyself, the precept written at Delphi, 437
Κόσμος, sense of, 282
Κύριος, the use of, 92

Laius, 197
Lateranus, Plautius, 6
Laticlave, the, 72
Law of life is the acting conformably to nature, 77
——, the divine, 150
Laws, the, sent from God, 325
Law, what it is, 350
——, nature of, 429
Learning and teaching, what they mean, 125
Levin's Lectures, 17, 80, 82
Liberty, what men do for, 321
Life and practice of the civilized world, the, 245
——, human, a warfare, 273, 274
——, the science of, 303, 312
—— of the dead rests in the remembrance of the living, 320
Lions, tame, 297
Logic is necessary, proof that, 192
Logical art is necessary, the, 52
Love, a divine power, 316
Loves mankind, who, 407
Love, to, is only in the power of the wise, 176
Lycurgus, 170, 415
Lycurgus' generous behaviour, 419

Man and other animals, 5, 20
—— and beasts, how distinguished, 123
—— a spectator of God and his works, and an interpreter, 20
Man's powers, 73, 74, 182
Man, powers in often no exercised, 73
—— and a stork, the difference between, 85
——, what is a, 111
——, what is he? 123
Man is improved or destroyed by corresponding acts, 124
——, a, who has looked after every thing rather than what he ought, 143
Man supposed to consist of a soul and a body, 252
Man's own, what it is, 277
Man, for what purpose God introduced him into the world, 310, 311
——, character of a, who is a fool and a beast, 336
Man's nature is to seek the Good; and Bp. Butler's opinion, 338
——, a, opinions only make his soul impregnable, 337
—— great faculties, 346
Man is that power which uses the parts of his body and understands the appearances of things, 350
——, a, contemptible when he is unable to do any good, 420
Manumission, 100
Marry, not to; and not to engage in public affairs, were Epicurean doctrines, 215
Marriage, 187
——, the Roman censor Metellus on, 187
——, Paul's opinion of; and the different opinion of Epictetus, 258
—— of a minister of God, in the opinion of Epictetus in the present state of things, 259
——, the true nature of, not understood by Paul, 317
Massurius and Cassius, Roman lawyers, 325
Masters, our, those who have the power over the things which we love and hate and fear, 302
Materials, ὕλαι, are neither good nor bad, 108
Matthew, c. vi., 31, 33
Measure of every act, 84
Medea, 155
Menoeceus, 242

Milesiaca, 358
Money not the best thing, 388
Murrhina vasa, 221

Names, examination of, the beginning of education, 53
——, a man must first understand, 142
Nature, acting according to, 37, 38
——, power of, 169
——, following; a manner of speaking, just and true, Bp. Butler, 198
——, living, according to; Zeno's principle, 198
—— of man, 313
—— of every thing which pleases or supplies a want, consider what is the, 381
——, the will of, how known, 389
——, the, of evil does not exist in the world, 390
Nero, 9
——, coins of, 335
News, not to be disturbed by, 239
Nicias, 420
Nicopolis, 63, 71, 112, 174

Obstinacy, on, 144
Obstinate person who is persuaded to change his mind, instance of an, 145
Opinion, 162, 386
Opinions, right, the consequences of the destruction of, 85
—— put in practice which are contrary to true opinions, 125
—— disturb us, 150
—— about things independent of the will, 207
Opinion the cause of a man's acting, 219
——, when the need of it comes, ought to be ready, 222
Opinions, the power of, 338
——, right and wrong, and their consequences, 346
——, not things disturb men, 381
——, fixed principles, how acquired, 420
Organs of sense and limbs are instruments used by the living man Bp. Butler, 350
'Ορμή, 15
Ostentation, those who read and discuss for, 264
Οὐσία, 29, 87
——, substance or nature of Good 214
——, Nature of man cannot be altogether pure, 367

Paedagogue, a, 425
Pancratium, Pentathlon, 195
Paradoxes, paralogies, 76
Partisan, an unseemly, 207
Patronus, the Roman word, 221
Paul, imperfect quotation from, by Mrs. Carter, 243
—— and Epictetus contemporary 283
—— and Epictetus do not agree about marriage, 317
Penalties for those who disobey the divine administration, 225
Perception, 82
Periodical renovation of things, 99
Peripatetics, the, 165
Persons who tell you all their affairs and wish to know yours, 375
Persuasion, a man has most power of, with himself, 359
Φαινόμενον, τὸ: φαντασία, 86
Φαντασίαι, visa animi, 161
——, visa animi, Gellius, 439
Φαντασία, an imagination of things to come, which will bring good 322
Phidias, 21, 121, 122
Philosophy, 387
——, what it promises, 49, 230
——, the beginning of, 79, 132
—— should be practical, 315
——, how to know that we have made progress in, 400
Philosopher, a, 401
——, the work of a, 140, 141
——, first business of a, 153
——, a real, described, 166
Philosophers in words only, 162

Philosophers' rules applied to practice, 328
Piety and a man's interest must be in the same thing, 81
——, and sanctity are good things, 170
—— to the Gods, what it is, 392
—— and a man's interest, how they are connected, 393
Pirate, how treated by a wise and good man, 427
Pittacus' teaching, that forgiveness is better than revenge, 419
Plato and Hippocrates, 28
—— says that every soul is unwillingly deprived of the truth, 83
Plato's saying, 160
—— doctrine that every mind is deprived of truth unwillingly, 181
—— Polity read by the women in Rome, 417
Pleasure, nature of, 416
Polemon and Xenocrates, 196
Polybius on the Roman state, 170
Polynices and Eteocles, 393
Poor, if, be content and happy, 410
Poverty and wealth, 411, 430
Practice in hearing, necessary for those who go to hear philosophers, 189
Praecognitions (προλήψεις), adaptation of, to particular cases, 66, 67
Preconception, πρόληψις, 8
Preconceptions, how fitted to the several things, 131
——, how to be adapted to their correspondent objects, 154
Principle, the ruling, of a bad man cannot be trusted, 180
Principles, general; and their application, 77
—— ought always to be in readiness, 105
Principle, the, on which depends every movement of man and God, 205
Principles, he who has great, knows his own powers, 357
Procrastination dangerous, 374
Προαιρετικὴ δύναμις, or προαίρεσις, in the larger sense, 183
Protagoras and Hippias, 211
Providence, 19, 41, 50, 51
——, πρόνοια, 141
——, on; προνοίας, περὶ, 238.
Publicani, εἰκοστῶναι, 298
Purity, cleanliness, a man is distinguished from other animals by, 366
Pyrrho, 80
—— and the Academics, 81
Pyrrho's saying, 424
Pythagoras' golden verses, 222
Pythagoras, 344
Pythian God, the, 394

Quails, how used by the Greeks, 237

Reading, Bp. Butler's remarks on, 326
——, what ought to be the purpose of, 326, 331
Reason; reasoning, the purpose of, 24, 52, 64
——, power of communing with God, 30
——, how it contemplates itself, 63
—— not given to man for the purpose of misery, 271
Reasoning, 26
Recitations, houses lent for, 267
—— at Rome, 396
Reformation of manners produced by the Gospel, 149
Relations, three, between a man and other things, 141
Resurrection of Christ; and Paul's doctrine of man's resurrection, 283
—— of the body, various opinions of divines of the English Church on, 284
Riches and happiness, 409
Rings, golden, worn by the Roman Equites, 299
Rome, dependents wait on great men at, 331
Rufus, C. Musonius, 7, 27, 34, 212, 236, 268

Rule, a, the value of, 86
Rules, by which things are tried, must be fixed; and then the rules may be applied, 133
Rules, certain, should be in readiness, 373

Sacred are the words by themselves, men say, 246
Sarpedon, son of Zeus, 81
Saturnalia, 74, 80, 302
Savigny on free will, 55
Sceptics, the, deny the knowledge and certainty of things, 81
Scholasticus, a, 41
School, who come to the, for the purpose of being improved? 174
——, the, with what mind it ought to be entered, 175
——, philosopher's, a surgery, 268
Secret matters require fidelity and corresponding opinions, 377
Seeming to be is not sufficient, 132
Self-knowledge, γνῶθι σεαυτόν, 256
Self-love, self-regard, 61
Sickness, how we ought to bear, 222, 223
Signal to quit life, God's, 89
——, the, to retire, 90
——, the, to retreat, 293
Simplicius, 1
——, commentary of, on the Encheiridion, 390, 404
Slave, a, why he wishes to be set free, 298
——, a, does not secure happiness by being made free, 298, 299
Socrates, 12, 30, 33, 41, 53, 76, 99, 101, 103, 104, 110, 115, 130, 160, 227, 228, 233, 237, 251, 267, 268, 284, 354, 400, 403
—— and his treatment by the Athenians, 88
—— preferred death to saying and doing things unworthy of him, 90
—— and the Phaedon of Plato, 95
—— taught that we must not do wrong for wrong, 129
Socrates, the method of, 134, 135
—— knew by what the rational soul is moved, 193
——, what he says to his judges, 197
Socrates did not profess to teach virtue, 210
——, imitators of, 217
—— loved his children, how, 277
——, Diogenes, and Cleanthes, as examples, 292
——, what he taught, 299
——, heroic acts of, 319
——, a brave soldier and a philosopher, 319
——, remembrance of what he did or said in his life, even more useful now, 320
—— in his prison wrote a hymn to Apollo, 329
—— avoided quarrels, 333
——, how he managed his household, 338
——, why he washed seldom, 369
——' opinion on divination, 394
—— and Diogenes, 151, 247, 275, 349, 358
Solitary, he is not, who sees the great objects of nature, 231
Solitude, on, 228
Solon's wise sayings, 421
Sophists, against the, 244
Sorrow of another, how far Epictetus would endeavour to stop, 272
Souls, human, parts of God, 47
Soul, body and things external relate to man's, 213
—— and body, severance of, no harm in the, 224
——, existence of the, independent of the body, perhaps not taught by Epictetus, 282
——, the probable opinion of Epictetus on the, 347
——, the impurity of the, is her own bad judgments (opinions), 367
Speaking, the power of, 182
Spirit, πνεῦμα, 182
Sportulae, 303

Stars, number of, neither even nor odd, 83
——, number of the, 147
Stobaeus, 405
Stoics, doctrine of the, 35
——, the language of the, formed long before that of the New Testament writers, 93
Stoic opinions, the mere knowledge of, does not make a man a Stoic, 126
——, who is a, 165
Stoics taught that a man should live an active life and should marry and beget children, 187
——, the, say one thing and do another, 215
——, practical teaching of the, 244
—— and the Pyrrhonists and Academics, dispute between, 82
Sufferings useful, whether we choose or not, 288
Suicide, 32, 33
Superiors, the many can only imitate their, 207
Swedenborg, 47, 120, 123
Sympathy, Epictetus' opinion on, 385
Symposium of Xenophon, 135, 333

Teacher, fitness of, and ordering of a, 247
Θαυμάζειν, admirari, to overvalue, 87
Θαυμάζειν, admirari, 305
Θέλειν, Βούλεσθαι, 308, 384
Themistocles, 430
Theopompus, 154
Θεωρήματα, 403
Theorems, why they are said to be useless, 175
——, the use of, 220
Thermopylae, the Spartans who died at, 171
Thersites, 249
Things, bond of union among, 46
—— under the inspection of God, 46
——, the power of using and estimating, 182
Things, a man is overpowered by before he is overpowered by a man, 279
——, some in our power and some not, 378, 435
—— not lost, but restored, 383
——, some, incomprehensible; and what is the use of them, if they are comprehended? 437
Thirty tyrants of Athens, the, 139
Thrasea, Paetus, 6
Three things in which a man should exercise himself, 201
Toreutic art, 216
Tranquil life, a, how secured, 382
Tranquillity, the product of virtue, 14, 17
——, of, 103
—— of mind and freedom, man should strive to attain, 152
——, to those who desire to pass life in, 325
Treasure, the, where it is, there the heart is also, 179
Trifles on which men employed themselves, 265, 269
Triumphs, Roman, 281
Truth, in, the nature of evil and good is, 104
——, 414
——, the nature of, 432
Tyranny in the time of Epictetus, 96
—— under the Roman Emperors, 102

Ulysses and Hercules, 271
—— and Nausicaa, 294
Unbelievers, the creed of, 170
Unhappiness is a man's own fault, 270
Universe, 21
——, the nature of the, 431
Unjust, that which is, a man cannot do without suffering for it, 312
Untaught, the, is a child in life, 241

Vespasian, 10
Victory, figure of, 121

Virtue's reward is in the acts of virtue, 276
Virtue is its own reward, 360
Visa animi, Gellius, 439

Wealth, 409
——, how gained, 421
What is a man? 123
Will, προαίρεσις, 6, 16, 23, 40, 45, 67
——, 109
—— to act, 39, 67
—— cannot be compelled to assent, 54
——, things independent of the, are neither good nor bad, 62
——, good and evil in the, 73, 147
—— only conquers will, 88
——, the, nothing superior to the faculty of, 127
——, friendship depends on the, 179, 180
——, the faculty of the, and its powers, 182, 184
——, perverted, 184
——, a faculty, and set over the other faculties, 184
——, when it is right, uses all the other faculties, 185
——, the cause of happiness, or of unhappiness, 186
——, the Good is in a right determination of the, 205
——, doing something useful for the exercise of the, 209
Will, the, can only hinder or damage itself, 241
—— of the Cynic and his use of appearances, 263
——, things out of the power of the, 329
——, the, must be exercised, 359
——, man's, put by God in obedience to himself only, 373
—— of God, conformity to, 42
Woman, war about a handsome, 179
Women being common by nature; what does it mean? 107
——, slaves to, 296, 297
World, the, one city, 271
Wrong, a man never does, in one thing and suffers in another, 240

Xanthippe, the ill-tempered wife of Socrates, 338
—— and Socrates, 436
Xenocrates and Polemon, 379
Ξύστρα, the Roman strigilis, 368

Zeno, founder of the Stoic sect, 65, 107
—— and Antigonus, 138
—— and Socrates, 274
Zeno's opinions, 353
Zeus, God, 12, 21
—— and the rest of the Gods, 156
——, the occupation of, 229
—— the father of men, 272

LONDON: PRINTED BY WILLIAM CLOWES AND SONS, STAMFORD STREET AND CHARING CROSS.

www.ingramcontent.com/pod-product-compliance
Lightning Source LLC
Chambersburg PA
CBHW032012110726
47901CB00004B/1055

* 9 7 8 3 3 3 7 8 1 8 3 9 5 *